Opera in Perspective

OPERA
in
Perspective

John D Drummond

University of Minnesota Press

Minneapolis

Copyright © 1980, Text, John D. Drummond
All rights reserved.
Published by the University of Minnesota Press,
2037 University Avenue Southeast,
Minneapolis, Minnesota 55414
Second printing, 1981
Printed in the United States of America

Library of Congress Cataloging in Publication Data

Drummond, John.
  Opera in perspective

  Bibliography: p. .
  Includes index.
  1. Opera-History and criticism. I. Title.
ML1700.D75   782.1–09   79-28697
ISBN 0-8166-0848-2

*The University of Minnesota
is an equal-opportunity
educator and employer*

Contents

Opera in Perspective

Figures

Musical Examples

To the memory of my father,

JAMES DODDS DRUMMOND,

who gave me a love of
music, and taught me
to think for myself.

Preface

This book is a personal view of Western European music-drama. It has no pretensions to be a comprehensive survey of opera, and does not set out the dates and details of all the important and less important operas written since 1600. There are other histories of opera which fulfil that task admirably. Here we are concerned not with the whats and whens of opera so much as with the hows and whys. My aim is to set opera as a whole within the context of man's music-drama, and its changing forms within the particular contexts of Western European cultural value-systems. In short, it takes the wider view.

Terminology is a problem. 'Opera' means, in general, the sort of music-drama written since 1600 and in particular that written since the late seventeenth century. 'Lyric drama' is a somewhat confusing term, for although the word 'lyric' does mean 'musical', we tend to associate it with poetry or with the text of song. 'Music-drama' is a literal translation of the German term *Musikdrama*, and suffers from particularly Wagnerian associations; nevertheless it seems the most useful general term to use, for it aptly describes that peculiar phenomenon in which music and drama are integrated.

The views on music-drama and opera put forward here are my own, and are the result of, or perhaps a reaction against, a conventional scholarly education. I have, however, been fortunate to have been taught by, and to have worked with, a number of people whose love and knowledge of music-drama have been formed from practical participation in opera. To them I owe a great deal. Among many it is right to mention Percy Lovell, James Brown, John Joubert, Ivor Keys, Jocelyn Powell, Jane Winearls and Martin Hindmarsh. I also owe much to those students who have suffered my opera productions, especially at Birmingham University.

I am particularly grateful to Dr Andrew Stewart, Dr Patrick Little, Professor John Steele and Professor Brian Trowell, who read parts or all of this book in typescript, corrected various factual errors and allowed me to learn from their expertise. They take, however, no responsibility for the

11

opinions expressed herein. Last but not least, I record my gratitude to my wife Susan, for her patience, her encouragement and her love.

John D. Drummond

Dunedin, 1978

1 The origins of music-drama

Music-drama and opera

Opera is, strictly speaking, one particular child in the family of music-drama. Born in Western Europe at the end of the sixteenth century, it is now, according to some, fast approaching its demise. It is essentially a regional art-form, although it has been exported along with the other trappings of Western civilization to many parts of the globe. It is also a comparatively short-lived child: in the span of human history four and three-quarter centuries is an insignificant length of time, a mere twenty-four generations, and many of opera's predecessors and siblings have had considerably longer lives.

Like any child, opera has developed a personality according to its genetic make-up and the particular qualities of its environment. The various forms of man's music-drama have some basic features in common, and others which reflect the cultures of which they are part. Music-drama has always been associated with religious belief and religious ritual, because music, dance, spectacle and narrative are ingredients of worship. Music-drama, too, has always provided an opportunity for man to delight in being playful, and catered for his love of pretending. In combining worship and make-believe music-drama has developed, in every culture, into an art-form; that is, it has become a structurally self-contained form of communication, expressing and stimulating experiences symbolic of some aspect of what it is to be a human being.

Even within the particular culture of Western Europe we can find examples of music-drama in which the three elements of religion, play and art are used, in different combinations. In the church service, music-drama has a primarily religious function. In the playground dance-songs of school-children, music-drama has primarily the function of play. In the opera-house, music-drama is primarily art. But art can be used in conjunction with religious elements, as in some of Handel's dramatic oratorios or in Britten's Church Parables. Britten's earlier setting of the Chester Miracle Play,

Noye's Fludde, is a musico-dramatic work of art using children's delight in play, and was written for performance in a church. If we accept that political ideology is a substitute for religion, we can find examples of 'political' music-drama in the collaborations of Bertolt Brecht and Kurt Weill in the 1920s and 1930s, and in the music-drama of Soviet Russia and Communist China.

There is, then, more to music-drama than merely opera in the opera-house. It is a tree whose roots lie deep in human history, perhaps deep in the human psyche, and the branch which we call 'opera' in the 'opera-house' can only be fully understood if we can learn about the nature of the tree itself. Because Western European culture has flourishing and separate musical and dramatic arts, we tend to think of 'opera' as being drama plus music, a combination of two distinct art-forms. From a historical point of view, however, it is a misleading way of looking at music-drama: the evidence shows that music-drama as a single entity has always been part of the life of man, from his earliest beginnings. Indeed, it shows lamentable cultural narrow-mindedness for systems-librarians to catalogue opera as a branch of music:[1] it is a branch of music-drama, as are masque, ballet, and other similar multi-media art forms.

The most compelling and direct evidence that music-drama is a single entity and not an amalgamation is provided by Classical Greek tragedy, which is universally agreed to have been the most important influence upon opera. The theorists of the late sixteenth and early seventeenth centuries deliberately attempted to recreate the experience of Greek tragedy in contemporary terms, and the great operatic reformers of the eighteenth and nineteenth centuries (Gluck and Wagner) also looked to it for support. Greek tragedy was not just spoken drama, it was music-drama: it was sung and danced. Also it was not just a secular, artistic activity: Greek tragedy sprang from, and retained a function of, religious ritual. Unfortunately, little is known about the musical side of Greek music-drama, and Greek tragedy has tended to receive rather short shrift in histories of opera, which are usually written by musicians rather than by music-dramatists.

Greek tragedy itself grew out of earlier forms of music-drama, which in most histories of opera receive even less attention. Donald Jay Grout, for example, in his *A Short History of Opera* — which is in most respects the most authoritative and informative single history of the art-form — disposes of Greek tragedy in four pages out of 583 (in the second edition) and discusses the family of music-drama only in the first three sentences of his introduction. Other historians of opera have shared this tendency. Presumably, and paradoxically, they have felt that to travel from the branch of opera to the trunk of music-drama is to move out on a limb: they have believed that our ignorance in regard to the music of early music-drama

14

absolves us from the necessity of discussing it.

Yet there is a fair amount of evidence about music in Greek tragedy, and even about the nature of earlier music-drama. Some of this evidence comes from archaeological and palaeological research, some from the studies of anthropologists and ethnomusicologists working with surviving primitive peoples.[2] There is never a great deal to go on, but it is enough to enable us to form working hypotheses about the early history of music-drama. And further research might enable more positive conclusions to be reached.

Beginnings

We do not know when music-drama began, because we do not know of a time when man had no music-drama. Even the most 'primitive' tribes which have survived to be studied by anthropologists have some kind of music-drama, and the archaeology of the most distant past has revealed clues that point to our early ancestors using ritual. While ritual and music-drama are not synonymous, all rituals contain ordered, organized physical movement with expressive or symbolic purpose; they therefore contain one ingredient of music-drama, and it is difficult to conceive of such rituals occurring without a simultaneous use of organized sound. It would seem appropriate, therefore, to begin a history of music-drama with the rituals of early man.

Despite intensive and extensive research, the origins of man on this planet are still shrouded in mystery. Before the Leakeys' researches in the Olduvai gorge, most prehistorians accepted a date of half a million years ago as marking the start of mankind. The Leakeys' work has pushed this date back to something like one and three-quarter million years ago, and each new discovery seems to push it back still further. Much depends on the point at which a higher primate can be regarded as a member of the genus Homo. We can perhaps leave that particular question aside: for our purposes it is enough to state what is generally agreed, that by half a million years ago a recognizable type of man was living in some numbers in Africa, Europe, India and the Far East, although we know virtually nothing about him. We know more about circumstances two hundred thousand years ago, when Neanderthal Man inhabited Europe, using tools and fire, practising cannibalism, living in caves, and hunting the mammoth, rhino, horse and bear. Common legend, and pictures of his reconstructed head, have given Neanderthal man the appearance and reputation of a stupid, clumsy humanoid; in fact, his brain capacity was slightly larger than our own, and he was superbly equipped, both physically and mentally, to meet the demands of a hostile environment. Recent research has led some archaeologists[3] to the conclusion that Neanderthal society was fairly complex; Alexander Marschack, with somewhat controversial views, maintains that Neanderthal man possessed a high level of intelligence, cognition, and culture.[4]

15

We can know but little of Neanderthal culture. The only remnants are burial sites, and caves showing signs of habitation. However, a number of skulls found in those caves show signs of having been opened for the purpose of eating the brains; until recently this rite was still practised by head-hunters in Borneo in the belief that they would thus acquire the virtues of the dead. Other skulls and stones are found placed in circles in Neanderthal caves, suggesting some deliberate arrangement, presumably for a ritual rather than a practical reason. In the Dordogne, in Southern France, there have been found the remains of adult and infant Neanderthalers who seem to have been buried with some ceremony; the ashes of offerings are present beside the bodies. One adult lies in an east-west orientation; another was buried with shells, flints, and with a stone axe in his hand.

Whatever conclusions we might draw from this fragmentary evidence, one thing is fairly clear. Neanderthal man performed some kind of ritual when burying his dead: the bodies were not just abandoned, but treated with care. What his precise beliefs were, we do not know — perhaps he believed in some kind of afterlife. Nor do we know for sure whether his burial ceremonies were communal affairs, though the existence of several similarly arranged graves does imply a generally agreed practice.

Evidence of a burial ceremony is not, as such, evidence of music-drama: what evidence is there that Neanderthal man was capable of using organized sound? Dr Carleton S. Coon[5] has suggested that the Neanderthalers communicated in speech, at least enough to be able to pass on skills from generation to generation. We know, too, that Neanderthalers had tools and weapons, made by chipping flint and stone. These facts suggest that Neanderthal man was aware of pitch and rhythm, the two basic ingredients of music, and even had to hand the materials to make simple musical instruments. We must be careful not to build too much out of too little, but let us raise the tentative possibility that man may have had some form of ritual music-drama as early as two hundred thousand years ago.

Though Neanderthal man is now long extinct, there is one race of people on this planet whose level of culture is regarded as not far removed from his. The Andaman archipelago in the Bay of Bengal is some two hundred and fifty miles distant from the nearest mainland, the coast of Burma. Because of this isolation, the inhabitants, pygmy Negritos, have regressed to a very primitive cultural level.[6] In the 1920s several tribes inhabited the islands living in groups of forty to fifty. Each group lived in a circle of huts surrounding a central, open area. At one end of the area stood a sounding log, a thick, hollow tree-trunk with one end embedded in the earth, which was struck with the foot to make a rhythm. At night, the women sat on the ground and sang, clapping their hands on their thighs, while the men danced.

In the dance of the Southern tribes, each dancer dances alternately on the right foot or on the left. When dancing on the right foot, the first movement is a slight hop with the right foot, then the left foot is raised and brought down with a backward scrape along the ground, then another hop on the right foot. These three movements, which occupy the time of two beats of the song, are repeated until the right leg is tired, and the dancer then changes the movement to a hop with the left foot, followed by a scrape with the right, and another hop with the left.[7]

The precise meaning of the steps is not made clear, but here there is irrefutable evidence of shaped physical movement to music in the rituals of these extremely primitive people. During their rites, enacted at important moments — birth, initiation, marriage and death — 'the individuals involved are defended from the powers of the moment by various types of ceremonial ornamentation — red paint, white clay, incised (scarified) designs, decorative plant fibers, shells, etc. — as well as by ceremonial dancing, ceremonial weeping, and the recitation of myths.'[8]

Costume, dancing, ceremonial weeping, narrative, an accompaniment of rhythmic drumming: these factors indicate that music-drama is present in Andaman culture. We must remember that Andaman culture may not have regressed as far in this respect as it has in others; nevertheless it is reasonable to suggest that music-drama in some form is here shown to be a natural part of an extremely primitive life-style.

For the Andamaners, as apparently for Neanderthal man, rituals are enacted at moments when the individual enters into a new 'life': birth, adulthood, marriage, and death; these 'rites of passage' show a link between music-drama and religion. At such moments, the individual faces a bio-logical or psychological transformation, and seeks reassurance and guid-ance from the community and tribal tradition. Music-drama and religion both provide that reassurance and guidance, and unite to do so in the single event of the ritual. It would seem that the activities of music-drama are a very ancient way to express, experience and explore religious beliefs.

Any conclusions we draw about the music-drama of such a remote period in human history must inevitably be tentative. But the evidence we can glean from Neanderthal man and the Andaman islanders points unwaveringly in one direction: music-drama arose during man's early history as part of the rituals associated with moments of literal or psychological death and rebirth. Music may have been used for non-religious purposes too, if tribal tradition allowed: we can certainly imagine that children then as now played games involving the ingredients of music-drama. But when the adults of the tribe gathered to celebrate or to mourn, their rituals took musico-dramatic form, and as we trace the continuing climb of man towards civilization we shall see that this primary interaction between music-drama and the mystery of death-rebirth remains, an immutable constant behind changing outer forms.

17

Man the hunter

Neanderthal culture seems to have existed for about one hundred and seventy-five thousand years (that is, approximately seven times the span of *homo sapiens* so far) and for all we know may have developed considerably during that time. But our bird's-eye view must now move to his successor, Cro-Magnon Man. By the period of twenty-five thousand years ago, a more temperate climate has changed man into a hunter of grazing animals. Although he is still a nomad, following the herds, he does select particular caves, to which he returns, and which form some sort of centre for the community; on the walls he daubs and scratches mysterious images of dancing animals and men. His hunting technology improves with the invention of the bow and arrow, and with the taming and training of the dog as his hunting-companion.

Man the hunter is entirely dependent, economically, on the animals he hunts. They provide him with food and clothing, with material for shelters, with bone tools, bone ornaments, ropes, and weapons. His entire way of life, and thus his outlook and his culture derive from this relationship with his animal victims. His society is male-dominated, for it is the men who hunt and the women who stay at home; yet women have a vital function to perform in child-bearing and -rearing, and it is this mysterious function of woman as a symbol of fertility that is celebrated in the female figurines preserved from this period. The major issue for man the hunter, however, is his almost personal relationship with the hunted, a relationship exemplified in the myth of a hunting tribe that survived well into the nineteenth century.

The Blackfoot Indians of Montana were hunters of the North American buffalo or bison. A favourite method of slaughtering or capturing the animals was to drive a herd over a low cliff, either to their deaths, or into corrals where they might be kept and slaughtered as necessary. The same method was used by palaeolithic man. One of the tribe's most important legends tells of a time when every attempt to kill or capture the buffaloes this way seemed doomed to failure; the tribe was growing alarmed.

> One day, a young woman of the tribe happened to be standing below a cliff, near the corrals. She looked up, and saw a great herd grazing at the very edge of the cliff. 'Oh,' she cried, 'if only you buffaloes will jump over the cliff, I shall gladly marry one of you.' To her amazement, the animals immediately began to leap over the cliff. One particularly large bull jumped over, and then leaped over the side of the corral, and came towards her.
>
> 'Come, then,' he said, and, tossing his horns, he led her up over the cliff and away.
>
> The tribe was delighted to see so many buffaloes in the corral, though they knew not how they came to be there. However, after a time, the young woman was missed in the encampment. Her father spoke to the chiefs. 'I shall go and seek her', he said. He took his bow and quiver, and set out across the plain.

He travelled a long way, and saw no sign of his daughter. Then he met a beautiful magpie. 'Ha, handsome bird,' he said, 'help me find my daughter. Fly about, look for her, and if you see her, tell her her father is waiting for her here by the water-hole.' The bird flew away, and shortly came to a large herd, led by a great bull. Near the bull stood the young woman.

'Young woman,' said the magpie, 'come quickly. Your father is waiting for you there by the water-hole.'

'Hush,' said the young woman, who was frightened that the bull would hear. At that moment the bull looked up.

'Go, wife,' he said, 'fetch me water.' The young woman took a horn, and hurried to the water-hole.

'Come,' said her father, 'let us hurry home.'

'No, not now', replied the young woman. 'Let us wait until my husband sleeps, then I shall try and slip away.' She returned to the bull, bearing the horn of water.

'Ha,' said the bull, 'there is someone close by here.'

'No,' replied the young woman, hastily, 'no one is here.' But the bull began roaring and bellowing, and stamping his feet, and presently the whole herd was roaring and bellowing and stamping, searching about for who might be there. They rushed about in wider and wider circles, and finally came to the water-hole, where they discovered the man. With great roars, they trampled him into the mud.

The daughter wailed. 'Oh, my father!' she cried.

'Aha', said the bull. 'You weep for your father. Now you may see how it is with us. We have seen our fathers, our mothers, driven over the cliff and slaughtered by your people. But I give you one chance: if you can bring your father back to life, you and he shall return to your own people.'

The young woman turned to the magpie. 'Help me now,' she said. 'Search in the mud, find my father's body, and bring it to me.' The bird flew about, searching, and digging in the mud with its beak. But all it could find was one small piece of backbone, which it brought to the young woman. She placed the piece of bone on the ground, and covered it with a robe. Then she knelt, and sang a certain song. She sang it twice, and when she removed the robe, she saw her father lying there. He stood up. The magpie flew about in delight.

'We have seen strange things today,' said the bull. 'The man we trampled to death is again alive. Now we shall teach you our dance and song. You must not forget them 'for these are the magical means by which the buffalo you kill are restored to life.' The bulls of the herd began to dance, the steps ponderous and deliberate, the song slow and solemn, as befits buffaloes. And when the dance and song were over, the bull spoke again. 'Now go home to your own people, and do not forget what you have seen. Teach this song and dance to your people. The sacred objects of the rite are a bull's head and a buffalo robe. All those who dance are to wear them.' He tossed his horns, and led the herd away.

The father and his daughter returned to their tribe. When they heard the story, the chiefs picked young men, called them I-khun-uh'-kah-tsi, and they were taught the song and dance of the buffalo. And that is why we dance the Buffalo Dance, and that is why, if anyone offends against the tribe, or if the rituals are not performed properly, then answer must be made to the I-khun-uh'-kah-tsi.[9]

This Indian legend provides the answer to several of the primitive hunter's questions about his life and the animals he hunts. It reassures him that there will always be a plentiful supply of bison to be hunted, so long as he follows the correct ritual procedures. It reassures him that the bison themselves do not object to being hunted and killed, for they are restored to life, again through the practice of proper rituals. It creates an interdependence between man and bison, not merely economically, but through the I-khun-uh'-kah-tsi, those who wear the bull's head and robe, dance the buffalo-dance, and are responsible for the moral and religious behaviour of the tribe.

More importantly, for our purpose, it tells us how a particular music-drama came about and why it is performed. The buffalo-dance, and that 'certain song' sung by the young woman, have the power to conquer death, the most final of events. It is through the buffalo-dance that man can come to terms with the animals he kills, and with the notion of death itself. And, just as the bison return to life to be hunted the next day, so the Indian is resurrected after death in the happy hunting grounds. The primitive hunter conquers death by making it a junction between two hunting lives, a painful moment, like the moment in an initiation ceremony when a boy becomes a man, or the moment of a baby's birth, but not ultimately an extinction of his being. As with the Andaman islanders, each of these moments has a ritual; the important events of man require some sort of ceremony in order for them to be registered as important and because they remind man of those things in his life which he cannot explain.

The Blackfoot legend appears to give the origins of the buffalo-dance; in fact, both the legend and the dance perform the same role, in different media. The legend is a typical myth story, with the characters acting as archetypes. The father is the archetypal hunter; the magpie is a typical medicine-man figure; the bull is the archetypal animal; the young woman is an archetypal female. Magpie, bull and young woman are also figures with mysterious associations: the medicine-man (whom we shall discuss later) possesses abnormal human powers; women have their own creative mystery; and the magical, mysterious power of the god-bull is the very essence of the story. Through these mystery-laden archetypes, the legend sets out to explain carefully how it is that death is followed by rebirth, why it is necessary to practise the buffalo-dance, and why man and animal have a closely-defined relationship. In passing, it stresses the role of women and medicine-men in the religious life of the tribe. Like any good narrative, the plot has character, tension and unexpected turns of event; beneath it all there lies a quality of inevitability. But the events are connected here in some non-rational way that we cannot easily comprehend.

What the legend does in a narrative medium, the buffalo-dance does in the medium of song and dance. Here it is not a matter of explanations, but a matter of actions and experiences. Instead of describing a buffalo, the performer 'acts' a buffalo. There is no story, developing through time, but a timeless, single experience. The dance, in fact, is not dependent upon the legend; indeed, it may have preceded it, and the myth-story may have been invented later in order to explain and justify it.

The possible age of the buffalo-dance is indicated by cave-paintings dating from about 30,000 B.C. In the Trois Frères caves in Southern France there are paintings showing buffaloes and, behind them, a man dancing in a bull's head and buffalo robes. In the Tuc d'Audoubert cave there is a chamber in which two buffaloes are represented in bas-relief on a raised mound; around the base of the mound are the imprints of foot-steps, as if some dance was regularly performed. In a nearby hunting-shrine may be found the famous Venus of Laussel (perhaps better named the Artemis of Laussel), a carved female figurine, holding in her uplifted right hand a buffalo horn. It would be absurd to suggest that the Venus illustrates the Blackfoot young woman offering a drink to her lord the bull; however, some kind of mysterious role for women in relation to animal magic is clearly indicated: the horn is a symbol of fertility and refreshment.

Some prehistorians maintain that the caves where paintings were drawn, where reliefs were etched out of the rock, and where little figurines were made were merely the hobby-rooms of ancient man. Others believe that their inaccessibility, and the nature of the 'art' left by primitive man, clearly prove that the caves were places of magical importance, perhaps the centres of secret societies with their own rituals, or perhaps the temples of whole tribes. Perhaps, indeed, they were the 'opera-houses' of man the hunter.

Just as the buffalo-dance is not dependent upon the legend that explains it, so these cave paintings are not dependent upon dancing; they are, again, a parallel expression of man's relationship to the animals he hunts, represented in the medium of painting. In each of these art forms — telling a story, dancing and singing, and painting — man is attempting to create: to make a buffalo. In the story, the words give a picture of a buffalo, and our imagination supplies the rest. In the dance and song, physical movements and sound and costumes suggest a buffalo, and, again, we imagine the rest. In the cave painting, a buffalo is shown in two dimensions, while we provide the third. In a sense, the created object (in whichever medium) is both buffalo and not buffalo; looked at objectively, it is not buffalo, but once we regard it subjectively, and supply imagination, it most definitely is buffalo.

This curious fact lies behind the whole of music-drama, and we should explore it a little more deeply.

Music-drama as image-making

A buffalo-dance, a painting of a buffalo, and a story about a buffalo have one common factor: imitation, 'image-making'. Each is an attempt to make an image of a buffalo; such an image is not an exact copy, but the imitator's version of a buffalo. Myths and works of art belong not to the world of logic, but to the world of the imagination in which objects are perceived for what they seem to be, or for what they can become, rather than for what they are. Thus a primitive dance portraying the hunting of a deer can take place with only human performers and in a small dancing area: an area twenty feet square seems to be, and can become, an area of plains many miles square; a man in a deer skin seems to be, and can become, a real deer. A gesture with a spear can represent a mortal blow to the heart of the animal. There is no need, in performing 'the hunting of the deer', for a real live deer to be pursued round the dancing area and finally slaughtered. (Indeed, to do so would be comic, for it would immediately point to the absurdity of the remaining pretence — that the dancing area can become the great plains.)

But why should man seek to imitate, to make images, at all? What benefit does it bring him?

The first reason is that it is enjoyable. We all have an inborn capacity for and delight in play, and the play element is basic to art. Leo Frobenius tells the story of a professor who was being pestered by his four-year-old daughter as he tried to work.[10] He gave her three burnt matches, and she sat down happily on the carpet to play Hansel, Gretel and the witch. After some time, the little girl suddenly jumped up and rushed, screaming, to her father. 'Daddy, daddy,' she cried, 'take the witch away, take the witch away!' Out of one burnt match the child had created an image of a witch, and that image had become frighteningly powerful and real. What began as a game took on a new dimension, for the imagination, once roused, went beyond the child's ability to control it. She knew, ultimately, and could be reassured, that the 'witch' was in fact only a burnt match; but this knowledge did not prevent her imagination taking flight. The ambiguity of an image enables us to participate in 'the game' and simultaneously to go beyond it. This is not the product of civilization, but a basic ability of man, as is shown in Frobenius's example of a child at play. R. R. Marett notes that 'the savage is a good actor who can be quite absorbed in his rôle, like a child at play; and also, like a child, a good spectator who can be frightened to death by the roaring of something he knows perfectly well to be no 'real' lion.'[11] Civilized man, like the 'savage' and the child, is able to accept pretence as reality in opera. Once the imagination is aroused, it does not matter that people sing all the time instead of speaking, nor does it matter that that eighteenth-century *château* is really a dozen painted stage flats. A match can become a witch — a fifteen-stone soprano can become a beautiful, slim Brünnhilde. Objectively, it is absurd; subjectively, and through the game, it is perfectly acceptable.

The second reason why man imitates is that through imitation he can share and gain the experience of the thing to be imitated. The Blackfoot Indian dances his buffalo-dance in order to understand more about the buffalo, by means of sympathetic magic. He wears a bull's head and a buffalo robe, so that he may look like a buffalo — and probably smells like one too. Stanislavsky stresses the importance for the actor of putting on costume and make-up as a means of achieving an immediate 'identity' with the character he is to portray.[12] Imitating outward appearances can lead to a perception of inner experiences. The simplest way to cheer oneself up is to do the things one does when one is cheerful. Related to this is the fact that imitation is also a learning process. A baby learns to speak by imitating the sounds made by its parents, even though it may not know at first the meanings of those sounds. Balinese children learn to make music not by being told what to do, but by watching, listening to, and then imitating the teacher as he makes music. Imitation has an immediacy of experience: the imitator is not held back by the limitations of verbal description.

There are, then, two reasons why we imitate: because it is fun, and in order to gain the experience of the thing we are imitating. The two reasons are not opposed. The little girl begins with play and finishes with gaining an immediate experience: she 'becomes' Gretel. The buffalo-dancer, it seems safe to assume, enjoys imitating the buffalo. Both use their imaginations to create images of magical power: the little girl is frightened by her image of the witch, while the buffalo-dancer's image of the buffalo is part of the magic which defeats death. The magic in the image lies in the fact that they are not the products of logical thought or literal fact. To see a match as a witch, or a man in buffalo-robes as a buffalo, is only possible when the power of imagination obliterates the power of objective thought.

However, we human beings do not constantly live according to our imaginations (unless we are schizophrenic): we live according to our powers of reason. We perceive things through our senses, process them according to our experience, and act reasonably on the basis of the evidence. Yet, were human beings only capable of input, processing and output in a logical way, we would be mere machines. We also have another set of faculties: the perception of something through the senses may arouse emotions in us; we are capable of creating in our minds things which do not literally exist. When faced with things outside our experience, or things we cannot logically analyse, we do not blow a fuse or stare blankly back and ask for more information. We attempt to come to some understanding of what we do not know, and, if our powers of reason fail us, we try something else.

The archetypal event that human beings find it most difficult to come to terms with is death. We find our logic incapable of coping with it, precisely because we do not have enough factual evidence from which to draw conclusions. In consequence, we attempt to provide non-logical explanations (a belief in the afterlife, or in re-incarnation, or in some superhuman figure into whose divine plan death fits neatly), and we can then happily indulge in logical reasoning about death, on the assumption that belief is fact. The trouble is that belief is not fact, and there remains an essential mystery about death that cannot be understood: more crucially, it cannot be avoided, for death is an experience which every man eventually has to face, and may face at any time.

It is no coincidence that primitive man should create rituals of music-drama to be performed at those moments in life where death or quasi-death (a significant biological and psychological change, like birth or adolescence) takes place. The rituals he devises are, equally significantly, concerned with the attempt to remove the permanence of death. These rituals, as we have seen, consist in the making of images through which the imagination can operate; it is the imagination that we use to penetrate the mystery and to bolster belief. And the images we create are substitutes for the facts we perceive in everyday life; we have an emotional reaction to them, and can even process them logically.

The images we create are also the products of ourselves, limited and shaped by our own human nature. The buffalo-dancer is limited by his own physique: he may imitate the pawing and stamping of a buffalo, but he has two feet and not four hoofs. A man may imitate a bird by putting on feathers, but he cannot actually fly: his imagination may take flight but he remains earthbound. Imitation is metamorphosis only in the imagination. Man the image-maker must create his images within his own limits. This itself creates a tension between desire and possibility which is part of the work of art (great art is perhaps that in which desire is almost fulfilled and the impossible almost achieved, and lesser art that in which desire has never attempted to challenge the impossible). Much, therefore, depends upon the imagination, for through it physical limits are temporarily forgotten. The young girl who turned a match into a witch in her imagination was more able to do so than a more adult, more educated person: she did not think of witches in terms of psychology as mother-figures, or in terms of orthodox religion as pagan priestesses. For her, a witch is someone living in a gingerbread house who eats little girls and boys for dinner. This quality of innocence, of the untrammelled imagination, is a particular feature of the creative artist.

The structure of an image also depends upon the medium used. Painting and dance, for instance, both have their own particular qualities as art-forms, and their individual characteristics provide both limits on and potential for expression. Each is a 'game' with its own 'rules', and we must have some understanding of those rules and their limitations in order to appreciate what is being expressed. Painting is two-dimensional: to paint a buffalo, therefore, is to create a two-dimensional image of a three-dimensional object — moreover, the painted image is incapable of actual movement. Dancing is a series of shaped and rhythmically related physical movements: they may have their roots in the natural movements of the human body, but they are not realistic. You can walk down a street or dance down a street, but to do the latter is not to do the former. Once we perceive the difference between 'the game' and reality, we are then in a position to see the game's potential as a mirror of reality. The young men of the Blackfoot tribe transform the movements of the buffalo into human dance-steps, within the structure of dance as an art-form. The everyday reality of a buffalo's steps undergoes a *transformation* through the medium of human dance, and our imaginations are stimulated. We perceive a meaning in what was hitherto mysterious, a meaning not arising from logical deduction but nevertheless striking us with the impact of truth.

It is this process that lends to artistic experiences an impact shared only by the most intense experiences of normal life. And it is those most intense experiences of normal life — birth, initiation and death — that bring about man's rituals, his exploration of mysteries in terms of the game of music-drama.

The images in music-drama can, therefore, be regarded as *reality transformed*. The transformation is begun by the author/composer/performer, who creates images according to 'the rules of the game', and is continued when our imaginations discover meanings within the images. When we grasp the rules, and allow our imaginations to be provoked, then even the realistic items employed in the image-making are transformed: paint on a canvas is not just paint, sound is not just frequencies and decibels, stage lighting is not just amps and volts. The theatre itself, like the art-gallery or the concert-hall, becomes more than a building; as with the tribal dancing-ground, the reality of bricks or mud is capable of being transformed into a world of images. And when we participate in the musico-dramatic experience, our everyday world is transformed into 'the no-place, no-time, no-when, no-where of the mythological age, which is here and now.'[13] The total image produces its own new reality, which our imaginations lead us to accept as naturally as though it were the reality of everyday.

Images and music

Music is the most abstract of the arts, or so it would appear. While representational painting is a transformation of what we naturally see, and dancing and acting are transformations of what we naturally do, music seems less directly related to the sounds we naturally hear. Obviously, the pitch-changes and rhythms of language have influenced music, and have done so quite strongly at times; similarly, the sounds of nature have had their effect; but it is not easy to trace a simple connection between, say, Mozart's G minor Symphony K.551 and human speech or natural sounds. What sort of images, then, does music provide? In what way is music *transformed reality*?

25

There are as many theories about the origins of music as there are historians of primitive music. Explanations include the 'yo-heave-ho' theory (to borrow and extend terms from the history of language[14]) — that music arose as an aid to rhythmic group work; the 'bow-wow' or 'tweet-tweet' theory — that music arose as an imitation of animal or bird noises; the 'help-help' theory — that music arose from the need to give signals; and the 'lovey-dovey' theory — that music arose from the rituals of courtship and mating. Other suggestions are that music is intensified speech, or that it arose simply as a way of alleviating boredom. Some authorities argue that rhythm preceded melody, others that melody came first; some suggest that singing preceded instruments, others suggest the opposite. Any of these theories might be correct: the simple fact is that no one has yet found any evidence of a time when man had no music, and we cannot, therefore, now trace its source.

The medium of music is sound, and the production of sound by a human being involves some physical exertion, whether it be striking something, plucking something, blowing into or across something, or simply taking breath and flexing the necessary muscles in order to sing. Human sound-making is, in short, the result of physical tension, as are human movements. Singing, playing an instrument, dancing, and gesture are parallel products of the same source. For musical sounds and physical movements to occur simultaneously is not an artificial partnership but one natural to man. But not all sounds made as the result of physical tension are musical, just as not all physical movements are 'dramatic'. Music is organized sound, caused voluntarily. If I accidentally drop a cup and saucer on the floor, the resulting sound of breaking china may well be rhythmic, but it is not music. If I stub my toe, and involuntarily give a scream, the sound I make well have distinct variations of pitch, but it is not music. In order to make musical sounds, a human being must deliberately create sound-shapes, and in order to do that, he must be able to imagine them before they occur.

This process happens automatically to us when we speak. Like music, speech is sound organized in pitch and rhythm. But there are significant differences between the two, which are bridged by poetry. Ordinary speech is a method developed by man to communicate specific facts, opinions, ideas and feelings. The components of speech are words, each of which has a meaning understood by those who are familiar with it, or who can work out its meaning in the context of other familiar words. Words are images representing things that are part of our everyday reality — the reality of everyday life, or the realities of our individual emotional and intellectual lives. Words are, furthermore, linked together grammatically: that is, according to logical rules that allow us to formulate and understand concepts of some complexity. Speech is, in short, composed of series of images whose meaning is *comprehensible* to other people.

26

Music, on the other hand, is composed of a series of images (notes and patterns of notes) whose meaning is not comprehensible in the same way, even though the sounds are linked by the rules of a musical grammar. Musical images, unlike the images of speech, are not specific: they do not relate to a common reality: they do not have specific meanings shared by all. This is not to say that musical sounds have no meaning, but rather, that they communicate in a different way from that of speech. They cannot communicate specific facts, ideas or opinions — they do not even communicate precisely the same feelings to everyone who hears them. Musical images retain a magic, a mystery that cannot be explained in any other but musical terms — and even then, such explanations may say little about the deepest meaning of the music.

Poetry stands somewhere between ordinary speech and music. It uses the materials of ordinary speech, but in such a way as to create images beyond the specific comprehensibility of the words used. From music it takes rhythm and metre, which introduce veils of artifice through which hidden meanings can be perceived. In Classical Greek tragedy, as we shall see, there was little distinction between 'poetry' and 'music' — the former almost automatically determined the latter. In more recent music-drama, it has been customary to provide an opera text which is at least in some way 'poetic', and many librettists and translators have discovered to their cost that ordinary speech and music are uncomfortable companions. Even in the most naturalistic of opera situations it is difficult to set and to sing a phrase like 'pass the mustard' without creating comic absurdity. On the other hand, there are examples from every period of opera in which a text is so poetic that it loses all comprehensibility when sung, for example, 'Now the Great Bear' in Britten's *Peter Grimes* (see chapter 8). If song is regarded as some form of heightened speech, then the text must have the potential to be heightened, without already being up amongst the stars.

However well-blended the words and the music may be in a particular music-drama, this does not disguise the fact that they operate in different ways. Verbal communication uses a language which is relatively explicit and comprehensible, while musical communication uses a language which is largely inexplicable but which is none the less understandable. We can grasp at music's meanings even if we can only imperfectly explain them: they are less *comprehensible* than *apprehensible*. Unlike words, music cannot be translated, but this very untranslatability allows it to communicate experiences which are themselves both understandable and untranslatable; it is peculiarly appropriate for the presentation of images symbolizing experiences beyond the reach of logic and words.

It is for this reason that music and religion have always been closely related. The relationship may take the form merely of using music as part of religious worship, or it may take a form like that of Indian Classical Music, in which musical sounds themselves have a deep-rooted religious significance. 'Primitive' and 'civilized' people alike have regarded music as being a natural and proper means to praise a deity, to inspire a worshipper, and to represent the presence of magical and mysterious forces in the life of man. Our modern, scientific investigations into the origins of music mean nothing to a member of a primitive tribe: more often than not, he will explain that music was not invented by man, but given to him by the gods: it is the language man and gods have in common.

In music-drama, words and music are put together simultaneously: two different sets of images are presented at the same time. Each informs the other: musical images take us beyond the text to what lies behind it, while verbal images give a focus to the implicit meanings of music.

Apollo and Dionysos

The blend of implicit and explicit in music-drama is not confined to the relationship between words and music: it is fundamental to the art-form (as it is to all art-forms). The interaction between apprehensible and comprehensible elements permeates its whole being. Viewed overall, a music-drama communicates indefinable experiences to us in definable ways; viewed at a much lower level, every musical sound, every word, every physical gesture has both a concrete comprehensibility and a hidden, implied meaning which we cannot easily explain. It is this which gives a music-drama its power, for it requires the response of all our faculties. It is a gigantic image operating visually and aurally, in time and in space, composed of a legion of constituent images, each of which contains the double-helix of implicit and explicit meaning.

To use the image of a double-spiral to describe the blend of implicit and explicit in music-drama is not accidental. One very ancient human symbol is the caduceus, or two intertwined snakes, representative of nature's regenerative powers. It appears as the staff of Hermes, mediator between the two worlds of life and death, as the famous Naga serpents of Indian mythology, and survives as a symbol of medicine and healing. More recently, and in a more scientific context, the double-helix has been revealed as the structural pattern of DNA. This ancient symbol therefore is not inappropriate to describe the internal workings of an art-form which, from our survey so far, would seem to have been born from man's need to understand in some way his own relationship to life and to death. Such an understanding could and can only come about through the exercise of both his rational and non-rational faculties, which can be stimulated through the double-helix of images.

The two ever-present spirals of music-drama, explicit and implicit, were interpreted in his own way by the German philosopher Friedrich Nietzsche. In *The Birth of Tragedy from the Spirit of Music* (1871) he uses the terms

'Apollonian' and 'Dionysiac' to describe the opposing forces which, in his view, came together to create Greek tragedy and which remain as the thesis and antithesis behind the synthesis of opera. Like the systematic categorizations of many German philosophers, Nietzsche's Apollo and Dionysos theory can be applied to almost every field of human activity, but this is something of an advantage in its application to the field of music-drama, which contains so many artistic elements and which creates its own microcosmic mirror of reality.

Figure 1 shows a wide range of characteristics that can be termed either Apollonian or Dionysiac, all of them relevant in some way to music-drama. Nietzsche borrows his terms from the gods of Ancient Greece: Apollo was (he says) the god of civilization, social order, and of musical structure, and encouraged the populace through his oracle at Delphi to practise moderation in all things and to acquire self-knowledge. Dionysos, on the other hand, was the god who encouraged his worshippers to throw off restraints, to liberate themselves from the prison of 'proper behaviour', and to experience truth directly and immediately. Thus, Nietzsche argues, all the ingredients in music-drama can be categorized as Apollonian or Dionysiac, and the total experience combines the two.

The subject-matter of Greek tragedy was taken from myth. As we have seen in the Blackfoot legend, myth has both Apollonian and Dionysiac aspects. The story of the young woman and the buffalo proceeds sometimes by cause and effect, sometimes mysteriously. It contains elements of the explicable and elements of the inexplicable. In reacting to it, we can follow it rationally but must also accept its irrational aspects. It communicates to us on a conscious level as a narrative of events, but it also demands that we liberate ourselves from the expectations of reality.

The myth is told in words, and words are able to communicate on both levels. At times, the words make perfect sense; at other times, they only appear to make sense, as when we read that the buffalo speaks. We know that buffaloes do not speak: however, in the world of myth, we move beyond that surface absurdity and are switched into another, Dionysiac reality in which all things are possible. The same thing happens in music-drama: the words here too have a subtextual reality.

A music-drama such as Greek tragedy arranges myth into words and music. Music too operates on an Apollonian and a Dionysiac level. As pure sound it has a physiological effect upon us, producing physical reactions: we tap our feet, or a shiver runs up our spines, or our pulse-rate and breathing-rate quickens or slows. It can arouse our emotions, making us want to weep in grief or joy. It can make us forget who we are, metaphorically sweeping us off our feet. These effects are familiar ones, particularly to anyone who listens to contemporary pop music or observes how its devotees react to it. They are Dionysiac effects. But music can also communicate on an

Fig. 1   Apollo and Dionysos

Apollonian art is	*Dionysiac art is*
concerned with	*concerned with*
concepts	feelings
knowledge	wisdom
cause and effect	coincidence
plans	impulses
moderation in behaviour	extreme behaviour
self-control	self-liberation
pattern and shape	effect and impact
the explicit	the implicit
the specific	the universally applicable
the explicable	the inexplicable
beauty	ecstasy

Our response to	*Our response to*
Apollonian art is	*Dionysiac art is*
rational	emotional, irrational
mental	physical
objective	subjective
observing	involved
self-aware	unaware of self
conscious	subconscious

Apollonian level: we perceive and appreciate the beautiful shape of a melody, or the well-planned structure of a movement. Often, we can 'follow' a piece of music, remaining disengaged from it. Music can be analysed, or at least a goodly part of it can be. Some pieces of music (one thinks of passages by Bach and others by Stravinsky) deliberately set out to appeal to our appreciation of sound-patterns; others (one thinks of passages by Beethoven and Wagner and Debussy) deliberately set out to involve us in sound-effects.

Nietzsche argues with considerable justification that music must contain both levels of communication if it is to operate properly: but he goes further, and suggests that, in the end, the Dionysiac sound-effects dominate Apollonian sound-patterns. In other words, when we listen to a piece of music, it requires an effort to remain objective; it is more natural to become subjectively involved. Our previous discussion of the nature of music would bear out this theory: it is the discrete, abstract, inexplicable nature of music which dominates everything else.

While music is therefore primarily, but not only, a Dionysiac medium, words are primarily, but not only, an Apollonian medium. The physical movement on the 'stage' can be either. In a narrative play the pseudo-realistic characters move in a manner close to the way we all move in everyday reality, and we therefore tend to recognize the purpose behind the movement: it is explicable, analysable, and therefore inclines towards the Apollonian. In dance or stylized movement, on the other hand, the physical action is further distanced from the way we move in everyday reality, and communicates on a more Dionysiac level, although its shapes and patterns have an Apollonian element as well. The visual setting (the stage set, costumes and lighting) can be Dionysiac or Apollonian according to the wish of the designer and director.

These ingredients in music-drama can be blended in a number of ways to produce an overall effect which may be more Dionysiac, more Apollonian, or evenly balanced. An opera in the opera-house may take its story from myth, and contain many Dionysiac inexplicabilities, or from history, where events may have a more Apollonian explicability. The characters can appear more realistic or less realistic; the text can be more naturalistic or more artificial, more informal or more poetic. The music can emphasize shape and pattern or incline more towards the involving quality of sound-effect. The production can affirm or contradict Dionysiac or Apollonian elements on any level.

It is impossible for music-drama to be totally Apollonian or totally Dionysiac. The images man creates must have shape to be images: as soon as words are used the consonants shape the vowels: as soon as a human being appears on a stage his nature as a human being gives shape to what he does. Music too, as organized sound, inevitably has some recognizable shape to it. But as soon as music sounds, Dionysos appears, for our imaginations are stimulated to explore what lies behind the shape of images.

It is for this reason that many people consider music to be the most important ingredient in music-drama — and presumably this is why opera is thought of as a branch of music. Dionysos dominates; we achieve our deepest experiences in the opera-house when we penetrate behind the text and the picture to the mystery beneath. And yet without Apollo those experiences would lack focus. As Nietzsche says, 'the Apollonian spirit rescues us from the Dionysiac universality and makes us attend, delightedly, to individual forms. It focuses our pity on these forms and so satisfies our instinct for beauty, which longs for great and noble embodiments.'[15]

Although Nietzsche was the first to explain the forces that combine to make music-drama (at least in such clear-cut terms), it was primitive man who first instinctively created that balance. We can see why music-drama has always been important to man. Together, Apollo and Dionysos provide a way to link the explicit (that which we know by direct experience) and the implicit (that which we come to sense, indirectly), the concrete (that which we can define and explain) and the discrete (that which we cannot define or explain). To 'primitive' man, music-drama offers a way of bringing together the worlds of reality and magic. It offers the same to 'civilized' man.

31

The image-maker

If music-drama was such a powerful and important element in the life of primitive man, we may ask how particular music-drama rituals came to be created. Who was it who made up that Blackfoot Indian legend about the buffalo? And who was it who actually made up the dance performed by the I-khun-uh'-kah-tsi?

The role of composer-dramatist was an honourable one in the primitive hunting-tribe.

Among the hunting Indians of North America, each adolescent boy was required as part of his initiation to go through an ordeal of isolation and fasting. He would remain at some deserted spot without food, and visited only occasionally by his father, until he experienced some kind of spiritual vision. Usually, the spirit of an ancestor would appear to him, and direct him into one of three careers: hunting, being a warrior, or shamanism.

In the Hollywood version of the American West an Indian shaman is called a medicine-man. But he was more than just a healer: the shaman was a mystic and an artist as well. While other members of the tribe related to their traditional myths and rituals in a conformist way, deriving comfort from their strict observance, the shaman related to these same myths and rituals in a creative way. His magical powers — and, whatever modern science may say, he did have magical powers — enabled him to experience directly the images of tribal ritual.

> I remember how, in the old days, the shamans bellowed during the seance like bulls. . . There used to live in our village a shaman whose name was Konnor. When his older sister died, he shamanised. When he did so, horns grew on his head. He stirred up the dry clay floor with them and ran about on all fours, as children do when they play 'bull'. He mooed loudly and bellowed like a bull. [16]

While the buffalo-dancers donned buffalo horns, the shaman 'grew' them, miraculously, out of his own head. For him, rituals were not ceremonials with fixed rules to be followed to the letter, they were living images of his own immediate experience. They were the starting-point from which his personal visions could soar, and in this respect, he was the prototype of the inspired creative artist.

The typical vision of the shaman is one of death and rebirth; the vision of the adolescent shaman is almost invariably of his own dismemberment and reconstitution. [17] This image is a typical psychological image in adolescent dreams; it is also a profound image of the creation of a work of art. The creative mind dismembers known material and reconstitutes it in new material. The extent of the dismemberment and reconstitution determines how 'new' or how 'derivative' the created work shall be (but not how 'great' it shall be). For most creative artists, this is an instinctive process — the new, reconstituted image emerges spontaneously into the consciousness through 'inspiration'. The process, like the visionary process of the shaman, can be helped by practice, but its essential feature is the moment of creative rapture, in which the 'idea' suddenly fills the mind to the exclusion of all else.

The act of artistic creation is, at least in its inspirational aspects, the act of a single man. A tribe cannot create a myth or a ritual.[18] The members of the tribe are the participants and beneficiaries, but the initial image-making is not theirs. The Blackfoot buffalo-dance is not created by the tribe as a whole, it is learnt by them from the report of a single person (in the legend, the young woman) who has seen the buffalo-dance in a 'vision'. In general terms, the gap between the primitive hunter's attempt to come to terms with death and the buffalo and the performance of some kind of buffalo-dance is filled by the creative visions of the shaman. In the Blackfoot legend, it is the magpie, the shaman-figure, who enables the story to reach its proper conclusion, by bringing father and daughter together and by finding the piece of backbone in the mud at the waterhole.[19] And the practising shaman is no solitary, he is part of the tribal community, available for consultation, and participating in tribal rites. He usually has a drum, or a drum-playing assistant; he sings and dances. Having seen his vision in private, he communicates it to the tribe in the form of song and dance, often going into a trance in which his body appears to perform impossible movements.

Behind the myths and rituals of primitive tribes there stands the ecstatically leaping figure of the shaman, the same figure that prances and dances among the buffalo in the cave-paintings of Trois Frères. He transmits images to the tribe, which they themselves take up and re-create in ritual. His visions are the images of immediate experience, shaped and structured by the ceremonial game.

Man the planter

The shaman, with his individualistic vision, is the product of a hunting society. Hunting, though it may be a group activity, depends essentially on individual bravery, and individual impulse is something to be encouraged in the community. Planting, on the other hand, is and must be a group activity, in which all take part as equals, men, women and children. Sowing and reaping are identical actions for all. Around 7500 B.C. life in the Near East changed from nomadic hunting to settled village life and the planting of crops (the Neolithic Revolution), and the individualistic shaman grew less important, to be replaced by the priest, the keeper of traditions, the temporary occupant of an office others have held and will hold after him.

The change in the pattern of life from hunting to planting was a profound one. Man's world was no longer dependent upon and related to the animal world. As a nomadic hunter, man had known death as the consequence of violence. Its very suddenness made it magical, unpredictable. And, when one could conceive of no other way of life than hunting, it followed that

33

rebirth must be into a happy hunting-ground. As a planter, on the other hand, man's life was now ruled by the changing seasons, the growth of plants, and the cultivation of a fertile earth. Settled village life, with a more reliable supply of food, led to an increased longevity and a greater likelihood of death from natural causes. The primitive hunter's view of life as a series of death-rebirth events in a single-line progression was replaced by the primitive planter's view of life as a continually revolving cycle of growth, decay, death and rebirth. Man now realized the connection between death, birth and fertility in the plant world on which he depended, and out of that realization grew new myths and rituals.

The most familiar planting myth is that of Demeter and Persephone, with its counterparts in the legends of Astarte and Adonis, Cybele and Attis, and Isis and Osiris. The Homeric *Hymn to Demeter,* written around 700 B.C. tells the story.

> The youthful Persephone, so runs the tale, was gathering roses and lilies, crocuses and violets, hyacinths and narcissuses in a lush meadow, when the earth gaped and Pluto, lord of the Dead, issuing from the abyss carried her off in his golden car to be his bride and queen in the gloomy subterranean world. Her sorrowing mother Demeter, with her yellow tresses veiled in a dark mourning mantle, sought her over land and sea, and learning from the Sun her daughter's fate she withdrew in high dudgeon from the gods and took up her abode at Eleusis, where she presented herself to the king's daughters in the guise of an old woman, sitting sadly under the shadow of an olive tree beside the Maiden's Well, to which the damsels had come to draw water in bronze pitchers for their father's house. In her wrath at her bereavement the goddess suffered not the seed to grow in the earth but kept it hidden under ground, and she vowed that never would she set foot on Olympus and never would she let the corn sprout till her lost daughter should be restored to her. Vainly the oxen dragged the ploughs to and fro in the fields: vainly the sower dropped the barley seed in the brown furrows; nothing came up from the parched and crumbling soil. Even the Rarian plain near Eleusis, which was wont to wave with yellow harvests, lay bare and fallow. Mankind would have perished of hunger and the gods would have been robbed of the sacrifices which were their due if Zeus in alarm had not commanded Pluto to disgorge his prey, to restore his bride Persephone to her mother Demeter. The grim lord of the Dead smiled and obeyed, but before he sent back his queen to the upper air on a golden car, he gave her the seed of a pomegranate to eat, which ensured that she would return to him. But Zeus stipulated that henceforth Persephone should spend two-thirds of every year with her mother and the gods in the upper world and one-third of the year with her husband in the nether world, from which she was to return year by year when the earth was gay with spring flowers. Gladly the daughter then returned to the sunshine, gladly her mother received her and fell upon her neck; and in her joy at recovering the lost one Demeter made the corn to sprout from the clods of the ploughed fields and all the broad earth to be heavy with leaves and blossoms. And straightway she went and showed this happy sight to the princes

of Eleusis, to Triptolemus, Eumolpus, Diocles, and to the king Celeus himself, and moreover she revealed to them her sacred rites and mysteries. Blessed, says the poet, is the mortal man who has seen these things, but he who has had no share of them in life will never be happy in death when he has descended into the darkness of the grave.[20]

Here, as in the myths of the hunters, we have the idea of the necessary ritual, but now the ritual is one of sacrifice. In order that Persephone — the crops — may emerge from the earth, payment must be made to Hades. Just as winter is necessary to spring, so death is to life. Man strikes a bargain with nature, and the bargain obliges him to ensure the annual death so that the annual rebirth can take place. Persephone must die to be reborn.

In Babylonian myth, it was Tammuz, the youthful lover of the great goddess Ishtar, who died each year, and was sought in the underworld by the goddess; his return in spring was celebrated with a sacred marriage.

His death appears to have been annually mourned, to the shrill music of flutes. . . The dirges were seemingly chanted over an effigy of the dead god, which was washed with pure water, anointed with oil, and clad in a red robe, while the fumes of incense rose into the air, as if to stir his dormant senses by their pungent fragrance and wake him from the sleep of death. In one of these dirges, inscribed *Lament of the Flutes for Tammuz,* we seem still to hear the voices of the singers chanting the sad refrain and to catch, like far-away music, the wailing notes of the flutes:

At his vanishing away she lifts up a lament,
'Oh my child!' at his vanishing away she lifts up a lament;
'My Damu!' at his vanishing away she lifts up a lament;
'My enchanter and priest!' at his vanishing away she lifts up a lament;
At the shining cedar, rooted in a spacious place,
In Eanna, above and below, she lifts up a lament. . .
Her lament is the lament for a herb that grows not in the bed,
Her lament is the lament for the corn that grows not in the ear. . .
Her lament is for meadows, where no plants grow.
Her lament is for a palace, where length of life grows not.[21]

The evidence of this, and other surviving Babylonian hymns, suggests that myth was presented in the form of music and drama, as it was with the Blackfoot Indians. Similarly, the Persephone myth was the subject of the Eleusinian Mysteries, one of the chief sources of Greek tragedy.

A further example of the music-drama of primitive planters may be found in the ceremonies of the Marind-Anim tribe of south New Guinea. Here the notion of necessary sacrifice is carried into musico-dramatic reality. Each year there occurs a series of complicated puberty rituals for adolescent boys and girls, which culminates in a terrifying rite. The whole tribe gathers at the dancing-ground, older members of the group being costumed as gods, or

35

Dema. Drums beat, bull-roarers[22] are whirled to represent the voices of the Dema rising from the earth. Everyone chants and dances, while a young girl, painted and costumed, is led into the centre of the dancing-ground. She lies down beneath a platform of heavy logs. One by one, the young male initiates are brought forward to copulate with her, while the dancing, drumming and chanting continues. While the youth chosen to be last is lying with her, the support of the log platform is knocked away, and the heavy logs drop on the couple, crushing them to death. Everyone howls and chants, and the drums beat long and loud. At last the rhythms change and a new ceremony begins: the dead girl and boy are dragged from beneath the logs, cut up, roasted, and finally eaten by the tribe.[23]

To those of us accustomed to less realistic horrors in our music-drama, this may seem unnecessarily bloodthirsty. But we must beware of judging it only in terms of twentieth-century morality. The love-death of the victims, and the eating of them, is a ritualistic representation of an ancient awareness of the importance of sex, sacrifice and death as symbols of the cycle of fertility in nature. What the Marind-Anim tribe does is to present, through the medium of music-drama, the fertilizing of the earth by dead matter. The sacrifice of the boy and girl, like the death of Persephone or Adonis, guarantees next year's crops, and the symbols of their sacrificial death are eaten by the other participants in the rite. While, literally, the participants are practising cannibalism, they are in religious terms merely eating the symbols, the visible representations of the idea of sacrifice, in much the same way as Christian communicants partake of the symbols of the blood and body of the crucified and risen Christ.

The difference between the symbolic eating of the body and blood of Christ in the Communion and the actual eating of the sacrificial victims by the Marind-Anim tribe is only one of degree. Though the girl and boy really die, they are, *within the rite,* merely actors in a music-drama and are considered as such by all. The young girl is painted and costumed, symbolic of the earth to be seeded, of fertility and potential birth. There is no reason to suppose that she is an unwilling sacrificial victim, any more than is the virgin who offers herself to death in Stravinsky's ballet *Le Sacre du Printemps.* To judge such acts as if they were solely reality, rather than *reality transformed,* is to miss the point.

The rituals of the Mysteries of Eleusis, centred on the myth of Demeter and Persephone, were less bloodthirsty than those of the Marind-Anim tribe: sacrificial symbols other than human beings were employed. With Eleusis we enter the world of Greece, which was to give birth to western European music-drama as we know it. But, though we move from pre-history to history, from the 'primitive' to the 'civilized', we are still dealing with the same basic human problems and needs that gave rise to music-drama in earlier cultures. Man is still concerned with exploring the mysteries of life through images which transform reality. His religious beliefs may alter, and the details of his music-drama change, but he perpetually remains the curious and mystified animal, seeking to find some connection between himself, the things he knows and the things he can imagine.

2 The music-drama of Ancient Greece

Predecessors

The link between the music-drama of primitive man and Western European opera is provided by the Classical Greek tragedy of the fifth century B.C. Greek tragedy is the earliest music-drama of which we have the preserved texts — the libretti, at least — and it is therefore easy to leap to the conclusion that the Greeks 'invented' music-drama. They certainly invented their own form of music-drama, but their city-state and culture was merely the latest in a series of cultures in the Near East stretching back to about 4000 B.C. Indeed, Classical Greek tragedy is chronologically closer to the present century than it is to the time when man first started living in cities: when we consider the amount and variety of music-drama there has been in the past two and a half millenia, we can at least begin to wonder what music-drama there might have been during the three and a half millenia between the foundation of Sumer and the first triumphs of Aeschylus.

That there was music-drama in the ages between primitive man and fifth century Athens can scarcely be doubted. We have traced the importance of music-drama to primitive man, and there is every reason to suppose that the Sumerians, the Akkadians, the Babylonians, the Egyptians and the Cretans all had their own types of music-drama. Although, therefore, music-drama may appear at first sight to have suddenly and miraculously burst into flower one day in late March, 534 B.C., when Peisistratos instituted the contests for tragic music-drama in Athens, this rather attractive idea must be discarded. In its religion, its political ideas, its social organization, its philosophy and its science Classical Greece owed much to its predecessors; there is every reason to suppose that this was the case with its music-drama as well.

Any attempt to show direct influences upon Classical Greece from earlier Middle and Near Eastern civilizations is, however, fraught with difficulties. In the first place, the course of civilization in its main locales ebbed and flowed with the rise and fall of dynasties, the regular incursions of barbarians from the north, the occurrence of natural disasters, and the natural

38

ambitions or laziness of men. These same factors mean that evidence of the various cultures is often very incomplete. In the second place, it is not always easy to establish the extent of the intercourse (if any) between contemporary civilizations when they were not actually at war. Nevertheless some facts can be stated, and interpretations drawn.

Of all the developments in the history of man, perhaps the most remarkable was that achieved by the Sumerians, in Mesopotamia around 4000 B.C. What they evolved was the city-state, and, along with it, mathematics, astronomy, writing and the wheel. Man the farmer, living in a tribal group, his life determined by the fertility of the earth, became urban man, living in a political-religious state, his life determined by the passage of the planets in the sky. Astronomy (or, more properly, astrology) determined the fixed patterns of planetary movement around the earth and the city-state was deliberately planned to reflect that pattern.

> The whole city, not simply the temple area, was now conceived as an imitation on earth of the cosmic order, a sociological 'middle cosmos', or mesocosm, established by priestcraft between the macrocosm of the universe and the microcosm of the individual, making visible the one essential form of all. The king was the center, as a human representative of the power made celestially manifest either in the sun or the moon, according to the focus of the local cult; the walled city was organized architecturally in the design of a quartered circle . . . centred around the pivotal sanctum of the palace or ziggurat . . . and there was a mathematically structured calendar to regulate the seasons of the city's life according to the passages of the sun and moon amongst the stars — as well as a highly developed system of liturgical arts including music, the art rendering audible to human ears the world-ordering harmony of the celestial spheres.[1]

The religion of the city-state did not, however, completely replace earlier beliefs. Man was still essentially a farmer, dependent upon water and sunlight for the cultivation of crops. His planter's rituals continued; now, however, they were fixed by priests and determined by law. Ritual sacrifices were still necessary — often of the king or his representative — and were presented in dramatic form to the accompaniment of music; the movement and music were symbolic of the actions of the gods and of man's relationship to the gods.

During the third millenium B.C. flourishing civilizations developed in Mesopotamia (Sumer-Akkad) and in Egypt (Old Kingdom); by about 2500 B.C. signs are evident of city-states emerging in Asia Minor and in Crete. What sort of music-drama did they have?

Inevitably the evidence is scanty. Third millenium Sumerian texts speak of temple music of some considerable sophistication. We know of the instruments used by the Akkadians and Babylonians after about 2250 B.C.: pipes of the flute and oboe type, drums of all kinds, stringed instruments (plucked rather than bowed) and metal and wooden trumpets. We know too that these instruments were often associated with animals, which suggests that their origins lie deep in human history, perhaps in the period when man was a hunter. In Mesopotamia they were used, along with singing, as part of temple rituals, and the sung liturgy seems to have been no less elaborate than that of the Catholic Church. We also have some evidence of secular music: as early as 2400 B.C., music in the form of a singer and *kithara*[2] was used for entertaining at royal banquets. There is evidence too of 'actors' — possibly priests, possibly not — dancing and singing in costume.

There is no doubt that music — and at least ritual music-drama — played an important part in Mesopotamian civilization. It may or may not have developed a great deal during the centuries: against man's natural instincts to find new ways of doing things we must set the traditionalism of the Mesopotamian city-state and the likelihood that music-drama rituals were fixed by the state religion. There may also have been an active, continually developing secular music-drama, perhaps even groups of strolling players, for the individualism that had produced shamans can scarcely have been obliterated by even the rigid totalitarianism of the Mesopotamian city-state: however (and perhaps not surprisingly) there is no extant direct evidence of this. All we do know is that travelling bards were in existence in Mesopotamia and Asia Minor around 2000 B.C. when the epic of Gilgamesh was written down.

Ancient Egyptian music seems from this distance to have been hardly different from Ancient Mesopotamian music. The same features are present, the same instruments, the same religious controls. But we can at least cite the description of an Egyptian music-drama ritual, the so-called Abydos Passion Play, dating probably from around 2000 B.C.

> The oldest documented Mystery, if we look at reliable remnants, is a report by the royal official I-kher-nefert of the Twelfth Dynasty of Egypt (*c*. 2000–1700 B.C.), which may be accepted without a doubt as the description of a performance of the most colossal organization. For several weeks a procession of ships moves along the Nile (it is also the longest-lasting festival known to us) and into its tributaries and canals. At least two barges are employed, probably a far higher number; the two main ones are those of Ap-uat and Osiris, both decorated with altars, with images of the divinity and, like all Egyptian theatre-ships, richly furnished with musicians, female dancers, and colossal decorations visible from far away. From the description in the report several landing-places are evident: at the site of a battle where Ap-uat was victorious, at the grave of Osiris at Peqer and finally at his temple in Abydos. Certainly a huge crowd of people will have followed the procession from the river banks, as is documented at similar events in Ancient Egypt. When the barges came into the shore, there was an 'act' of the festival play: in Peqer doubtless the death of Osiris, who was dismembered by his brother Seth; in Abydos, as the inscription clearly states, his resurrection amid

the endless jubilation of the participants and the public, for the leader of the play 'caused great happiness, when they saw beauty brought ashore, in bringing the lord of Abydos into his palace'.[3]

By 2100 B.C., Crete was a wealthy island, standing as it does at the crossroads of the eastern Mediterranean. Cretan ritual centred round the worship of the great mother-goddess (of whom Demeter may be regarded as a descendant), and certainly included ceremonial music and dance. Archaeology has revealed the existence, at Phaestus and Knossos, of tiered open-air theatres, built about 2000 B.C., and although we do not know exactly what was performed there, we do have pictures of Cretans in other contexts watching dancers and singers. It seems not altogether unlikely that Crete had some form of secular music-drama, since the Cretan theatres were obviously designed for audience and performers rather than as temples for worship. For musical instruments, the Cretans had the seven-stringed lyre, trumpet and drum, pipes and reed-pipes (including the double-pipe — two pipes blown simultaneously); these are included among the instruments of Ancient Greece.

One of the important ritual activities in Crete was 'bull-leaping', which seems to have been a mixture between a sport and an initiation-rite, much as bull-fighting is today. But it is also had a religious side, for the bull was an important animal in the Cretan pantheon. There is some evidence to suggest that singing and dancing took place as part of bull-leaping ceremonies, and this again reminds of more primitive rituals such as the buffalo-dance and the cave-paintings of Trois-Frères.

After about 1800 B.C. there seems to have been considerable contact between the various civilizations of the Near and Middle East: Egypt, Mesopotamia, Crete — and the emerging Hittite Empire in Asia Minor and the Mycenaean kingdom in mainland Greece.

The Mycenaean culture was created, it seems, by Indo-European peoples who entered Greece from the north around 2000 B.C.; from around 1600 B.C. signs of great wealth appear in their tombs (the so-called Shaft Graves at Mycenae and elsewhere), wealth perhaps gained in service as mercenaries in the Egyptian wars of the Hyksos Pharaohs (around 1720 to 1570 B.C.). In about 1400 B.C. the Mycenaeans appear to have occupied Crete, and here and on the Greek mainland developed a civilization of considerable material prosperity. This same period marks a highpoint in Babylonian culture, and in the New Kingdom in Egypt with the radical ideas of the Pharaoh Akhenaton.

Little is left of Mycenaean culture: no amphitheatres of this period have been found in Greece, so we must presume that the Mycenaeans did not bring this aspect of Cretan culture back across the Aegean. As a rather warlike people they presumably had at least martial music. The Mycenaeans were the Greeks who fought, according to legend, at the walls of Troy, and if Homer is a reliable reporter, then they enjoyed singing and dancing and the narration of epic stories, as in Odysseus' account of his own adventures in books nine to twelve of the *Odyssey*.

Epic poetry (of which Homer's *Iliad* and *Odyssey* are our most familiar examples) is of very ancient ancestry. Correspondences in phraseology, metrical structure, and terminology between Vedic (i.e. Indian), Slavic, Celtic and Greek epic poetry suggest that all sprang from a common Indo-European tradition. That tradition clearly ante-dated the invention of writing; epic poetry was transmitted orally. Like the buffalo-myth of the Blackfoot Indian, the epic poem tells a story, often with its source in history, but embroidered as necessary by the poet to include moral or religious messages, to add entertaining digressions, or simply as the result of some creative fancy. For our purposes, epic poetry is important because it was sung, and the recitation of it may have been accompanied by gesture and movement.

The epic poet may be an important link between the primitive shaman, the musical traditions of the pre-Greek city-states, and the music-drama of Classical Greece. As a teller of tales, an upholder of tribal tradition, and a creator and developer of legends, he seems to share much with the shaman, although magic is now transmuted into the magic of poetical and musical improvisation. As a user of strict poetic metres, and as a skilful instrumental player, he seems to reflect the artistic skills of a civilised culture. That the Mycenaeans had their own form of sung epic (the ancestor of Homeric epic) is proved by a number of Mycenaean 'survivals' in the *Iliad* and *Odyssey*.[4] The tradition was to be maintained and developed through the subsequent Dark Age by travelling bards, particularly in Ionia (see Fig. 2) and culminated in the eighth century in the Homeric epics themselves.

Clearly, epic poetry and dramatic poetry are not the same, and it would be unwise to draw hasty conclusions. But we can, again, see the epic poet as a link between the temple priest addressing his worshippers and the dramatic actor addressing his audiences; he provides one element in an explanation for the emergence of Greek music-drama.

But whatever the Mycenaeans might have acquired from their neighbours, or evolved themselves, very little survived the disasters which swept across the Eastern Mediterranean about 1200 B.C. Around this time the Mycenaean and Hittite cultures collapsed, apparently under the onslaught of the mysterious 'Sea Peoples', who destroyed but did not settle. Only Egypt successfully resisted them. The consequence, in the Aegean at any rate, was the onset of a Dark Age, when literacy vanished, populations declined, and the Mycenaean Greeks were reduced to isolated, struggling communities. We must presume that precious little in the way of music-drama survived, at least in any sophisticated form. Perhaps in Egypt, which

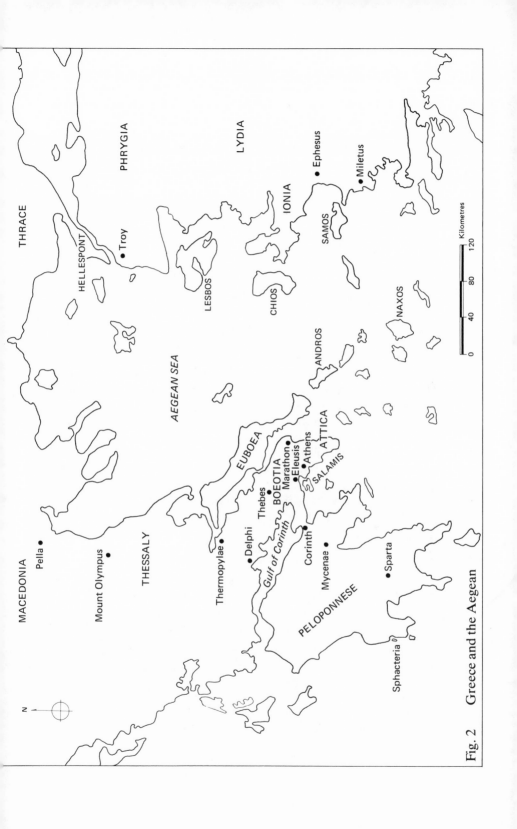

Fig. 2   Greece and the Aegean

was being gradually taken over by Libyan immigrants, something was preserved; perhaps also in Crete. In Mesopotamia the Assyrians were in control and gradually expanding westwards: they are better known for their military exploits than for any major contribution to the arts.

In Greece itself a new settlement from the north, by the Dorians, was taking place, yet another in the series of quiet or noisy invasions by barbarians from the north which punctuate the history of the Near and Middle East from about 3500 B.C. to the time of Alexander.

According to Campbell, these continuing invasions from the north by hunting nomad peoples, who settled and met the civilized societies of the Middle East, resulted in a series of clashes between patriarchal and matriarchal cultures. In Sumer, growing as it did from neolithic village culture, the Great Goddess stood behind everything as 'the arch personification of the power of Space, Time and Matter, within whose bound all beings rise and die: the substance of their bodies, configurator of their lives and thoughts, and receiver of their dead.'[5]

In contrast, the warrior tribesmen who invaded from the north had a masculine and patriarchal view of life. The result was continual clash and interplay between patriarchal and matriarchal cultural elements, with a tendency for the patriarchal to dominate. Thus in Mycenae we find that the usual offerings were female figurines, but that Zeus, Poseidon and other male deities were also worshipped. The duality seems to lie at the root of Greek culture, and was possibly one element in the tensions which gave rise to the glories of the Classical period.

In Greek religion and mythology we can see the patriarchal-matriarchal conflict through the stories of Odysseus' adventures with the fair sex in the *Odyssey*[6] and the legends of Zeus' many conquests of women. The matriarchal culture personified the great Mother-goddess in the form of local cult goddesses, representatives of her power within the village community. Zeus, the male god, dominates them, and makes them his own. In at least one legend, he significantly assumes the form of a bull as part of his amorous pursuit. It was a peculiarly Near Eastern (and particularly Greek) achievement that the conquest of the local goddesses did not lead to their obliteration: on the contrary, they remained as part of the male-dominated Pantheon. This is illustrated in Apuleius' *The Golden Ass*, when the initiate successfully undergoes his ordeals and hears the words of Queen Isis:

> I am Nature, the universal Mother, mistress of all the elements, primordial child of time, sovereign of all things spiritual, queen of the dead, queen also of the immortals, the single manifestation of all gods and goddesses that are. My nod governs the shining heights of Heaven, the wholesome sea-breezes, the lamentable silences of the world below. Though I am worshipped in many aspects, known by countless names, and propitiated with all manner of different rites, yet the whole round earth venerates me. The primeval Phrygians

call me Pessinuntica, Mother of the gods; the Athenians, sprung from their own soil, call me Cecropian Artemis; for the islanders of Cyprus I am Paphian Aphrodite; for the archers of Crete I am Dictynna; for the trilingual Sicilians, Stygian Proserpine; and for the Eleusinians their ancient Mother of the Corn.

Some know me as Juno, some as Bellona of the Battles; others as Hecate, others again as Rhamnubia, but both races of Aethiopians, whose lands the morning sun first shines upon, and the Egyptians, who excel in ancient learning and worship me with ceremonies proper to my godhead, call me by my true name, namely, Queen Isis. I have come in pity of your plight, I have come to favour and aid you. Weep no more, lament no longer; the hour of deliverance, shone over by my watchful light, is at hand.[7]

When, therefore, Greece began to emerge from her Dark Age, she was the descendant of two cultures. One was the culture of her predecessors, Egypt, Crete, and Mesopotamia, with its matriarchal ancestry and its sophistications in the city-state, in music, and possibly also in music-drama. The other was the culture of the patriarchal hunting peoples of the north. The emergence seems to have begun rather suddenly, about 1050 B.C., when a new form of pottery (Protogeometric) appears, and when iron begins to be used more widely. By 750 B.C. the population had grown: colonies were established on the Ionian coast, in Sicily and southern Italy. Contacts were spreading across the Aegean and the Eastern Mediterranean; from Phoenicia, for instance, the Greeks adopted and adapted the recently developed alphabet. Already developments were being made in science, philosophy and the arts. After 750 B.C., despite wars between the Greek city-states, contacts increased, ideas circulated, and colonial expansion continued. Only one peril was in sight on the horizon: the growing power of the Persian Empire, whose culture had remained predominantly matriarchal.

The conflicts between Greece and Persia during the fifth century B.C. provide the historical background to Classical Greek tragedy. Around 500 B.C. the Greek settlements in Ionia rebelled against Persian occupying forces: by 494 the revolt was crushed, and the Persians under Darius invaded mainland Greece. In 490 this first assault was defeated by Athens and her allies at the battle of Marathon, in which the playwright Aeschylus fought.

Darius' successor, Xerxes, crossed the Hellespont in 480 at the head of a second expedition against the Greeks. The Spartans resisted in vain at Thermopylae; Athens was evacuated. But the Greek navies succeeded in defeating the Persian at Salamis (where Aeschylus again fought) and the Persian army was vanquished at Platea. The playwright Sophocles led the chorus in the ensuing victory celebrations.

By 469, the date of Socrates' birth, the Persians had been cleared out of mainland Greece, and Athens was about to enjoy its Golden Age. Pericles was elected to office in 467, and in 447 the Parthenon was begun. This was a time of considerable dramatic activity, which was to continue even when the wars with Sparta began in 431. In fact, apart from a brief period between 468 and 431, and an even briefer interlude in the Spartan Wars between 421 and 418, Athens was constantly at war during the fifth century; this may be one reason why conflict was so important in Greek tragedy.

Greek music-drama

The duality in Greek culture is illustrated in their attitude to their gods: a blend of belief and cynicism, of serious ritual and delighted mockery. The oracle at Delphi, the most important shrine in the Greek peninsula, was fervently consulted on every matter, large or small, and yet everyone knew the priests could be bribed to deliver helpful (or at least not harmful) oracles. Even Homer's *Iliad* describes the gods as idols with feet of clay. In short, the Greeks humanized their gods and resisted the Mesopotamians' unquestioning faith in a divine cosmic order. Order there might be, but they wanted it to be reasonable, analysable, and comprehensible. It was the Greeks who practised most ably among these early civilizations the human being's delight in questioning, in working things out. Thus they (and in particular the Athenians) experimented with and evolved different forms of government: for them, the city-state was certainly not an institution whose structure was ordained by the movement of the planets.

This freedom of thought, this humanizing of the relationship between man and the gods, is the single most important ingredient in Greek music-drama; it was because the Renaissance in Western Europe shared the same attitudes that Greek music-drama became the inspiration for 'opera'. And it is because these attitudes have remained the cornerstones of West-European civilization that we can read the plays of Aeschylus, Sophocles and Euripides and find them striking a sympathetic note today.

But below the enlightened surface of Greek culture there lay mystery and magic. Reason might well be applied to the solving of problems; Pythagoras, Socrates, Plato, Aristotle, Euclid and the rest might well place science and philosophy upon the secure foundations of logic: but there lingered basic uncertainties. Sacrifices must still be made to the gods. Music might be, as the Pythagoreans suggested, the embodiment of mathematical relationships (themselves symbolic), but it was also, as Socrates pointed out, a divine madness. The Greek ships may have defeated the Persian fleet at Salamis through better strategy; but if the wind had not blown from the right quarter at the right time. . . Behind the complex and ordered funeral rites of the Greeks, as of every tribe or civilization, there lurked the primitive scream of fear made by man in the presence of the unknown, the unknowable.

Rationalism and uncertainty came together in the mystic cults of Greece. Of these, the most important (in the fifth century) were the Eleusinian Mysteries. Eleusis, fourteen miles from Athens, was a city basking in the patronage of Demeter (as Athens was under the protection of Athene, Delphi of Apollo, and Corinth of Aphrodite). Athens appears to have taken over the Mysteries early in the sixth century (under Solon). The Greater Mysteries were celebrated in autumn, in Greece the time of sowing, and can be seen as celebrating and encouraging the fertility of the soil. Four days were devoted to the festival, including sessions open only to those appropriately initiated: many of the details of the more secret ceremonies have remained secret. But we do know that the mysteries included a musico-dramatic presentation of the myth of Demeter and Persephone, and a symbolic procession through subterranean darkness and back up to the light of day. Here already are the basic ingredients of Greek music-drama: the presentation of myth in musico-dramatic form, a literal participation by an audience in the experience of the myth, and the whole enclosed in a mixture of ritual, festival and entertainment.[8] The subject is, as it was for man the hunter and man the planter, death and rebirth.

During the period of Peisistratos' rule in Athens (off and on between 560 and 527) the Greater Eleusinian Mysteries were augmented by the addition of Dionysos in the story. According to myth, Dionysos was twice-born (he was saved by Zeus when about to be murdered, sewn into his father's thigh, and born again); he therefore bears a close relationship to the Mesopotamian god Tammuz and the Greeks' own Adonis, both of whom died and were resurrected. Dionysos, as a cult-figure, was of Thracian origin (see fig. 2) and was worshipped with the typical orgiastic rites of a fertility god; the climax of the Dionysiac orgy was the dismemberment of a live sacrificial animal. Dionysos became to the Greeks, as he was to Nietzsche, a symbol of liberation from rationality. Clearly, Dionysos was not irrelevant to the Demeter-Persephone myth, and he became a more and more influential figure in Attica during the sixth century — ironically, perhaps, since this was the time of the great developments in rational science and philosophy.

In 534 Peisistratos established in Athens the spring festival called the Great Dionysia, during which the great drama festivals took place. Some authorities have made much of this, suggesting that Greek tragedy sprang from the worship of Dionysos. It may be so; certainly, there is enough evidence (discarding the questionable) to show that Dionysos-worship was *one* of the sources of Attic tragedy. But many other factors were involved. William Ridgeway[9] has suggested that tragedy arose from the worship of dead ancestors: this may ultimately be true, if we bear in mind the origins of music-drama itself, but is certainly open to question so far as the immediate paternity of Greek tragedy is concerned.

The technical ingredients of Greek tragedy were present in Grecian culture by the late sixth century. The Greeks of a thousand years before must have known of the theatres of Crete; priests and priestesses engaged in rituals like the Eleusinian Mysteries must have been practised performers of music-drama; all the instruments of Mesopotamia, Egypt and Crete were in current use in Greece; the Greeks had oral and literary traditions of story-telling and sophisticated forms of poetry. The enlightened Greek mind was posing questions, raising issues, wondering how much freedom man has or should have — not only politically, but in relation to his gods. All these ingredients were brought together in a music-drama of such compelling power that Pericles arranged for the works of Aeschylus, Sophocles and Euripides to be preserved. But what of the music in these music-dramas?

The basic element of Greek music was the tetrachord: two notes a perfect fourth apart with two more notes filling the gap. While the interval of the perfect fourth was absolute, in the same way as it is in our conventional organization of pitch, the intervals between the two middle notes and between them and the outer notes were extremely flexible. Three sets of four-note tetrachords were used by the Greeks, known as the diatonic genus, the chromatic genus and the enharmonic genus.

In the diatonic genus, the descending order of intervals was tone-tone-semitone; thus, within the fourth from *a* down to *e* the notes would be called by us *a—g—f—e*. In the chromatic genus, the notes are more difficult to represent, but might be described as *a* — a sort of *f* sharp or *g* flat — *f* — *e*. In the enharmonic genus similar difficulties arise, and the notes are best described as *a* — a rather sharp *f* — a rather sharp *e* and *e*. It is evident that the Greeks did not divide the octave into twelve equal semitones, but allowed other microtonal intervals between notes.[10] Even the intervals between notes in the tetrachords of the three genera described above are only approximate, for the Greeks knew at least two varieties of the diatonic genus and three of the chromatic genus. From all of this it will be clear that even the basic elements of Greek music show enormous expressive potential.

Several tetrachords were put together to make a scale. Four diatonic tetrachords (with an additional lower note) could be assembled in a two-octave scale. The two upper tetrachords shared a common note, as did the two lower tetrachords, as shown in Fig. 3. This scale, with its lowest and

Fig. 3   The Dorian scale

highest notes shown as *a*, is the so-called Dorian scale. It was capable of transposition, to suit the practical requirements of a singer, and since the intervallic relationships of the tetrachord (tone-tone-semitone) must be preserved, it is clear that what we would call 'accidentals' were used. To these transpositions the Greeks gave names, themselves based upon the two

other diatonic tetrachords which automatically follow from such trans-
positional procedures.

If we transpose the Dorian scale of Fig. 3 up one tone, this yields the notes
b — a — g — f sharp — e — d — c sharp — b. If, however, we reassert the *a* in
this new scale as the important note, and consider the tetrachord which
descends from it, we find we have a new series of note relationships: *a — g —
f sharp — e,* or tone — semitone — tone. This is the Phrygian tetrachord. If
we transpose our Dorian scale up one tone more, and follow the same
procedure, we get another new tetrachord of *a — g sharp — f sharp — e*
(semitone — tone — tone): the so-called Lydian tetrachord. Authorities
differ on whether these new tetrachords developed from transposition of the
Dorian scale, or whether they are as old as the Dorian tetrachord itself, and
merely enabled transposition to take place more easily.

Fig. 4 The Greater Perfect System

49

Figure 4 shows the range of the Greek scales in the Greater Perfect System: that is, the seven available transpositions of the Dorian diatonic scale, with their Greek names. Additionally, the Dorian, Phrygian and Lydian tetrachords are shown. The dotted rectangle shows the disposition of Dorian, Phrygian and Lydian tetrachords within the scales. Similar series of scales can be made up for the chromatic and enharmonic genera, as used by the Greeks. These provided the background pitch-structure to the choices made by a composer. His first decision would be which of the three genera to use, and it seems that the enharmonic genus was thought to be the one most suitable to the recitation of tragedy. Within the enharmonic genus, then, the composer could select the scales and tetrachords most suitable to express dramatic situations.

In his composition, the Greek composer or performer of tragedy was restricted by a number of factors. One was rhythm; another was the narrow range and the selectiveness of the notes used in each melodic passage (suggested by the few relics of Greeks music we have); a third was the presence, in vocal music, of a verbal text.

The verbal text of Greek poetry (as in tragedy for example) influenced the music in two very natural ways — through pitch and metre. Classical Greek was a very 'musical' language, requiring a rise and fall of up to a fifth on each word (the so-called pitch accent); meaning thus depended on the rise and fall of the voice. In poetry, the verbal text determined the rise and fall of pitch (within the key, scale and mode used) and also the rhythm, through the metrical structure of the lines. These metrical structures could be very complex: the Greeks knew of and used duple rhythm, triple rhythm, and rhythms of fives and sevens, combined in sophisticated ways. In tragedy, the rhythm determined not only text and music but also the dancing of the chorus. This is not to say that rhythm had the banal mindlessness of some modern pop music with its unshakeably conforming beat. On the contrary, it is clear even from the little Greek music we have that melody was not the slave of the varying pitches of a verbal text, and we can imagine that music, text and movement might be blended in tragedy with rich subtlety.

The accompaniment to vocal singing was provided by an *aulós* (reed pipe) in chorus passages, and probably by a stringed instrument in solo passages. The extent to which such accompaniment was independent of the vocal melody is a matter hotly debated: it would seem that there was probably some variation. The instrumentalist perhaps played only some of the sung notes, or followed the vocal line with some rhythmic independence. Passages in Plato suggest more: it is evident that the Greeks understood a difference between consonance and dissonance, and Sachs for one argues that this is only possible if two independent lines are sounded simultaneously.

Whatever may have been the precise sound of Classical Greek music —

and we remain largely in the dark about that — it was governed by two overriding principles. Firstly, music reflected *harmonia*, the 'balance' that pervades the Universe and which Man should seek to imitate. The Indo-European root *harm* means the unification of disparate or conflicting elements into an ordered whole, that Mesopotamian dogma which the Greek intellect sought to define and explain. Pythagorean theorists therefore sought to analyse the relationships between notes in a mathematical way.

Secondly, and here we again meet that other side of the Greek outlook, musical sounds were capable of a deep and powerful influence upon the mind of the listener. According to Greek *ethos*, Mixolydian melodies (see Fig. 4) were pathetic and plaintive, and Lydian were mournful. Music in the Phrygian key was agitated and Dionysiac, liable to inspire ecstatic enthusiasm. Dorian music on the other hand was virile and bellicose (patriarchal?), but at the same time it moderated and settled the temper. Hypolydian melodies were thought of as dissolute and voluptuous, Hypophrygian as 'active', and Hypodorian as majestic.

Such descriptions of the expressive power of music may seem as credible or incredible as more recent attempts to do the same thing for the keys of tonal music. They may reflect a Greek response to the names of the keys as much as to the sounds themselves. Sachs argues that one factor may be the relative pitches of the Greek keys. But there is no doubt that the Greeks associated particular musical sounds — rhythms as well as melodic shapes — with moral and even political or religious values.

This may have been an important factor in the development of Greek music-drama, for the Attic tragedies are more than entertainment: they discuss moral issues, and in the discussion musical sounds must have played their part.

Attic tragedy seems originally to have been performed in the *agora* adjoining the northern slope of the Acropolis. Here the earliest play-contests were probably held, although other contests in honour of Dionysos took place at his shrine on the south-eastern slope of the hill. The *agora* contained an *orchestra*, a semicircular area where the chorus performers sang and danced, while the audience watched from a grandstand of wooden seats. In about 470 B.C. the grandstand collapsed, and the contests were transferred to the shrine of Dionysos: here the theatre was enlarged in about 450 to 440, and the adjoining temple rebuilt about twenty years later. At about the same time the *Odeion* was built nearby to hold choral and solo singing contests.

In the Theatre of Dionysos an audience of about five thousand sat or stood in the *theatron*, semicircular rows cut from the rock of the Acropolis, and gazed down at the *orchestra*, where there was a small altar to Dionysos (see Fig. 5). Behind the *orchestra* stood a low semicircular platform, the

51

proskenion, on which the solo actors performed, and further back the *skene*, a wooden structure through which actors might enter and which served to represent scenery or to support scenery. It is possible that the roof of the *skene* was used for the appearances of gods. At the rear stage-left of the performing area, and therefore further downhill, stood a small temple to Dionysos.

Fig. 5　　The Theatre of Dionysos, late fifth century B.C.
　　　　　　(from J. Travlos, *Pictorial Dictionary of Ancient Athens*)

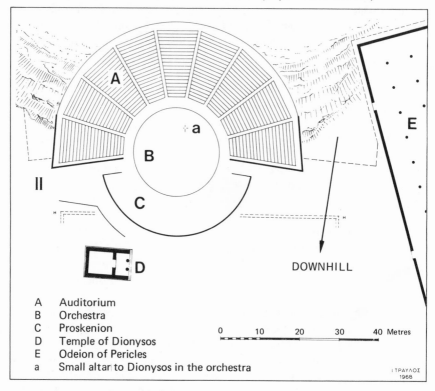

A　Auditorium
B　Orchestra
C　Proskenion
D　Temple of Dionysos
E　Odeion of Pericles
a　Small altar to Dionysos in the orchestra

0　　10　　20　　30　　40 Metres

ΙΤΡΑΥΛΟΣ
1968

DOWNHILL

Both the original Theatre of Dionysos and the fifth century alteration described here can only be deduced from archaeological investigation and occasional references in texts. In the late fourth century a further reconstruction took place, resulting in the 17,000 seat theatre visible today.

The earliest music-dramas in the Theatre of Dionysos seem to have been performed by chorus only. However unlikely this may seem, it becomes more plausible when considered as part of the strong Greek tradition for choral music. So far as we can determine, unison singing by massed male voices was the predominant form for public music: it was virtually the only form permitted in Sparta, and remained in Athens a prerequisite of all festival celebrations even after tragedy had been introduced. The performers were amateurs, although their leader had professional experience (and perhaps status). A prominent citizen was appointed *choregos*, and together with the author/composer he was responsible for the costuming and rehearsing of the group, which consisted of between fifteen and fifty men and youths.

During the fifth century, the importance of the chorus in tragedy declined as the role of the chorus leader grew more prominent. Originally there seems to have been one solo actor/singer — perhaps the author; Aeschylus' plays require two, and Sophocles' three. In 449 a prize was established for solo performance, which must have encouraged this particular skill and helped to establish the profession. All roles, male and female, were played by men. The actors wore both costumes and masks, designed to express in a typical way the main features of character or social status. Sometimes a special mask was used for a particular scene, as in Oedipus' appearance after putting out his eyes.

Masks and costumes had the effect then, as they do now, of transforming reality: the 'actor' lost his everyday reality and became the character in the drama. They also had a practical function in a theatre as large as the Theatre of Dionysos: small facial gestures are invisible at a distance, and a mask creates an easily identifiable image for the spectators. The actors' chief means of expression were gesture and voice: there was little in the way of movement. Vase-paintings show us that gesture was highly stylized, and much of the performer's individual characterization must have been achieved through skilful vocal improvization around the composer-dramatist's text.

Chorus and solo actors had different functions in Greek tragedy. The solo actor represented an individual personality, while the chorus symbolized the group, the community. Some authorities (including Nietzsche) have seen in this a similarity to the priest and a congregation in religious ritual: certainly the chorus tends to voice reactions rather than initiate actions. The chorus-members provide a bridge between silent spectators and the characters in the drama: often they interpret, comment upon and generalize what happens on the stage. Usually what they say makes the specific events more universal: they stress the emotional content of the story, and thus arouse in the audience a Dionysiac response to what it sees and hears.

Greek music-drama was such a sophisticated art-form that it is difficult to believe it sprang suddenly into existence. The music was based on practices and ideas that are at least as subtle as those of Western European tonality; the poetic language and skill in characterization shown in the texts is the work of brilliant and expert dramatic composers. In no way does it seem to be the beginnings of an art-form; rather, the evidence would suggest that it

53

relies upon an ancient ancestry, though precisely how the heritage was handed down remains as yet a mystery.

It therefore becomes all the more intriguing to wonder about the music-drama of Greece's predecessors in the Near East. There is no reason to suppose that Egyptian or Cretan or Mesopotamian music was any less sophisticated, nor is there any reason to suppose that their music-drama was entirely restricted to temple rituals. If the Egyptians honoured a dead king by presenting the Abydos Passion Play — in much the same way as Oberammergau in Bavaria presents a Christian Passion Play every ten years — what music-dramas were performed in honour of the generations of the kings of Babylon? And can we suppose that the minstrels who journeyed through Greece singing the tales of Homer never presented scenes in dramatic form? In Mesopotamia, similar wandering minstrels sang episodes of the Epic of Gilgamesh before 2000 B.C. — perhaps they too acted and danced. The I-khun-uh'-kah-tsi became the temple priests with their ritual music-drama, but perhaps the shaman survived, making his magic images in music and movement through the thousands of years of man's struggle against nature and himself. What wealth of music-drama, now lost, stands behind that isolated survival from more recent antiquity that we call Attic tragedy?

Aeschylus' The Persians

Aeschylus' *The Persians* is the earliest fifth-century play to have been preserved complete; it is therefore our earliest musico-dramatic text. The chorus opens the drama by stating that it is the Persian Council, left to rule Persia in the absence of King Xerxes (who has departed with the army to conquer Greece: these are the events of 480 B.C.). This statement is brief, and is immediately followed by a much lengthier passage in which the splendid sight of the departing army is emotionally remembered, interspersed with expressions of alarm at the lack of news from the front. Within this framework are placed clues to the moral theme of the play, which is that King Xerxes has committed the crime of *hubris*, excessive pride, and that the consequence of his *hubris* will be disaster (the battle of Salamis).

Here, immediately, within the first one hundred and fifty lines of the play, we are presented with a precise situation, its universal application through emotional expression, and its universal application as moral law. A magic image is being created in movement and music: that image is specific, concerning particular human beings (historical figures, no less), but also universalized, firstly through emotional expression, for which Dionysiac music provides an instant communication, and secondly in terms of ethics, as a cause and effect argument (of obvious appeal to Greek rationality). The same result was achieved by the buffalo-dance, the sacrificial rites of the Marind-Anim tribe, the mysteries of Eleusis, even, perhaps, by the burial rituals of Neanderthal man. In short, the spectator-listeners are subjectively involved and objectively 'taught' at the same time.

Aristotle's term for this tragic effect was *catharsis* — purification, achieved through the audience experiencing pity and terror. Our pity, he says, is aroused by seeing a man fall 'from prosperity to misery, and it will be due, not to depravity, but to some great error. . .'[11] A man commits an error: the tragedy is caused by human actions, and thus arouses our human feelings. We experience pity: we recognize that we are capable of the same or a similar error (if not, perhaps, on the same scale). We comprehend the image. But in so doing, we also experience the misery that results from the error, for the misery brings the sufferer into contact with the mysteries behind the surface of life. We apprehend what lies behind the image: we experience that primeval scream which expresses man's terror in the presence of death.

In *The Persians*, the lengthy opening chorus is followed by the appearance of Queen Atossa, Xerxes' mother, who focusses the anxieties of the chorus in her first words: 'that fear is mine; I too am torn by anxious thoughts. Therefore I have left the golden-furnished chamber which I shared with king Darius, to tell you my own dread. . .'[12] Atossa goes on to say that she knows the reason for her fear: the Persians have been rash. Again we are presented with the twin poles of Athenian thought: a focussed experience of dreaded mystery, and a rational explanation. The play develops these together, reaching its climax in the appearance of the ghost of Darius, who explains all.

Darius' ghost is summoned by the chorus, reminding us of primitive man's reverence for his dead ancestors, his belief that death is merely a stepping-stone between lives. Just as the great leader of the buffalo comunicated the truth to the I-kuhn-uh'-kah-tsi, and just as the image of Persephone risen from Hades brings the truth to man the farmer, so the great king Darius rises from death to speak to his people. He expounds the moral truth:

> . . .dead heaped on dead
> Shall bear dumb witness to three generations hence
> That man is mortal, and must learn to curb his pride.
> For pride will blossom; soon its ripening kernel is
> Infatuation; and its bitter harvest, tears.[13]

These words were probably sung: while the verbal images specify the moral law (summarised in the Delphic axiom *meden agan* — moderation in all things), the musical images would have contained that Dionysiac irrationality of sheer sound-effect, arousing dread. And in experiencing dread, the awareness of the final limitations on our *hubris*, we become wiser, we are purified.

The Persians affected its Greek audience (and can still affect us) in the

55

same way that tribal music-drama had affected primitive man: those who witnessed it were brought to a deeper understanding of the mysteries of life. But Aeschylus' play was also of immediate local relevance, and this must have added to the depth of its impact. It was written and performed a mere eight years after Salamis, the event at the centre of the play, and a battle in which Aeschylus himself had fought. Considering how the Athenians probably felt at the time, Aeschylus was remarkably bold in presenting Salamis from the Persian point of view. It is as if, to paraphrase H. C. Baldry,[14] an opera were staged in 1952 portraying the events of D-Day sympathetically from the point of view of Hitler and his generals. It is clear, however, that Greek tragedies were often written and staged to make political points, if not always with the astonishing magnanimity of *The Persians*. Phrynichos' *The Capture of Miletus*, performed in 492, reputedly aroused the audience to tears with its portrayal of the Persian conquest in 494 of the Ionian city of Miletus; it may well have formed part of Themistocles' political campaign to get the Athenians to prepare for war with Persia. The brutal devastation of the island of Melos by the Athenians in 416 inspired Euripides' *The Trojan Women* as a protest: indeed, the plays that Euripides wrote during the Peloponnesian War raise important issues in relation to its conduct. Greek music-drama was not escapist entertainment, but relevant in all respects, both specific and universal, to the life of the inhabitants of Athens.

Sophocles' King Oedipus

Aeschylus' plays are the earliest surviving examples of Western European music-drama. By the time Aeschylus died in 456, Sophocles, his immediate successor, was forty years old, with a number of successes to his credit. Sophocles was born at Kolonos, about a mile north-west of Athens, a village famous as the site of the tomb of the legendary king Oedipus. Of Sophocles' seventy tragedies, of which only seven are extant, it is his *King Oedipus* which has become the most popular in the twentieth century: not simply because Freud drew our attention to the psychological depth of the legend, but because it is, in the view of many commentators, Sophocles' masterpiece.

The subject of Oedipus had already been treated by Aeschylus, in 467. Sophocles' play is dated in the period 429–420, that is, during the years of the first Spartan War, when Sophocles was in his seventies, and at the height of his dramatic powers. Here we have a music-drama which, at first sight, seems less ritualistic than those of Aeschylus, and closer to our more modern idea of play as plot. The basic story is familiar, and was familiar to Sophocles' audience. King Laius and Queen Jocasta of Thebes have a son, but the Delphic oracle predicts that he will murder his father and marry his mother. In order to avert this disaster, the baby boy is given to a shepherd with orders that he should be killed. The kind-hearted shepherd in fact gives the child to a friend, and the boy is finally adopted by the king of Corinth and named Oedipus. Oedipus grows up believing that he is the son of the Corinthian king, but, on learning of the prophecy that he will kill his father, he flees the city. By chance he meets King Laius on a lonely road: after a quarrel, and still ignorant of his true birth, he kills Laius. Thebes is at this time menaced by a monster, a Sphinx, which spreads famine and plague and destroys all who cannot answer its riddles. Oedipus succeeds in doing so, kills the Sphinx, is hailed as King, marries Jocasta and has children by her. This then, is the background of the story which unfolds in Sophocles' drama: fifteen years have past, and Thebes is again struck by plague and famine. What happens is quite simple: Oedipus is gradually led to full awareness of the cause of the renewed disasters – he is guilty of a dreadful crime.

Here we are concerned not with *hubris* and its consequences so much as with fate and its inevitability. Laius, Jocasta and in his turn Oedipus have done their utmost to avoid the fulfilment of the oracle's prophecy, but all has been in vain. Fate, or the gods, are relentless: what will happen must happen. Oedipus is no deliberate criminal — he has not wilfully committed any error. What is it, then, that awakens our pity and terror?

King Oedipus is an essay in dawning realization. From scene to scene the evidence of Oedipus' unintentional crimes, of his destiny, mounts up relentlessly, until he is forced to acknowledge the truth. In his pursuit of the facts Oedipus calls upon the aid of Apollo, representative of the rationality of man, symbol of Greek enlightenment. It is in fact Apollo (whose oracle at Delphi had foretold all) who is responsible for Oedipus' tragic realization, as he himself acknowledges:

> Apollo, friends, Apollo
> Has laid this agony upon me. . .[15]

But we must set Oedipus' apparent dedication to Apollo against its religious background, one which would have been familiar to Sophocles and the Athenian audience.

The patron goddess of Thebes was Artemis, whom the Romans called Diana. Like Athena, the patron of Athens, Artemis was originally a local representative of the mother-goddess. Traditionally, the story of King Oedipus is dated to the mid-thirteenth century; Oedipus is the great-grandson of Cadmus, whom we may think of as the invader who established patriarchal Zeus-worship in Thebes. Oedipus' victory over the Sphinx may be taken as a symbol of his re-assertion of patriarchal culture over the native earth-mother worship of Thebes. Ephesus, in Ionian Asia Minor, was the chief centre of Artemis-worship, and there is no doubt at all that here Artemis was a symbol of the mother-goddess.

Although Artemis, like Athena, was assimilated into the Olympian family, she retained many of her ancient characteristics. To the Greeks she was not only the model for chaste Greek girlhood, but also the goddess of motherhood and female fertility. Every fifth year, in August, Attica celebrated, at Brauron, a special festival to Artemis, blending piety and debauchery. Campbell[16] compares Artemis with the female-goddess of primitive hunting peoples, as represented in ancient statuettes; Frazer[17] considers her a personification of the teeming life of nature, both animal and vegetable. She is, in fact, a survival in the Greek pantheon of that ancient and constant symbol, the Great Goddess.

The ancient and Olympian sides of Artemis are brought together in her role as goddess of the hunt: here she seems to relate to that Blackfoot Indian girl, while at the same time she symbolizes the domination of man over nature. The duality is also brought out in the traditional legends in which a huntsman chances to meet and gaze on Artemis, or Diana, and is punished with death: her mysteries are not easily penetrated. It is also interesting to note that the image of hunting, of pursuit and capture, is a relevant image to describe Oedipus' pursuit and capture of the truth.

While Oedipus is, apparently, governed by Apollo, it is clear that his quest is also part of an Artemisian mystery. Throughout the play Sophocles uses the terms life and death in describing Oedipus' search for the facts, and this imagery suggests that the drama is concerned with more than the rational pursuit of truth.

From the start, the Theban priest speaks of Oedipus as

> the first of men.
> Whether in the ordinary business of mortal life
> Or in the encounters of man with more than man.[18]

He calls on Oedipus to restore the city to life. Later, the chorus calls upon the gods to slay death — an image for the present troubles of Thebes.

> Slay with thy golden bow, Lycean! Slay him,
> Artemis, over the Lycian hills resplendent!
> Bacchus, our name-god, golden in the dance
> Of Maenad revelry.
> Evoe! thy fiery torch advance
> To slay the Death-god, the grim enemy,
> God whom all other gods abhor to see.[19]

Three gods are invoked: Apollo Lyceus, Artemis (in the Lycian hills of Asia Minor), and Bacchus or Dionysos. Dionysos was closely associated with Thebes, as our discussion of Euripides' *The Bacchae* will show. These lines show that, although Apollo's aid is needed, so also are the gods of mystery and magic: in short, we are concerned here with man face to face with the inexplicable, and mere rationality is insufficient. Sophocles shows this within the context of Oedipus' rationality: he first suspects the truth of his past before all the evidence is accumulated, and it is an apprehension (in

58

both senses of the word) not a comprehension.

> My wife, what you have said has troubled me.
> My mind goes back . . . and something in me moves. . .[20]

Indeed, when Oedipus brings the truth to light, and sees clearly, his response is impulsive, instinctive: he puts out his eyes with Jocasta's brooch. This action is not a rational one — indeed, it is not the punishment he had decreed for whomever might be found guilty. It is close to the sort of self-mutilation practised by god-kings in earlier times:

> When his time came, the king had a wooden scaffolding constructed and spread over with hangings of silk. And when he had ritually bathed in a tank, with great ceremonies and to the sound of music, he proceeded to the temple, where he paid worship to the divinity. Then he mounted the scaffolding and, before the people, took some very sharp knives and began to cut off parts of his body — nose, ears, lips, and all his members, and as much of his flesh as he was able — throwing them away and round about, until so much of his blood was spilled that he began to faint, whereupon he slit his throat.[21]

Oedipus' self-mutilation can be seen as a ritual sacrifice, part of a necessary offering by the king to the mother-goddess. In this sense, Jocasta becomes a symbol for Artemis, and the whole work links with the rituals of primitive man. Oedipus is the new seed (a product of the old, Laius) sown in the earth, the womb of the earth-mother (Jocasta/Artemis): inevitably the harvest is reaped. Thus the inevitability of Oedipus' fate is the inevitable march of the seasons. As he himself says

> I am the child of Fortune,
> The giver of good, and I shall not be shamed.
> *She* is my mother; my sisters are the Seasons;
> My rising and my falling march with theirs.[22]

In *King Oedipus* we again find the duality of the Greek mind. On the surface, we observe the process of a rational pursuit of truth to its conclusion. But, underlying this, we are in a world of magic and mystery, in which is explored once more that age-old experience of the cycle of death and rebirth. Sophocles presents these two levels in the structure of his play: the truth is revealed in scenes of Apollonian dialogue confrontation (duets, trios) interspersed with Dionysiac choral interludes. In the final scene (which contains every device calculated to make stunning theatre, including the arrival of Oedipus' and Jocasta's children) the two levels and textures are brought together, and Apollo and Dionysos are united.

Euripides' The Bacchae
The third in the great trinity of fifth-century Athenian dramatists was Euripides. Born in Athens, eighteen years younger than Sophocles (and

dying before him), he did not win first prize until he was forty-two years old. Eighteen of Euripides' plays survive, nineteen if one includes the *Rhesus* of doubtful attribution. Euripides' contemporaries saw him as an innovator. Certainly the quality of his music-dramas is variable, and he seems not to have been a very popular figure.

Euripides was some fifteen years older than Socrates, and his working life coincided with those developments in intellectual thought we associate with the philosopher. It was a time of growing scepticism about traditional religious belief: at his trial Socrates was indicted on two counts, that he corrupted the youth of Athens, but also that he did not recognise the 'official' gods of the state, and introduced new ones. Developments in philosophical thought were giving man more confidence in himself and in his ability to work things out rationally. Euripides and Socrates admired each other and were apparently, good friends. Aristophanes, whose satirical arrows are delivered from a conservative shoulder, attacked both. Like Socrates, Euripides was indicted for impiety, in 410, unsuccessfully as it turned out; but in 408 he voluntarily left Athens and settled in Pella in Macedonia, where he wrote his last plays. After his death, and particularly in the Hellenistic period (about 330 to 100 B.C.), Euripides' works won enormous popularity: his and Socrates' ideas had achieved broader acceptance.

The Bacchae, Euripides' last work, is in some respects not typical. He takes his theme from traditional legend, and in style returns to an earlier period. Some authorities maintain it is his most incisive and best constructed play: certainly some of his other works have a wanton complexity.

The background to the story is the coming of the cult of Dionysos into Greece, and the opposition of the Apollonian state to this new and disturbing cult. The events are set in Thebes, at the time of Cadmus: that is, three generations before Oedipus.[23] According to Theban legend, Cadmus' daughter Semele was beloved by Zeus, but Hera (Zeus' wife), enraged at her husband's infidelity, persuaded Semele to ask Zeus to reveal himself in all his glory, knowing that for a mortal to behold divine Zeus was fatal. Although Semele consequently died, her unborn child Dionysos was rescued by Zeus and sewn into his father's thigh, whence he was later born again. When *The Bacchae* opens, Cadmus has handed over power to his grandson Pentheus, who refuses to honour either Semele or Dionysos: Dionysos himself has appeared in disguise at Thebes, determined to re-establish the worship of his mother and himself.

The music-drama is concerned with the struggle for power between Pentheus and Dionysos. Dionysos has already infected the Theban populace, especially the women, who are joyously celebrating the orgiastic rites of the god on nearby Mount Cithaeron. Cadmus and the blind prophet Teiresias (who also, curiously, appears in *King Oedipus*) have also become

Dionysos-worshippers. Pentheus, who finds worship of 'the effeminate Oriental' distasteful and immoral, commands that the Dionysiac priest (in fact, Dionysos himself) be arrested. They confront each other: Pentheus questions the priest without success, and imprisons him, but he miraculously escapes. A messenger brings to Pentheus the news that his mother Agave has joined the worshipping women. Dionysos appears and suggests that Pentheus should go and see for himself. Pentheus, dressed in women's clothes, and entirely under Dionysos' influence, witnesses the rites. Dionysos incites the worshippers to ritual murder, with Pentheus as the victim. Agave returns to the palace, still in a state of orgiastic exaltation, and clutching Pentheus' head, while (a marvellously ironic touch) the chorus dances around Dionysos' altar in the *orchestra*. Cadmus gently shows her what she has done. Dionysos appears, banishes Cadmus and Agave, and prophesies the destruction of Thebes.

It has been suggested that *The Bacchae* makes the typically Euripidean point that blind faith in the gods is humbug. This interpretation, while it has the merit of trying to fit the play to one of the consistent themes of Euripides' thought, is difficult to maintain from the evidence of the music-drama itself. Basically, it is concerned with the battle between Apollo and Dionysos, a battle in which Dionysos is inevitably victorious. Euripides seems to have little sympathy either with Pentheus or with Dionysos, although he does treat Agave as a tragic figure. What he is concerned with is the dialectics of opposition between the two central characters, and with the gradual domination of Dionysos over Pentheus, the man of reason whose rationality hides an inner irrationality which responds to the beguiling promptings of the god. Euripides argues that the irrational side of man will inevitably dominate his rationality. In stating this, he seems to be neither criticizing nor approving: he simply presents it through the medium of music-drama as a fact.

The conflict between Dionysos and Pentheus is between Orient and Occident, between liberating madness (*enthousiasmos*) and proper observance of the law. To Pentheus, the worship of Dionysos is lunacy, a disease, an inferior Oriental mystery, an impurity to be stamped out. To the chorus of Dionysiac worshippers, their rituals have an ancient and proper foundation:

> Blest is the happy man
> Who knows the mysteries the gods ordain,
> And sanctifies his life,
> Joins soul with soul in mystic unity,
> And, by due ritual made pure,
> Enters the ecstasy of mountain solitudes;
> Who observes the mystic rites
> Made lawful by Cybele the Great Mother;

Who crowns his head with ivy,
And shakes aloft his wand in worship of Dionysos.[24]

Indeed, this speech is a precise definition of the function of ritual music-drama in primitive cultures: a direct knowledge of divine mystery, not interpreted through law or reason; a losing of individuality in the communal rite; a purification (removal of problems) through ritual; an ecstatic identification with nature; participation in rites to the great earth-mother. It is a definition too of the continuing role of music-drama in the life of the Greeks. Once again Artemis triumphs in Thebes, this time through the agency of Dionysos. Once again the chorus in the Theatre of Dionysos involves the audience in the great mystery, brushes aside their Pentheus-like resistance, and makes them participate in the necessary sacrifice of the god-king. However sophisticated *The Bacchae* may seem, it is basically a story of human sacrifice.

It is perhaps not fanciful to see Euripides' last music-drama as a return by the great master to the roots of his art. For the victory of Dionysos is a victory for what lies behind the transformed reality of music-drama — the direct experience of mystery. In the end, verbal images alone and rational explanation are insufficient. Perhaps Euripides' scepticism was finally turned upon the very sceptism for which he was noted: perhaps he realized that rational, human self-assertion is, after all, brought to nothing by the magic of mystery.

Hellenistic culture

The fourth century was marked by internecine strife in Greece. A brief period of prosperity in Athens was followed by economic and social collapse. Egyptian and Asiatic mystic cults came more and more to replace the traditional worship of the Olympian gods. To the north, Macedon was growing in power under the leadership of Philip: his intervention in yet another of the interminable wars between Thebes, Sparta and Athens was to culminate, eventually, in the Macedonians taking over the leadership of a united Hellas (except the Peloponnese) in 338. From this point on, Greek culture is customarily called Hellenistic.

In spite of disturbance and political decline, fourth century Greece was intellectually very much alive. Perhaps the very social turmoil prompted the tremendous developments in ethical and political philosophy epitomized by the careers and writings of Plato (428–348) and Aristotle (384–322). Plato had the distinction of founding the Academy in Athens in 386, which was to survive as the intellectual centre of Greece for nine hundred years. Aristotle had the distinction of being tutor to Alexander, and his ideas had undoubted influence on the young conqueror of Asia.

Music-drama continued in the Theatre of Dionysos until the first century, but we know little beyond the names of authors and titles of plays — no complete works have survived. It would seem that the dramatists of the previous century were revered: from about 386 it became customary to present a play by either Aeschylus, Sophocles, or Euripides as a prelude to the new plays. We know that in the three years 341–339 the prize was 'won' by Euripides, who had been dead for sixty-seven years! It would seem that innovation was not encouraged, and contemporary playwrights modelled their work on their predecessors. We learn too, from Aristotle and others, that many of the 'new' works were written as vehicles for solo performers: apparently the actor's prize was considered more important than the prize for new music-drama. We may surmise that virtuosity and self-indulgence were preferred to dramatic content.

Another characteristic in fourth-century music-drama was the continuing decline of the chorus. In *The Bacchae* the chorus tends to be restricted to interludes between scenes for solo actors in which the main dramatic action takes place. As the chorus grew more expensive, and the solo actor more important, playwrights began to introduce intermezzi into music-dramas, often unrelated to the main plays themselves.

Perhaps fourth-century Athenians found that their musico-dramatic needs could be satisfied more directly through participation in the growing mystic cults. Orphism, developed from the Dionysos cult, was influenced by Egyptian Isis-worship, and took its name from the legendary Thracian musician Orpheus. Orpheus is yet another death-rebirth figure: according to legend he descended into the realm of death to rescue his wife Eurydice. Through his music he charmed the god Hades, and was allowed to return with Eurydice to life, so long as he did not look at her on the way. Yielding at the last moment to temptation, he lost her a second time. Unwilling to console his sorrows in the company of other women of Thrace, he was torn to pieces by them. His severed head, still singing, we are told, floated to the island of Lebos, was buried there, and became an oracle. Orpheus is commonly regarded as a disciple of both Apollo and Dionysos, and we shall discuss his role as a symbol of the creative music-dramatist in a later chapter. At this stage we may note that he became the figure-head of a mystical cult based upon the process of suffering, death and resurrection. Orphism bridges the gap between fertility rite and Christianity; indeed, it may be regarded in more ways than this as a forerunner of Christianity. Orphic worship was also based upon a series of hymns purporting to have been written by Orpheus, and we can assume that Orphism included musico-dramatic rituals of some sophistication.

Music itself was undergoing radical development during the fourth century. Plato accused contemporary musicians and music-dramatists of anarchy, of overthrowing tradition, of replacing music written according to established forms with music designed to be sensational. Plato in the

Republic describes Timotheus' (446–357) music-drama *The Persae* as a 'bombastic libretto . . . written for programme-music of the sort which attempted to make the noises of thunder, wind, hail, cats, dogs, cattle, bird-song, and all kinds of instruments, with frequent and startling modulations.'[25] One is reminded of early nineteenth-century (A.D.) music: certainly Timotheus was a 'young Romantic', as his manifesto suggests: 'I do not sing the old things, Because the new are winners. Zeus the young is king today: Once it was Cronos ruling. Get out, old dame Music.'[26]

By the beginnings of the Hellenistic period, the next step in a familiar process had occurred: the revolutionary new music had become conventional. To Aristoxenos, the leading musical theoretician of the last decades of the fourth century and a pupil of Aristotle, contemporary music was more saccharine than shocking.[27]

The latter years of the fourth century were dominated by political events, and in particular by Alexander the Great's conquest of the Persian Empire. In thirteen years, between 335 and 323 (when Alexander was aged between 19 and 33), he took Greek thought to the gates of India, and in the process sent back Oriental thought to Greece. The empire he created stretched from Western Greece three thousand miles east to the Indus valley, and from the Caspian to the Nile. Such an empire could not be held together by force of arms — his army was anyway only thirty-five thousand strong. Alexander's policy, despite occasional acts of ferocious cruelty, was to respect the people he conquered, and to permit them to govern themselves. He encouraged his soldiers and officers to settle and to marry Persian women, and conceived the notion of a Greco-Persian empire, rather than a Greek empire dominating Persia.

This policy was a practical extension of the Greek respect for the individual; it was born, moreover, in an age of philosophical enquiry. The result was an assimilation of Persian, Egyptian, and of more distant Oriental cultures and ideas and an attempt to find common ground between them. In religion, as we have noted, Oriental mysticism began to play a more important part. Often Greek and Oriental deities were paired off in such cults: Zeus-Ammon, of whom Alexander declared himself to be the divine offspring (in 324), Demeter-Isis, Dionysos-Shiva, and so on. Hellenistic religion, then, was a marriage of East and West; we can presume that its music-drama rituals also took on a mixture of Greek and Oriental flavours.

But once philosophy and man's enquiring rationality got hold of religion it was not long before magic and mystery were lost. In about 300, Euhemerus of Sicily published a book in which he argued that the gods were merely deified humans: Zeus was a conquering chieftain who died in Crete, Aphrodite a famous early prostitute, and the legend of Kronos eating his children a memory of times of cannibalism. He was probably quite right, but his book did little to stimulate the artistic imagination. Greek religion had been, historically, a link between primitive mystery and modern rationality, and in the gap had arisen fifth century tragedy. Once rationality had done away with the bases of belief, music-drama in the same form could not survive.

Alexander's sudden death in 323 plunged his empire into chaos. His generals, fighting over the spoils, lacked Alexander's breadth of vision and were concerned only with the power and wealth to be achieved through military victory over each other. That remarkable conjunction of influences which had led to the golden age of Athens withered away into anarchy and despotism. The most that Athens could offer the world was the sentimental comedy of Menander, and poor imitations of fifth century tragedy, precious little to set against the triumphs of military despots. Under the twin assaults of rational philosophy and military tyranny, music-drama as the fifth century had known it collapsed into oblivion.

Enthusiasm, ceremony and narrative

Our survey of the musico-dramatic history of man from primitive times up to the Hellenistic period has inevitably covered large areas where evidence is scanty. Only in discussing Greek tragedy have we been on slightly firmer ground, as here at least we have some musico-dramatic materials to work with. For much of the time we have been forced to look for clues amongst other, larger surveys of man's cultural history.

And yet these clues have tended to point in a single direction, and we have gradually evolved a hypothesis which fits the facts as they are. That hypothesis is simply that music-drama arose as one of man's attempts to come to some understanding of the mysteries that surround his existence. In one sense, it could be argued that this is an unchallengeable hypothesis, for perhaps everything man does has that function. But our hypothesis would seem right in a more particular way, in that we have observed a close and continuing connection between man's music-drama and his religious rituals. At the most distant historical point we have asked whether Neanderthal Man's rituals could have existed without the ingredients of music-drama, and have shown that the potentiality was there. At the most recent historical point we have investigated the religious themes of Greek music-drama. In between, we have noted firstly, the development of man's religious ideas as a series of responses to death and rebirth, and secondly, the possible development of his music-drama towards the climax of Attic tragedy. We have also noted how suitable music-drama is, *by its very nature*, to man's task of exploring the inexplicable. While, therefore, our hypothesis cannot be proved, it does have the virtue of making sense.

Absence of proof inevitably invites challenges to a theory. Quite probably, our hypothesis can be challenged in some of its details. But if it be deemed to be complete nonsense, then a challenger must face a number of questions. What alternative reasons can be adduced for man's constant interest in creating, performing and witnessing music-drama? Why should every culture we now know, from the 'primitive' to the 'civilized', have some form of music-drama? If it is merely a game, then why should it have been linked so consistently to activities man has considered magical or holy? And, most importantly, if music-drama is not linked to man's deepest and most serious preoccupations, why on earth should he have so determinedly indulged in an activity which from a rational point of view is so patently absurd?

Whatever may be the merits or demerits of our hypothesis, it does at least answer all of those questions. And we can test it, not only through our own experience of opera in the opera-house, but by investigating further its implications. Where do they take us, these ideas that music-drama is somehow part of our explorations of the inexplicable, and that it is closely related to those of our activities we call religious?

Man's mythologies, cults and religions are attempts to perceive the apparently unperceivable, to explain the apparently inexplicable, and to bring order to the apparently chaotic. Once a myth, cult or religion is evolved, it provides an answer, which, while it may masquerade as rational, is in fact based upon a fundamental acceptance of something which cannot be logically proved: it is based upon belief.

But so, too, is music-drama. When we enter the opera-house, we must suspend our disbelief, and allow our imaginations to dominate our intellects. In chapter 1, music-drama was described as images which transform reality, allowing direct perception of experiences. This description might also be used to describe myth, man's first attempt at 'religious' explanations of the inexplicable, and to describe the modern Communion Service. In all three cases — music-drama, myth, and church service — images are used to symbolize basic human experiences. We can only penetrate these images if we suspend our disbelief.

The singular phenomenon of Attic tragedy can be explained in relation to the development of man's religious ideas during the eras before Christianity, and this approach also offers some assistance when we attempt to explain the dark ages of music-drama between the fifth century B.C. and the European Renaissance.

The mythology of primitive man developed in two directions, which Campbell[28] defines as Occidental and Oriental. The dividing line between the two occurs geographically, he suggests, in the Middle East.

Oriental religious thought starts from the premise that God is indefinable; He cannot be described or imagined. Religious rituals, deities, myths are merely means to an end: through them man achieves identity with God. 'Prayers and chants, images, temples, gods, sages, definitions and cosmologies are but ferries to a shore of experience far beyond the categories of thought, (and are) to be abandoned on arrival. . .'

According to Oriental religious thought, then, music-drama rituals would have as their aim a direct identification with God, the ultimate source of being. We have met this idea already, in the sacrificial rituals of the Marind-Amin tribe, and in the shape of Dionysos, whose rites inspired his worshippers with *enthousiasmos* — possession by the God. Even Aristotle accepts the notion in his description of *catharsis* — the purification resulting from audience involvement in the experience of pity and terror. We have also seen the primitive source of this in the shamanising of the medicine-man. We may describe this Oriental/Dionysiac element as *enthusiastic music-drama*.

Occidental religious thought starts from a different premise: that God is something quite separate from man, and that we cannot identify with Him. Religious rituals, deities and myths have the function of defining the relationship between Man and God. The idea of the separateness of God and Man leads to two possible approaches. The first approach is to say that Man's relationship with God is fixed by ritual, which must be rigorously observed (Zoroastrianism, Judaism, most forms of Christianity, and Islam). The second approach is to say that the relationship between Man and God is open to negotiation and investigation (the native mythologies of Europe: Greek, Roman, Celtic and Germanic). Both of these approaches are evident in the music-drama of pre-Christian eras. The first, which we can call *ceremonial music-drama*, is evident in the ritual dance of the I-khun-uh'-kah-tsi and the astrologically determined liturgies of Mesopotamia. The second approach is evident in the Indian myth of man's negotiations with the buffalo, and in the myth of Demeter and Persephone.

The special characteristic of this second approach is that negotiation and investigation are not immediate things, but take place gradually. *Enthusiastic* identification takes place instantaneously (though it may be long prepared); *ceremonial* worship is the expansion of a single moment; but negotiation and investigation take more time, and the processes are as important as the results (hence theological tracts and philosophical tomes). In terms of myth and music-drama, these processes can only be expressed through *narrative*, the gradual unfolding of event to event. Hence we can speak of *narrative music-drama*.

These three forms of music-drama, and their mythological/religious sources, can be shown diagrammatically.

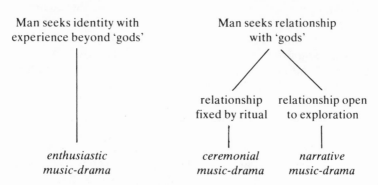

It is now possible to see what made Attic tragedy: a coincidence of all three forms. The *narrative* elements were the source of the play in myth or legend, and the development of the action through the scenes for solo actors. The *ceremonial* elements were the choral hymns and dithyrambs, and the Apollonian verbal and musical forms. The *enthusiastic* elements were the Dionysiac character of the chorus, and the sound-effects of the words and music.

The special ingredient in the recipe was *narrative*, presented on the stage for an audience to see and hear. *Ceremonial* had been present in Mesopotamia, and *enthusiasm* in numerous mother-goddess cults and rituals. What drove the Greeks to create *narrative music-drama* was the same healthy scepticism and intellectual curiosity that also impelled them towards philosophical speculation. In the end, scepticism and philosophy were to destroy belief and break the link between the three elements by setting up *narrative* on its own, divorced from *ceremonial* and *enthusiasm*. The poverty of music-drama in the Hellenistic period may be due to the fact that intellectual speculation and musico-dramatic speculation are ultimately antithetical, as can be shown by reference to Plato's famous simile of the Cave.[29]

Plato likens man to a prisoner, forced to sit in a cave facing the wall: behind him people and objects pass between him and the cave-entrance, throwing their shadows on the wall. All he sees are the shadows, and he therefore gives to this illusion the name of reality. Yet if he were to be liberated he would turn round and (once his eyes were accustomed to the light) would see that what he had thought was reality is nothing but illusion. Plato uses the simile to illustrate his point that we can only perceive the truth if we will free ourselves from the shadowy darkness of our normal perception.

This is the intellectual, rational approach, but music-drama offers the converse interpretation of the image of the cave. Plato's belief that the truth can best be sought by turning away from images is only one side of the matter. The painter of Trois Frères deliberately cast his images on the cave-walls in order to penetrate the mysteries of reality more deeply, and the dramatic arts, like the visual arts, derive their power from the fact that images provide us with a way of transforming reality so that we may *better* understand it.

Death and rebirth

The one constant theme of the music-drama we have so far investigated is that of death and rebirth. It was seemingly an important issue for Neanderthal man, and certainly for the hunters of the great plains. So, too, it was for man the farmer, for whom the issue now extended from the death and rebirth of animals to the death and rebirth of crops. We have seen the influence of fertility rites on Greek drama through the influence of the Eleusinian Mysteries and the cult of Dionysos. It is interesting to note in this connection that the Greater Mysteries of Eleusis were held in September and October, the time of planting in Attica, and that the music-dramas of the Great Dionysia were performed in March and April, harvest time.

The rites of death and rebirth were performed by primitive man for a practical reason: within his hunting or farming mythology it was necessary for death to be followed by rebirth — on this he depended for survival. What will happen if all the buffalo die? asks the hunter. They die only to be reborn, says the shaman, and these are the things you must do to bring them back to life. Will the earth bring forth its fruits? asks the farmer. Only if the earth receives its toll of blood, comes the reply: you must make the proper sacrifice. Out of these beliefs, implanted deep in the collective unconscious of man, comes a basic imagery of death and rebirth, an awareness of cyclical balance in nature.

One of man's earliest perceptions must have been of the passage of time — his own circadian and other bodily rhythms cannot be ignored. And this perception must have been matched by his perception of the rhythms of nature: day and night, the passing of the seasons, the waxing and waning of the moon. He would soon notice the connection between the moon and menstruation: clearly, nature's cycles and human cycles were related. Growth and decay in nature, and birth and death in animal life, were both somehow connected to his own personal cycles of birth, growth, decay and death. Thus he evolved rites not only to guarantee nature's cycles, but to mark the important moments in his own biological cycle: the birth of a baby, the loss of sexual innocence and beginnings of adulthood, marriage and the conception of children, and death. Moments of change in nature and moments of change in himself were moments to be noted, celebrated, explored. Whatever mysteries governed change in nature presumably governed change in man. Thus the idea of death and rebirth becomes attached to all moments of change: if a bull is sacrificed to guarantee the

69

resurrection of bulls, then a bull is also sacrificed to mark a marriage ceremony, or the birth of a baby, or a boy's admission to adulthood.

But it was not until the twentieth century that a terminology was evolved to explain how the idea of death and rebirth relates precisely to the continuing life of a human being. The terminology was that of psychology, and its chief proposer was Carl Jung. Jung evolved the idea of psychological death and rebirth, providing almost incidentally an explanation for Aristotle's *catharsis*, which itself had been a Greek explanation for something already instinctively perceived by primitive man.

According to Jung, the human mind has two distinct areas: the conscious and the unconscious. The conscious, through the ego (our knowledge of ourselves) and persona (the image we wish to present to other people) governs and controls our everyday thoughts and actions. The conscious builds up a basic view of the world, in which we fit, and interprets and judges the information we receive in accordance with that basic view. Behind or beneath the conscious, however, lies the unconscious, consisting of id (those areas of the mind containing ideas and experiences of which we are not normally aware) and libido (an energy which tends to force unconscious contents into the conscious). Our development as individuals consists of our creating successive egos and personas in response to the pressures from id and libido. Normally this process occurs quite naturally ('changing one's mind'). But if the ego establishes a control which resists libido, then the images swirling about in the id become repressed, and will in the end break-out, shattering the ego and persona, and it may be difficult to re-establish new controls.

Jung suggests that the unconscious mind contains images that are part of our own personal experiences, but also images that are part of our human heritage and are shared by others. He therefore speaks of a personal unconscious and a collective unconscious, the latter built up over the generations of human experience on this planet, and at least partly a function of our biological make-up.

In psychological terms, then, we can speak of the natural death and rebirth of successive egos in our own psyches, as a constantly recurring phenomenon; we can also speak of the death and rebirth which occurs at particular moments of psychological crisis. There is a clear relationship here to *enthousiasmos* and *catharsis*. It has already been suggested that *enthousiasmos* is a loss of identity, a submergence of self in divine rapture. This can be interpreted, psychologically, as a loss of ego and a liberation of libido. *Enthousiasmos* is an opportunity for psychic renewal.

We have now found a psychological reason why Dionysiac rapture is often regarded as dangerous: it can bring possibly disturbing unconscious contents to our notice. Pentheus' opposition to the celebrations on Mount Cithaeron continues in the opposition to modern pop-festivals — indeed, to anything which liberates unconscious contents from the id, such as erotic art and literature. It is interesting to note that primitive man's musico-dramatic rituals were often erotic, for sexual excitement is a strong liberating force.

Enthousiasmos is the vital ingredient in *catharsis*, which we may interpret psychologically as a liberation of unconscious contents. When Aristotle speaks of purification, he means, psychologically, the healthy coming together of conscious and unconscious. Music-drama, in short, provides one of the few safely controlled opportunities for psychological death and rebirth. Its safety lies in the presence of Apollo, who provides the comprehensible structure of images. Without rules the game is dangerous; with them it can be both involving and fun to watch.

The music-drama of ancient Greece is concerned with death and rebirth on three levels. Firstly, the subject-matter is concerned with death and rebirth, presented in the form of *narrative music-drama*. Secondly, it stems from continuing rituals designed to guarantee the death and rebirth of animals and crops: on this level it takes the form of *ceremonial music-drama*. Thirdly, it awakens the process of psychological death and rebirth in ourselves, by means of *enthusiastic music-drama*.

Death and rebirth is also an image which aptly describes the history of music-drama, in the Greek fashion at least, over the two thousand years between Euripides and Monteverdi.

3　Rome and the Middle Ages

The music-drama of Rome

Two years after the death of Alexander, in 323 B.C., the army of a small town calling itself the Republic of Rome was trapped and defeated in the pass of Caudium by a neighbouring tribe, the Samnites. The obvious course of action for Rome would have been surrender to Samnite domination. However, the Romans refused that alternative, and, after a further thirty years of war, themselves dominated the Samnites. Within another twenty years Rome controlled the whole of central and southern Italy. In another one hundred and fifty years Rome ruled the Mediterranean from Spain to Palestine.

The remarkable tenacity of Rome in the Samnite Wars shows the basis of the Roman attitude to life. The Romans were men with a mission: it was their destiny to win. Their virtues were those of discipline, firmness of purpose, manliness, severity, and service: a true Roman was obedient to orders, loyal to his family, and above all faithful to Rome.

In conquering most of Europe and the Near and Middle East, the Romans brought security, peace (by and large), roads, baths and law, but precious little in the way of artistic achievement. Magnificent examples of lyric and epic poetry, of history and oratory are certainly evident in Roman culture, but scarcely anything original in music, sculpture, painting or drama. In these fields the Romans seemed to have relied on the Greeks, for whom they had some respect. As we shall see, even this respect was grudging at times, and it certainly seems that the cultures of other conquered races and nations scarcely aroused any interest at all. The reason for this may be the simple patriotism of the Roman: although the Romans came into contact with every range of human culture from the primitive hunter to the sophisticated city-state, all cultural activities were measured, accepted or rejected, in terms of their Roman-ness.

This was certainly true of 'foreign' religions. Rome's gods were 'Olympian', in the sense that they were a patriarchal family. However, in

204 B.C., threatened by the armies of Hannibal, Rome followed the advice of an oracle and introduced the cult of Cybele the mother-goddess into the city. Such an opposition of patriarchal and matriarchal beliefs had been one of the foundations of Greek tragedy. But Rome did not go the whole way; having fulfilled the oracle's advice by admitting the exotic ceremonies and priestesses into the Temple of Victory, her rulers then forbade the people to take part. In 186 B.C., the worship of Dionysos (or Bacchus) gained enthusiastic followers: the Senate banned it. The only religions permitted in Rome were those recognized by law (i.e. those which did not conflict with Roman ideas). Only the Persian mystic cult of Mithras, which was founded upon ancient death-rebirth beliefs, gained a hold in Rome, and that was largely amongst professional soldiers, who are not known for creating music-drama.

A similar xenophobia may be seen in the way the Romans adopted Greek culture. When the Romans conquered southern Italy, they came across the flourishing artistic life of the Greek colonies there: the Roman occupation of Greek Sicily during the first Punic War brought young, aristocratic Roman officers into close contact with Greek music-drama. As soon as the war ended, in 240, Greek dramas began to be performed in Rome, translated and adapted by Livius Andronicus and Gnaeus Scaevius. Despite a barren interlude during the second Punic War (218–201) Greek tragedy was gaining a foothold, and Naevius was writing his own tragedies based on episodes in Roman history. However, such activities were un-Roman, in the eyes of Cato the Elder: he succeeded in preventing the establishment of permanent theatres. Not until 55 B.C. was the first stone theatre built in Rome.

In spite of Cato's opposition, Rome enjoyed a brief period of flourishing music-drama in the Greek style: the chief authors were Quintus Ennius (239–169), Marcus Pacuvius (c. 210–130), and Lucius Accius (170–c. 86). Only titles and fragments have been preserved of their works. It would seem that music-drama in the Greek style did not greatly appeal to Roman audiences, who preferred spectacular entertainments: the first gladiatorial contests had been established in 264.

The performances of music-drama in Rome were part of festivals dedicated to other activities: there was no festival, as there was in Athens, specially devoted to music-drama. Nevertheless, three stone theatres were eventually built: the theatre of Pompey in 55 B.C., the theatre of Balbus in 13 B.C. and the theatre of Marcellus in 11 B.C. The total capacity of all three theatres together was approximately 30,000 people, as compared with the Colosseum (built A.D. 65–80) which could seat 45,000. It is clear where Roman taste lay.

Indeed, it is doubtful whether complete dramas were ever performed in the three Roman theatres. What was performed was farce, spectacular

73

'variety' entertainments, pantomime (mime by a solo actor to musical accompaniment) and tragic recitation, a form Nero enjoyed to the extent of performing in it himself.

Why did music-drama never become popular in Rome as it did in Greece? There are several reasons. Firstly, Rome clung to things Roman; secondly, the scepticism and freedom of thought that characterized fifth century Greece had no place in a Rome that clung to traditional answers and, under the Caesars, enforced the strictest censorship; thirdly, the Hellenistic star-system was imported into Rome to the detriment of drama itself (at the reopening of the Theatre of Marcellus, the Emperor Vespasian paid the actor Apollinaus £3,500 for his performance, and £1,800 to each of the two *kithara*-players); fourthly, Roman religious ritual found a secular expression in a different way, in the arena.

The Roman arenas, such as the Circus Maximus, rebuilt by Trajan to seat 200,000 spectators, the Circus Flaminius, built in 220 B.C., the Circus Gai (scene of the first Christian martyrdoms in A.D. 63), and of course the Colosseum, were the chief places to which the Roman people resorted for their music-drama entertainments. Events included horse-racing, dancing displays, mock battles (including sea-battles), cavalry displays, gladiatorial combats, and animal hunts (the Caesars effectively depopulated North Africa of elephants, Upper Egypt of hippopotami and Mesopotamia of lions.) All of these events, apart from displays, were competitive in some way: man against man, men against animals, even animals against animals; they reflected the deep-seated Roman interest in winning, and winners.

The ultimate 'winning' in combat is the death of the opponent, and there is no doubt that the Romans, in Imperial times at least, enjoyed the spectacle of death in the arena. It is possible to see, in this, that primitive ritual was barely concealed beneath the surface of Roman life, for the death of animals or gladiators has some resemblance to the sacrifices of fertility rites. Certainly the death of a gladiator was framed in ritual, from the first 'Ave, Imperator, morituri te salutant!' ('Hail, Emperor; those about to die salute thee!') through the opening of the duels while the band of trumpets and hydraulic organ played, to the final sign of thumbs up (mercy to the fallen) or thumbs down (death to the loser). Sacrifice (at least of animals) was a necessary ritual in man's ceremonial relationship to the gods. In the arena, however, sacred rite had become purely secular, no matter what its origins might have been. In consequence, the letting of blood lost its symbolic function, and became brutal reality rather than reality transformed.

No better example can be found of this than the performances of Catullus' mime-drama *Laureolus* under the emperor Domitian, a play which ends with the crucifixion and dismemberment of the brigand hero: Domitian's contribution to the production was to substitute for the actor a criminal who was actually put to death in the prescribed manner. The audience, apparently,

74

loved it.

Such revolting exhibitions were part of the Imperial policy of 'bread and circuses', a method of pleasing the masses to gain support. That it was necessary to do so in quite this way betrays the failure of traditional Roman religion, and the essential poverty of a restrictive politico-ethical system which could offer no alternative means for the individual to experience intense emotion.

The events in the arena were designed to appeal to the mob. Roman music, too, seems to have consisted almost exclusively of pop-songs. Curiously, from our viewpoint, this was accompanied by an interest amongst the intellectual and cultural élite in experimental music and in musicological research into the music of the past, i.e. Greek music. *Plus ça change, plus c'est la même chose.*

Oddly enough, Roman drama did have an influence upon European drama during and after the Renaissance. The polished comedies of Terence (*c.* 195–159 B.C.), based upon the Greek New Comedy of Menander, were widely read in the seventeenth century, and earlier Renaissance drama acknowledged the influence of Seneca's plays (*c.* 55 B.C.–*c.* A.D. 41). These latter, which formed a part of the intellectual élite's interest in drama, were written to be read or recited, but not to be performed.

The collapse of the Roman Empire

Three factors led to the collapse of the Roman Empire: all three were attacks upon the basic Roman view of life.

The first was the influx, from the third century A.D., of Oriental cults and ideas, this time virtually unstoppable. In 222 a new Sassanid dynasty arose in Persia, and over the next century much of Rome's power was diverted to meet the threat that it posed. Diocletian, in 284, moved the centre of government to Asia Minor, and became virtually an Oriental despot. His adoption of Oriental customs quickly spread through the Empire, markedly affecting the traditional attitudes of Romans.

The second factor was the pressure of barbarian tribes from the north. In 167, despite initial resistance by Rome, barbarians invaded and settled in northern Italy; in 250 Rome was fighting the Goths in Thrace. For the next hundred and fifty years, the Roman legions fought a losing battle against Germans, Franks, Goths, Visigoths and Huns, as they poured south across the Alps and Caucasus, over the Rhine and Danube. In the end, weight of numbers and loss of morale defeated Rome: the Visigoths under Alaric sacked Rome in 410, and the Vandals had their turn in 450. The barbarians were basically nomadic herdsmen, and they brought with them their traditional hunting religion. But this was not to become the religion of post-Roman Europe, because of the third factor in the collapse of the Empire — Christianity.

Christianity, centred round the crucifixion and resurrection of Jesus Christ, is clearly a religion concerned with death and rebirth; as such, it was a natural successor to the religions of the hunter and the farmer. But, while pre-Christian and non-Christian religions (with the exception of Islam) regard death and rebirth as a cycle in nature, Christianity bases its thought upon a single death and a single rebirth. The Fall of Adam in the garden of Eden is the event of 'death' for man, which introduced 'sin' into the world, and the crucifixion and Resurrection of Christ is the 'rebirth' of man, offering the abolition of 'sin'. 'As in Adam all men die, so in Christ all will be brought to life. . .'[1]

In the early years of Christianity, three different interpretations of the meaning of Christ's life and death emerged. The view of the Jewish Christians of Palestine was that Christ was the Messiah, and that Christianity was both a renewed promise of and a means for the political establishment of the Kingdom of God (the Hebrew Yahweh) on earth. Other Christians, called Gnostics, related the message of Christianity to other mystic cults, and saw Christ's death as an affirmation of the immanent and transcendent nature of God, a universal with whom we can achieve identity. Gnosticism flowered during the period of the Antonine emperors (Antoninus Pius, who ruled from 138 to 161, and Marcus Aurelius, who ruled from 161 to 180); its religious writings included, in the text *The Acts of John,* a remarkable description of what we might call the Mysteries of Christ.[2] The third view was that Christ's life is a fulfilment of Old Testament prophecy, but in a spiritual rather than political terms. It was this third view which was to triumph when Constantine the Great adopted Christianity in 312: at the Council of Nicaea, May 20th to July 25th 325, a creed was established, heretics anathematised, and Catholic (i.e. universal) Orthodox Christianity established. Theodosius I (ruled 379–395) proscribed all non-Christian rituals, and Christianity became the only religion tolerated in the Roman Empire, or what was left of it. Finally, in 438, Theodosius decreed the death penalty for Christian unorthodoxy. The dark ages had begun.

The Christian Church usually took a firm stand against paganism. Dionysos, the half-goat, half-man, was transmuted into the popular image of the devil, horned and hoofed, and his female worshippers were later to be burnt at the stake as witches. For many years Christians in Asia Minor celebrated Easter on March 25th, the vernal equinox, traditionally the day on which the fertility-god Attis rose from the dead: the Church opposed this. At the same time, some concessions were made: the date of Christmas was moved from January 6th to December 25th, the winter solstice. Most remarkably, Christianity accepted pagan worship of the earth-mother, by establishing the divinity of the Virgin Mary, the mother of the dying and resurrected God. There were, indeed, many ways in which the pagan could relate his beliefs to Christianity: Jesus' biographies in the Gospels were similar to the biographical legends of pagan cult-figures — prophecies, mysterious conception, miracles, suffering, death, resurrection — and the ritual Eucharist meal of 'bread' and 'wine' had many ancient parallels. In Alexandria, Christian philosophers set about the task of building up a theology and doctrine based upon a mixture of Greek philosophy and Christian belief. This embryonic religious and social institution, which was given fresh impetus in the writings of St Augustine, stepped into the political and religious vacuum caused by the sack of Rome by Alaric in 410.

Christianity was established not as a path to a direct experience of God, but as a ceremonial, ritualized barrier between man and God. For this, St. Paul had been chiefly responsible. As a Roman citizen, he believed in the virtues of law and order; for him the Christian message was a liberation from the old ways, but must also provide a new order. Christianity, based upon his teachings, became an organization with fixed traditions, in which the unorthodox was anathematized. Under the well-intentioned guidance of the Catholic Church, freedom of thought was banned, questioning of man's relationship with God discouraged; any attempt to become 'enthusiastically' united with God was treated with suspicion, if not severity. Mysticism and enthusiasm were banished to solitary desert hermitages, or went underground, to emerge only occasionally in esoteric works such as the letters of St. Teresa of Avila. It is not surprising, therefore, that Christianity in its public and communal form should permit only *ceremonial music-drama;* there was little room for *narrative music-drama,* except as a function of the liturgy, and certainly no place for *enthusiastic music-drama.* The Catholic Church's predecessors in the history of man were the state religions of Mesopotamia and Egypt, not those of primitive man or Greece.

Christian ritual as music-drama

Philo of Alexandria (first century A.D.) made a strict distinction between music used in the theatre, which was effeminate and sensual, and music appropriate for Christian worship, which must be moral and properly regulated. Clement of Alexandria (*c.* A.D. 200) rejected the use of wind instruments in Christian ritual: they were, he said, more suitable to animals than to men. The two wind instruments he referred to were the *syrinx,* a flute with two pipes associated by the Greeks with the fertility god Pan, and the *aulós,* associated with Dionysos. Both Philo and Clement had read the lessons of history and realized that Christian worship needed a music that was Apollonian, not Dionysiac. Their admonitions were squarely in the Old Testament tradition of the prophets (if not of King David). Isaiah had raged against those who neglected the work of the Lord, and spent their time in drunkenness and feasting, to the music of the lyre, *kithara, aulós* and tambourine (*Isaiah* 5:16). Many early Christian writings reprove the brethren for singing 'heathen' tunes borrowed from pagan cults. The battle between Apollonian and Dionysiac music continued for centuries: the Council of Trent (1545–63) thought it necessary to ban 'impious and lascivious' music, and as recently as 1903 Pope Pius X was to condemn the use of 'theatrical' music in Christian worship: he maintained that music must serve the liturgy, not the liturgy serve music.[3]

The first step taken by early Christians to purify their music was to go further than Clement of Alexandria, and to ban instrumental music totally from their ritual. The introduction of the organ (a Roman invention, much used in music for the arena) is attributed to Pope Vitalian (reigned 657–72); by his time Christianity had long established vocal music as the proper means of worshipping the Lord. St. Paul had already encouraged the brethren to sing psalms, hymns and spiritual songs (*Colossians* 3:16): he appreciated, with his successors, the value of making Dionysiac music submit to an Apollonian text. Liturgical singing was therefore the basis of Christian worship from early times. It was based upon the ceremonial chant of the synagogue, itself related to the tradition of temple ceremony first developed at Sumer. The musical language was that of the Near East, related therefore to the music of Greece and Rome, though we know little of the details of early Christian ritual music before the codifications of Ambrose.

Bishop Ambrose of Milan (*c.* 340–97) classified the forms of liturgical music and allocated appropriate music to particular feasts. But he went further, and codified musical chant according to what he believed was Greek practice. He was right in speaking of 'modes', and eight-note scales in which the end-note ('final') and middle-note ('reciting' note) are considered more important than the remainder, but he unfortunately got the names of the modes wrong. The Ambrosian system is also exclusively diatonic. During the papacy of Gregory I (from 590 to 604) a further four 'modes' were derived from Ambrose's four, thus completing the modal classification of what we call Gregorian chant, the Christian equivalent to the codified liturgical music of earlier religions.

The central ritual of the Catholic Chruch was codified in the eleventh century, as the Ordinary of the Mass,[4] and can be regarded as an example of *ceremonial music-drama.* The Church has always looked with suspicion upon attempts to analyse the Mass as music-drama, wishing to stress the ritual rather than the theatrical aspects of the ceremony; nevertheless, no one who has attended High Mass at St. Peter's in Rome can deny that it contains a strong theatrical element. As early as A.D. 821 Bishop Amalarius of Metz published, in Book III of his *Liber officialis,* an analysis of the Mass as music-drama.[5] The analysis of the Mass that follows leans heavily on Amalarius' work.

The Mass contains the basic ingredients of music-drama: solo performers, chorus, audience, representational physical movement, characters (i.e.

human beings disguised in costume in order to imitate other human beings), verbal and musical texts. Within the music-drama, several symbolic levels can be traced. Firstly, a *ceremony* is being performed, which symbolizes the partaking by communicants of the body and blood of Christ (compare the ritual but more realistic cannibalism of the Marind-Anim tribe); on this level we can see a trace element of *enthusiasm*, in the identification between the communicant and his deity. Secondly, the Mass is a symbolic allegory of the life, death, and resurrection of Christ; on this level there is an element of *narrative*. Thirdly, the Mass is based upon miraculously transformed reality. Bread and wine are miraculously transformed into the body and blood of Christ; the celebrant (officiating priest) acts at times as Christ himself, and may appear to the imaginative worshipper to have become the crucified victim. Fourthly, the idea of sacrificial death leading to rebirth, which lies at the heart of the Christian faith, is symbolically expressed in the visual, textual and structural content of the Mass.

Before the Mass begins, the chief solo actor (the celebrant) is required to go through rituals of preparation. He affirms his belief in the ritual he is about to perform, expresses hope that his performance will meet with (God's) approval, acknowledges his doubts about his ability and worthiness, and finally recognizes that through his performance he may become united with God, the ultimate universal. These rituals are not dissimilar to the normal preparations of an actor about to go on to the stage. Having prepared himself mentally, the celebrant prepares himself physically, by donning a symbolic costume: his costume is perhaps closer to that of the primitive buffalo-dancer than to that of the modern actor, in that each garment or part of a garment has a symbolic function. In putting on his vestments the celebrant protects himself against Satan (the amice), affirms his integrity (alb), controls his physical desires (girdle), accepts the sorrowful lot of man (maniple), affirms his essential immortality (stole), and gains strength to bear his burden (chasuble). Each of these acquired characteristics is a characteristic of Christ: in donning the vestments the celebrant is putting on the costume of Christ, the character he is about to play.

The stage on which he is going to perform is the altar area. We may note the presence of an altar in the *orchestra* of the Theatre of Dionysos, and that theatre's ancestry as a religous shrine. It is clear that the medieval Christian church attached symbolic importance to the different areas around the altar: stage-right (i.e. the right-hand side when facing the audience) represented paradise and safety, while stage-left represented hell, the temporal world, strife and danger. The movements of the actors upon the stage therefore have visual symbolic importance.

When the actors are prepared, and the audience-congregation has assembled, the *ceremonial music-drama* can begin.

Opera in Perspective

Introit The celebrant and his assistants enter in procession while a short antiphon and psalm-verse are sung. The singers represent, on the narrative level, the Hebrews awaiting the coming of Christ. The celebrant moves to the altar. The Kyrie is recited or sung, nine supplications to the Lord.

Gloria Suddenly, in a loud voice, the celebrant sings *'Gloria in excelsis deo';* the choir takes up the song. These are the words sung by the angels at the birth of Jesus; on the narrative level we have suddenly arrived at the Nativity, while on the ceremonial level the spirit of Christ has come among the people.

Collect, Epistle, Gradual, Gospel, Creed At this point, the celebrant becomes identified with Christ, the chief character in the drama. He greets the congregation (*dominus vobiscum*) and they reply (*et cum spiritu tuo*), shouting the words, at least in the Middle Ages, in acclamation. The celebrant makes a short prayer on behalf of the congregation (the Collect) and there follows a sequence of 'scenes' which build up to the first climax. The Epistle is read, followed by the singing of the Gradual and Alleluia. The celebrant marks the importance of the forthcoming Gospel reading by blessing it and the reader. Then the Gospel extract is read. This sequence of scenes represents, on the narrative level, the teachings of Christ; on the ceremonial level, it stresses the importance of the word of God as recorded in the Bible and proclaimed by the Church. It is at this point, therefore, that a sermon may be preached. The climax of the sequence occurs with the congregation reciting the Creed. This has the dramatic effect of uniting the audience as a single body, brought into 'tribal unity' by the preceding events, and about to take part in the deeper mysteries that follow. In the terminology of secular music-drama, it marks the end of Act One.

Offertory Act Two represents, on the narrative level, the events in Jerusalem before, during and after crucifixion. The Offertory opens with the same greeting and response *'Dominus vobiscum — et cum spiritu tuo'.* During this scene the bread and wine, symbolizing the body and blood of Christ, are ceremonially prepared for sacrifice. The Offertory antiphon is performed; the celebrant takes the offerings to the altar and blesses them. The duality of Christ's (the celebrant's) sacrifice and that of the congregation, seeking its own salvation through death, is emphasized when the celebrant says 'Brethren, pray that my sacrifice and yours may be acceptable to God. . .' He then kneels and prays silently (the Secreta); on the narrative level this parallels Christ's prayers in the Garden of Gethsemane after the last supper, here symbolized in the offering of bread and wine.

Preface and Canon Once again the greeting and reply *'Dominus vobiscum*

— *et cum spiritu tuo'* are heard. The choir sings the Sanctus and Benedictus at this point (or after the canon): these choruses symbolize the mystery and joy felt by the participants in the miracle that is about to occur (or has just occurred). The celebrant now elevates the bread and wine above the altar, 'the sacramental immolation of the divine Victim'; in medieval times he remained with arms outstretched, representing Christ on the cross. The imitation of the crucifixion, in the elevation of the symbols of Christ (and the position of the celebrant) miraculously transforms bread and wine into body and blood.

Communion The celebrant recites the Lord's prayer (*'Pater noster. . .'*) and the congregation joins in the final line 'but deliver us from evil', representing the liberation of man from sin through the sacrifice of Christ. At this point in the medieval liturgy it was possible at Easter-tide to insert the story of the women visiting the sepulchre, the so-called *Quem quaeritis,* to which we shall return later. The celebrant now drops a particle of bread/body into the chalice of wine/blood to symbolize the redintegration of the body and blood of the resurrected Christ. The choir sings the Agnus Dei (sacrificial lamb — sacrificial victim — Christ) and asks the resurrected Christ to bring mercy and peace. The celebrant gives the kiss of peace to his assistants (in medieval times the kiss was passed on to and through the congregation), representing Christ's return to the disciples with his message of peace and salvation. The celebrant, and then the congregation, perform the symbolic partaking of the body and blood of the sacrificed victim by partaking of the bread and wine: 'may the body of our Lord Jesus Christ preserve thy soul to life everlasting'. Thus the death and rebirth of Christ becomes more than a story: it is 'cathartically' transmitted into the direct experience of the congregation.

Post communion 'Dominus vobiscum — et cum spiritu tuo' is reiterated. The celebrant announces *'Ite missa est'* (go, you are dismissed); the congregation replies *'Deo gratias'*. Prayers of thanksgiving are offered, the celebrant blesses the congregation, and concludes with a reading from St. John's Gospel, which places the entire ceremony in its context: 'In the beginning was the Word. . . and the Word was made Flesh and dwelt among us.'

Figure 6 summarizes the structure and content of the Mass as music-drama. The final column, showing the *narrative* level, presents the kind of structure which one might find in Greek tragedy, but it is important to stress that this is a level beneath the *ceremonial*: the primary aim of the Mass is not to tell us the story of Christ's life and death. Nor does the division into scenes, signalled by the reiterated greeting of priest to people and their

Fig. 6   The Mass as music-drama

ACT ONE   The Coming of the Lord

scene one	*Introit*	Entry of celebrant.	Hebrews await the coming of Christ.
scene two	*Gloria*	Readings from the word of God.	Jesus is born; he preaches.
	Creed	Congregation united.	

ACT TWO   Jesus in Jerusalem

scene one	*Offertory*	Blessing of bread and wine; Secreta.	Last Supper; visit to Gethsemane.
scene two	*Preface and Canon*	Elevation of the bread and wine; transformation into body and blood.	Crucifixion.
scene three	*Communion*	Paternoster, Agnus Dei, kiss of peace, communion meal.	Death and resurrection; cathartic participation in mystery.
scene four	*Postcommunion*	*Ite, missa est;* Readings from St. John.	Moral.

reply, follow conventional dramatic practice: there is no change of location or alteration in the number of 'characters' on stage.

Nevertheless, the inherent musico-dramatic qualities of the Mass must have been appreciated by medieval congregations, as they were by theologians like Amalarius. Whether it was intended to or not, the Mass fulfilled a need for the cathartic experience of mystery in man.

Popular medieval music and drama.

Medieval man found other outlets for his yearning for music and drama. The Church by no means had a monopoly on these activities; indeed, the occasional and continuing admonitions from church writers against dramatic activities and the profession of acting show that a thriving secular 'alternative' culture was firmly established. Nor was there an absolute schism between the two: many of the dramatic activities we shall meet were initiated by clerics, monks, nuns and teachers in church schools.

Richard Axton cites three traditional elements in the European secular drama of the Middle Ages:[6] mime, combat-games, and dancing-games. Mime was a popular activity in Roman times.[7] It includes performance with gestures and movements (but no words), dance, juggling, acrobatics and puppetry. Many of the practitioners of the art in the Middle Ages seem to have been professionals, either permanently attached to courts as jesters, or possibly as touring individuals or groups. In the tenth century King Edgar complained of the detrimental effect of such players visiting monasteries. The activities of mimes are not recorded in detail, but evidence of them appears in thirteenth century vernacular texts such as the Flemish comic play *Le Garçon et l'Aveugle* (c. 1270). It would seem that in mime there was considerable use of social and religious satire, vulgarity, and knockabout farce. Songs were often included.

The relationship between combat and drama is also evident in the Roman theatre. An interesting example of the medieval combat-play was performed at the Gothic Byzantine court around 953, apparently to entertain and keep awake the sleepy Emperor Constantine VII Porphyrogenitus.

> A 'director of the theatrical games' rode (or pretended to ride) horseback in a circle about the Emperor's dining table and hall. He then called two teams of warriors into this prescribed playing circle. Each team had a leader and was accompanied by musicians playing instruments. The warriors were clothed in reindeer skin cloaks and wore various kinds of mask, carried shields in their left hands and staves in their right. At a command from the master of ceremonies, the leaders signalled their men to combat; the teams danced, rushed together in perfect symmetry, striking their shields together and crying in one voice the battle chant, 'Tul, tul'. One party surrounded the other and circled three times in stylized battle. Falling back into facing ranks they began an antiphonal chant, telling of Gothic heroes. . . followed by Greek verses in which the warriors commemorated the battles of the Old Testament, won by the heroes of the Christian God. Finally, the Goths sang in praise of the Emperor, hailing him as the inheritor of the fief of Rome, sun-like in his virtue, and invoking Christ's blessing on his empire.[8]

Here we can see a blend of dramatic elements drawn from several sources: the dances of primitive tribes, with their stylizations of naturalistic movement to the accompaniment of music; the recitation of heroic deeds as in epic poetry; and an application of the whole to the immediate political circumstances. Clearly a cultural synthesis between the hunting world of the barbarian Goths and the more sophisticated world of the Christian state is taking place.

We can also trace the influence of Roman written comedy upon the drama of the Middle Ages. The plays of Terence and Plautus were widely studied from the ninth century, and it is clear that medieval scholars believed (wrongly) that the plays of Terence were recited by a narrator while mimes performed the action. Imitations of Terence (with Christian morals added) were written by Canoness Hroswitha of Gandersheim (*fl. c. 960*). Other churchmen seem to have been familiar with other Classical dramatic forms. As early as 790 Stephanos the Sabaite had written a religious drama modelled on Greek tragedy entitled *The Death of Christ*. In the tenth

83

century Johann Tzetzes (probably) wrote *Christ's Passion,* using passages from the works of Aeschylus and Euripides. Knowledge of the classics must inevitably have brought an appreciation of the style and techniques involved in writing polished drama, even if the original content or the medieval product might be viewed with some alarm by the church.

The stylized movement of communal dance has always been a vital ingredient of nature-rituals, and remains an important one in Western European music-drama. It is a way of uniting the community in images of magical power, and as such still survives today as part of the folk-culture of all nations. In the Middle Ages it was a normal activity, associated not only with Church feasts but also with seasonal festivals. One example of apparently ancient ancestry is recorded in a Scots plough-song of about 1500. Here we have a dance-play in celebration of the new year, concerning the preparation of ox and plough for the forthcoming work in the fields. The old ox is sacrificed, the new ox summoned, the plough-boys 'initiated'. The whole is an amalgam of dance, mime and song, with the performance of ritual activities in an obviously enjoyable way.

The dance-play was also an opportunity to reflect contemporary images of behaviour, as we can see in thirteenth century Old French and Provençal dance-songs. These seem to have been sung as accompaniment to mime and round-dances, in which games of courtly love were enacted. The most famous example of the sung dance-play is Adam de la Halle's *Jeu de Robin et Marion* (*c.* 1283). The first part is narrative, in which a knight unsuccessfully woos the shepherdess Marion: she remains faithful to her Robin. In the second part games and dances are performed in celebration of the fidelity of the young and exceedingly innocent couple. A dance-song of great popularity was *La bele Aelis,* which begins by describing how the beautiful Aelis rose early, put on her most beautiful dress and make-up, and then departed to the garden to meet her courtly lover. A song like this was sung as accompaniment to mime, usually improvised. A more familiar example may be found in the Beuren manuscript (*c.* 1230) and was set by Carl Orff in *Carmina Burana.* It begins 'Chramer gip die warwe mir' and is a vernacular secular dancing-song with a story similar to that of *La bele Aelis;* but the context here is a Passion Play, and the song is that of Mary Magdalene before her repentance.

This last example shows that some Churchmen at least had no objection to the use of secular musico-dramatic forms in a sacred context. A similar example may be found in the Saint-Martial manuscript of the late eleventh century, where a popular dancing-song tune is used for a vernacular song of the Annunciation, *Mei amic e mei fiel* and for the Latin Christmas hymn *In hoc anni circulo.* But other churchmen were less enthusiastic. An irritated Jacques de Vitry in the early thirteenth century informed his congregation that by the time the beautiful Aelis had risen, washed herself, dressed and adorned herself, Mass was already over, and devils carried her off.

Some Church writers were vehemently opposed to all forms of drama, not only popular activities, but those that arose as part of the Church's own moves into the field of music-drama. Gerhoh of Reichersberg, writing around 1160, objected particularly to ecclesiastical drama, on the grounds that the performers who portray the likenesses of Biblical characters 'participate in the very mystery of iniquity'.[9] This perceptive comment shows why the secular tradition of music-drama should have persisted: it was, as ever, the mystery (iniquitous or not) of the musico-dramatic experience which made it so attractive and rewarding. The same innate characteristic may have been an important factor in the development of music-drama within the church; churchmen were not immune to music-drama's power, and the particular mystery that lies at the heart of the Christian message was an obvious subject for expression in musico-dramatic terms.

Ecclesiastical music-drama

Theologically, the central event in the Christian story is the crucifixion, the sacrifice of Christ, who takes upon him the sins of the world, and offers the hope of man's redemption from the state of sin acquired at Adam's Fall. The linking of the two 'events' of Adam's Fall and Christ's Sacrifice is not logical or rational, but a matter of belief, consequent upon a particular interpretation of legendary or historical events. As such, it is a mystery. But the event of Christ's life contain other mysteries, from his nativity through his miracles to the climactic mystery of his resurrection. The corpus of Christian history also includes other mysteries, particulary in the miracles performed by early saints. In the imaginative writing of early Christians we can also see an extension of the story-sequence, from Adam through Old Testament history to Jesus and the New Testament, on to the history of the Church itself, and then through 'new' prophecy to the apocalyptic Last Judgment. To medieval man, this sequence had a ring of truth, and provided a simple trilogy of events: the Fall of Adam representing the Fall from grace of man; the crucifixion of Christ representing atonement on behalf of man, and his resurrection representing the hope for man's return to grace; and the Last Judgement representing man's attainment of grace, when the dead actually arise and all are reborn into the kingdom of heaven. Each of these events contains mystery, and each is an event whose symbolic meaning is fixed by doctrine.

From about the tenth century onwards (there are isolated earlier examples) music-drama began to occupy an important place in the church's liturgical activities. This ecclesiastical music-drama developed quite naturally as an acting-out of the moments of mystery in the Christian story, whether from the Old Testament, the New Testament, the stories of saints, or the prophecies of future history. By the fourteenth century cycles of

Mystery Plays were being performed which covered the whole range of history from Genesis to the Last Judgment.

Initially, such ecclesiastical music-drama retained its religious function: the characters involved in the stories were treated symbolically rather than as human beings; performance took place in the church and as part of the liturgy; little attempt was made at naturalistic costuming; the text was in Latin and the music was strictly in the church style. There is nevertheless evidence of some influence from secular drama in the dramatic techniques employed. Quite swiftly, however, secular elements began to exert a stronger influence: secular musical styles appeared, together with occasional lines in the vernacular; performances began to take place outside the church; non-clerical performers began to take part. By the time of the Mystery Play cycles, music-drama had become a mixture of sacred and secular traditions, performed for all in the vernacular and on a day (Corpus Christi) sanctified by the Church for this purpose. And while the Mystery Plays purported to retain a doctrinal purpose, it is nevertheless clear that they made their appeal largely as secular popular entertainment.

The two are not necessarily opposed, of course. Lessons can be learned in an environment of enjoyment; and it is quite probable that the ecclesiastical drama arose because some churchmen thought it would be fun to act out a portion of the liturgy. That portion which seems to have been first selected was the moment in the Easter story at which the three Marys approach the sepulchre and find it is empty. During the tenth century and thereafter the *Visitatio Sepulchri* play achieved enormous popularity as a dramatic interlude enacted by priests during the Easter Mass. [10] It is customarily known as the *Quem quaeritis* from its opening words:

ANGEL	Whom do you seek in the sepulchre,
	O Christian women?
WOMEN	Jesus of Nazareth, who was crucified,
	O heavenly one.
ANGEL	He is not here: he has arisen, as it
	was foretold. Go and announce that he has
	arisen. [11]

This Latin text was sung by the priest-performers and acted out in the church near the altar. The text makes it clear what the point is: the sudden revelation of the mystery of Christ's resurrection. In Aristotelian terms we would call this moment in the Passion narrative *peripeteia,* an abrupt reversal, and *anagnorisis,* a moment of the recognition of a truth. It has its counterpart in the death-rebirth rituals of primitive man, or in the Eleusinian Mysteries, or even in a play such as Sophocles' *Oedipus.*

In the conventional *Quem quaeritis* the doctrinal framework is clear: expansion into music-drama at this moment merely gives force to the liturgical message. But in the Easter Play performed at Ripoll *c.* 1100, the three Marys approach the sepulchre and *command* Christ to rise. This is magical conjuring, and betrays an ancestry in ancient ritual: the performers here are thought of as capable of *making things happen* through their actions.

The *Visitatio Sepulchri* focusses our attention upon the mystery of Christ's death and rebirth; it is capable also of being transferred to the moment of Christ's mysterious birth. *Quem quaeritis in sepulchro* becomes *quem quaeritis in praesepe*, spoken by the angel to the three shepherds approaching the manger. A similar extension is possible to portray the arrival of the three Magi.

Such interpolations into the services of appropriate Feasts were common in the tenth, eleventh and twelfth centuries. All had Latin texts and were sung throughout in plainsong style. By the thirteenth century, however, further developments were taking place, particularly in monasteries and in the church schools of northern France, with the writing of more lengthy and more sophisticated Latin music-dramas. The subject-matter still took its source from Christian history, and the plays retained a liturgical and didactic purpose, but larger forces and more ambitious stage requirements are employed.

The 'Fleury-playbook' from the monastery of St-Benoît-sur-Loire contains nine plays of this kind (four miracle-plays of St. Nicholas, a Herod play, a Rachel play, a Journey to Emmaus play, a Conversion of St. Paul play, a Raising of Lazarus play) and one *Visitatio Sepulchri*. Dating from the thirteenth century, these works show the blending of dramatic ingredients from many sources. The Herod play, for instance[12] includes liturgical antiphons, Latin narrative and even quotations from Virgil.

The Beauvais thirteenth-century *Play of Daniel* shows a more radical departure from a liturgical context. The chorus is not a church choir *per se* but a group of costumed attendants involved in the stage action. The staging is spectacular, the music relies little upon plainchant and makes use of a variety of invented or popular melodies. The performing area is less symbolic and more representational. This is not to say that it is completely divorced from church musico-dramatic practice: it retains a formalization of structure and stylization in gesture, and is clearly didactic theatre. But one is drawn to the conclusion that here the potential of music-drama is beginning to be fully explored by the anonymous composer/dramatist, though we cannot know whether he thought of such exploration as a service to his faith or as an adventure in itself.

Perhaps the most extraordinary Latin music-drama of the early Middle Ages is Hildegard of Bingen's *Ordo Virtutem*, or *Play of the Virtues*. This is a musico-dramatic allegory in which sixteen or seventeen 'Virtues' argue with the Devil for the possession of Anima, the soul. The stage, a series of steps, is symbolic, as is the costuming. The Virtues dance and sing monodic (single-line) melody based on Gregorian chant while the Devil speaks or shouts in prose. Here symbolist drama is taken out of the liturgy and related to secular dance-plays, in a fashion which seems to anticipate the Masque and *ballet de cour* of the seventeenth century; the notion of the ascent of the soul forecasts, as we shall see, an image of the early Renaissance.

All the ecclesiastical plays mentioned so far were written and performed in Latin. It was however not unusual for Latin plays to make some use of the vernacular. The *Sponsus* (Play of the Wise and Foolish Virgins) in the eleventh-century Saint-Martial manuscript goes so far as to use Latin and Provençal in alternate sections. Here the vernacular is set to secular musical styles and forms. To use the vernacular language of the people instead of the Latin of the church and scholarship implies a wish to make details of a story or characters more interesting and understandable to a popular audience. While it is clear that some of the Latin ecclesiastical music-dramas were probably written only for private monastic performance, it is equally clear that most were given before a congregation or even an audience. It must at times have been a puzzling experience for those unversed in Latin, and one can see why clerics should wish to help by writing passages in the vernacular. At the same time, this involved the risk of losing the symbolism of the story and the ceremony of its presentation. All too easily ecclesiastical drama could take on the undignified aspects of secular drama.

And yet by the mid-twelfth century ecclesiastical plays were being written in the vernacular, in Spain and in Northern France. Of these the most interesting is *Le Mystère d'Adam* (c. 1160). The action (from Genesis) is represented in spoken Norman-French dialogue by the main characters, who use strictly stylized gesture and wear suitable costumes. A mime element is present in the dancing and cavorting of Satan and his devils. A third, more liturgical element is provided by a church choir which opens, punctuates and closes the work by singing responsories in Latin. This mixture of styles is highly individual for the time, but anticipates the Mystery cycles of the fourteenth century, which brought together the current available forms of music-drama, both secular and ecclesiastical.

Most of the medieval forms of music-drama have now been mentioned, and an overall picture has begun to emerge. Despite being a Dark Age — and in many respects it was, not least so far as full-scale music-drama is concerned — the medieval period was a time of considerable vitality in drama. At one end of the spectrum there were the dance-songs, and mime-songs of folk ritual. At the other end there was liturgical drama sung in Latin. In between stood the world of the court, drawing its entertainment from folk-song and -dance and creating its images of courtly love in minstrelsy and in Arcadian music-dramas such as *Le Jeu de Robin et Marion*. Across the spectrum flow the lines of influence between sacred and secular, Latin and vernacular, to create an astonishing variety of spoken dramas and sung dramas, on Biblical subjects or with plots in the style of Terence or Plautus. Gradually more sophisticated techniques are being developed, in the use of the stage, the structuring of dramatic material, and not the least in the world of music, where complex polyphonic textures are now being used alongside simpler ecclesiastical and secular forms. Here and there musico-dramatic works of startling originality are being written.

What emerges into the foreground is the constant influence of the secular upon the ecclesiastical. We do not know how the *Quem quaeritis* came about: perhaps from a wish to combat secular music-drama, perhaps from a wish to parallel its popularity, perhaps from a desire of clerics themselves to participate in what seemed to be an enjoyable secular activity. By the twelfth century we can see ecclesiastical music-drama employing many of the techniques and methods of secular music-drama, from the vernacular spoken text to the more human representation of character. The causes of this are not easy to determine: perhaps the limited approval given to music-drama by the church encouraged a wider creative search by authors. There was certainly, it seems, a continuing struggle between some churchmen and the power of secular musical and dramatic celebrations. The activities of some town populaces on Feast Days were regarded with horror by many ecclesiastical critics; nevertheless it may have been in these activities of dancing, mime, drama, song and revelry that some ecclesiastical dramatists found an inspiration (at least in technique) for their own works, and the more restrained celebrations of courtly life must also have played a part.

The English Mystery Plays

It is in the English Mystery Plays that we see how closely the secular and sacred worlds are interwoven. Four complete cycles from the fourteenth century are preserved: The York Plays, the Beverley Plays, the Towneley Plays and the so-called 'Coventry' Plays. These play-cycles were concerned with the events of Christian history from Genesis to the Last Judgment, in other words with the overall 'mystery' as established in Christian doctrine. But that history was also presented as a succession of individual episodes, each a 'mystery' in itself, an inexplicable event understandable only by reference to the established faith. From an ecclesiastical point of view, the Mystery Plays were doctrinally acceptable and had a clear Christian didactic purpose. It is however plain that Mystery Plays were not unopposed. The Lollards in particular considered them iniquitous, and a famous treatise includes (in order to rebut them) six arguments in defence of Mystery Plays:

1 Mystery plays are acted in honour of God.
2 Men are converted to virtuous living by seeing the mystery plays, for they learn from them the folly of pride and the wiliness of the devils in their attempts to ensnare people.
3 By seeing the sufferings of Christ people are moved by compassion and

devotion, and they weep bitter tears.
4   There are some people who can only be converted through the device of entertainment.
5   People must be given some entertainment for refreshment after their work, and religious plays are far better than the frivolous pastimes with which they would otherwise occupy themselves
6   Since it is permissible to portray the work of the Redemption in art, it must be permissible to portray it also in drama, the latter being yet more memorable and effective than art, for the one 'is a deed bok, the tother a quick'.[13]

Two of these arguments (4 and 5) are flimsy, and are attempts to justify the fact that the Mystery Play was obviously a form of popular entertainment. Argument 2 stresses didactic purpose; argument 1 is not an argument but a bald statement. Arguments 3 and 6 are more interesting, for both grant particular powers to the dramatic arts.

The 'moving of people to compassion, devotion and tears' bears comparison with Aristotelian theory, which speaks of tragedy arousing our 'pity' and 'terror'. It is the 'emotional' appeal of dramatic images which is stressed here, an appeal in which man's sufferings speak to men, in a stage-to-audience relationship with which we are familiar. The same idea is implicit in the final argument which speaks of drama as a 'live' (quick) art compared with the 'dead' art of painting. In drama the images are alive in the human sense: hence their power to involve us so deeply. But in these arguments the Aristotelian interpretation is not accepted without qualification: we are told that people are moved to compassion and *devotion*: our Dionysiac involvement is here 'rescued' by high moral purpose. Images, in short, are not idolatrous (as the Lollards maintained) but an acceptable part of didactic teaching, a view which reminds us of the function of Apollo in the Nietzschean interpretation of music-drama.

The Mystery Play cycles were large-scale affairs. The York Cycle (in the extant text of *c.* 1450) contains some forty-eight separate plays, each of which was performed on its own 'pageant waggon' at one of the 'stations' in the city during Corpus Christi day.[14] Each play was the responsibility of a different Guild of craftsmen or tradesmen, and the whole was supervised by the City Corporation. It is interesting to note that the church did not have over-all control. Although the texts were written by scholars, and church musicians played an important role, this is not ecclesiastical drama in church performance, but secular drama on a church subject. The plays are written in the vernacular (with an occasional Latin line) but with directions in Latin. The verse text is not sung but spoken.

Music in the Mystery Play cycles had several functions.[15] Firstly, music in the church style was associated with God, Heaven and angels. This was in keeping with the medieval belief that music reflects in some way the indefinable music of the Universe. The source of such a belief may be found, as we have seen, in Sumer, and the Greeks had their own version of it. In practical terms, God's music meant plainchant, in the Mystery Plays as elsewhere, either sung as simple melody or in some polyphonic arrangement. In the York cycle specific instructions for angels to sing are given in twelve plays; in one Mary sings a Magnificat, and in another the Jews sing in praise of God. Possibly these songs were accompanied by instruments. The effect of using church music was twofold: in the first place it provided a proper formalization for any representation of divine beings, and in the second place it reminded the audience, by association, of the over-all religious and didactic purpose of the plays.

A second use of music was for ceremonial, a use probably adopted from courtly practice. Here fanfares or short, dignified instrumental pieces marked the entrances, exits and commands of important persons such as Herod or Pilate. Occasionally the York Plays indicate some spectacular stage effect, as in the Curriers Play when 'a cloud descends, the Father in the cloud': possibly ceremonial music was used at this moment rather than church music.

Music was also used for scenes involving mime. The classic example in the Mystery Play cycle is the building of Noah's Ark — in the York cycle this is appropriately performed by the Guild of Shipwrights. The style must have been secular, perhaps even a folk-song, probably performed on pipe and drum. An extension of this principle occurs in the music for the appearances of devils: it seems that one common practice was to use musical instruments for sound-effects — real music would be inappropriate for the agents of Lucifer. The York cycle also indicates, in the Lytsteres Play of Herod, that court revelries, including dancing, take place, for which, presumably, music was required.

Finally, music in a popular form makes an appearance at moments of comedy, especially those associated with the shepherds. The association of shepherds with music belongs to the folk-tradition, but, as we have seen, was adopted into the tradition of courtly love in works such as *Le Jeu de Robin et Marion*. The shepherds in the York cycle are in no way courtly, however. At the appearance of the angel they rustically exclaim 'Ah! Ooh! Ah! Hoo!'.[16] The angel sings, to which the third shepherd remarks:

> I can sing it as well as he,
> And on essay it shall be soon
> > Proved ere we pass.
> If ye will help, hold on. Let's see;
> > For thus it was.
> > (*The shepherds sing*)

2nd SHEPHERD   Haha! This was a merry note,
By the death that I shall die.
I have so croaked in my throat
That my lips are near dry.

3rd SHEPHERD   No boasting, boys.[17]

A little later the shepherds sing again, and this song 'covers' their journey from the fields to the manger at Bethlehem.

The lack of respect shown to the angel relates to the tradition of popular comedy, and might be thought to verge on the blasphemous. The idea that shepherds singing a secular (and possibly vulgar) song could compete with the angel singing of the birth of Jesus was an adventurous one, but such adventures seem to play a part in all the shepherd plays in the Mystery cycles. The shepherds are the most obvious example of the popular entertainment element in the plays; they are the most 'ordinary' people involved, and the audience would find them easy to identify with.

Evidence that the shepherds might sing a fairly sophisticated music comes from the *Secunda Pastorum* play of the Towneley cycle. The text clearly indicates that a three-part song is sung. Indeed, the shepherds are no mean musicians, for they discuss the angel's musical and vocal technique. What impresses them most is not the sound-effect of the Gloria but the singer's skill in ornamentation and the rhythmic complexity of the piece.[18] This may be satirical of musical attitudes of the time, or merely a delicious comic incongruity in portraying simple shepherds as scholars. Either way, its humour depends on the audience accepting that there is a gulf between 'popular' and 'church', a gulf which the Mystery Plays were in fact bridging most sucessfully.

We can apply to medieval music-drama the terms we have been using to describe previous examples of the *genre*. The *Quem quaeritis* must be regarded as purely *ceremonial*, with *narrative* elements scarcely present at all. As ecclesiastical drama develops, using the vernacular and, occasionally, secular musical styles, *narrative* elements increase, in so far as the characters begin to assume more human interest, for it is only when we see human beings enmeshed in great events that our minds are engaged in the action. So long as the drama retains an ideological framework, the *ceremonial* aspects triumph. It is only in moments such as the shepherds' plays in the Mystery cycles that the *narrative* element begins to grow important, for, until they are caught up in the business of adoring the child, the shepherds are ordinary human beings faced with mystery — in this case, an angel singing. This is scarcely on the level of the deepest and most mysterious of close encounters perhaps, but what makes the shepherds' plays so interesting is that we see them engage in attempts to come to terms with what they face. The York shepherds deal with an angel's song by singing their own, which is precisely the 'irrational' solution to mystery that music-drama offers.

Enthusiasm is not present in ecclesiastical music-drama (for obvious reasons). It is present, however, in the popular music-drama that derives from nature-rites, where involvement is a method for learning truths. And we can see it as an ingredient in the York shepherds' response to the angel:

the mystery of song is penetrated by directly participating in song oneself. Yet this is a brief moment in a cycle of plays whose fundamental aspect is *ceremonial,* and cannot be regarded as significant except in so far as it betrays the enduring quality of folk-ritual, which we have taken as the fundamental example of music-drama.

The most important aspect of the Mystery Play is, as the first 'argument for the defence' put it, that it is acted in honour of God. It is an act of Christian faith, illustrative and didactic, not exploratory. This is why it differs from Greek tragedy. The Mystery Play *reiterates* history/myth and *celebrates* a solution to life's mystery, while Greek tragedy *explores* history/ myth in order to *seek* a solution to life's mystery. While the Greek looked for answers, medieval man had found an answer, and praised it.

4 Rebirth

Orpheus

In 1471 or 1472 (that is, some twenty years after the date of the York Mystery Play texts) a young man aged about eighteen named Angelo Ambrogini, usually called Poliziano, after his birthplace, produced upon the stage at Mantua a verse drama with music called *La Favola d'Orfeo*. One hundred and thirty-five years later that same city was to see the production of another *favola* called *L'Orfeo*, this time by Alessandro Striggio the younger and Claudio Monteverdi. Poliziano's work marks the start of the birth-pangs of music-drama as 'opera'; Monteverdi's registers its successful delivery.

Even as a young man Poliziano was recognized as a talented writer and Greek scholar. We do not know what actually led him to conceive a drama on the Orpheus myth, but it is surely no coincidence that both he and Monteverdi should choose this subject, for the story of Orpheus is one of the death and rebirth of a man, an allegory from pagan Classical rather than strictly Christian sources, and is furthermore 'about' the processes of artistic creation. It is therefore highly appropriate to any attempt to re-create the music-drama of pre-Christian Europe.

There are several versions of the Greek legend. Orpheus was the son of Calliope, the muse of epic poetry; his father was either Apollo or the Thracian king Oeagrus. It was Apollo who gave him a lyre and taught him music, apparently, although other versions make him a follower of Dionysos. Orpheus' musical powers were such that he could move not only his human listeners, but animals, birds, and even trees and rocks. Having fallen in love with the wood-nymph Eurydice, he married her; but Eurydice one day was pursued by Aristaeus (another son of Apollo by the nymph Cyrene, and the protector of cattle and orchards) and in fleeing from him she was fatally bitten by a snake. Orpheus resolved to descend into the underworld to rescue her.

Hades, ruler of the underworld, was so moved by Orpheus' singing that he

94

agreed to release Eurydice, on condition that Orpheus did not look at her until they regained the upper world. At the very border between the two worlds, however, Orpheus was so overcome by anxiety and desire that he broke the condition, turned and looked at her: and Eurydice was lost.

The original ending to the story, usually modified by composers of opera, is as follows. Orpheus emerged from the underworld stricken by grief, and resisted the attempts of Thracian women to console him. Angered by his rejection of them and, some say, in a frenzy inspired by Dionysos, the women seized him and tore him to pieces. The Muses collected the fragments of his body together and buried them near the foot of Mount Olympus, but his head, thrown into the river Hebrus, floated down to the Aegean Sea; it was finally washed up on the island of Lesbos, where it became a famous oracle. His lyre, apparently, was placed among the stars.

The complete legend of Orpheus is really a combination of two legends. The first legend is the story of Orpheus' descent into Hades and his 'resurrection', a parable of death and rebirth that relates to the ancient myths of the dying and resurrected God. The second legend is the story of an Apollonian individual who, like Pentheus in *The Bacchae*, objects to the cult of Dionysos and finally suffers the traditional fate: it was this story which Aeschylus used in his lost Orpheus-play *The Bassarids*. Both legends are, of course, essentially about the same thing: death and rebirth.

Both Poliziano and Monteverdi allow Christian elements into the texts of their Orpheus music-dramas. This is neither unexpected, for they were Christians living in a Christian culture, nor inappropriate, for the Greek cult of Orphism which grew out of the legends associated with Orpheus was close enough to Christian belief to be made much of by the early Gnostic Christians. It emphasized the importance of leading a pure life, and was based on a belief in the immortality of the soul. In order to purify the soul from the bodily temptations of evil, Orphic worshippers took part in symbolic rituals. The combination of moral probity, strict ritual and a belief in the immortality of the soul places Orphism clearly in the Christian tradition: its single most non-Christian characteristic was its central (and Oriental) faith that the soul could become one with the divinity, an *enthousiasmos* which the Christianity of St Paul bitterly opposed. At the same time, *enthousiasmos* was perhaps what most attracted the music-dramatists of the Renaissance and early Baroque.

What distinguishes Orpheus from the other heroes of the myths of death and rebirth is the fact that he is a poet-musician, a creative artist. His own death at the hands of Dionysos' followers is symbolic of the experience of the Apollonian creative artist whose dedication to shapes is swept away by a rapturous involvement in Dionysiac sound-effects. This part of the legend is therefore of immediate appeal to the musician or music-dramatist who is discontented with a musical style fixed by convention or law, and who seeks to re-assert music's power to express innermost experiences. Certainly this was the aim of those who brought about the rebirth of music-drama at the end of the sixteenth century, and a more generalized support of Greek freedom of expression in contrast to Christian restrictions on expression undoubtedly lay behind Poliziano's youthful experiment.

But the legend of Orpheus is more than an allegory about the relative powers of Apollo and Dionysos in music. The first part of the story may also be interpreted as a symbol of the act of artistic creation.

The act of artistic creation is inspiration plus perspiration (according to Bernard Shaw, ten per cent of the former and ninety per cent of the latter), a process which begins with the arrival of an 'idea' and continues through the process of working on, with and around that idea until a finished work of art is produced. As Shakespeare puts it in *A Midsummer Night's Dream* (*c.* 1594), Act V scene 1:

> . . . as imagination bodies forth
> The forms of things unknown, the poet's pen
> Turns them to shapes, and gives to airy nothing
> A local habitation and a name.

The initial idea emerges from the unconscious through imagination: it is indefinable and inexplicit until the creative artist gives it shape, place and identity. The similarity between the artistic 'idea' and the unconscious content which stimulates psychological rebirth is obvious, and provides another connection between Orpheus as creative artist and the theme of death and rebirth.

In the legend of Orpheus, Eurydice is a symbol of the creative 'idea'. She is a dryad, a nature-spirit, an embodiment in semi-human form of part of the mysterious forces that govern nature. Orpheus, the creative artist, perceives the idea, and begins to process it. His marriage to Eurydice symbolizes his wish to make the idea his own: to turn dryad into wife is to give the idea 'a local habitation and a name'. However, the idea is elusive: Eurydice is bitten by the snake (a symbol of the forces of the unconscious) and disappears from the conscious. She goes in fact to the *under*world (*sub*conscious); Orpheus, the creative artist, realizing that 'Eurydice' is the best 'idea' he ever had, pursues her. Psychologically this is very dangerous, for Orpheus is opening himself to the full force of his repressed unconscious. Creatively, it is also dangerous, for the ideas born of inspiration are generally best left to make their presence felt without detailed analysis.

Indeed, this is the meaning of the condition imposed on Eurydice's return: Orpheus is warned not to repeat his first error in seeking to identify the inspired 'idea'. He must trust it. But he cannot do so, and inevitably the 'idea' is lost. The story so far makes a moral point about the act of creativity: Orpheus' first and second losses of Eurydice are both caused by the same error, his wishing to give too soon 'a local habitation and a name' to 'airy nothing'.

After this point in the story several endings are possible, depending upon the attitudes of the dramatist or composer telling the story. Monteverdi's ending, as we shall see, makes a second and more emphatic moral point about creativity. The original ending emphasizes the terrible danger of doing what Orpheus did: unable to extract his 'idea' from the unconscious he slams the lid down, refusing to acknowledge its claims. Such severe repression serves only to build up pressures, until the libido, in the form of Dionysos' frenzied Maenads, breaks through and dismembers the personality. Orpheus becomes schizophrenic, his body being buried at Olympus and his head at Lesbos.

This interpretation of the Orpheus legend is, of course, a twentieth-century interpretation, a re-reading of the myth in contemporary terminology. But the modernity of the terminology does not mean that Greek or Renaissance man did not perceive the same moral in the legend. A myth is an image, a way of saying something in story-form; each age interprets myths in its own way. Freud's 'invention' of the Oedipus-complex is not a sudden dawning of the truth but a re-defining in modern terms of a truth contained already in the particular circumstances of the Oedipus story.

Poliziano's *La Favola d'Orfeo* was something of a departure for its period: it anticipates the *pastorale* of the following century, but, more than that, as its title suggests, it tells a story. After a Prologue by Mercury, scene 1 is a dailogue between Mopsus, an old shepherd, and Aristaeus, a young one. Aristaeus declares his love for Euridice, and sings a song in four stanzas, accompanied on the reed-pipe. In the second scene Aristaeus is seen pursuing Euridice. In the third scene a dryad informs her companions of Euridice's death: a simple homophonic chorus of lament follows. The fourth scene opens with Orpheus singing a lengthy song in Latin, accompanying himself on the lyre (possibly a viola da braccia); a shepherd enters and informs him of Euridice's death. He resolves to rescue her. Scene 5 contains the rest of the action: Orpheus' singing persuades Pluto and Proserpina; the condition is stated; Orpheus breaks it and loses Euridice; he denounces women. A chorus of Maenads rush in, drag off Orpheus and kill him, returning with his severed head (cf. *The Bacchae*) to sing and dance in praise of Bacchus.

This version of the story seems to stress an Apollo-Dionysos confrontation. Aristaeus and Mopsus (in original Greek legend a prophet, the grandson of Tiresias, though possibly here taken from Virgil) sing and dance to Dionysos' instrument, the *aulós*; Orpheus sings in Latin, which for Poliziano, who was to be called 'the father of vernacular Italian poetry', was the language not only of courtly compliment but also of traditional church religion. The Maenads are Dionysiac worshippers, and the play ends with

97

praises to Bacchus.

The first performance must have been a startling event. We do not know who wrote the music (perhaps a mysterious Signor Germi), but it was apparently entirely in a simple secular style. Nor was the performance half-hearted or amateur. A temporary stage was erected in the hall of the Gonzaga Palace, and partitioned down the middle. Stage-right was the Thracian pastoral scene, stage-left was Hades. The scenery was carefully painted (possibly by Botticelli?). The starring role of Orfeo was played by the famous Florentine *improvisatore* and singer Baccio Ugolino.

Poliziano's work is not 'opera'; it was the product of the growing influence of Greek models, and of the particular cultural hot-houses of Florence, where, a century later, music-drama was to be reborn. The text was published and widely circulated, and was probably known to the later Florentines: perhaps they saw in it the relevance of the Orpheus myth to the rebirth of an art-form.

Renaissance and Reformation

The great significance of Poliziano's *Orfeo* is that it breaks with Christianity and takes its subject from Classical Greece. The reawakening of interest in Classical Greece was a general one in the late Middle Ages, and was one of the driving forces in the creation of Renaissance culture. Medieval Universities had always studied Greek and Roman classics, and Christian theologians since the time of St. Augustine had embodied Greek philosophy in Christian religious thinking. But much of the study of Greek thought had been through Roman translations and mistranslations. In the early fifteenth century scholars began to be interested in the originals, and diligent searching brought them to light. By the end of the century scholars were discovering the true Aristotle, for instance, and finding he was rather more than a buttress to Catholic Christianity. This desire to distinguish Greek thought from Christian theology was one of the factors contributing to a new humanist outlook.

Another contributory factor was the gradual development of commercially prosperous towns, which reproduced many of the cultural conditions that had obtained in the social environment of Classical Greece and the Roman Empire. Material prosperity tends to bring with it an interest in this life rather than the next; for the medieval peasant the next life must at times have seemed the only hope. Though the Church might announce that this life was a shadowy vale of tears in which sinful man must suffer, it became clear to men with money in their pockets that there were ways of making this life an Arcadian vale of laughter and pleasure. Prosperous urban man was consequently attracted to that secular enjoyment of life revealed in the literature of the Classics.

At this time, too, Europe was looking outward. Commercial pressures, and the invention of a fairly reliable system of oceanic navigation, led in the fifteenth and sixteenth centuries to voyages of exploration and discovery round Africa, to China, and across the Atlantic. The Treaty of Saragossa in 1529 partitioned the known world outside Europe into Spanish and Portuguese spheres of influence.[1]

Growing prosperity brought with it both greed and an appreciation of wealth; it was noticed that the Catholic Church was exceptionally wealthy, and, moreover, imposed heavy ecclesiastical taxation. To many, and particularly to the rising class of capitalist merchants and bankers, this seemed unjust. Commercial enterprise also brought with it the phenomenon of the self-made man, who achieved wealth and respect entirely through his own actions and hard work. Such a man was naturally suspicious of easy promises such as the sale of indulgences by the church, and the miraculous claims made about the relics of Saints.[2]

These factors led to two new developments: the rebirth of humanism, and the Reformation.

Humanism may be defined as an attitude which places emphasis upon this world, and upon man in this world. Renaissance humanism took two forms. In the first, Man was celebrated: the most notable visual example is Michelangelo's painted ceiling in the Sistine Chapel, peopled with idealized human physiques. In the famous panel *The Creation of Adam* it is God who is stretching out his hand towards Adam, who reclines almost nonchalantly, though not disrespectfully. The second form of Renaissance humanism was a resurgence of individualism, an emphasis on the freedom of the individual mind, a belief in the right of a man to express himself. In literature the notable example is Montaigne (1533–92) whose essays reflect this intellectual self-assertion.

In general, Renaissance humanists were Catholics, though they tended to play down the ritual and doctrinal aspects of Catholicism. The typical solution to a possible dilemma of faith between Catholicism and Classical humanism was that of Erasmus (1466–1536).

> The first place must indeed be given to the authority of the Scriptures; but, nevertheless, I sometimes find some things said or written by the ancients, nay, even by the heathens, nay, by the poets themselves, so chastely, so holily, and so divinely, that I cannot persuade myself but that, when they wrote them, they were divinely inspired, and perhaps the spirit of Christ diffuses itself farther than we imagine. . .[3]

This statement, so tentative and conciliatory in expression and so positive in content, reveals the prime source of humanist ideas — Classical literature and poetry. It was the arts which were the vehicle for the Renaissance humanist's views. Through the arts transcendental experiences could be enjoyed. Through the arts morality would triumph (see Sir Philip Sydney's *An Apologie for Poetrie*). Through the arts humanity could be portrayed in

99

all its aspects — even the grosser or comic ones (*Pantagruel* (1533) and *Gargantua* (1535) of Rabelais). Through the arts man's heroism and sentiment — and wit — could be revealed (Ariosto's *Orlando Furioso* (1516 and 1532)).

While humanism lay at the foundation of the Renaissance of the arts in Europe, similar pressures were leading in another direction. Discontent within the Church led eventually to a split, and to the formation of the Protestant religions. Martin Luther (1483–1546), John Calvin (1509–64), Ulrich Zwingli (1484–1531) and John Knox (1505–72) opposed the excessive ritualism, central control, wealth and corruption of the Catholic Church. They strove for a simpler and more direct form of worship than the spectacular Latin Mass, and questioned the supernatural transformation of wine and bread into the actual blood and body of Christ. They opposed the idea that the only path to salvation was via the sacrament administered by an ordained priesthood. In short, they opposed the Church machine.

In the event, the new Protestant religions differed little from Catholicism in many aspects: both accpeted the Bible as sacred truth, both accepted the doctrines of heaven, hell and salvation, and both denounced intellectual freedom. The moral severity of Protestantism was matched by the Catholic Counter-Reformation and the founding of the Jesuit Order in 1534, closely followed by the College of Inquisition in 1542. Both churches partook in the witch-hunts of the sixteenth and seventeenth centuries. The tolerance of the early Renaissance gave way to intolerance; by this time, however, the humanist arts were well-established.

Renaissance (re-birth) and Reformation (re-shaping) are the key-words of this period for the arts. The principles of the Classical Age were born again and shaped anew in contemporary forms.

The Music of the Spheres
One of the most curious of those forms was the symbolic diagram, of which Franchino Gafori's (or Gafurius') *Music of the Spheres* (Milan, 1496) is an interesting example (see Fig. 7). It represents Gafori's view of the relationship between (from the left) the Greek muses, the notes of the Greek scale,[4] the Greek 'modes' (with the intervals between notes indicated) and the astronomical spheres, with Roman names. At the top of the picture sits Apollo, to his right the three Graces: Euphrosyne (Joy), Aglaia (Splendour) and Thalia (Abundance). In his left hand he holds a lyre with which he causes the music of the spheres. Further to his left stands a vase of flowers, which according to Edgar Wind[5] signifies the *crater* through which the divine spirit descends. At the base of the picture is Cerberus, with two lupine or canine heads and one central lion's head. Below stands Thalia once more, now in the underworld. Down through the centre of the diagram lies a serpentine creature with a curling tail.

Fig. 7   *The Music of the Spheres*

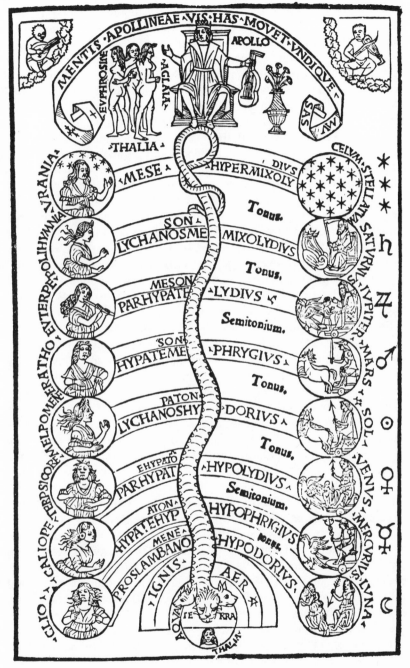

This diagram is open to a number of interesting interpretations. Wind[6] suggests that it shows the *descent* of a spiritual force which emanates from Apollo and permeates the Universe. But more intriguing meanings arise if we regard the diagram as suggesting *ascent*, the ascent of the human spirit from 'earth' to 'heaven' through the arts. Such an ascent is via the snake. The snake sheds and renews its skin, and is an age-old symbol of the cycles of life and death. It is also a particular symbol in Christian mythology, representing the cause of the Fall of Man, and while a specifically Christian interpretation is not what Gafori had in mind, the imagery may be useful.

Ascent begins by entry into the lion's mouth, a surrender to death. This surrender of individuality (loss of *individuation* in Jungian terms) can be related to the loss of identity we experience as we become involved in a Dionysiac experience. What leads us to enter the jaws is the image of Thalia, the goddess of abundance, an Artemis-Persephone figure, the personification of nature's promise of rebirth. That rebirth occurs over eight stages, the function of each stage suggested by the appropriate muse and by a heavenly body which we can interpret according to Roman mythology. In climbing the eight stages we ascend a musical octave. But first we must pass through earth, water, air and fire, which are the constituents of matter. Once 'dematerialized' the soul can begin its journey.

The first experience brings us to Clio, the muse of history, and Luna, who measures time. The second brings us to Calliope, the muse of epic poetry, and Mercury, who guides souls to eternity. Epic poetry is history made timeless; under Mercury's guidance we break free of time, and are beginning to enter the 'no-time, no-when' of artistic experiences. On the third level we reach Terpsichore, the muse of dance and choral song, and Venus the goddess of love: timeless images and experiences concern us here. On the fourth level we find Melpomene, the muse of tragedy, and the searing, illuminating power of the sun. Here we perceive the universals represented in tragic images, with their tremendous power to illuminate our understanding.

This experience leads us to examine ourselves. On the fifth level we are made aware of the conflict (Mars) between our spiritual and baser natures: Eratho is the muse of lyric and erotic poetry. On the sixth level we come under the fatherly protection of Jupiter and find the purity of Euterpe's flute music. On the seventh level Polyhymnia's sacred song frees us, like Saturn's scythe, from all links with the world, so that we may attain the stars, on the eighth level, under the watchful eye of Urania, goddess of Astronomy. Thus we complete the octave and regain the upper 'tonic'.

But though we have ascended the serpent to the feet of Apollo, our journey is not yet ended. We have caught a glimpse of Euphrosyne, Aglaia and Thalia, but in a Christian world our aim is not enthusiastic identification with the deity. We must follow the serpent's tail back down to level seven, to sacred song and to Saturn, for it is the liturgy that guarantees our freedom.

We might also observe that the 'notes' up which we have ascended are those from *a* to *a* (the Hypodorian scale: our progress has been 'majestic'). In Gregorian chant the most important notes in this mode are *d* and *f*.[7] By association the important moments in the journey have been the cathartic moment in tragedy and the timeless experience of pure music.

An interpretation such as this is of course wider than Gafori intended. But symbols have a power that cannot always be circumscribed, and the world of the late Middle Ages and early Renaissance was one which sought to find systematic explanations for the Universe which would include Classical images. Nor is it inappropriate to interpret our diagram in terms of transformation, for this was clearly an important concept to Gafori and his contemporaries. Indeed, since *The Music of the Spheres* positively invites allegorical interpretation, we can investigate it as an image of transformation in relation to the Mass, the Christian ceremonial through which bread and wine are transformed into the body and blood of Christ, and in which the Christian soul finds its own hope of rebirth (see fig. 6).

The measurement of time (level one) is presented by the reiterated Kyries of the Introit, and heroic poetry, guiding souls towards the eternal, by the Introit's psalm (level two). The Gloria is choral song (level three). The sequence of teachings from the Bible 'illuminates' the congregation (level four), which is thus united and expresses its unity in the Creed. The Offertory turns the base reality of bread and wine into the incorruptible symbols of body and blood. The Sanctus and Benedictus express the protectiveness of God ('*Benedictus qui venit in nomine domini*') and his glory (level six). The Elevation of the Host symbolically frees us from the corruptibility of the world (level seven). In participating in the Communion we ourselves gain entry into the kingdom of heaven (level eight). The Postcommunion brings us back down the serpent's tail to receive the liturgical moral. The validity of this interpretation is, of course, open to question: it is doubtful whether Gafori would have approved.

Gafori's diagram has all the pantheistic syncretism of the Renaissance attempt to find answers. That search is itself indicative of the Greek influence: medieval man knew the answers. It is the sort of diagram which invites interpretation in as many ways as possible and suggests correspondences with contemporary ideas. We might, for instance, see Thalia as a Eurydice figure, whose proper place is by Apollo/Orpheus, but who has been bitten by the snake/serpent and is now in the underworld, whence she must be rescued by a descending and ascending Orpheus. We might note that the two semitones involved in the eight-note scale connect heroic poetry with dance and choral song (which is a possible historical connection, in Greece), and lyric poetry with flute music (which is a certain connection in Greece). We might further note the connection between the 'Dorian' mode

103

and tragedy (thus the occurrence of tragedy in Greece) and the associations of erotic (Dionysiac?) poetry and flute music with the 'Lydian' and 'Phrygian' areas of Asia Minor. A more curious (and therefore more intriguing) connection is between the two notes of the octave, the lower one of history and time and the upper one of astronomy and the stars. Does this suggest a Sumerian view of astrological forces determining events? The reader is invited to explore further the potentialities of Gafori's diagram.

Music and drama in the Italian Renaissance

Although the cultural rebirth of the Renaissance occurred throughout Europe, the important developments in relation to music-drama took place in Italy. Italy in the sixteenth century was not a united country, but (with the exception of the Papal territories) a collection of independent states, each under the rule of a prominent family (see fig. 8). The Duchy of Milan was

Fig. 8   The city-states of Renaissance Italy, late fifteenth and early sixteenth centuries

ruled by the Sforza family, the Duchy of Ferrara by the Este family, the Marquisate of Mantua by the Gonzaga family, and the Republic of Florence by the Medicis. Intermarriages and the fact that cardinals and Popes tended to be selected from these same families lent, despite occasional skirmishes, a sense of a common culture; musicians, painters and scholars often moved from one state to another. The ruling families were mostly enthusiastic about the arts, and gave opportunities for artists to work in their palaces, churches and courts.

In the latter part of the fifteenth century the most flourishing hive of cultural activity was Florence, under the rule of Lorenzo the Magnificent (1448–92), father of Pope Leo X (ruled from 1513 to 1521), and uncle to Pope Clement VIII (ruled from 1523 to 1534). Here Botticelli lived and worked, and Michelangelo until 1496. Here too lived Angelo Poliziano, a member of what we may call the First Florentine Academy (to distinguish it from the Academy of a century later). The Academy was a group of intellectuals and artists who met to discuss philosophical and artistic matters, to perform music and to recite poetry. Similar academies grew up in other Italian towns during the century. It was as a member of the Academy that Poliziano established through his own works the worth of poetry written in Italian, rather than Latin. His Academic colleagues included Marsilio Ficino (1433–99), a philosopher and musician, who maintained that music added an extra dimension to poetry, because of its moral power. Also in the group were Pico della Mirandola, poet, philosopher and singer, Domenico Benivieni, a noted instrumentalist and improviser, and Leon Battista Alberti, musician and architect, who argued that buildings and music must observe the laws of simple proportion.

Here was a unique gathering of ideas and talent. In typical Renaissance fashion, it was dedicated under Lorenzo's guidance to the establishment of secular music as an art form distinct from the traditional complex polyphony of church music. The issue was a live one in Italy at the time: a Spaniard working in Bologna, called Bartolomeo Ramos de Pareja, was advocating a new simplicity in melody and harmony, derived from popular music, and opposed to the extravagance and overcomplexity of Flemish-dominated church styles. Ramos' ideas sparked off endless debate in which even Leonardo da Vinci got involved. Amongst Lorenzo's court composers was Heinrich Isaac (or Isaak), Flemish by birth, a practised polyphonist but naturally sympathetic to Lorenzo's views. During the 1480s and up to Lorenzo's death in 1492 Lorenzo and Isaac wrote a number of popular songs for Florentine carnivals, and others for the masquerades which provided the staple musico-dramatic diet of the Court: spectacles with dances and songs, usually based loosely on mythological allegories or scenes from history.

The dedication of Lorenzo and his Academy to the elevation of poetic and musical expression, and their interest in drama, might have led to the

105

invention of opera a century early, but they had no real interest in music-drama as such. The death of Lorenzo in 1492 ushered in a brief Dark Age under the rule of Savonarola, who turned the carnivals into religious festivals, and burned musical instruments and 'books of lascivious music' on 'Bonfires of Vanity'. Savonarola's Catholic piety did him little good: he was condemned as a heretic and himself burnt at the stake in 1498. That year was also the one in which Machiavelli first took office in Florence.

Meanwhile, Renaissance drama was re-forming the drama of Rome and Greece in two ways. The first path was the imitation of Seneca's suave historical dramas, as in Giovanni Rucellai's *Rosmunda* (performed in Florence in 1515). The influence of Greek models, interpreted through typical misunderstandings of Aristotle's *Poetics*, is shown in Trissino's *Sofonisba*, which, like Seneca's plays, achieved immense popularity even though it was intended for study, not for performance. It was misconceptions of Aristotle which hindered progress in Italian Renaissance drama: theorists came to the conclusion that tragedy must have unity of action (only one plot), unity of place (no change of scene) and unity of time (the action must take place within the space of a day). Most Attic tragedy does in fact conform to these unities, but they were not calculated to appeal to the Renaissance Italian, who liked a complicated intrigue (which was provided in his comedy), spectacular changes of scene (provided in *sacre rappresentazione* and other courtly spectacles), and the panorama of history (provided in the epics of Ariosto and Tasso). The failure of tragedy to appeal led some authors into sensationalism: Giraldi Cinthio's *Orbecche*, performed in Ferrara in 1541, contains incest, ghosts, at least two murders by decapitation, and a suicide. Speroni's *Carace*, performed in Padua in the following year, is even more bloodthirsty.

Even this was not enough. Audiences attended performances of tragedy less for the plays and more for the *intermedii*, spectacular interludes of music and dance between the acts. All the resources of Renaissance music were employed in these interludes, both vocal and instrumental. Often the interludes were related in theme to the themes of the plays, but this was about as close as music came to drama in this context.

Greek influence was also felt in the Arcadian *pastorale*. This development of the medieval courtly dance-play or mime-play with song assumed a distinctive literary form, and an image of legendary Greece was created in which man was an innocent child of nature, his only concern to enjoy fine weather, pretty scenery, and sentimentalized sex. Sannazaro's *Arcadia* in 1504 set the pattern: shepherds and shepherdesses mildly flirting in the sunshine. The *pastorale* was basically a lyric-dramatic poem, with dialogues and monologues written in exquisite verse. Occasionally songs were sung. The *pastorale* illustrates the domination of poetry during the Italian Renaissance: both music and drama were subservient to it. The most famous and popular examples of the Italian *pastorale* were Tasso's *Aminta* (Ferrara, 1583), and Guarini's *Il Pastor Fido (The Faithful Shepherd)*, written between 1581 and 1590.

The main function of music in these dramatic entertainments was to provide songs, though *Il Pastor Fido* contains an important dance scene. Secular song under the generic title *frottola* had been particularly practised at Ferrara since the beginning of the sixteenth century, when the city became a remarkable centre of music, under Ercole I d'Este. Ercole's two daughters spread the influence of Ferrara more widely. Beatrice married Lodovico Sforza of Milan, who employed Leonardo da Vinci to design (amongst other things) the costumes and scenery for court entertainments. Isabella married Francesco Gonzaga of Mantua: while he earned a reputation in the military field, Isabella stayed at home and patronised the arts. The *frottola* was a simple part-song, either to be sung by four voices, or by one voice with instruments playing the other lines.

In the second quarter of the century the *frottola* developed into the *madrigal*. The causes are exemplified in the ideals of the Accademia Filarmonica at Verona, whose members were anxious to unite poetry and music as closely as possible. Music must follow the text pictorially: some madrigal composers went so far as to illustrate the words in the way they wrote the music down on paper. Madrigals developed in intensity and complexity. Usually in five parts, they employed all the sophistication of polyphony and the textural contrast between imitative counterpoint and homophony. The *frottola* and later the madrigal became the chief forms of music used in dramatic interludes, though sometimes extended in form to meet particular needs. Besides the conventional madrigal expressing sentiments of love or anguish, there developed less serious, more humorous kinds, such as the *villanella* and the *balletto*. An example of the latter is the Florentine Alessandro Striggio's *The Chatter of Women at their Washing* (1567): here too, clearly, musical pictorialism is in evidence. We shall meet Striggio's son later.

Some madrigal composers made moves in the direction of drama, by writing madrigal-cycles, or madrigal-comedies. These were sequences of madrigals telling a story, monologue-madrigals and dialogue-madrigals. Normally they were not staged, but there is evidence that some were mimed by actors while the singers sang.

In surveying the interaction of music and drama in Italy in the sixteenth century, one gains the impression that music-drama was continually on the verge of rebirth. Nearly all the ingredients were there: Greek humanism, a sophisticated and expressive musical language, a sense of ceremony in courtly spectacles. Two things only were lacking: firstly, an accurate, or more accurate view of Greek music-drama, for Renaissance dramatists generally believed that drama must be expressed in spoken verse, and

107

secondly, a means of expressing a developing *narrative* in music: song-forms were essentially expressions of single experiences through polyphony.

The Florentine Camerata

The Renaissance interest in Greek drama was pioneered in Florence. Ficino, the philosopher-musician of the 'first' Florentine Academy, and Poliziano both taught Diacceto (1466–1522), who formed an academy in Florence to study the works of Plato. Here studied Piero Vettori (1499–1585), who was later to become the first professor of moral philosophy and Greek and Latin rhetoric at Florence University. Vettori was concerned to study Greek sources rather than Latin translations, and, together with a student, Girolamo Mei (1519–94), embarked on a search for lost Greek manuscripts. Among other things they rediscovered Euripides' *Electra* and restored the previously incomplete *Agamemnon* of Aeschylus. Mei was clearly extremely talented: he was admitted in 1540 (aged 21) to the illustrious Accademia Fiorentina. In 1560 he moved to Rome, entering the service of Cardinal Montepulciano (those who are attracted by coincidence may find it interesting that Montepulciano is the town from which Angelo Poliziano took his name). Over the next fourteen years Mei pursued his life's work: a scholarly study of Greek music and drama. He worked in the Vatican library, where he had access to virtually all that had been written or printed on the subject. His bible was Vettori's scholarly edition of Aristotle's *Poetics* in the original Greek. In 1574 he published *De modis musicis antiquorum* which was by far the most complete and accurate analysis of Greek musical history and theory up to that date: furthermore, it is almost entirely right.

Mei was a scholar, not a practical musician. He had no interest whatsoever in turning theory into practice. But in 1572 he received a letter from Vincenzo Galilei, a forty-year-old composer living in Florence, asking for information about Greek music. Mei's lengthy answer was later published, in 1602, as the *Discorso sopra la musica antica e moderna.* Galilei sent more letters, and apparently visited Mei: the result was that in 1581 Galilei published in Florence his *Dialogo della musica antica et della moderna,* in which Mei's ideas about Greek music were used as the basis for a vicious polemic against the polyphonic madrigal. The *Dialogo* became the theoretical justification for the new music-drama. (Galilei's other chief claim to fame lies in his being the father of Galileo the astronomer.)

Galilei was a member of what has become known as the Florentine Camerata, a group of writers, poets and musicians living in Florence between about 1567 and about 1600. Literally a *camerata* is a room shared by a number of people, in artistic terminology a *salon*. In fact, there were several groups of like-minded artists and scholars who met in different nobles' houses in Florence, and often opposed each others' ideas and projects; a better term to use is 'academy', in the sense in which we used it to describe the 'first' Florentine Academy: not as a building, but as a large group of people, in different factions, all engaged in discussions about basically the same things.

Galilei belonged to the faction that met at the house of Count Giovanni Bardi, a banker and businessman, philologist, mathematician, playwright, composer of sorts and author of a treatise on football. The group included the composer Giulio Caccini (*c.* 1546–1618), but ceased operations when Count Bardi took up a position in Rome in 1592, taking Caccini with him. Its contributions to the birth of opera were twofold, theoretical and practical. Galilei's *Dialogo* set out to answer a question: why was Greek music so much more expressive than contemporary music? Mei had provided the answer: Greek music was monodic, a single melodic line expressing the meaning of a text. Galilei was able to contrast this with contemporary polyphonic writing, which, despite its pictorialisms, succeeded only in obscuring the text. Borrowing again from Mei, Galilei argued that Greek harmony was not the same as the ecclesiastical modes, but was based on principles closer to what we would call tonal harmony. He challenged the view that music operates with moral force because it appeals to the intellect, and argued that its moral force lay in its power to express and therefore to arouse emotions.

Curiously, Galilei says nothing about drama or music's relationship to it: he is only concerned with music and poetry. Not surprisingly, then, the main practical product of the Bardi Camerata was a collection of songs by Caccini, printed in 1602 under the title *Le Nuove Musiche*. Here polyphony is abandoned in favour of the simple texture of a vocal line and a bass line or *basso continuo;* the accompanist's task was to improvise harmonies from the bass notes and from the figures given with it, which indicated the intervals above the bass required to make the chords. Neither solo song nor *basso continuo* were new: what was new was to have them on their own without any middle parts for other voices or for instruments. This was one step on the road towards opera: the expressive solo vocal line had been evolved.

A second Camerata group centred around Emilio de' Cavalieri (*c.* 1550–1602). Cavalieri was brought to Florence in 1588 by the new Grand Duke, Cardinal Ferdinand de'Medici, possibly to oppose the influence of Count Bardi, who had been a supporter of the previous Grand Duke Francis. Cavalieri was of a different mould from Bardi, less devoted to scholarship, more devoted to the pleasures of life: he was a famous dancer and conversationalist. However, Cavalieri's and Bardi's groups combined in 1589 to mount a spectacular celebration for the wedding of Grand Duke Ferdinand to Christine of Lorraine. A comedy called *La Pellegrina* by Girolamo Bargagli was to be performed, with six *intermedii*. Bardi was in overall charge, Cavalieri supervised the music, choreography and production, and Bernardo Buontalenti was designer.

Bardi chose as theme for the *intermedii* the power of ancient music, and commissioned contributions form the leading court madrigal composers Striggio, Marenzio and Malvezzi, as well as from Caccini and a young composer named Jacopo Peri (1561–1633), one of Malvezzi's pupils. Cavalieri also contributed to the music. Florence was famous for the quality and quantity of its spectacular *intermedii,* and contemporary prints show that this occasion was no exception. The visual magnificence was matched by musically grand choruses and madrigals, and a large orchestra was used.

The six tableaux as a group reflected Renaissance thinking about music. The first represented the harmony of the spheres (medieval/classical tradition), the second the rivalry of the Muses, and the third the victory of Apollo over the python (the victory of Classical form). The fourth *intermedio* was entitled 'The Song of Arion', a Greek poet and singer who lived *c.* 625 B.C.; the part was played by Peri, who sang a song by Caccini. The fifth interlude portrayed the descent to earth of Apollo and Bacchus, together with Rhythm and Harmony: it is interesting that Bardi should have introduced Apollo and Bacchus/Dionysos together: Nietzsche's theories were three centuries away. The final tableau was the underworld scene traditional to the *intermedii*: spirits in Hades foretold the golden age (Arcadia) that would follow the royal marriage.

The Florentine wedding festival of 1589 was magnificent, but it was not opera. Bardi was not interested in music-drama, and Cavalieri believed in variety in stage spectacle, with music performing whatever function was necessary. Only Caccini's material was in the style of *Le Nuove Musiche,* and here the vocal line was elaborate and spectacular, to suit the requirements of the occasion.

Neither Bardi nor Cavalieri was responsible for the creation of opera: its invention was the work of a third Camerata group under the patronage of the aristocrat Jacopo Corsi, who succeeded to the position of Bardi after the latter's move to Rome in 1592. Corsi was a favourite of Duke Ferdinand, and was sought out by, amongst others, the poet Tasso and the composer Monteverdi. Corsi and his two particular adherents, Peri, who had become director of court music in 1591, and the poet Ottavio Rinuccini (1562–1621), seem to have been the ones who saw a possible application of melody plus *basso continuo* to the problem of setting an entire narrative verse text. They took the dramatic form of the *pastorale,* and applied it to the Greek legend of Daphne, who was pursued by Apollo and metamorphosed into a laurel.

Perhaps they considered the legend symbolic. Daphne was a local Theban version of the Great Goddess, conquered by Apollo, but still retaining her nature symbolism in her metamorphosed state. Perhaps the legend was deeply appropriate to the rebirth of the musico-dramatic experience, and the duality of its images. At any rate, with music by Corsi, Peri, and perhaps from Caccini too, after four years the work was ready to be performed in

1597: it was successful enough to be repeated in the next two years. Only fragments of the music remain, but circumstantial evidence suggests that *Dafne* was sung throughout, and may therefore be deemed the first opera.

The different members of the 'second Florentine Academy' had all played a part. Galilei and Bardi had brought Mei's scholarly discoveries about Greek music to the notice of their fellow musicians, without however following his ideas through to their natural conclusion and reviving music-drama. Caccini had proved the power of simple one-line vocal melody over a basso continuo. Cavalieri had involved them all in a stage production. Finally, Corsi had financed, Rinuccini had written, and Peri had set, a completely sung drama. But the experiment needed to be repeated before real success could be claimed.

Peri's L'Euridice
The opportunity to write a second fully-sung drama arose with the marriage (by proxy) of Maria de' Medici to Henry IV of France, on 6th October 1600. Clearly something even more splendid than the *intermedii* of 1589 was required. However, by this time Peri and Caccini were bitter rivals. Perhaps Caccini was jealous of the younger man: certainly he was to claim later that he and not Peri had invented the new music-drama. In 1600 the rivalry was such that Caccini would not allow his singers to perform music by Peri, and he went so far as to insist that he write the songs for the role of Eurydice, and two choruses, in the forthcoming work, Peri's *L'Euridice*. Such Machiavellian tactics were scarcely necessary: the chief honour for the festival was given to Caccini anyway, for the major theatrical event was the performance on 9th October (from 1 a.m. to 5 a.m.!) of Gabriello Chiabrera's *pastorale, Il Rapimento di Cefalo,* with music by Caccini, in the Uffizi Theatre before an audience of three thousand eight hundred. A hundred musicians took part under Caccini's direction; scenery and stage machinery were by Buontalenti.

In comparison, the first performance of Rinuccini's and Peri's *L'Euridice,* in a small room on an upstairs floor of the Pitti Palace, before an audience of two to three hundred, must have seemed insignificant. Curiously enough, as soon as *Il Rapimento* was over, Caccini started to write a complete setting of Rinuccini's text, and succeeded in getting it into print a month before Peri's. But Caccini's efforts were in vain: history has come down on the side of Peri, on the grounds that his talent for music-drama was considerably greater than his rival's. The planning and execution of *Il Rapimento* clearly had some effect upon the first performance of *L'Euridice*; apparently the scenery was not completed in time, and Cavalieri, who was in charge, left Florence for Rome in a huff as soon as the wedding celebrations were over. Here he and Bardi both spoke scornfully of Peri's work. In fact, *Il Rapimento* sounds more to Cavalieri's taste: four hours' worth of spectacular variety.

111

In Greek legend, Cephalus was married to Procris: like Guglielmo and Ferrando in *Cosi fan tutte* he resolved to test his wife's faithfulness by appearing disguised as a stranger bearing gifts. Procris yielded, whereupon Cephalus revealed his true identity. Procris fled in shame to Crete, where she hit upon the idea of playing the same trick, returning to Cephalus in the disguise of a youth. Cephalus offered himself as the youth's lover, whereupon Procris in her turn revealed her true identity and the two were reconciled, or apparently so. Procris however still suspected her husband and watched him closely especially when he was out hunting. One day, hearing a noise in the bushes, he abruptly flung his spear, accidently killing Procris. Discovering what he had done, he committed suicide. One wonders at the suitability of any part of this story to a wedding celebration; on the other hand, it was not normal for a poet to make up his own story. The only remnant we have of the work is the final chorus, printed in Caccini's *Le Nuove Musiche,* 'concerted', says the composer proudly, 'with voices and instruments by seventy-five persons in a semicircle for the entire scene, after which there followed other music and a ballo. . .'[8] This chorus at least was suitable: it is an apotheosis of love.

Rinuccini's version of the Orpheus myth was, in contrast, particularly appropriate to a wedding. Not only did he omit the second part of the Orpheus myth; he even went so far as to omit the condition decreed for Eurydice's return, so that Orpheus and Eurydice might emerge at the end as a reunited couple. It could be argued that to make this alteration so drastically affects the story that there was little point in using the Orpheus legend at all; however, the alteration had the result of making Orpheus' musical and vocal powers the key to a successful rescue, and this was certainly the point that Rinuccini and Peri wished to make.

Rinuccini's text can be divided into a prologue and six scenes.

Prologue: In a strophic song Tragedy introduces herself and the drama to be played.

Scene 1: A nymph and a shepherd set the scene: this is the day on which Orfeo has married Euridice. The chorus sings its joy. Euridice expresses her own happiness, and Amintà, one of her companions, says all nature is affected by love. Euridice leaves the stage; the scene concludes with a set piece in which solos are answered by a dance-chorus.

Scene 2: Orfeo recalls the sad songs he sang before meeting Euridice. One of his companions, Tirsi, sings a cheerful strophic song. Suddenly Dafne arrives and relates the news of Euridice's death (which, in Greek fashion, has occurred offstage). Orfeo resolves to join her in the realm of death. The scene ends with a chorus of mourning interspersed by soles and a trio.

112

Scene 3: Arcetro reports that as Orfeo was about to commit suicide Venus descended in a chariot and carried him away. The chorus rejoices.

Scene 4: Venus has led Orfeo to the gates of the underworld, and advises him to use his powers of singing. Alone, he sings a lament (in recitative). Pluto hears the music; so does Proserpina (Persephone), who persuades Pluto to release Euridice, despite the warning of Charon (guardian of the entrance). Two choirs in dialogue reflect that no one has ever before been freed from the underworld, and then praise the triumph of Orfeo and his lyre.

Scene 5: Arcetro sets the scene: it is dawn. Amintà brings the news of the return of Orfeo and Euridice.

Scene 6: They enter. Orfeo rejoices in a song in two verses, the second a variation of the first. Euridice tells how she was rescued. Orfeo acknowledges the aid of Venus, and the music-drama ends with a dance-chorus of rejoicing.

It will be seen that the structure of the plot conforms, generally, to Greek models. The opening scenes of joy are abruptly turned to lament with the news of Euridice's death. Lament is abruptly turned to hope with the news of Venus' intervention, and hope is fulfilled with the successful return of the happy couple to earth. This story is told in passages of narrative monologue and dialogue for solo actors, interspersed and punctuated with passages for the chorus which explore the emotional experiences behind the action.

The passages for the chorus are set in the style of contemporary song, that is, in a mainly homophonic manner. Peri's contribution lies less in this than in his development of monodic recitative as a way of setting the narrative text. His monody differs from Greek monody in that, instead of a solo flute player accompanying the vocal line heterophonically, Peri writes an accompaniment of changing chords, to be played on a continuo instrument or instruments. Expression is thus created in four ways: firstly in the pitch of the vocal line and its rhythm, both based for much of the time upon the declamatory style of an actor reciting verse (and therefore closely related to the text); secondly in the extension of vocal melody into song, when what lies behind the textual surface can be explored; thirdly in the harmonic changes in the accompaniment, which provide an interpretation of the inner sense of the text in relation to the emotional experience of the characters; and fourthly in the interaction between vocal line and accompaniment, to express the relationship between what is said and the experience behind what is said.

Essentially, Peri communicates the personal experiences of the characters. Rinuccini's text gives us what they say, but Peri's music tells us how they say it and why. In other words, it penetrates behind the text, and enables us, as audience, to share directly in the experiences of those whose actions we witness. This is, basically, Aristotle's *catharsis*. Through the music we eventually experience pity and terror.

The difference between Peri's method and that of the contemporary madrigalians cannot be emphasized too strongly. The madrigal was based upon the assumption that music relates to a text, and to life, by expanding and exploring isolated moments: hence the pictorial treatment of particular words, and the form of madrigal-comedy — and of the conventional *intermedio* and *pastorale* — as a series of tableaux. Tableau music-drama, on the large-scale or the small-scale, is a form of *ceremonial music-drama;* it tends to concentrate upon Apollonian shapes, upon musical structure. Peri's monody, on the other hand, is based upon the assumption that music can relate to a text, and to life, by expressing them as a developing continuum. Monodic music-drama, on the large-scale or the small-scale, is a form of *narrative music-drama*; it tends to concentrate less upon Apollonian shape and musical structure. Peri's invention, then, was a rebirth of Greek music-drama after two thousand years of darkness.

Peri's *L'Euridice* contains both monody and tableaux, but it is clear which he considered to be the most important, for Orpheus' plea in the underworld, which leads to his victory, is set as monodic recitative. There is a necessary structural element: his prayer is punctuated three times by the phrase '*Lagrimate al mio pianto, Ombre d'Inferno*' (Weep at my complaint, infernal shades). But this too is expressive, a rhetorical device of progressive intensification germane to his purpose, and it is therefore musico-dramatic rather than merely musical.

This is not to say that Peri's monody is musically shapeless. It is written within what we may now call the tonal system, which inevitably gives a shape to the relationships between notes. The poetic text also provides a musical shape through the rhythm of the words. More importantly, the characterization too gives it shape, the shape of human experiences, which communicate immediately to us.

How exactly does Peri's monody create character? Example 1[9] is Peri's interpretation of Orfeo's reaction to the news of Euridice's death. Musico-dramatic analysis shows how Peri uses melody and harmony (in particular) to recreate Orfeo's experience.

An A minor chord, held for five bars, shows that, for Orfeo, time stops. He can scarcely, in his vocal line, move away from the tonic, except to sing the dissonant *b* in bar 3. The dissonance implies tension: he ought to weep, and knows it, but his grief is too deep for tears. He thinks of Euridice: under his held *c*, stressing the minor third, the chord changes in bar 6 to make a dominant seventh, a more open, yearning sound. The vocal *c* falls to a *b* flat (we expect *b* natural) as he sings her name; a dissonant *g* in the accompaniment forces the harmony to a chord of D major. Peri adds a further dissonance immediately by interposing an *e* at the end of bar 7, en route to the reiterated D major chord. Already we are given insight into Orfeo's

Ex. 1   Peri: *L'Euridice*

mind: the change in the bass from *a* to *d* has occurred when his thoughts change from grief to his beloved, and the new thought focuses his grief, for the harmony contains both more dissonance and a sense of cadence. His emotion is welling up inside him: in bars eight to ten he continues to protest that he cannot sigh and weep, but his vocal line (the repeated *b* flats against the D major chord, the change from a *b* flat in bar 8 to a *b* natural in bar 9) betrays the fact that he is less able to control his emotions than he would wish. This is reinforced by the two harmonizations of the bass notes *d* and *e*: from D major to a first inversion in C major which could lead in many directions, and from D major to a firmer root position chord E major, the dominant chord of the opening *a* minor. Orfeo is fighting for control, trying to reconcile his reaction to death (A minor) and his feelings for Euridice (D major).

116

The words '*Cadavero infelice*' (unhappy corpse) bring the concepts of death and Euridice together: A minor becomes A major, the dominant chord of D major, and a perfect cadence occurs, representing Orfeo's acceptance of Euridice's death. Significantly this occurs in the middle of the word 'cadavero' — it is while he is saying the word that the reconciliation takes place. But the D major itself becomes a dominant chord leading to G major in bar 13: the process of acceptance carries on as he realizes the true 'infelicity' of the facts. He breaks out in protest on a high note, an *e*, anticipating the coming shift to a chord of A minor; this stands out against the G major chord. The harmony resumes A minor, emphasizing the dominant E major. Orfeo's words are emotional: the facts have sunk in and the floodgates are now opened. The chords change frequently at first, with the release of tension, but the outcry quietens (bars 16 and 17).

In bar 18 Orfeo suddenly switches key from E major to G minor. In tonal terms this is an abrupt and unprepared modulation. It is, however, not the first time in the opera that an opposition between A major/E major and G minor has occurred. Example 2[10] shows the moment when Dafne bursts in with the news of Euridice's death. She interrupts in G minor after Orfeo's A major cadence (bars 4 and 5), switching immediately to G major, then back to G minor. Her phrase

Ex. 2 Peri: *L'Euridice*

'my heart freezes within me' anticipates, harmonically, Orfeo's lamenting 'O my dear Euridice'.[11] At bar nineteen she resumes G minor, and the harmony shifts suddenly to E major. A little later in the same scene Dafne sings 'O day full of anguish and full of woe', cadencing in A major: a chord of G minor sounds immediately as Orfeo asks 'What hateful news. . .?' Dafne's narration is full of implicit contrasts between these key areas. Example 3,[12] an extract from Orfeo's prayer to Pluto, shows a further example of this key-shift, by now become less dissonant. Orfeo's '*ohimè*' in bars 7 to 8 moves from G major to E major, and is surely reminiscent of Dafne's '*ohimè*' in Ex. 2, bars 19 to 20.

Ex. 3   Peri: *L'Euridice*

It would be unwise to suggest that Peri's *L'Euridice* contains a harmonic *leitmotiv*, but it is clear that this particular opposition of key areas is of some expressive importance in the opera. In Orfeo's lament, to return to Ex. 1, it is not fanciful to suppose that the shift from E major to G minor in bar eighteen not only expresses a stab of emotion, but indicates his remembering how he heard the news of Euridice's death: after all, Peri could have chosen a different key-shift. Orfeo's '*ohimè*' can therefore be seen as expressing his own personal sadness on hearing the news — it leads naturally into his complaint 'who has taken you from me?' also in G minor. (In bar 21, G major is briefly sounded, but G minor reasserts itself immediately.) The repetition of the words suggests that Orfeo cannot find an answer to his anguished question the first time; the second time the harmony moves to D minor, and then to the A minor of his opening words. Though no answer is given, the mere act of verbalising his anguish has brought it under control.

The two questions Orfeo asks (in bars 19 to 26) are: 'Who is responsible?' and 'Where have you gone?' They indicate that he is beginning to think of Euridice's death in specific terms: to interpret via the allegory of creativity, he is giving to his experience 'a local habitation (where) and a name (who)'. The experience is being assimilated and understood, which must automatically lead to decision and action.

Bars 26 to 27 present once more the E major to G minor key shift, but this time the musical symbol for Orfeo's dreadful experience leads into a more strictly rhythmical section, representing his decision to act. In harmonic terms, the chords flow cadentially; there is an air of determination about what he says. Even the final word 'death' is treated without dissonance: Orfeo can now speak the word (and he has not mentioned it before) without his emotions overcoming him. Action, he has discovered, is the best antidote to self-pity; the action he chooses is, moreover, going to solve the emotional problem resulting from his sense of loss, for he means to be reunited with Euridice.

This musico-dramatic analysis is summarized in Fig. 9. It reveals that Peri's music portrays Orfeo as a living human being, whose thoughts and emotions develop. Orfeo is not a figure in a tableau. The music is psychological narrative, and it is through the impact of the music that we as listeners become involved in Orfeo's experiences. We are not objectively aware of this or that modulation, any more, perhaps, than Peri was, for Dionysos' sound-effects arouse a subjective response in us which dominates Apollonian objectivity.

Fig. 9 Orfeo's lament

Bars		
1— 4	I feel nothing, though I ought to.	Emotion
5— 7	I love Euridice, but I have lost her.	is
8—10	I must not weep, though I want to.	repressed
11—13	'She is dead'.	THE EXPERIENCE
14—15	I protest.	Emotion is
16—17	I accept.	accepted
17—19	I remember when I was told.	THE EXPERIENCE
19—26	I seek to understand my loss. Who is responsible? Where is she now?	Emotion is explored
26—27	We are apart.	THE EXPERIENCE
27—35	I shall reunite us.	Action

Peri's *L'Euridice* is the first music-drama since the fifth century B.C. to unite *narrative music-drama, ceremonial music-drama* and *enthusiastic music-drama.* Many commentators have called it a dull work, which is not true, though it has suffered from being overshadowed by Monteverdi's *L'Orfeo* of seven years later. This should not blind us to Peri's achievement: many actors contributed to the rebirth of opera, but without Peri's develop-ment of and deeply effective use of expressive narrative monody it would never have happened at all.

Monteverdi's L'Orfeo

In the February before Peri's *L'Euridice* was first performed, Emilio de' Cavalieri had written and directed a music-drama in Rome. Just as Peri had applied monody to the *pastorale*, so Cavalieri introduced monody into the *sacra rappresentazione.* The work was called *La Rappresentazione di Anima e di Corpo* and was an extravaganza typical of its composer. The personages on the stage had names such as Body, Soul, Intellect and Pleasure, and the forms used included a spoken prologue, dances, instrumental interludes, choruses, songs and some monody. But sacred drama (except as static oratorio) was no longer significant; humanist drama in partnership with music based on secular styles was to become the music-drama of the future.

The work which established secular music-drama as the leading form of the age was Monteverdi's *La favola d'Orfeo*, first performed in 1607 in Mantua. Claudio Monteverdi was by then forty years old and an established composer of madrigals; his fifth volume, published in 1605, includes *basso continuo.* He had, it is thought, visited Jacopo Corsi in Florence; he may or may not have seen performances of Peri's *Dafne* or *L'Euridice*, but it is obvious from his own work that he was familiar with the monodic style, and certain internal evidence that we shall discuss later suggests that he must have known the score of Peri's *L'Euridice* (published in 1601). It is also more than likely that Monteverdi's librettist knew Peri's work, for he was Alessandro Striggio, son of the Florentine composer who had contributed with Peri to the grand celebrations of 1589.

Striggio's first version of *L'Orfeo* concluded authentically with the death of Orpheus at the hands of the Maenads. By the time the composition was published, however, the ending had been drastically revised, for reasons that are not difficult to detect. Monteverdi approached music-drama from the point of view of music; as an immensely skilled musical craftsman he was concerned that his music should be properly structured. Although he threw himself wholeheartedly, at least temporarily, into the monodic style, he saw the danger that monodic music-drama might become shapeless. His major contribution to the nurture of the infant opera, therefore, was in the field of musical — and musico-dramatic — structure. This is not to say that *L'Orfeo* is cold-blooded; far from it. But Apollo receives more worship from Monteverdi than he had from Peri.

Indeed, Monteverdi's ending to the Orpheus legend replaces the

121

Dionysiac sacrifice of Orpheus with the spectacular appearance of Apollo himself, who descends to the Thracian fields and raises the distraught Orfeo up to heaven to join Euridice. Orfeo the musician is made eternal not through Dionysos but through the god of musical form. Indeed, the text of the final scene reminds us emphatically that Orfeo is the son of Apollo. Not surprisingly, therefore, Monteverdi sets Orfeo's plea at the gates of Hades not in recitative, as Peri had done, but as an Apollonian, virtuosic strophic song, '*Possente spirto*' (O mighty spirit. . .). Dionysos' power of affective sound is controlled and focussed by Apollonian musical structure. In the same way, the Prologue to *L'Orfeo* is sung not by Tragedy (as had been the Prologue to Peri's *L'Euridice*) but by La Musica, the spirit of music. There is no such deity in the Classical pantheon: Striggio has La Musica announce that she comes from Permessus, which, as Malipiero tells us,[13] is a river in Boeotia sacred to Apollo and the Muses. Thus Peri's Tragedy, dedicated to Dionysos, gives way to Monteverdi's Music, dedicated to Apollo.

Monteverdi was faced with a problem new to Western European music but which lies at the centre of 'opera': how to give musical shape to developing narrative drama. The musical shapes favoured in post-Renaissance Western music rely upon the repetition of remembered sounds to make their effect; repetition is however difficult to achieve in circumstances where dramatic action is continually developing. Later generations of composers were to evolve various ways of reconciling the demands of developing narrative and musical repetition, in such forms as the *da capo aria*, the sonata-form ensemble, and Wagner's symphonic structures. All these methods are based upon the principle of varied repetition, that is, the re-presentation in a new disguise or context of material already heard. If any single composer can claim credit for inventing the idea of varied repetition in music-drama, it is Monteverdi.

His problems in *L'Orfeo* were made somewhat easier in two respects: firstly Striggio's libretto is extremely well-structured, particularly on the large-scale, and secondly it is not until the middle of Act II that real narrative begins. By this time Monteverdi has established in the opera a number of well-defined structural elements.

The Prologue is in five verses, each accompanied by a virtually identical bass line. The sequence is preceded by a ritornello which reappears in shortened form between each verse. La Musica's words forecast the action: verse 1 celebrates the glorious deeds of heroes, as Act I is to celebrate the glorious marriage of Orfeo and Euridice. Verse 2 speaks of the power of music to soothe the troubled heart: in Act II Orfeo's heart is certainly troubled when he receives the news of Euridice's death. Verse 3 speaks of music charming the soul, as Orfeo is to charm Charon in Act III. Verse 4 mentions Orfeo moving the powers of Hades, which he does in Act IV. Verse 5 speaks of the power of music over nature: Act V brings the miraculous appearance of Apollo, who promises to reunite Orfeo and Euridice in heaven. The anticipatory quality of Striggio's Prologue text is matched in Monteverdi's music. The ritornello is built over a series of cadential bass phrases, in D minor, A minor, F major and D minor again (with a major third in the final chord). (See Ex. 4).[14]

Ex. 4   Monteverdi: *L'Orfeo*

These cadential phrases present us with the keys closest to D minor: A minor is the dominant, F major is the relative major, and the implied D major of the final bar is the tonic major. In the first speech of Act I, a shepherd establishes particular associations between these keys and various dramatic ingredients in the opera, in the following way (see Ex. 5).[15]

On this happy and fortunate day,	D minor
which has put an end to love's sufferings for our demigod,	A minor
let us sing, shepherds, in such sweet accents that	F major

Ex. 5   Monteverdi: *L'Orfeo*

-sto - ri, in si so - a -vi a -ccen - ti che sian de - gni d'Or-
shepherds, in such sweet accents that worthy of

-feo no - stri con - cen - ti. Og - gi fat -ta è pie -
Orfeo shall be our songs. Today has been made

Fine

-to - sa l'al - ma gia si sde - gno sa de la bell' Eu - ri - di — ce.
merciful the soul, once so disdainful, of the lovely Euridice.

Og - gi fat -.to è fe -li — ce Or - feo nel sen di le - i.
Today happy is Orfeo on her breast;

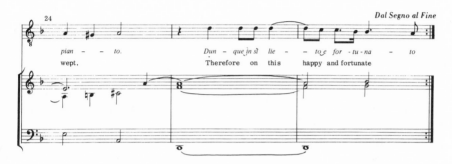

worthy of Orfeo
shall be our songs.   D major

The shepherd continues (bars 13–23) to other closely related keys as follows:

Today, has been made merciful the soul, once so   G major
disdainful, of the lovely Euridice.
Today, happy is Orfeo on her breast   C major
so much for her through these woods   A minor
he has signed and wept.   to   A major

The shepherd's text compares Orfeo's previous state of mind (suffering and sighing for love) with the present situation, when Orfeo's loving union with Euridice is to be celebrated. The keys A minor and A major are used to represent the suffering and sighing, and F major, D major and G major to represent the celebrations: more precisely, F major represents celebratory song, G major the new-found tenderness of Euridice's heart, and C major his happiness in her embrace.

In the tonal cycle of fifths, A major/minor is on the sharp side of D major/minor (the key of the Prologue); G major/minor, C major/minor and F major/minor are on the flat side of that key (see fig. 10). We may therefore deduce that Monteverdi, while using only a portion of the cycle, is basically equating sharper keys with suffering and flatter keys with celebration. These associations are in no way odd: to sharpen tonally is to increase tension; to flatten tonally is to reduce tension. Monteverdi therefore uses a more tense key to represent the emotional tension in Orfeo's previous state of mind, and more relaxed keys to represent the present situation.

Fig. 10   The cycle of fifths (1): major and minor modes connected at the tonic

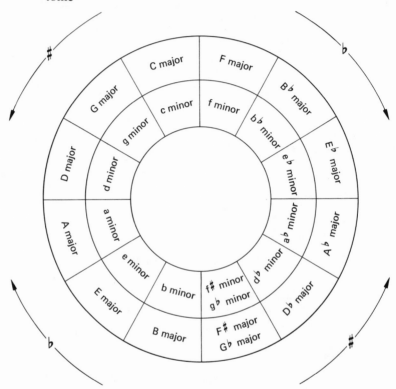

In Fig. 10 D major is shown in the same position in the circle as D minor; they have the same tonic note (*d*), the same dominant note (*a*) and the same subdominant note (*g*). What differentiates them is the major third (*f* sharp) or minor third (*f* natural) and hence the key signature: D major has two sharps and D minor one flat. But major and minor keys can relate to each other in another way, through sharing a common key signature. D minor is the tonic minor of D major, but it is also the relative minor of F major, which has an identical key signature of one flat, and has, moreover, more notes in common with D minor than has D major. Figure 11 shows the cycle of fifths with major and minor keys connected relatively.

126

Fig. 11   The cycle of fifths (2): major and minor modes connected at the relative

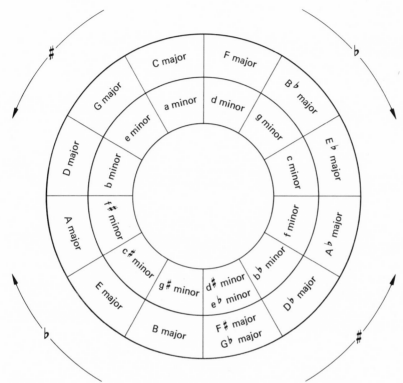

If the two versions of the cycle of fifths are put together, it is evident that a system of key associations that employs both major and minor modes allows for the relationships between keys to operate on a complex level: thus, both D major and F major can be regarded as the closest major keys to D minor, though for different reasons. Furthermore, while A minor is the dominant key to D minor, the dominant chord (the one used before D minor in a perfect cadence) is A major. By analogy, the D minor can 'borrow' G major instead of G minor in the subdominant direction, although this is an unusual move. In short, each of the following keys is equidistantly one step away from D minor: A minor, A major (in the sharp direction), G minor, G major (in the flat direction); D major (as the tonic major), and F major (as the relative major) are particularly close. Figure 12 shows what we might term the nine closest keys to D minor.[16]

Although Monteverdi's *L'Orfeo* was written at a time when the tonal system was only gradually beginning to evolve, he uses the relationships between keys with evident understanding of these principles. In the music-

127

drama, he does not stray outside the field of D minor as shown in Fig. 12. The key-associations outlined in the first speech for the shepherd at the beginning of Act I are maintained — and developed somewhat — during the course of the work.

Fig. 12   Keys related closely to D minor

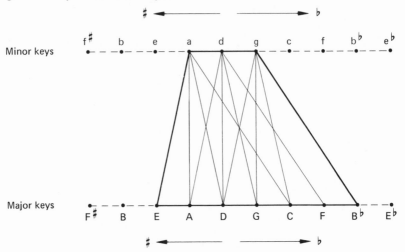

The basic key-associations (for the first two acts, at any rate) are as follows.

E major	anguish of no love
A minor/major	desire for love
D minor/major	'La Musica'
G minor/major	tenderness of love
C major	loving union
F major	joyful celebration
B flat major	

As we move 'downwards', from the sharpest key, E major, to the flattest key, B flat major, we pass from the extreme anguish of loneliness through to the delight of partnership: the D minor/major of La Musica occupies the centre. The relationship between Orfeo and Euridice, upon which the drama is built, can thus be represented in musical terms.

After the shepherd's opening words in Act I the chorus prays to Hymen, the god of marriage, in G minor/major. A nymph calls upon the Muses to assist in the celebrations, her text set in F major. The chorus sings and dances in G major and G minor; an orchestral ritornello follows in G major. A shepherd asks Orfeo to speak, mentioning the hero's laments (A minor) and his instrumental skills (D major), and begs him to sing a song inspired

128

by love (A major). Orfeo does so, beginning in G minor, moving to F major when he speaks of his joy, and ending in D major.

Euridice's reply (see Ex. 6)[17] is a masterly example of the subtle use of key to express what lies behind a text. Striggio provides Euridice with a somewhat indirect way of confessing her love for Orfeo.

Her first statement (bars 1–4) raises an element of doubt: Euridice teasingly refuses to say that she shares Orfeo's joy. Monteverdi accordingly moves from D minor through an A major chord to E major in bar two, thus reflecting Euridice's teasing words — but also associating Euridice with this key in a manner which becomes important later. In bar three we move back to A minor and thence to a chord of F major and to C major, as if to reassure

Ex. 6   Monteverdi: *L'Orfeo*

129

bra - mi quan - to lie - to gio - i - sca e quan - to t'a - - mi.
how happily I rejoice and how much I love you.

that celebration and union are really the issues here. As Euridice begins her second statement, with a tender reference to her emotions, Monteverdi takes us to G major; as love is mentioned, the harmony resolves into D minor (it could be D major). The two sides of D minor are recapitulated in Euridice's third statement: her teasing shift of focus from herself to 'her heart' is reflected in the shift to A minor, while her final acknowledgment of joy and love for Orfeo is set in F major, and through a chord of G minor to a final cadence in D major.

Monteverdi's setting of this passage gives us insight into Euridice: like all great opera composers he is 'inside' the character, and presents their personalities in musical sounds.

The remainder of Act I is celebration and sticks firmly to G major, reflecting the tender feelings of Orfeo and Euridice. The first part of Act II is also celebratory: Orfeo and his companions are visiting the Thracian woods where first he saw Euridice, and where he had sighed for her. This scene is beautifully structured in a growing crescendo of songs and duets:

1 *G minor*, $\dfrac{3}{2}$

  Orfeo greets the woodlands

2 *F major*, $\dfrac{2}{2}$

  a Ritornello.
  b A shepherd describes the play of sun and shadow.
  a Ritornello.
  b A shepherd suggests all sing to the murmur of the stream.

3 *G minor*, $\dfrac{6}{4}$

  a Ritornello.
  b Shepherds duet: woodland gods dwell here.
  a Ritornello.
  b Shepherds duet: here Pan is heard, lamenting his lost love.

4 *G major,* $\dfrac{2}{2}$

  a Ritornello.
  b Shepherds' duet (the bass line relates to that of the ritornello):
    wood-nymphs gather roses here.
  a Ritornello.
  b The chorus repeats the music of the previous shepherds duet,
    encouraging Orfeo to sing.

5 *G major,* $\dfrac{3}{4}$ and $\dfrac{6}{8}$

    Orfeo sings four verses of a song, each verse preceded by a ritornello, recalling,
    his previous suffering and celebrating his present happiness.

With telling effect, Orfeo has remained silent between his opening remarks and his song: the entire scene with its gradual Dionysiac sinking into a unity with nature has been described by the shepherds. A small-scale allegory of the act of creation is thus described: a drift into the dream-world of the unconscious, out of which emerges Orfeo's song. More significantly, the dream-world contains an image of what is to happen later in the act: the shepherds mention Pan lamenting his lost love.

Orfeo ends his song abruptly. A shepherd marvels (in C major) at the way nature responds to Orfeo's music and invites him to continue. Suddenly we hear a voice raised in lament. This is the moment of *peripeteia*, of abrupt reversal. A messenger, Dafne, has come, bringing news of a disaster. She sings in A minor. One of the shepherds protests at the interruption (in F major and C major); Dafne wonders how to give her news. Another shepherd (in C major) asks the gods to protect them. 'Shepherd, end your song,' says Dafne in G major: 'all our lightheartedness is turned to grief' (A minor). Orfeo clearly has a premonition — at least Monteverdi believes so. 'Whence do you come?' he asks, with chords of F major and C major. 'Where are you going?' (G major/D major chords) 'Nymph, what news do you bear?' (A minor/E major chords). His mounting alarm is expressed here in a sequence, each step higher and (in the vocal line) more rhythmically vehement than the previous one. The messenger begins to tell him (Ex. 7),[18] in A minor, with emphasis on an E major chord. Orfeo interrupts in G minor as he senses what she is going to say. Relentlessly Dafne resumes in E major: 'Your beloved wife is dead.' Once again Monteverdi shows the depth of his characterization of Orfeo and his musico-dramatic skill: Orfeo's 'alas' is not an anguished cry or a sob of agony, but a murmur. Silence follows, before the messenger begins to relate the full story.

The similarity to Peri's *L'Euridice* is close, particularly in the opposition between G minor and E major. Monteverdi recapitulates this opposition whenever Euridice's death is mentioned during the remainder of the act:

131

Ex. 7   Monteverdi: *L'Orfeo*

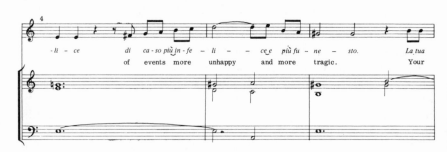

when the messenger recalls the snake sinking its fangs into Euridice's foot, when she recalls Euridice's last despairing cry ('Orfeo!'), and when Orfeo himself begins to try to come to terms with the facts he has been told (Ex. 8).[19] The same key-opposition returns in Act IV, at the climactic

Ex. 8   Monteverdi: *L'Orfeo*

moment when Orfeo breaks the condition, and turns round to look at Euridice (Ex. 9a),[20] and when Euridice voices her grief at this second parting (Ex. 9b).[21]

Officially, the *leitmotiv* was not invented until the nineteenth century, but if a *leitmotiv* is defined as a memorable musical idea which recurs to mirror the return of a dramatic idea, and whose repetitions have a structural

133

Ex. 9 Monteverdi: *L'Orfeo*

(a)

ORFEO

O_____ dol - cis - si - mi lu – mi io pur vi veg – gio,
O   sweetest   eyes,   I   can   see you,

io pur...   Ma qua - le e - clis - si, ohi – mè, v'os - cu – ra?
I   can ...   But   what   eclipse, alas,   obscures   you?

(b)

EURIDICE

Ahi _____   vis - ta trop - po dol – ce,   e trop - po a - ma – ra;
Ah   sight   too   sweet   and   too   bitter ...

function, then Monteverdi's G minor/E major opposition must be regarded as a *leitmotiv*. It is, simply, a way of communicating drama through music, or as seventeenth-century composers termed it, *dramma per musica*. As a structural ingredient it is purely musical, requiring no particular words, but it encapsulates the central idea of the drama.

Monteverdi's problem was to provide a musical structure in a narrative drama. This he provides not only on the rather deep and hidden level of key-association, but also in more obvious ways. The ritornello used to frame La Musica's Prologue returns at the end of Act II and the beginning of Act V, thus separating the action in three ways. Firstly, it reminds us of the importance of La Musica, as narrator and as guiding force in the work; secondly, these re-appearances frame Acts III and IV, the scenes in Hades in which Orfeo is put to the test; thirdly, they follow acts in which Euridice is 'lost' and precede acts in which Euridice is to be regained (Act V includes Apollo's promise of reunion). The role of music in the story is thus reinforced. The ritornello to '*Possente spirto*', the Apollonian aria by means of which Orfeo gains entry into Hades, is recapitulated, appropriately, to introduce Apollo's entry in Act V. These reappearances of previous material help to give shape to the narrative.

The five-act music-drama is balanced in its overall dramatic structure, as several commentators have noted. This is Striggio's doing. The central point is '*Possente spirto*', in the middle of the third act; the bringing of the news of Euridice's death in Act II is matched by Orfeo's second loss of her in Act IV. The appearance of La Musica at the very beginning is balanced by the appearance of Apollo in the last scene. Such symmetrical balance only exists on paper however, for the pace of the action accelerates through the opera. The actual mid-point in performance is not '*Possente spirto*' but the end of Act II. While, therefore, Monteverdi has reflected Striggio's symmetries, he has also followed the narrative requirement for forward-moving action. It is this ultimate balance between the needs of music and drama that makes Monteverdi a great music-dramatist: the third element in his greatness is his ability to see characters as human beings and to enable us to identify with them as if they were real individuals.

The tendency of opera historians in discussing early seventeenth-century opera is to dismiss Monteverdi's predecessors and to elevate Monteverdi himself to a pedestal. The argument is based upon the idea that in the first opera's music was subservient to other music-dramatic elements. Thus Grout speaks of a

> kind of opera . . . in which the music is definitely subordinated to the other features. As a matter of fact, the very earliest operas were of this kind; but it was found that their appeal was limited and that it was necessary to admit a fuller participation of music in order to establish the form on a sound basis.[22]

The earliest operas arose from the determined efforts of theorists to find, as they said themselves, a relationship between words and music in which the words would retain a clarity of meaning. Peri and his colleagues are therefore accused of subordinating music to the text; Monteverdi is revered for establishing a leading position for music.

Reverence for Monteverdi is not misplaced, but he should be revered, in *L'Orfeo* at least, not as a musician but as a music-dramatist. Music-drama is not a compilation of ingredients: words plus music plus a mysterious thing called drama that no one can really define; it is an integrated whole, whose constituents can only be separated intellectually. The music in *L'Orfeo* is not

135

pure music, and cannot properly be judged as if there were no text: it is meaningless to say that Monteverdi's music is *per se* 'better' or even 'more important' than is Peri's. Monteverdi's music-drama may well be 'better' than Peri's, but this is not due solely to musical considerations, and Striggio may well have had something to do with it. It is extremely dangerous, and may hinder the pursuit of truth, to set up a critical judgment which argues that the quality of music-drama is dependent upon the quality of the music alone: such a critical judgment is part of that attitude which regards opera as a branch of music, rather than as a branch of music-drama.

Peri may have had, as his conscious aim, the idea of providing music more expressive of a text, of 'seeking out the kind of imitation necessary for these poems.'[23] But his broader purpose was not merely to imitate the superficialities of the text, but to find the means to express what lay behind the text: the emotional experiences of those who speak the text. In other words, he was returning music to its *proper* function in music-drama, that of communicating what is implicit. In *L'Euridice*, as in *L'Orfeo*, text and music interact to create 'drama'.

This principle is of primary importance in discussing 'opera'. We have seen that music-drama is a particular form of human activity, quite distinct from music alone; it makes its effects in a different way. It is necessary therefore to judge it on its own terms, and not solely on musical grounds. We must be careful to avoid dismissing Peri on purely musical grounds ('all that recitative is boring') even though some of his musical contemporaries took that view. We must be careful, similarly, to avoid adulating a music-dramatist like Mozart purely on the grounds that he wrote good tunes.

The invention of monody had been a reaction against the formalism and artifice of the madrigal, a move towards a more direct expression of human experience, and thus a rebirth of the Dionysiac side of Greek music-drama. Peri and Rinuccini had perhaps been too involved with the anti-madrigalian, revolutionary mood of the 'second Florentine Academy' to be able to capture the true Greek balance between Dionysos and Apollo — although *L'Euridice* is more structured than might at first appear. It was Monteverdi and Striggio in Mantua who perceived that an image must be shaped to have its full impact, and succeeded in re-establishing the Apollonian side without losing the gains made by Peri and Rinuccini. *L'Orfeo* is music-drama reborn in the context of its time; it is not a reproduction of Attic tragedy, but a renaissance of the spirit of music-drama, and a re-formation of Aristotelian principles and Attic practice in terms of contemporary conditions. It marks the establishment of a distinctly Western European type of music-drama founded on ancient tradition as modified by the Greek experience.

5 Opera seria

Baroque and Classical

Music historians customarily call the period from about 1600 to about 1760 the Baroque era, and the period from about 1760 to about 1800 or 1820 the Classical era. To distinguish the periods in this way is useful, for it reflects the apparently fundamental changes that appear to have occurred around 1600, about 1760, and at the beginning of the Romantic period. However, to use the terms Baroque and Classical can be misleading if that is taken to imply that Classicism was something new in 1760. In fact the Baroque period was also a Classical period, for the ideas which became explicit in the mid-eighteenth century were implicit in the preceding century and a half and had their roots in the Renaissance. But it is not merely that Handel's so-called Baroque operas contain strongly Classical elements: Gluck's so-called Classical operas also contain strong elements of the Baroque. We shall therefore use the terms baroque and classical (without capital letters) in discussing aesthetic elements in *opera seria,* and the terms Baroque and Classical to describe the conventional division of historical period.

There is also a chronological overlap between this and the following chapters. During the eighteenth century two sorts of European music-drama were being written, *opera seria* and *opera buffa,* and they were to be integrated into Early Romantic Opera at the beginning of the nineteenth century. *Opera seria,* the subject of this chapter, stems from the traditions of music-drama we have discussed so far, while *opera buffa* stems from the comic tradition and must be examined in that context. The music-dramas to be treated in this chapter are therefore those of the baroque-classical Handel and Gluck, while the main music-dramatist to be discussed in chapter 6 is Mozart, who utilized baroque and classical aesthetics in the genre of comic opera.

The actual meaning of the word 'baroque' is shrouded in mystery. The word itself has various possible etymological sources. It was originally used in the eighteenth century as a term of abuse, with the meaning bizarre, unusual, or badly-made. Those who used it were artists and writers who adopted the classical point of view and believed they were the inheritors of Renaissance principles which baroque artists had confused and distorted. More recent authorities have defined it in a number of different ways, many apparently contradictory. It is basically a term employed by historians of the visual arts, and while it can be applied to music and to music-drama, this extension of its use is best approached by concentrating upon the aesthetics which lie behind it. The classical writers and artists were right in one respect: it is essentially a reaction to the Renaissance, or, more precisely, to a problem arising out of the late Renaissance.

We have already seen that Renaissance Humanism inevitably came into conflict with its antithesis, the established Christian church. Catholicism took the line that the truth about man, in relation to God and the Universe, had been revealed and was codified in the Bible and in Christian doctrine, although certain concessions were made to the idea that this truth might also have been partially expressed, in a different way, by the philosophers of Ancient Greece and Rome. Renaissance humanism, on the other hand, saw in the writings of the Classical past less a reinforcement of orthodox Christian belief than a series of examples of man working things out for himself by rational investigation and discussion. If the results could be interpreted as coinciding with orthodox belief, all well and good: but they might go beyond it or even undermine it. There consequently grew the idea that the results of rational investigation, since they could be 'proved', must be true even if they did not coincide with orthodox belief.

In the field of astronomy, the church had adopted the Ptolemaic view that the earth was the centre of the Universe. In 1543 Copernicus had put forward the theory that the earth and its sister planets in fact revolved around the sun. This idea not only challenged the Church's view of the Universe, it also attacked the associated belief that man, as God's special creation, is at the centre of the Universe. Copernicus' ideas were condemned by the church: only his own death saved him from being indicted for heresy. The issue came to a head once more, however, in 1633. Galileo Galilei, the son of Vincenzo Galilei of the 'Second Florentine Academy', succeeded in establishing, through research with the newly-invented telescope, that Copernicus was right, and in 1632 published his *Dialogue on the Great World Systems* to say so. Inevitably, he was brought before the Inquisition. The trial was rigged: a forged document was produced in which it was stated that Galileo had undertaken in 1616 not to support Copernicus' views. Galileo was unwilling to suffer death as a heretic and recanted, though legend has him muttering in an aside that he knew he was really right.

Galileo's trial epitomizes the dilemma lying behind the attitudes to life and art of the Baroque period: a dilemma between order and self-expression. The Renaissance had rediscovered these two ideas in the art and

138

thought of Ancient Greece and had developed them into aesthetic and scientific principles. The idea of order corresponded with the Christian idea of a planned universe: God's plan could be discerned in everything. If men were to imitate the divine in a work of art, that is 'to create beauty', it was therefore vital for them to aim for a clearly defined, ordered shape. The idea of self-expression arose from the way in which Greek scientists and philosophers has so obviously worked things out for themselves, and from the obvious emphasis placed in Greek politics, history and art upon the freedom of the individual; aesthetically this became an attitude which emphasized the individual, human aspects in the work of art.

Both ideas are present in Monteverdi's *L'Orfeo*. On the one hand Monteverdi strives for clearly-defined structures; on the other he is concerned to express the individual, human situations of the characters. In *L'Orfeo*, as we have seen, this becomes a matter of reconciling the static and the dynamic, of presenting dynamic, onward-moving narrative without losing static, recognizable musico-dramatic shapes. Over the following century and a half, however, Monteverdi's comparatively simple solution was not automatically followed, and this for several reasons. Firstly, the conflict between static and dynamic was not solely a musico-dramatic problem, and the possible solutions put forward in other areas of human activity exerted an influence upon music-dramatists. Secondly, Peri and Monteverdi had created music-drama out of the *pastorale,* and this was by no means the only dramatic form available or possible: different sorts of drama could be integrated with music in different ways. Thirdly, the grammar and forms of the musical language were continually developing, and therefore new ways of integrating music and drama were becoming available. Behind all these developments, however, lies the basic Baroque polarity of order and self-expression, of static and dynamic.

Rhetoric

In order to explain *opera seria* we must also take into account a second element in Baroque aesthetics. Unlike the music-drama of Classical Greece, opera evolved at the same time as a separate spoken drama was developing; the presence of spoken drama separately from music-drama is the chief reason why opera is customarily thought of as a play with music or music with a play, rather than a distinct, integrated art-form. The public singing of words and the public speaking of words were for the Greeks quite different things: the former was music-drama, and is analysed in Aristotle's *Poetics,* while the latter was oratory, and is analysed in Aristotle's *Rhetoric.* The spoken drama of the Baroque period blurred the distinction between poetics and rhetoric; in consequence, the music-drama of the period was strongly affected by the rhetorical principles of the time.

In the Baroque period the influence of rhetoric was not confined to

139

spoken drama and music-drama. Germain Bazin[1] maintains that rhetoric lay at the centre of baroque thinking and therefore of all the arts. He suggests that, like rhetoric, baroque art was the art of persuasion. While the Renaissance artist pursued absolute truth, which could be perceived objectively, the baroque artist presented the truth subjectively, arousing a subjective response in the spectator: truth was portrayed from a human point of view, engaging the spectator in a human response. The baroque work of art, he says, was not an end in itself, reflecting beautiful order, but a means to the end of evoking a reaction. He therefore relates baroque art to Cicero's definition of oratory: that it instructs (docere) by delighting (delectare) and moving (movere) its audience.

If as Bazin suggests, rhetoric or the art of persuasion lies at the heart of baroque aesthetics, we must investigate precisely what rhetoric is. In the seventeenth and eighteenth centuries, it was an essential part of a young man's education, as it had been since medieval times. The composers of the day, like the dramatists, poets and politicians, studied rhetoric if they received any education beyond mere literacy. While rhetoric is not a subject in the twentieth-century school curriculum, the matters it deals with are familiar, not only in terms of what we may have studied at school under the title literary style analysis, but also in the form of political speeches and commercial advertisements: television commercials in particular are concerned with the art of persuasion, and a knowledge of the tricks of rhetoric is an ideal defence against their often too persuasive effect.

The terms 'rhetoric' and 'rhetorical' have become pejorative terms, because rhetoric is concerned not merely with stating the simple truth, but with presenting the truth in the most persuasive way: its techniques can therefore be used to present lies or half-truths in the most persuasive way. In this, rhetoric and music-drama are close allies: both are fundamentally based upon deceit, or, as we have termed it, pretence or illusion, *reality transformed*. The rhetor, like the actor, assumes a mask for the duration of the performance, but whereas the actor's performance is part of an overall masquerade that is obviously so, the rhetor's performance pretends to be no masquerade at all: he aims to persuade us within the everyday world rather than through the image of another world. From the time of the Ancient Greeks, writers on rhetoric have emphasized that he who uses rhetoric must do so virtuously and honourably, but none has suggested exactly how this can be guaranteed: indeed, discussions about rhetorical devices and methods seldom seem to include any comment about what may be honourable or dishonourable uses of them.

But if we today admit a distinction between honest, truthful, plain speaking and dishonest, deceitful rhetoric, the distinction was less important in the Baroque period. It was a time when emphasis was put upon appearances rather than on substance, when display and ostentation were to be admired. In seventeenth-century France, for instance, the *précieuses* (ridiculed by Molière) who met in the salons of the nobility spent much of their time discussing and evolving elegant and ornamental ways of expressing the simple; their ideas were born of rhetorical practice and reflected a tendency of the times. It is this delight in disguise, ostentation, and ornament which is so clearly evident in certain aspects of baroque art; it is no coincidence that the theatre played an important part in the courtly entertainments of the period.

Rhetoric is concerned not with what is said, but with the way of saying it. In using rhetoric it is all important to make the strongest possible appeal to the audience through carefully planned structure and suitably embellished language. Rhetorical manuals of the Baroque period took the textbooks of Aristotle, Cicero and Quintilian for models and divided the subject into five parts: *inventio*, deciding on the means of persuasion most suitable to the issue; *dispositio*, the planning of the speech, which would usually begin with an exordium, in which the speaker tries to gain the goodwill of the audience, and end with an appeal to the emotions in the peroration; *elocutio*, the use of elegant and appropriate figures of speech which will set the arguments in the most favourable light; *memoria*, the importance of appearing to speak spontaneously; and *pronuntiatio*, the art of verbal delivery, including facial and physical gestures. Many of the particular rhetorical devices discussed in these textbooks have parallels in the musical devices of the period: the use of verbal sequences to build to a climax, for instance, is reflected in the use of musical sequences for the same purpose. More broadly, the essential rhetorical device, that of amplifying and expanding a simple idea into something impressive or elegant, is central to baroque musical style.

By far the largest section in a rhetorical textbook is devoted to *elocutio*. Here are enumerated the many devices by which a thought or idea can be garbed in such a way as to stir or delight an audience. The various kinds of metaphorical language are explained, and the dozens of artificial turns of phrase and figures of speech set out in detail. Metaphor was considered a device particularly to be encouraged, for it is a way of encapsulating a thought in a powerful image (e.g. 'he was a lion among men'). Metaphorical images, since they are essentially transformations of the ordinary into the emotionally persuasive, are of particular appeal: the commonplace dons a disguise of the unusual or special. Metaphor, however, easily degenerates into cliché: every leader can be described by his advocate as a lion among men, and in the end the phrase becomes meaningless and its use counterproductive. The *précieuses* developed cliché expressions too, particularly ones that described emotions in a circumlocutory way. In music this tendency was reflected in the doctrine of aria-types: particular tempi, textures, rhythms and figurations were used to reflect the emotions of the characters as described in their words. And just as an expert but shallow rhetor could

141

weave a speech out of elegant circumlocutions without saying anything at all, so an expert but shallow baroque composer could spin endless patterns of notes, all most elegant, all most effective, but completely lacking in substance. This was the danger of placing a high value on rhetoric, and it was only avoided by the rhetor or composer who had a sincere or passionate belief in the substance of what he wanted to say.

So far, two principles of baroque aesthetics have been discussed: the conflict between static and dynamic, and the importance of rhetorical elegance and ornament in the way things are said. The latter too can be seen in Monteverdi's *L'Orfeo*: Orfeo overcomes Caronte's resistance at the gates of Hades by singing the highly ornamented aria *'Possente spirto'*. Here sophisticated musical rhetoric is employed, justified only by Orfeo's (and Monteverdi's) passionate conviction. Before we turn to a detailed examination of *opera seria* in terms of these principles, however, it is necessary to discuss the place of the theatre in seventeenth- and eighteenth-century courtly life, and the particular influence on *opera seria* of French drama.

The opera-house in the Baroque period

Both Peri's *L'Euridice* and Monteverdi's *L'Orfeo* were performed, like all Renaissance drama and music-drama, on temporary stages set up in the halls of aristocrats' houses. During the seventeenth and eighteenth centuries, however, theatrical activity of one kind or another came to occupy a more and more important position in courtly (and in public) life; in consequence, permanent stone theatres and opera-houses were built. It is not surprising that theatrical activities should have been so important in the life of the baroque courtier: his language was formed by rhetoric, his physical movement was carefully calculated to be elegant and expressive, indeed, his whole life was a dramatically heightened, stylized image of living. In consequence, the division between theatre and life was at times a tenuous one: Louis XIV could take part in a courtly musico-dramatic ballet without there being any clash between reality and transformed reality. The palace of Versailles was designed as a colossal stage-set reflecting the glory of the Sun-King; the theatrical décor of the period used the same symmetrical perspectives and allegorical figures as the Versailles gardens. For the baroque courtier, all the world was a stage, and he and his fellows were the players on it.

At first, the permanent theatres were built on Roman models (see Fig. 13), as was the Teatro Olimpico in Vicenza, designed by Palladio and built in 1584. The seats were arranged in rising tiers in the semi-circular amphitheatre style. The stage itself was broad and shallow. For the back of the stage, Palladio designed a wall with a central opening in the form of a broad arch, and with smaller doorways to each side, the whole ornately decorated with pillars and tiers of statues in niches. For the first performance in the

Fig. 13   The typical Roman theatre (after Vitruvius)

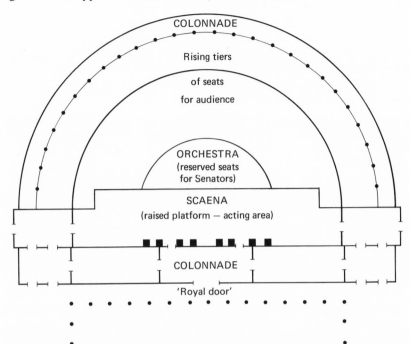

theatre (Sophocles' *King Oedipus,* 1585) Scamozzi designed perspective vistas for each of the openings.[2] The symmetry of the whole is striking; clearly, whatever self-expression might occur on the stage was to be heard and seen against a background of strict classical order.

The similarity between life on the stage and life in the auditorium meant that there was no need for the audience all to face the stage, for the auditorium was full of actors too. And the chief actor might not, indeed, be a person on the stage, but the prince or king in the audience. Accordingly, the amphitheatre idea was usually replaced with a system of boxes lining the walls, and the auditorium assumed the shape of a horseshoe or even an ellipse. At one end was the stage; at the other (in the typical theatre of this kind) the splendid royal box. The floor of the theatre was left as an open space: seats could be put there for stage performances, or the area could be used for balls and other festivities.[3]

The designs of theatres of this kind show a deliberate intent to blur the distinction between stage and auditorium. The proscenium arch acted as a visual link between the ornate decoration of the audience's surroundings and the ornate décor on the stage. Much of the action was brought forward onto the apron-stage in front of the proscenium arch, without any sense of

143

incongruity. At the same time the proscenium arch and stage-set did provide a visual framework for the stage action, enclosing it in a suitable classical order. Similarly, each of the ornately decorated boxes in the auditorium was a picture frame, inhabited by courtiers acting out their theatrical lives. And the whole world of baroque pretence is shown by the fact that stage-sets painted in perspective inevitably looked distorted to the viewers from three quarters of the boxes around the sides of the opera-house.

In two respects, however, the dramatic spectacle in the auditorium could not compete with that on the stage. Firstly, the stage contained all the machinery necessary for spectacle: storms at sea, the descent of gods and goddesses in chariots and the like. Secondly, the actors on the stage were virtuoso singers.

Virtuosity, the ability to perform a skill better than ordinary people, and to impress others by means of this technical mastery, was part of the baroque admiration of technique. We have seen that in rhetoric skilful persuasion was emphasized rather than truth. Virtuosity similarly emphasizes the how rather than the what of singing. The adulation of the virtuoso (which reminds one of Ancient Rome) was also related to the principle of absolutism in government. Louis XIV established the idea of the absolute monarch: '*L'état, c'est moi*', he said: 'I am the state'. This idea had two consequences. Firstly, the importance of the absolute monarch must be reflected in an appropriately grand manner (hence Versailles); and secondly, it suggested that an individual could obediently serve and reflect the absolute mastery of the monarch by himself achieving absolute mastery over something. One path was to become a master of some technique or other, the path of the virtuoso; another was to achieve complete mastery over oneself, so that everything one did was calculated — the path of the baroque courtier. To be a virtuoso was not an act of Romantic rebellion, it was an image of absolute control, reflecting the absolute control of the autocrat over his subjects. In applauding the virtuoso opera singer, the audience was applauding a principle.

Virtuoso singing in *opera seria* took place in the aria, in which a particular emotion was encapsulated and expressed. For a singer to express emotion through the medium of virtuoso technical brilliance was a supreme example of rhetorical device: the simple was made persuasive through musical metaphor. Certainly, on occasion, the original emotion vanished in a welter of empty display, but if delivered with conviction, and clearly consistent with the emotional circumstances of the character, such vocal ornamentation added much to the impact of an aria.

To judge from some contemporary account of the performances of *opera seria* in the seventeenth and eighteenth centuries, the audience paid scant attention to the events upon the stage, except in the arias. Dinner was served, gaming tables were set up, conversations took place, and many

144

members of the audience seem to have spent much of their time touring around from box to box visiting their friends. It is clear that the opera-house was a place of entertainment, but it was more than that: it was an opportunity for the baroque courtier to show what a good actor he was too. Although he might not be involved in the stage action, he was certainly involved in his own drama: like the plot of the opera, it was compounded of intrigue, love, the exercise of power, and the balance of relationships between superiors and subordinates: it was expressed in elegant language which both concealed and revealed emotion.

The seventeenth- and eighteenth-century opera-house was obviously very different from the Theatre of Dionysos in Athens, and far removed from the dancing ground of primitive man. While primitive man and the fifth-century Athenian participated in his music-drama in the open air, Baroque man went into a totally enclosed and roofed hall. The Baroque audience's participation in its own drama does seem to have some similarity to the participation by the primitive audience in ritual music-drama, but the baroque audience-drama was concerned quite as much with form as with content: for the baroque courtier the drama of life was playing games. Accordingly, a curious relationship evolved between audience and performance in baroque music-drama. On the one hand there is evidence that performances of a form of music-drama so close to life provoked deep emotional involvement in the audience, which was both delighted and moved. On the other hand there is also evidence that performances were treated as if they were part of everyday life, with little attention paid except at the more delightful moments. Both responses are understandable in the context of the times. Presumably reactions depended not only upon the quality of performance, but on the attitudes shown by the more influential members of the courtly hierarchy. In towns such as Venice and Hamburg, where there were traditions of public opera, it seems clear that audiences were very much involved in the works performed before them.

Many of the reports about poor behaviour of the audience in *opera seria* were written by those who disapproved of the baroque-ness of the genre: their descriptions of the audience paying scant attention to the stage may not be objectively accurate. It seems at first sight unlikely that librettists, composers and performers would spend so much time writing and rehearsing new works at the rate they did, if the products of their efforts were going to be ignored. If, as many suggest, audiences paid attention only in arias, then why did anyone bother to write and learn lengthy passages of recitative? It would seem likely that at least some members of the audience did attend *opera seria* for its music-drama; perhaps it was only a small proportion. Even today audiences in opera-houses are comprised of those who go to see and those who go to be seen, and there is no reason to suppose that an eighteenth-century audience was markedly different in this respect. One

145

of the most enduring features of Western European 'opera' is its image as a high-brow, snob cultural activity, and this image was born in the seventeenth century, when opera was an activity of the court, its spectacle reflecting the splendour of the monarch.

Care is therefore needed in assessing the reactions of seventeenth- and eighteenth-century audiences to *opera seria*. Undoubtedly there was an element of drama in the auditorium, in the playing of the courtier, but the extent to which this occurred varied from court to court and from opera-house to opera-house. Much depended upon the particular shape of the auditorium, and whether it was made up of rows of boxes round the walls or tiered semicircles of seats. Much too must have depended on the quality of the music-drama: we must not suppose that the baroque courtier was insensitive to artistic quality nor that there were no connoisseurs. A composer who cared about music-drama could, given the right circumstances, create works of the highest quality within the *opera seria* genre. Such a composer was Handel: in London between 1710 and 1741 he wrote opera for a public which was, in general, appreciative. Until 1734 he wrote for the King's Theatre in the Haymarket, which had an auditorium arranged in amphitheatre style, with semicircular rows of seats facing the stage, and with the royal boxes arranged over the sides of the stage. Here was an environment in which, clearly, an audience came to see and hear what was provided for them by the music-dramatist.

French drama and opera

The model for the late Baroque palace was Versailles, and the French court under Louis XIV the model for courtly behaviour throughout Europe. Louis XIV ruled from 1643 until 1715, acting as absolute monarch from 1661. He was a firm believer in the importance of appearances and ceremonial, and his courtiers followed suit. As an absolute monarch, he delegated power at will: those seeking power had of necessity to vie with each other to achieve positions close to him. Such intrigue demanded expertise and secrecy: a mask of calm elegance concealed unscrupulous conspiracy.

Louis was a great patron of the arts, which he saw as a reflection of his own glory. Lully, the great music-dramatist of France, became head of the *Académie Royale de Musique* in 1673 by dint of the favour he enjoyed as the King's dancing-master and dance-composer, a position that as a master of intrigue he knew how to exploit. Lully's operas were themselves reflections of the glory of *le roi soleil:* spectacle was an essential ingredient. The plots, usually based upon classical mythology, provided opportunities for often irrelevant choruses, dances and instrumental items. Ceremony dominated narrative, in the same way that ceremony in the court came before the actual process of governing France: Louis XIV bankrupted the country in order to celebrate the trappings of his position.

In such an atmosphere, it seems extraordinary that great drama could arise, but arise it did in the plays of Pierre Corneille (1606–84) and Jean Racine (1639–99). Their works form the high point of French Classical Tragedy, a genre which was to exert enormous influence upon *opera seria*. Indeed, Lully's librettist, Philippe Quinault, was a failed writer of tragedy, and Lully's music-dramas show some Cornelian influence too.

French Classical Tragedy was a product of its age. (Corneille and Racine differed to a certain extent in their concepts of tragedy, but both were in general agreement about the motivations of tragic action: we shall concentrate upon Corneille, who had a direct influence upon the particular *opera seria* to be discussed later in this chapter.) The issues and dilemmas in the plots arose from the clash of baroque and classical attitudes. Corneille's characters are caught up in the conflict between personal emotion and duty, between baroque self-expression and a classical devotion to order. In sympathy with the absolutism of the French court, the characters could attain heroic stature only by subduing their personal passions: this was the path of *vertu*, leading to *gloire*. The truly *généreux* hero or heroine was able to effect a reconciliation between the two poles of his or her dilemma: in the end he or she was to prove capable only of loving the honourable, and of choosing the virtuous course of action. This might lead to death or apparent dishonour, but no matter: therein lay the tragedy, the aspiration to higher things despite circumstances.

Essentially, French Classical Tragedy is concerned with inner action. The conflicts and resolutions that occur are within the characters, and are expressed in their dialogue. It is a drama of human character, in which the events are human decisions and the motives are moral qualities. (Consequently, many playgoers find French Classical Tragedy 'boring' — nothing seems to happen; the same criticism is often made of *opera seria*.[4]) This narrative of decision-making was organized in French Classical Tragedy according to strict notions of classical structure. The Classical Unities were (nearly always) observed: there should be one central action, to which all else contributed; there should be a single locale (though one might show several different rooms in the same palace, for instance); the events should all take place in a single day. The text was written (with rare exceptions) in twelve-syllable 'alexandrine' rhyming complets. The number of important characters was restricted generally to five or six, usually connected in a series of complex emotional relationships. These structural arrangements lend a certain similarity to the plays, but provide a basic and recognizably patterned world within which playwright and audience can concentrate upon the particular conflicts of the characters.

The rigorous structure of French Classical Tragedy provided a ceremonial framework for the narrative, and the tension between the two helped to create dramatic climaxes, through which tragic catharsis could occur. In this respect as in others it was a precursor of *opera seria*.

The conventions of opera seria

By Handel's time *opera seria* had become a form of music-drama with rigorously fixed conventions. Today these conventions may seem excessively artificial and stylized: it may be difficult to see what purpose they served. But they are based, like French Classical Tragedy, upon the twin attitudes of baroque and classical, and succeed in uniting the apparently contradictory demands of these two aesthetics.

The *opera seria* plot (after the reforms of Zeno and Metastasio between 1690 and 1730) was based upon historical events or classical legend. The 'heroic' type of *opera seria*, to which this discussion will be confined, was concerned with the political and amorous intrigues of about six characters. The main issues at stake were the conflicts between inclination and duty, between temptation and fidelity, and between resisting and yielding to the pressures exerted by those more powerful than oneself. As such, therefore, the subject-matter reflected the activities of an autocratic court; the jockeying for positions of influence, the extent to which absolutism must be obeyed no matter what the cost, the use and misuse of power, and human relationships garbed in rhetoric. The baroque courtier's concern with appearance was reflected in the frequent use of disguises, dissimulations and deceit in *opera seria* plots; in short, the audience was familiar — more familiar perhaps than we are — with the superficial aspects of the narrative.

But the issues raised in these plots of complex interaction were and are of more than passing relevance. Often, they involve questions of life and death, either literally, or figuratively in the sense that to adopt a particular course of action may involve the 'death' of deeply-held principles, or the 'death' of one's previous image of honourable behaviour. Although the surface action may be comprised of lies, deceits and disguises, the 'good' characters at least are concerned with the preservation of *vertu*, and their dilemmas are moral conflicts and psychological crises. A twentieth-century cynic finds it easy to scoff at the moral probity of the heroes and heroines of *opera seria* and their reluctance to be morally pragmatic: indeed, one might have expected baroque man to join in the mockery. However, the baroque concentration upon appearances was the result of deep, unresolved conflicts, and this is why *opera seria* plots presented the inner conflicts behind appearances: they responded to the deepest needs of their audiences.

The conventional structure of *opera seria* supports this view. The story was arranged as a sequence of passages of *recitativo secco* (i.e. recitative accompanied only by continuo) punctuated by arias for solo characters (accompanied by the orchestra). Occasionally, recitative accompanied by

148

the orchestra was used, or arioso (a fragment of aria-type material); ensembles were present only in the form of a rare duet and a final homophonic '*coro*' for the solo singers. Virtually all the musical attention in *opera seria* is therefore focused on the arias, each of which portrays a character's reaction to his or her situation. It is in the arias that dilemmas are discussed, emotions released, and experiences explored and processed. In other words, what matters musico-dramatically in *opera seria* is the personal lives of the characters involved. Deceit, deception and disguise, and the forwarding of the interactions of the plot, take place in the recitatives: but the true motivation for the plot is revealed in the arias.

The *opera seria* aria was conventionally in what is called *da capo* ('from the beginning') form: a first section was followed by a contrasting middle section, which was followed by a repeat, from the beginning, of the first section. This structure is well-suited to the character's task of exploring a situation. First thoughts or feelings are examined, and followed by second thoughts or feelings, which must inevitably cause some reconsideration or intensification of the initial ideas. Thus in the repeat of the first section of the aria it was conventional to ornament the musical material. The *da capo* aria thus provides a simple and effective solution to the problem of static versus dynamic: the basic ABA form has classical symmetry, while the variation of A on its return creates and shows a dynamic forward motion in the action.

Within this typical *da capo* aria-form a great variety of relationships is possible between the A and B sections. Much depends upon the particular dramatic situation and the character: the text to the B section may be a complete switch to a new topic or merely a slight modification of what was said before. (Much depended, too, on the poet's skill in writing two couplets with the correct rhymes while trying to say something positive about the situation from the character's point of view.) Similarly, the music of the B section may be closer to or more distant from that of the A section. In Handel's operas (such as *Rodelinda* which we shall discuss in a moment) one generally finds that the texture of the B section is lighter (there are exceptions); modulation to more distant keys is a common feature. The thematic material is often new for the voice, although the original ritornello idea from A often makes brief appearances.

Since the dramatic, and therefore textual and musical relationship between A and B depends upon circumstances, it is not possible to come to any general conclusions about how B affects A on its return. In some arias we find that A seems to be recapitulated in order to reject the second thoughts of B; in others a more valid dramatic approach from the point of view of character suggests that A must be recapitulated with B's second thoughts very much in mind.

It is considerations of this kind, that is, *dramatic* considerations, which must determine the nature of the ornamentation in the reprise of A.

149

Composers usually specify nothing, leaving ornamentation to the discretion, taste, creative and virtuoso powers of the singer.[5] Later critics of *opera seria* devote much attention to virtuoso ornamentation, arguing that it was almost always absurdly excessive. Perhaps it often was: *opera seria* was wide open to the sort of abuse in which the singer arouses admiration for himself at the expense of character and drama. But if we accept that the *da capo* aria is a *musico-dramatic* form, then it follows that musical decisions (such as the nature of the ornamentation) must take into account the dramatic elements of situation and character.

The same elements must also be taken into account by the continuo keyboard player in *opera seria*. All he is given in the recitative is the vocal line and the bass notes of chords, sometimes figured. In creating the composer's intended chords considerable dramatic discretion is required, particularly in timing. To suggest, as modern writers often do, that very little happens musically, never mind musico-dramatically, in the recitatives of *opera seria*, is to be blinded by the appearance of the printed page of the score. A close investigation of Handel's recitatives, for instance, shows them to be dramatically extremely subtle in their portrayal of character, and musically very much part of the overall structure in the way the melodic ideas and modulations prepare for subsequent arias.

As a whole, the *opera seria* structure plays with time in what seems to be a most unnatural way. Recitatives proceed at a pace more or less equivalent to the pace of natural speech. In arias, however, time seems to expand: words are repeated, indeed a whole section is repeated. It seems as if the opera is governed by a most erratic clock. Yet this alternation between time-scales is not particularly unnatural: the arias are expressions of deeply-felt emotion, and the human mind loses its sense of the normal passage of time at such moments. During arias the characters and the audience enter that no-time, no-place of the imagination.

Thus it is that *opera seria* uses the basic ingredients of opera, blending them in its own way. *Narrative music-drama*, the dynamic attitude, is present on the large scale in the narrative plot, and on the small scale in the *da capo* aria. *Ceremonial music-drama*, the classical attitude, is present in the large-scale organization of the narrative into recitative and aria, and in the ABA symmetry of the aria. *Enthusiastic music-drama* is present in the power of musical expression in the aria to take us out of reality (our own and that of the circumstances of the plot) and into the heart of human experiences. The music-drama is essentially humanist, being concerned with human emotions and human decisions. In accordance with baroque ideas, the element of pretence, implicit in all music-drama, is here brought into the open more perhaps than in any form of Western European opera.

Opera seria is the product of the taste of the urban courtier: it may seem far removed from the world of the Athenian democrat, never mind the primitive hunter. But the essential elements of music-drama are there, re-arranged and disguised according to the cultural values of the historical period. Hidden behind the superficial intrigue there is even the issue of death and rebirth, as we shall see in investigating one of Handel's greatest operas.

Handel's Rodelinda

Rodelinda, composed by Handel before 20th January 1725 to a libretto by Nicola Haym, is taken from Corneille's tragedy *Pertharite*, 1652 (revised after 1656). Haym's text follows Corneille's very closely in some respects (though there may have been intervening plays or libretti). In changing the title from the name of the hero to that of the heroine, Haym was reflecting what is already present in Corneille's play: Rodelinde is the most *généreux* of the characters. (The French names of the original are translated into Italian in the opera.)

The events in the story centre around Queen Rodelinda, who, in the Cornelian tradition, is caught in a series of dilemmas which test her *vertu* and in resolving which she achieves *gloire*. When the opera opens, a *coup d'état* has just occurred: the throne has been seized by Grimoaldo, and King Bertharido, Rodelinda's husband, has vanished and is presumed dead. Grimoaldo approaches Rodelinda, to ask for her hand in marriage: not only has his love for her been a prime motive in the *coup d'état*, but marriage to the queen will assure his position. Rodelinda is in a difficult position: she has a young son, the legitimate heir to the throne, and to marry Grimoaldo would ensure his safety. However, to marry him would also be to abandon her loyalty to the 'dead' Bertharido, and would thus be in conflict with her sense of *vertu* and *gloire*. In consequence, and heroically, she rejects Grimoaldo: 'leave me my *gloire* and take the throne.' Grimoaldo, who is, despite his seizure of the throne, potentially *généreux* himself, is impressed with Rodelinda's reply. However, Garibaldo, a villain with no *généreux* qualities, and who himself has an eye on the throne, persuades Grimoaldo to allow him to convince Rodelinda of the wisdom of the proposed marriage.

Garibaldo proceeds to threaten Rodelinda: unless you marry Grimoaldo, he says, your son will be killed. Rodelinda at first yields under this pressure, but when Grimoaldo comes to check Garibaldo's report, announces that she will marry him *only if* he will murder her son.

This is not merely a tactical bluff: it springs from Rodelinda's sense of *vertu*. Her *vertu* will not allow her to be both mother to the legitimate heir and wife to the usurper of the throne. Her love and duty towards the 'dead' Bertharido have produced in her a 'virtuous hatred' for Grimoaldo (who, as a *généreux* character, is worthy of virtuous hatred), and if he kills her son, her hatred will be properly augmented. As Rodelinda herself puts it in

151

Corneille's play (Act III, scene 3), and almost identically in the opera (Act II, scene 3):

> Since he [my son] must die, better sooner than later. Let it be a crime rather than an accident. Let the memory of his innocence fill my soul, and demand of me a great sacrifice. Let the death of the young king by your hand make you abominable in the eyes of the whole human race. Let it arouse everywhere hatred of you, let it make rebels of all your subjects. Then I shall marry you, and do what I must, to better serve my hatred, to seek a better revenge, to strengthen my will against your barbarity, to be at all times mistress of my life, to have a free opportunity to unleash my fury, and to better choose the moment when I can stab you in the heart.

Rodelinda sounds a ferocious woman, but her position is clear. Grimoaldo, by killing her son, will dishonour himself, and her hatred will be even more *glorieux*.

Not surprisingly, but from *généreux* motives, Grimoaldo cannot do what Rodelinda suggests: but her glorious solution to her difficult situation provides him with a dilemma. Should he give up the throne in an 'act of generosity' corresponding to hers? Can he stay on the throne without marrying Rodelinda, and with her son still alive? Garibaldo's recommendation is simple: murder the boy and take the queen. Grimoaldo, however, is not prepared to sacrifice his *vertu* for political security.

Rodelinda's battle to preserve her *gloire* despite the pressures from Grimoaldo and Garibaldo is thrown into relief by the other main strand of the plot. Bertarido has not in fact died, but has returned in disguise, and awaits the opportunity to reclaim his throne. From the sidelines he watches Rodelinda's dilemmas, through the eyes of his servant Unulfo. Bertarido quite correctly sees events as a test of Rodelinda's constancy: when Unulfo suggests that the queen should be told her husband lives, Bertarido disagrees: 'a constancy forced by necessity is no sign of *vertu*.' Only when his wife has proved her *vertu* in a free decision does he reveal himself to her.

Their embrace of greeting in Rodelinda's apartments is interrupted by the arrival of Grimoaldo. He does not recognize Bertarido in his disguise, and accuses Rodelinda of being faithless to him and to the memory of her husband. Both Rodelinda and Bertarido are in a dilemma here: the question is whether they ought to reveal the true identity of Bertarido. Bertarido, to preserve Rodelinda's *vertu*, confesses who he is, in an act of *généreux* self-sacrifice. Rodelinda immediately denies it, in order to preserve Bertarido's life. Grimoaldo, non-plussed, has 'the man', whoever he is, consigned to the dungeons.

But all is not yet lost. Bertarido's sister, Eduige, had been engaged to Grimoaldo, but has been discarded in Grimoaldo's passion to marry Rodelinda. This attack upon her *gloire* has caused her to seek revenge, at first by agreeing to help Garibaldo gain the throne. Now she has recognized

Bertharido, and, rather more virtuously, sees a way to redeem her *vertu* by helping him escape. She drops a sword through his dungeon window, gives Unulfo a key to a secret passage from the dungeons to the royal gardens, and brings Rodelinda to see Bertharido.

These arrangements are made in haste, and Bertharido is not informed. When Unulfo arrives to rescue Bertharido, the imprisoned king thinks it is a minion of Grimoaldo, come to murder him, and stabs him with the sword. Unulfo is not badly hurt, but bleeds copiously. After he and Bertarido have escaped along the secret passage to the gardens, Eduige and Rodelinda arrive at the dungeon. Finding it empty, and fresh blood on the floor, Rodelinda leaps to the conclusion that Bertarido has been murdered.

Meanwhile, Bertarido is hiding in the garden. Grimoaldo arrives, in the throes of a new dilemma: could he now marry Rodelinda at all, after finding a stranger in her arms? His crime of usurping the throne can only be exonerated by the love of a virtuous Rodelinda: is she virtuous? Exhausted, he falls asleep. Garibaldo arrives, and sees his opportunity to assassinate Grimoaldo and seize the throne himself. Bertarido emerges, foils Garibaldo and kills him. Grimoaldo awakens: he recognizes Bertarido and the *vertu* Bertarido showed in saving an enemy's life. Willingly, he gives up the throne to Bertarido and Rodelinda, and thus becomes virtuous himself.

Apart from the somewhat melodramatic and contrived events in the escape scenes, the plot provides maximum opportunity for the four main characters to make decisions, and each finally achieves *vertu*.

The plot of *Rodelinda* has been discussed fairly fully because, at least until fairly recently, writers on *opera seria* have in general seemed to think the plots unimportant. However, as we shall see, the moral ideas lying behind the plot of *Rodelinda* also govern the progress and structure of Handel's music. Traditionally, too, the narrative structure of *opera seria* has been thought to consist of long passages of recitative that serve only to provide an excuse for arias. This view is nonsensical: the narrative of the plot is entirely motivated by the dilemmas of the characters, and these are what are presented in the arias. In other words, it is the dramatic content of the arias that provides the motivation for the recitative. The arias tell us what the characters think and feel, and it is their thoughts and feelings which govern their actions as presented in recitative. Although superficially there may appear to be a structure of recitative leading to aria, dramatically it would be more correct to speak of aria giving rise to recitative. This dichotomy between apparent musical structure and underlying dramatic structure might be expected to set up irreconcileable tensions, but in the hands of a great music-dramatist like Handel the tension becomes part of the overall impact of the work.

The music for *Rodelinda* consists of an overture, a final homophonic 'moral' ensemble for all, two accompanied recitatives, two arioso passages, one *da capo* duet and twenty-eight *da capo* arias.[6] Such an arrangement of the music into an overture and thirty-one separate numbers seems hardly conducive to a conception of large-scale structure: that Handel was able to use the conventions and at the same time conceive the whole opera as a structural entity is a mark of his genius.

Fig. 14   Handel's *Rodelinda*. The arias

ACT I, scene 1: Rodelinda's apartments.
  1 *Rodelinda* faces the situation of having lost her husband. *Largo, C minor.*
   a Can I bear the pain?
   b I must do what I can for my son.

  2 *Rodelinda* rejects Grimoaldo's proposal: to marry him would be contrary to *vertu* and *gloire.Allegro, G minor.*
   a Fate cannot make me dishonourable, though it makes me unhappy.
   b Tyrant, you will never placate me.

  3 *Grimoaldo* discards Eduige. *Allegro, B flat major.*
   a Once I loved you, but you rejected me;
   b I do not wish to have a queen who despised me.

  4 *Eduige* plans revenge. *Allegro, F major.*
   a I shall break completely with him. . .
   b . . . and turn to you, Garibaldo.

  5 *Garibaldo* plans to gain the throne. *Allegro, C minor.*
   a I'll use love to gain the throne, though I love only power.
   b Deceit is best; true feelings are an obstacle.

ACT I, scene 2: a wood with sepulchres.
  6 *Bertarido* seeks love and consolation.
   (Accompanied recit.) He speaks ironically of death, and reads his own epitaph. *Largo, G minor.*
  (Aria) *a* Come, love, to console me. *Largo, E major*
       b I am oppressed by torments.

  7 *Rodelinda* seeks comfort from the spirits of the dead. *Largo, B minor.*
   a You know the delight in my heart.
   b Among you I might find well-being.

  8 *Rodelinda* tells Garibaldo that, though she yields to blackmail, he will suffer. *Allegro, E major.*
   a You shall die;
   b That is the sweetest gift my new husband could give me.

  9 *Grimoaldo* reassures Garibaldo of his protection. *Allegro, F major.*
   a What, whom should you fear?
   b I command, I am king.

10 *Unulfo* reassures Bertarido. *(Allegro), D major.*
   a A strong heart is proof against the blows of fate.
   b Love's blows can hurt most but make the heart more noble.

11 *Bertarido* doubts Rodelinda's loyalty. *Allegro, B minor.*
   a She is faithless.
   b Her lamenting for me was false.

ACT II, scene 1: a room in the palace.
   12 *Eduige's* fury against Grimoaldo is renewed. *Allegro, G minor.*
      a I shall avenge his betrayal.
      b My cruelty shall match his.

   13 *Rodelinda* warns Grimoaldo. *Allegro, B flat major.*
      a If you spare my son you will preserve grief and anxiety;
      b I would still kill you: you are the cause of my grief.

   14 *Grimoaldo* speaks of his feelings for Rodelinda. *Allegro, A major.*
      a I am imprisoned in sweet chains and do not seek my freedom.
      b I am sad, but the feeling delights me.

   15 *Garibaldo* speaks of kingship. *Allegro, D minor.*
      a The kingdom is his who rules with rigour;
      b The foundation of ruling is strictness.

   16 *Unulfo* will tell Bertarido that Rodelinda is faithful to him. *Allegro, G major.*
      a In tempests a star brings hope of peace.
      b Faithfulness shines to the anxious heart.

ACT II, scene 2: a pleasant spot in the gardens.
   17 *Bertarido* shares his unhappiness with nature. *Larghetto, E flat major.*
      a The streams join in my lament. . .
      b . . . and the rocks echo my complaint.

   18 *Bertarido* is reassured of Rodelinda's fidelity. *Allegro, C minor.*
      a The swallow flies about without complaint. . .
      b . . . for he has a faithful companion.

ACT II, scene 3: Rodelinda's apartments.
   19 *Rodelinda* awaits Bertarido's arrival. *Andante, G major.*
      a Come, beloved, and ease my heart.
      b You will comfort my anguish.

   20 *Grimoaldo* accuses the lovers. *Allegro, G minor.*
      a Whore, you shall die.
      b (to Bertarido) Your actions prove you guilty.

   21 *Rodelinda and Bertarido* say farewell to each other. *Larghetto, F sharp minor.*
      a Our love is stronger than death.
      b Tyranny shall not defeat it.

ACT III, scene 1: a gallery in the palace.
   22 *Unulfo* is optimistic about rescuing Bertarido. *(Andante), F major.*
      a I feel hope and shall bear it to you.
      b In saving my lord I ease his cares.

   23 *Eudige* sees her part in the rescue as a cancellation of her mistakes. *Allegro D major.*
      a The more the tempest roars the more hope I have;
      b I shall reach the port of safety.

   24 *Grimoaldo* cannot decide what to do. *Allegro, A minor.*
      a My heart is full of conflicting emotions.
      b Should I repent or be angry?

ACT III, scene 2: the darkest dungeon.
   25 *Bertarido* considers his position: did Fate or love betray him?
      (Arioso, leading to accompanied recitative.) *Largo, B flat minor.*

   26 *Rodelinda* laments the supposed death of Bertarido. *Larghetto, C minor.*
      a Why, O heavens, so much pain?
      b Come, my son, weep with me.

   27 *Rodelinda* contemplates suicide. *Largo, F minor.*
      a Is my grief not strong enough to kill me?
      b To suffer thus without release is a cruel fate.

ACT III, scene 3: the royal garden.
   28 *Bertarido* celebrates his freedom. *Allegro, C major.*
      a The beast freed from its chains rejoices to be free.
      b It knows not how to show mercy.

   29 *Grimoaldo* wonders what to do.
      (Arioso) *E minor, F sharp major.* He is torn by envy, disdain, love, and remorse for his deeds. He seeks the healing power of sleep.
      (Aria). *(Larghetto), E minor.*
      a The humble shepherd sleeps content.
      b But I, the king, can find no repose.

   30 *Rodelinda* lovingly greets her husband. *Allegro, G major.*
      a My beloved, I suffer no more.
      b To see you happy fills my heart with love.

   31 *All* sing in celebration. *(Allegro), F major.*
      a After dark night the sun is welcome.
      b Out of misfortune and suffering is born joyful *vertu.*

Figure 14 shows the basic content of the sung numbers; that of each *da capo* aria is shown in the two constituent sections (a) and (b). It will be seen that each scene tends to have a key structure. Act I, scene 1 moves through the 'flat keys' C minor, G minor, B flat major, F major, and closes in C minor. In the following scene the prevailing 'sharp' tonalities are broken only by Grimoaldo's F major aria. In other scenes the key-shifts from aria to aria can be seen to have general significance: in Act II scene 3, for example, Rodelinda's G major is turned to the minor by Grimoaldo's accusations, and the situation is lowered in pitch but 'sharpened' in key-quality for the duet of farewell. In Act III Handel achieves a masterly effect at the scene-change between scenes one and two by shifting from A minor up a semitone to B flat minor. This kind of semitonal progression is also shown in the way Handel begins Act I in C minor and ends it in B minor, and begins Act II in G minor and ends it in F sharp minor. These structural and expressive uses of key suggest that Handel is not selecting keys by chance: indeed, if he wished to give some overall musico-dramatic structure to the opera, he could use little other than keys to do so.

We have established that the primary function of music in music-drama is to reveal what lies behind, and is implicit in, the outer words and actions of the characters. *Rodelinda* is drawn specifically, and generally as an *opera seria*, from French Classical Tragedy, and what lies behind a Cornelian dramatic text is a series of moral issues. The decisions the characters make reveal their motives, which may be the selfish pursuit of personal power (*ambition*), an unselfish concern for another person (*amour*), uncontrolled emotion (*passion*), or a highly controlled pursuit of virtue (*vertu*). There may be other motives involved, but *Rodelinda* at least can be analysed in these terms. In expressing what is implicit in the music-drama, Handel uses keys to represent these four ethical characteristics. Figure 15 shows how.

The outer circle of keys arranges major keys in the cycle of fifths: clockwise movement leads to sharper keys and anti-clockwise movement to flatter keys. The inner circle of keys shows the cycle of minor keys: since a minor key is closely related to both its tonic major and its relative major, the minor keys are sited here at a point equidistant between these two related majors. The keys indicated in brackets are not used by Handel for arias or ariosos.

Although this diagram was arrived at by careful examination of the score, it is most simply explained by applying it to the chart of arias in Fig. 14. The issue or issues lying behind each aria will thus become evident.

In No. 1 Rodelinda is motivated by *vertu*, which demands she comes to terms with the situation, and by *ambition* for her son: the keys of C major and E flat major thus interact to produce C minor. It is notable that the (b) section of the aria is resolutely in B flat major and E flat major, the *ambition* keys. In No. 2 the same issues are involved, but *vertu* is much stronger as a motivating force; hence the key sharpens to G minor. In No. 3, Grimoaldo's *ambition* dominates all else: the aria is in B flat major. Eduige's *vertu* is

157

Fig. 15   Key-associations in Handel's *Rodelinda*

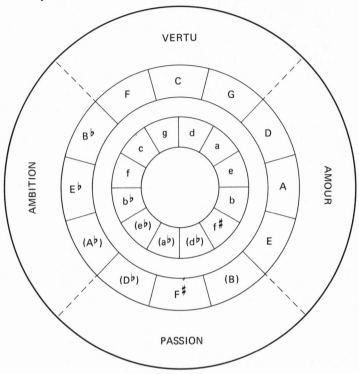

challenged: she responds in No. 4 in F major. Garibaldo's *ambition* is reflected in No. 5's C minor; if *vertu* is hardly present, he is at least totally in control of himself and his destiny. In Nos. 6 and 7 we move into the world of *amour*, which is diametrically opposed to *ambition*. No. 8's E major is difficult to explain: perhaps Handel wishes to suggest this opposition to Garibaldo's *ambition*. Rodelinda herself is hardly motivated by either *vertu* or *ambition*, so to choose a key on the borderline of *amour* and *passion* seems not entirely inappropriate. In No. 9 Grimoaldo reassures Garibaldo of his own *vertu*. In No. 10 Unulfo sings in a key at the *vertu* end of the *amour* group, most suitably. In No. 11 Bertarido's feelings of love for Rodelinda are what motivate his accusing her of infidenlity: he is, moreover, in the sway of *passion*, for nothing Unulfo has said gives him cause for this outburst.

Nearly all the arias in Acts II and III can be interpreted in the light of Fig. 15, and such analysis reveals the depth and complexity of the characters' motivations. The two arias most difficult to resolve are Nos. 15 and 17. It is not easy to understand why Garibaldo in No. 15 shold choose a key relating to D major (*amour*) and F major (*vertu*) when maintaining the need for tyrannous government. Nor is it clear why Bertarido in No. 17 should pick the central key of the *ambition* group when lamenting Rodelinda's faithlessness: E major might have been more suitable, as B minor might have been in No. 18.

But even if three numbers out of thirty-one are difficult to interpret in the light of Figure 15, the evidence at least suggests that Handel used keys with considerable care to express the motives that drive the characters to make the decisions. In other words, Handel's arias are not just pretty songs, nor glittering ornamental displays, nor even artificial pictures arranged in a musical gallery. On the contrary, each is a miniature music-drama, in which Handel is expressing the humanity of the characters, not just as an emotional outburst, but in psychological terms. And behind the arias there lies a musical representation of that inner world that lies behind the text and action.

A further example of relationships between the arias, illustrating the way Handel thinks beyond the surface structure and into the lives of the dramatic characters, can be seen in the first two arias for Rodelinda (Nos. 1 and 2). A clear thematic relationship is evident here. Example 10 (a) shows the opening four bars of No. 1: 'I have lost my dear husband'; (b) reduces the melodic shape of this to its bare outline, transposed into G minor; (c) shows the opening four bars of No. 2: 'The cruel rigour of fate. . .' and (d) reduces this to its melodic shape. Brackets show that the constituent motifs of No. 1's opening have been shuffled to create No. 2's opening: in other words, the cruel rigour of fate lies in the fact that Rodelinda has lost her dear husband.

Ex. 10   Handel: *Rodelinda*

(e)

se mi - se - ra — mi fè

(f)

se m'hai — le - ga - to il piè, — se m'hai le - ga - - - - to il piè, se m'hai le - ga-to il piè.

(g)

Ahi, per - chè, giu - sto ciel, tan - ta pe - na a ques - to cor?

(h)

Ri - tor - na, oh ca - ro e dol - ce mio — te - so - ro,

No. 2 continues with an almost exact repeat of the opening phrase, in B flat major, to the words 'dishonourable it (fate) cannot make me,' and then follow the words 'though it has made me unhappy,' set to the melody shown in (e). This melody is the first part of the opening bars of the aria; the portion left is motif *x* in (d), which is precisely the constituent notes of 'I have lost. . .' in No. 1. 'The cruel rigour of fate' is therefore comprised of 'it makes me unhappy/I have lost. . .', a delightfully neat way of Handel's to describe the particular experience behind the words. In the second section of No. 2 Rodelinda says 'And you, harsh tyrant, in vain try to placate me, through you have shackled my foot', these final words sung to the melodic phrase shown in (f). The melodic line here looks very much like a melodic expansion — in the same key — of 'I have lost my dear husband' from No. 1.

In No. 26, Rodelinda's lament for her apparently murdered husband, C minor returns, and with it a melody born of the same shapes: 'Ah, why, just heavens, [bring] such pain to this heart?' (Ex. 10(g)). In No. 19 Rodelinda eagerly awaits the imminent arrival of Bertarido. 'Return, o dear, sweet treasure,' she sings, in G major. The end of misery is clearly shown in the melody (Ex. 10 (h)): the notes and shape of 'unhappiness' (e) are retained but put in a major key. As if to emphasize the similarity, Handel retains an *f* natural, although we would expect an *f* sharp in G major.

Two cases of thematic correspondence in Bertarido's arias are shown in Ex. 11. No. 6 opens with his seeking consolation: 'Where are you [my beloved]?' (a), a phrase which glides easily from recitative into aria. In No. 17, still lamenting, Bertarido shares his weeping 'with the harsh murmurs (of streams and fountains). . .' (b). The similarity is obvious. In the second example, a ritornello with slightly different material precedes

160

Ex. 11   Handel: *Rodelinda*

(a)

Do - ve   se - i?

(b)

Con   rau - co   mor - mo - ri - o ...

(c)

Con - fu - sa   si   mi - ri   l'in - fi - da   con - sor - te ...

(d)

Mà   poi da' la - cci sciol-ta ___   in   fu - ga ogn'un ri - vol - ta ...

(e)

Pa - sto - re - llo d'un po - ve-ro ar-men-to pur dor-me con-ten-to ...

(f)

Or   ch'io son   Rè,   non   vo - glio ...

this, and would normally have been taken up by the voice: for Bertarido to sing something new is therefore significant — and his new material is justified by overall structural considerations. (c) is the opening material of No. 11, in which Bertarido states he is 'confounded to see [his] unfaithful wife.' The same material recurs in the middle section of No. 28 (d): perhaps not too much should be made of this, for it is a by no means unusual melodic phrase and also appears in Vivaldi's Violin Concerto in A minor! An interesting relationship to (a) is provided in Grimoaldo's self-pitying search for peace in No. 29 (e): the same falling phrase is used. But a more significant connection is between this and Grimoaldo's 'now I am king I seek not [you Eduige as my queen]' in the second section of No. 3 (f).

Key-associations and thematic relationships in *Rodelinda* have been discussed here at some length (though by no means exhaustively) in order to show that Handel was concerned with the overall shape of the music-drama. A procession of thirty-one apparently self-contained and isolated arias is in fact more than this: the separate numbers are constituent parts of a total music-drama, which Handel thought through as a whole. We know his practice was to begin at the beginning of a text and work through it, and this already suggests an interest in the development of dramatic action. Having composed the arias, he turned to the recitatives, but even this was no mere hack-work.

For example, in the recitative between Nos. 1 and 2 Rodelinda informs Grimoaldo she cannot marry him, and concludes with the statement 'leave my *gloire*, and take the throne'. This statement summarizes her motivation: in consequence, Handel sets it to the melodic phrase (Ex. 12) which binds together the material of arias Nos. 1 and 2. The choice of D minor is not

Ex. 12   Handel: *Rodelinda*

La-scia-mi la mia glo-ria, e tien-ti il tro-no.

see Example 10 (b)

accidental: indeed, Handel's use of keys in recitative is often quite deliberate. In No. 8 Rodelinda warns Garibaldo that he shall die for forcing her into marriage: the aria is in E major. After the aria, and Rodelinda's exit, Grimoaldo enters to a chord of C major, and asks Garibaldo whether the plan was successful.

GARIBALDO	You shall be happy, and I my lord am dead.	G major
GRIMOALDO	Dead? Why?	B minor
GARIBALDO	When she regains the throne all her hatred will fall on me.	E minor
GRIMOALDO	Do not fear, for my protection in your defense against her anger will be a strong shield.	C major F major B flat major F major

Grimoaldo's aria of reassurance (No. 9) follows in F major. Handel begins the recitative in C major, the dominant of the key he must eventually reach: it is therefore not strictly necessary to have the moves to B minor and E minor. These keys are used for an expressive reason, to refer back to the key of Rodelinda's threat, and therefore have symbolic force.

We may conclude that *Rodelinda* is an apparently highly artificial kind of music-drama, but that behind the veneer of artifice the music provides an expression of the unfolding human experiences that are implicit in the narrative. *Ceremonial music-drama* it certainly is, but we have now seen that the music also has narrative characteristics: behind the thirty-one separate numbers lies *narrative music-drama*. There is an *enthusiastic* element present too in the use of music to stir the audience to pity and terror.

The dramatic situations seem to be so rooted in the ethos of the time that they have little relevance to us nowadays. The concepts of *vertu, gloire, générosité* and so on are, perhaps sadly, neglected in twentieth-century materialist culture, though they linger in the concept of the English gentleman. Nevertheless, tragedy has seldom been a direct representation of everyday life: you and I may not be Renaissance royalty, but we are not princes of Denmark either. Tragedy is concerned with exploring the deepest human experiences, and *Rodelinda* is no exception. All the major characters hover between Apollo and Dionysos, between *vertu* and *passion,* and each achieves his own final balance after experiencing a death-rebirth experience.

Rodelinda, faced with tremendous political pressure, takes refuge in consultation with the spirits of the dead (No. 7); she opens her mind to supernatural — or unconscious — forces. It is after this experience that she faces Garibaldo and then Grimoaldo with reborn strength — the E major of No. 8 perhaps shows this. Bertarido at first believes Rodelinda to be unfaithful, but in No. 17 he opens his mind to nature, and is reborn: in No. 18 he is able to rejoice in his wife's fidelity — not only because of Unulfo's assurances, but because his state of mind has altered. The third major character, Grimoaldo, is forced with an impossible decision to make: to lose Rodelinda whom he loves, or to take her at appalling cost. In No. 29 he takes refuge in sleep, and during sleep the problems is solved: Bertarido saves his life. His renunciation of the throne is motivated not just out of gratitude, but out of a psychological rebirth.

Ghosts, submerging oneself in nature and sleep are archetypal images of the process of psychological death and rebirth. In each of these arias we as audience die and are reborn, through the involving power of music. And so we too attain *vertu* and *générosité.* We are rescued from excessive baroque expression and from rhetorical artifice by the music's reinforcement of two elements: the moral continuum of the story, which makes the characters into real people, and the moments of mystery, through which we enter the characters' experiences.

Gluck's Orfeo ed Euridice

Through the first half of the eighteenth century *opera seria* came under severe critical attack. In *Il Teatro alla Moda* of 1720 Benedetto Marcello satirized certain practices of conventional *opera seria*, such as the singer dominating all, the poor quality of the acting, and irrelevant ornamentation. These views were echoed by Addison in his articles for *The Spectator*. In short, *opera seria* was considered to be over-stylized and lacking in immediate dramatic impact. Apollo was dominating, and even excluding, Dionysos.

There is some justification in these claims. Although we have seen that Handel thought of *opera seria* as more than mere artifice, his musico-dramatic narrative techniques lie well below the surface; furthermore, most of his contemporaries were far less able than he. There can be no doubt that the *opera seria* conventions lent themselves only too easily to a treatment that would arouse strong criticism from those who believed that *narrative* and *enthusiasm* were as important (if not more important) than *ceremonial*.

By the middle of the eighteenth century more positive suggestions were being made about opera. In 1755 Francesco Algarotti published his *Saggio sopra l'opera in musica*. Algarotti's book was important and influential, for it laid the foundations of a new approach, which reflected changing aesthetic values. The new outlook was something of a revolt against the values of the Baroque. Rhetoric, artifice and deceit were now no longer considered to be virtues: in place of them were raised the banners of truth, reason, and simplicity.

Classicism was breaking free of the dilemmas of the Baroque period. A fresh impulse had been given to classicism, in a renewed assertion of the clarity, reason and humanism of Greek thought. The German classical scholar Winckelmann was rediscovering in Greek art the characteristics of 'noble simplicity and tranquil grandeur'. In France Voltaire was using his sharply critical pen against religion, intolerance, and fanaticism, and arguing for a greater use of reason and common sense. Writers on ethics were taking a more reasoned and secular view of their subject, exposing the hypocrisy of the baroque in its pretended pursuit of *vertu* and its actual pursuit of *ambition*. The idea was growing that a human being has certain rights, immortalized in the American Constitution's 'life, liberty and the pursuit of happiness'. Such an idea would have been incomprehensible to Louis XIV. Intellectually European man was beginning to stand rather more firmly on his own feet: in France the *Encyclopédistes* pursued knowledge relentlessly and were dedicated to enlightening their fellows.

It was ideas such as these which led Algarotti to state that an opera poet should 'exert all his judgement and taste in choosing the subject of his drama, that thereby he may attain his end, which is to delight the eyes and the ears, to rouse up and to affect the hearts of an audience, without the risk of sinning against reason or common sense.'[7] Here the rhetorical aims of *delectare* and *movere* are accepted, but the falseness of rhetoric is abjured.

Algarotti's central argument is that *opera seria* had strayed too far from the music-drama of the early seventeenth century,[8] and therefore from that of the Greeks. The chief reason for this straying from 'true music-drama' was, Algarotti argued, the dictatorship of music, the

> authority, power and supreme command usurped in its name; because the composer, in consequence, acts like a despotic sovereign, contracting all the views of pleasing to his department alone. It is almost impossible to persuade him that he ought to be in a subordinate position, that music derives its greatest merit from being no more than an auxiliary, the handmaid to poetry. His chief business, then is to predispose the minds of the audience for receiving the impression to be excited by the poet's verse, to infuse such a general tendency in their affections as to make them analogous with those particular ideas which the poet means to inspire.[9]

Algarotti was not a composer; had he been, he might have understood rather better the composer's reluctance to be persuaded. Indeed, Algarotti may go too far in his argument. But his point of view is a reasonable one, and not without merit. He points out, correctly, that music's role is to provide the universal human experiences behind the particular experiences represented in the poetic text. From his classical Apollonian outlook, the particular has more importance than the general: hence he believed that music is subordinate to poetry.

Later, Algarotti seems to be more in favour of a partnership between poetry and music. The operas of the present age, he argues, have improperly separated them, and thus opera tends to become a purely musical *genre*.

> Now that the twin sisters, poetry and music, go no longer hand in hand, it is not at all surprising, if the business of one is to add colouring to what the other has designated, that the colouring, separately considered, appears beautiful; yet, upon a nice examination of the whole, the contours offend by not being properly rounded and by the absence of a . . . blending of the parts throughout.[10]

Algarotti goes on to make specific suggestions. An operatic overture should not be a rhetorical exordium, but a preparation for the action. Recitative should be written to achieve the expressive strength of Peri's, the harmony 'chastely following nature step by step'. Perhaps accompanied recitative and arioso could be employed more often. Arias should be more simple. Words should not be endlessly repeated, but 'treated in no other manner but according as the passion dictates'; the *da capo* form is, he says, 'repugnant to the natural process of our speech and passions'. He concludes that 'the duty of a composer is to express the sense, not of this or that particular word, but the comprehensive meaning of all the words in the air. . .'[11] in other words, music must keep to the universal and implicit, and not attempt to represent the specific and explicit.

We do not know whether Christoph Willibald Gluck read Algarotti's book; if he did not, then his operas provide some startling coincidences with

Algarotti's suggestions, for theory is here put into very effective practice.

Gluck was no young revolutionary. His first opera was performed in 1742 (the year after Handel's last): it was an Italian *opera seria*, performed in Milan. In the following twenty-one years, Gluck wrote over twenty *opere serie*, about ten rather light-weight French operas, and three ballets. Only then, in 1762, aged forty-eight, did he write his first 'reformed' opera, *Orfeo ed Euridice*. In the following seventeen years of his working life he composed six more operas in the new style, three French comic operas, and four or five *opere serie*. It is truly astonishing that Gluck seems to have treated his own reform so lightly, especially since the power of his works in the new style is so evident.

He was initially persuaded to write serious opera in a different manner by Durazzo, director of the Vienna Court Theatre, and Raniero da Calzabigi, who provided 'reformed' libretti. Two choreographers were also involved: Gasparo Angiolini, who had already collaborated with Gluck and Calzabigi in the creation of 'reformed ballets', and who was to arrange the dances in *Orfeo ed Euridice*, and Jean Georges Noverre, the most important dance-reformer of this period, and who was to stage the dances in *Alceste* in 1767. Noverre also played a large part in the creation and production of the third of Gluck's three Vienna 'reformed' operas, *Paride ed Elena* (1770). From 1770 until 1778 Gluck worked mostly in Paris, where they were more receptive to his ideas, and it was there that he produced French revisions of *Orfeo* and *Alceste*,[12] and wrote four more operas in the new style: *Iphigénie en Aulide* (1774), *Armide* (1777) to a libretto by Quinault, first set by Lully, *Iphigénie en Tauride,* and *Echo et Narcisse* (both 1778). The final nine years of his life Gluck spent in retirement in Vienna, enjoying productions of Mozart's operas.

It should by now come as no surprise to the reader to discover that the subject of the first 'reform' opera of Durazzo, Calzabigi and Gluck was the legend of Orpheus. It was almost as though Algarotti's encouragement to reurn to the principles of early opera had been taken literally. But the Calzabigi/Gluck version of the story differs considerably from those of Rinuccini/Peri and Striggio/Monteverdi. The aim here was not to establish narrative music-drama, nor well-structured narrative music-drama, but to find an alternative to the artifice and complexity of *opera seria*. *Orfeo ed Euridice* was new for its time, but from our point of view it is a reinstatement of ideas and principles we have already discussed. The overall principles of the work can be described as 'noble simplicity and tranquil grandeur' — a new-found awareness of Classical Greek aesthetics — and 'narrative expression' — an interest in musical expression as a developing continuum rather than the structural isolation of expressive moments which occurred, at least apparently, in the *da capo* arias of *opera seria*. 'Narrative expression' was a throwback to early opera, particularly in the use of orchestrally

166

accompanied recitative, but the principle was re-stated using the musical language and orchestral resources of the mid-eighteenth century.

Calzabigi's version and arrangement of the story is simple and neat. Act I opens with Orfeo and his companions lamenting the death of Euridice. Orfeo begs for the gods' pity: Amor, the god of love, appears, and tells Orfeo he will help. Orfeo shall regain Euridice from Hell, so long as he neither looks at her nor tells her of this condition. In the first scene of Act II Orfeo succeeds in persuading the Spectres and Furies of Hell to let him pass: they do so out of pity, being moved by his grief-stricken state and the simple appeal of his song rather than by any display of vocal virtuosity. In scene 2 Orfeo arrives in the Elysian Fields where the Blessed Spirits, the heroes and heroines of antiquity, pass their pleasant days. They welcome him, and return Euridice to him. In Act III, Orfeo and Euridice are on their way back to the world. Euridice cannot understand Orfeo's taciturnity and refusal to look at her. She complains bitterly, accusing him of not loving her: finally he turns — and loses her. He resolves to kill himself: Amor reappears and says there will be no more tests of Orfeo's love. He restores Euridice to life, and the scene changes to the Temple of Love, where general celebrations are held.

The focus of the story shifts, in this version, from concern with Orfeo the musician to a more simple tale of love. Only once in the text, in fact, is any overt reference made to Orfeo as a musician. What is emphasized is the love element in the story: as Amor indicates, Orfeo's love is being tested; by this is meant the extent to which Orfeo is prepared to endure danger, suffering, and finally death itself for the sake of his love for Euridice. This has certain similarities with the dilemmas placed before the characters of French Classical Tragedy and Baroque *opera seria*, but the issue is made more universal by the move from a world of courtly intrigue into the no-place, no-time of myth.

This move into another world is emphasized by the recurrence in the opera of choruses and ballets, which have the function of universalizing, as did the choral singing and dancing in Greek tragedy. They are the natural activities of man in myth, as they were of the primitive men who invented myth. There is no doubt that Calzabigi and Gluck (and of course Angiolini) considered them important: only four scenes (Orfeo's lament and his conversation with Amor in Act I, and his dialogue with Euridice and the second appearance of Amor in Act III) contain neither choruses nor dances.

In contrast to previous *opera seria*, Gluck's *Orfeo* is very plainly composed in units comprising whole scenes and acts. Calzabigi called the work not an opera but an *azione teatrale per musica*, 'theatrical' because of the spectacular element of dancing. 'Action through music' is an apt description: it is the developing narrative action that interests Gluck, and the music returns to Monteverdian principles in this respect.

167

Gluck uses a method of key-association much more obviously than does Handel, for he is eager that the narrative should be perceived as having an overall unity. Briefly, flat keys are associated with death, Hell, and love lost, while sharp keys are associated with life, Heaven, and love regained. Thus the opening laments for Euridice are in C minor and E flat major; Orfeo's plea for her return is in F major, and Amor's promise of hope brings the first Act to an end in D major. The scene of Orfeo with the Furies is in C minor, E flat major and F minor, and the scene in Elysium with the Blessed Spirits is in F major and its surrounding keys. Act III opens with recitative; Orfeo's famous lament *Che farò* is in C major, while the final celebrations are in D major. But this system of key-associations operates not only on the large-scale but on the small-scale too, in the recitatives.

The following extract is the text to the recitative section in Act I where Orfeo's lamenting is interrupted by the arrival and promise of Amor. The sharps and flats represent the keys to which the music modulates: thus G minor and B flat major are represented by ♭♭ , the former by ♭♭– and the latter by ♭♭ + . It is thus easy to see how the music reflects what lies behind the text, in terms of the polarities of love lost (flat) and love regained (sharp).

ORFEO: Gods, barbarous gods, the pale inhabitants of Acheron and Avernus,	♭ ♭ –
whose hands, greedy for the dead, never hold back from	♭ ♭ ♭+
beauty or youth!	♭ ♭ ♭ ♭ –
You have robbed me of the beautiful	♭ ♭+
Euridice (o cruel memory!) in the flower of her years.	♭ ♭ –
To you I speak, tyrant gods. I have	♭ –
heart enough to search, in the tracks of more intrepid heroes, for my wife and	♮ –
beloved amongst your horrors.	
AMOR (enters): Amor will assist you.	♯–
Orfeo, Jove has pity on your anguish.	♮ –
You are permitted to travel alive through the dark waters of Lethe;	♮ +
Through the dark abysses shall be your path,	♭+
Your singing shall placate Furies, monsters and cruel death.	♭ ♭ –
You shall bring the lovely Euridice back to daylight.	♭ –
ORFEO: What? When? Is it possible?	♭ +
Explain!	♭ ♭ –
AMOR: Have you the courage for this extreme ordeal?	
ORFEO: You promise me Euridice,	♯ ♯+
and wonder if I tremble?	
AMOR: Then know the condition that goes with this.	♯–
ORFEO: Speak it.	
AMOR: At Euridice you are forbidden to	♮+
look until you past the gates of Styx, and ban you may not	♭+

168

reveal. If you do, you	♭ ♭+
lose her, again, and forever.	♭ ♭ ♭−
You shall live lost in unhappiness.	♭ ♭−
Think of this. Farewell. (*Exit*)	♭−
ORFEO: What did he say? What did I hear?	♮+
Shall Euridice live by my side?	♭−
And after so much disquiet, must I then not	♮−
look, nor press her to my breast?	♯−
Unhappy wife? What will she say? What will she think?	♯ ♯−
I foresee her anger	♯−
and feel my own anguish —	♯ ♯ ♯−
merely to think of it makes my	♯ ♯ ♯ ♯−
blood freeze and my heart tremble.	
Yet, I can do it;	♯ ♯ ♯−
I will do it; I am decided.	♯ ♯ ♯ ♯ −
The most intolerable of	♯ ♯ ♯+
ills is to be deprived of that unity of	(♮+)
soul, of the object of one's love.	♭−
Assist me, O Gods!	♯+
I accept your law.	♯ ♯+

Orfeo's forecast of Euridice's reaction is accurate in emotional content, and in key to an extent, but while here he is filled with the hope of love regained, later he is filled with the dread of love lost.

Gluck's structures in *Orfeo ed Euridice* are well-defined. He is clearly thinking in terms of scenes; at the same time his use of structure gives insight into the experiences of the characters. Act I, scene 1 is concerned with Orfeo's reaction to the news of Euridice's death.

Part One: (*a*) The chorus laments, while Orfeo cries 'Euridice!' three times. He, unlike the chorus, is too overcome to verbalize his emotions: he stands apart. The principle of using silence to represent overpowering emotion was used in exactly the same place by Monteverdi: one cannot imagine it occurring in *opera seria.* (*b*) In a short recitative, Orfeo begs the chorus to be silent, to decorate Euridice's grave with flowers, and to leave him here alone. (*c*) A dance follows, during which the grave is decorated. (*d*) The chorus departs, singing a reprise of (*a*), while Orfeo remains silent. This leads into

Part Two: Orfeo sings a simple song whose three stanzas have essentially the same music, the verses separated by short recitatives. Each verse is an image of loneliness: I call for my beloved but she does not reply; I weep for my beloved but only the river replies; I seek my beloved but only Echo replies.

169

The recitatives are moments of outburst, the first one of begging and lament, the second an avowal of his love. The structure here is entirely appropriate to the situation of Orfeo fighting to control his experience: we observed a similar use of freer and more structured music in Peri's Orfeo's response to the same situation. In the end, here, emotion cannot be controlled: after the third verse Orfeo breaks out into an arioso challenge to the gods. (see the extract on p. 168).

Ex. 13   Gluck: *Orfeo ed Euridice*

Orfeo's situation in the opera is focussed in three moments. The first is his initial experience of Euridice's death (expressed in the opening chorus). The second is his song as he arrives in Elysium in Act II (Gluck's equivalent to Monteverdi's '*Possente spirto*'). The third is the song he sings after losing Euridice for the second time, the famous '*Che farò*. . .' The opening musical phrases of these three moments are connected, as is shown in Ex. 13. (a) is the opening chorus, (b) the song in Elysium, and (c) is '*Che farò*'. *The* similarities are too obvious to require explanation.

Gluck's opera is a powerful work: its power lies in its simplicity and grandeur. Nothing is irrelevant; all the parts relate to the whole; the action begins slowly but works up swiftly to the climax in Act III; the music is planned to provide both narrative and overall structure. The aim of Gluck and Calzabigi was simplicity, and this is what they achieved.

But why should they have chosen the Orpheus legend? In relation to previous Orpheus operas we have interpreted the myth in terms of artistic creativity and psychological rebirth. Here the issue is less artistic and more psychological, at first sight. As an allegory of psychological rebirth, the story begins at a traumatic moment and continues by portraying attempts to find a new synthesis between ego and id. We may transplant this interpretation into aesthetic terms: a new synthesis must be found between structure and content. This version of the Orpheus legend does not begin with a happy marriage, but with a situation of separation: as Algarotti maintains, the

170

partnership between text and music has been shattered, and needs to be built anew.

In this sense, the condition imposed upon the partnership is that structure should not seek to dominate expression: Eurydice must work things out for herself. Whatever form expression takes must be drawn from itself, not imposed from outside. Thus Gluck avoids the strictness of *da capo* arias and arranges structures to suit the expression within scenes. The demands that expression makes are aptly symbolized in Euridice's demands on Orfeo; he finally succumbs because, in this interpretation, structure must succumb to expression. But having succumbed, and having gone so far as to suggest that structure must sacrifice itself absolutely to expression, Orfeo is saved by the intervention of Amor, and structure and expression — Apollo and Dionysos — are united.

Once again we see a music-drama operating on several levels. On one level it tells a story, behind which lies an image of psychological rebirth. On a second level it is 'about' music-drama. On a third level the way the story is presented reflects the aesthetic solution portrayed in the story. We have no way of knowing whether Gluck and Calzabigi consciously intended the work to have a single idea permeating its aesthetics, its subject matter and its musico-dramatic structure. To suppose that they did explains the unity of the levels, but one may be reluctant to accept such a hypothesis on the grounds that it makes them appear cold-blooded. At the same time, creativity does involve thought as well as instinct, and we must not assume that the detailed planning of a work of art necessarily precludes any visits from the muses.

There are several ways in which we can regard the overall development of music-drama between Peri's *L'Euridice* and its quasi-resurrection in Gluck's *Orfeo ed Euridice*. Many consider the intervening Baroque opera, culminating in *opera seria*, an aberration, a move away from the essential principles of music-drama into a type of opera whose artificiality stands in the way of immediate dramatic effect. Others see Baroque opera as a triumph for music: all other elements are properly subordinated, and the *da capo* aria provides the essence of music-drama. Some think of Baroque opera as an aristocratic entertainment irrelevant to the rest of us; some regard it approvingly or disapprovingly as a glorification of vocal viruosity.

Let us take a more objective view. *Opera seria* is very much a product of its time: the virtuosity, the *da capo* aria, the ethical motivation of the characters all spring from baroque problems and ideas. Absolutism, rhetoric, and extravagance all contribute to its outer forms, and the inherent tension between expression and content in the *da capo* aria is a product of the clash between baroque and classical. But behind its outer forms, *opera seria* contains the same elements as all music-drama: it is a means to explore the otherwise inexplicable, and it provides through music a direct entry into the

171

human experiences that lie behind the events of the plot.

Between Monteverdi and Handel we can see a growing emphasis on *ceremonial music-drama*, perhaps at the expense of *narrative* and *enthusiasm:* Apollo's shadow grows longer. By the time of *opera seria, narrative,* apparently, is sacrificed to single moments of *ceremonial* and *enthusiasm.* With Gluck we return to a more obvious emphasis on *narrative* and *enthusiasm,* with *ceremonial* now applied to long-term structure. Here Dionysos, perhaps, has the slightly upper hand.

Peri's *L'Euridice* looked back to Greece for inspiration: so too did Gluck's *Orfeo ed Euridice,* to a certain extent, but it was a reforming of opera and not a rebirth of Greek tragedy. The musico-dramatic conditions of 1762 were different from those of 1600, not least in that comic music-drama was flourishing and offering alternatives to the sort of music-drama we have discussed so far.

6　Comic music-drama

So far we have concentrated upon 'serious' music-drama; 'comedy' has received only passing reference. During the eighteenth century, however, comic opera developed into a *genre* in its own right, and it is neither possible nor proper to continue an analysis of opera as music-drama after the time of Gluck without examining the nature of comedy.

Comedy and tragedy
The traditional visual symbols for tragedy and comedy are two masks. The tragic mask wears an expression of lament or despair, while that of the comic mask is of confident glee. One weeps; the other laughs.

The first point to be made is that both are masks: both are images which transform reality, according to particular points of view. The face inside the mask, that of the human being, remains the same. Man adopts one mask or the other, according to his mood, but does so in order to explore the same essential human problems that drama and music-drama have always explored.

Right from the start man has used image-making as a way to discover the hidden meaning of life. Music-drama was born out of the attempt to understand a mystery, the mystery of life versus death, the transient versus the eternal. To have perceived the mystery at all is the most curious thing about man; at some point in the past it occurred to him that there might be a reality other than the reality of his everyday life. This thought, which seems to have become deeply ingrained in the mind of man, sets up a conflict between the reality he knows and its alternative. Music-drama has been and is an exploration of this conflict. Its plots are concerned with dilemma and choice and the consequences of choice, with the aspiration towards something beyond everyday reality, the demands of that everyday reality, and the tension between the two: it is about Man, stretched between earth and heaven.

We may distinguish between tragedy and comedy by saying that tragedy

173

engages our sympathy towards aspiration, while comedy points out the difficulties involved in breaking free of earth. Thus a tragic ending brings us the joy of having shared a character's aspiration, and the grief of realizing the truth that in the end he and we are earthbound, while comedy continually reminds us of our earthly nature, but finally, in the 'happy' ending, reassures us that conflict can be resolved. The tragic plot builds to the cathartic moment when a higher truth dominates lower truth: the Persians hear it from the lips of Darius' terrible ghost, Oedipus discovers the terrible truth himself, Pentheus is lost in the truth of Dionysos' terrible power. The moment is one of terror and dread as we see what we could not or would not see before. The comic plot proceeds rather differently: although it may build up to a climax it proceeds (generally speaking) through a series of small-scale crescendos and climaxes in individual scenes and moments. And the comic climax, on the large or small scale, is not a straightforward move away from reality, but a sudden double-perception of reality itself.

We can illustrate comic structure — 'single-meaning' building up to 'double-meaning' — by examining two comic moments. (I beg the reader's indulgence: the comic effect will inevitably and unfortunately be spoilt by analysis.) The first is a line spoken by Lady Bracknell in Wilde's *The Importance of Being Earnest*.

> To lose one parent, Mr Worthing, may be regarded as a misfortune; to lose both looks like carelessness.[1]

Here the first perception, of Mr Worthing having 'lost' one of his parents, arouses our sympathy, because we interpret the word 'lost' to mean that fate or death has intervened and Mr Worthing is a victim. The final phrase however gives a second interpretation to the word 'lose', that of misplacing something; we see Mr Worthing not as a victim but as a fool. This clash of meanings — Mr Worthing is a victim, Mr Worthing is a fool — is something that confuses our emotions; our sympathy is both engaged and disengaged. Because our emotions cannot switch as quickly as our thoughts, the emotional tension aroused in the first half of the sentence explodes into laughter.[2]

A similar process takes place in the second example, which comes not from dramatic literature but from common parlance, and which betrays the prejudices of the English culture in which it was born.

> Have you heard about the Irish woman who broke her leg ironing the curtains? She fell out of the window.

Here the double-meaning, or, as Koestler terms it, bisociation, is between our initial assumption that anyone ironing curtains would take them down and put them on an ironing-board, and the realization forced abruptly on us that the woman approached the problem of ironing curtains in a different

174

way. Actually, the woman's solution is a fine example of what de Bono calls 'lateral thinking';[3] it is not itself a totally absurd solution. But the joke pre-empts our accepting her solution as a good one by announcing from the start that it did not work — she broke her leg — and this information is given before we know of the problem or its solution. Furthermore, our possible sympathy for the woman who broke her leg is pre-empted by our being told she is Irish; whom the English like to regard as possessing natural stupidity. The joke could of course be applied to any 'outside' group. A further level of comedy is provided by our imagined vision of the woman on top of a pair of steps, believing she has found the right solution. Her pride and confidence lead however to catastrophe: the high and mighty are brought low. This joke (which must by now have been almost completely destroyed) therefore works on a number of levels; they combine to produce one basic process: expectation — clash of meaning — explosion of tension.

Several elements in this Irish joke show the close relationship between comedy and tragedy. Firstly, the situation described is actually tragic for the woman: were our sympathies for her sustained, we would indeed see it as a tragedy. In other words, the line between tragic and comic is a matter of how our emotions are engaged or disengaged. This is often shown when, in tragedy, something occurs to disengage our sympathy. Let us imagine the climax of Shakespeare's *Othello*: Othello stands by the bed of the sleeping Desdemona, about to smother her and her infidelity with the pillow. Suddenly, he gets a fit of hiccups. 'Put out the light . . . hic! . . . and then put out . . . hic! . . . the light . . . hic!' It would take the greatest actor in the world to prevent the audience bursting into laughter. The hiccups disengage our emotions: we cannot cope with the possibility that Othello suffers indigestion (the normal world) while he speaks Shakespeare's rolling pentameters (the world of heroic image). A more trivial illustration of the narrow line between tragedy and comedy can be seen by comparing similar scenes in two 'dramas'. In *Götterdämmerung,* Siegfried is speared in the back by Hagen, and Wagner sustains our emotional involvement through the scene of Siegfried's final reminiscence of Brünnhilde and his Funeral March: Siegfried's death has the emotional effect of tragedy. In one of the James Bond spy-films, a character is gruesomely killed by being shot in the chest with a spear from a harpoon-gun. Lest we become involved sympathetically with the character, the script-writer and director switch to a shot of James Bond, who murmurs 'I think he got the point.' The pun on the word 'point' explodes our tension; our emotions are disengaged.

Just as a tragic situation can easily become comic, so a comic situation can become tragic, and here a more complicated set of emotions is aroused. Let us suppose we are watching a film of a fat man walking down the street, behaving pompously; he suddenly steps on a banana-skin. His feet are swept from under him and he is reduced to an undignified heap on the pavement.

175

We laugh: the comic event is archetypal. However, it transpires that the man has actually injured his back: he cannot move, and lies there screaming in pain. The situation is no longer 'funny', but, although we may recognize its new seriousness, we may still have difficulty in stifling our laughter. We may know we ought to compose our faces into an expression of sympathy — indeed, we probably feel sympathy — but somehow the absurdity of the initial downfall of pomposity persists. We are in the midst of a complicated experience in which we perceive the tragic moment and the comic moment simultaneously, and the urge to laugh tends to dominate our sensitivities, perhaps because the bisociation between the comic and the tragic sets up new tensions which explode in laughter.

A second elementary connection between comedy and tragedy is shown in the joke about the Irish woman, admittedly on a trivial level. Two possible ways of ironing curtains are proposed in the joke, and the clash of the two makes us see the problem, however briefly, in a new light. This phenomenon is the same as that which takes place in creativity, whether artistic or scientific: out of the clash of two different ways of looking at a single problem is born a new idea. One thinks of Archimedes' shout of 'Eureka' as he discovers a truth about mass and volume; his discovery occurs through his applying scientific thought-processes to something as ordinary as climbing into a bath of water. Such a moment of discovery is irrational (although de Bono argues that a secondary type of 'rational' thought is employed). The solution hits blindingly: it is there without warning. The inexplicability of the sudden dawning of truth is a phenomenon experienced in tragedy: however well we and Oedipus might be prepared for the truth about his parentage, the moment of realization is still shattering. Thus it is that comic bisociation can communicate 'truth' in the same way as the cathartic moment in tragedy.

The ability of comedy to stretch the mind in this way can be shown in several examples. The first is a cartoon by Charles Addams, which shows rows of audience in a darkened cinema. Every member of the audience has tears streaming down his or her face, except one man, who is grinning from ear to ear. The effect is comic, an obvious bisociation between the overall picture and one single, contrary element. At the same time the cartoon arouses questions: what sort of man is he? What conditions could produce these contradictory reactions? Charles Addams is a 'horror'-cartoonist, and this scene sends a shiver through us, for it raises questions to which the answers are horrifying. Another cartoon, this time by Gerard Hoffnung, and called 'Jazz', shows a man playing a saxophone: out of the bell rises the figure of a girl in a tight, revealing dress, with a look of invitation in her eyes. The comedy lies in the bisociation between our knowledge that musical sounds are what come out of a saxophone, and the fact that we see the girl. The mind is stretched into exploring the association between jazz and sex.

One of the most fundamental comic devices is that of disguise. In comic plays, characters often deliberately disguise themselves as other people; the important thing is that the audience should know that the disguise has occurred. We know that X is really Y, although some characters in the play do not. The effect is comic, not just through dramatic irony (we know more than the characters) but because a permanent bisociation is set up. Yet it is more than just comic, for it raises questions about what individual identity really is. Someone whom we know to have a certain look and certain behavioural characteristics adopts other features and characteristics convincingly enough to fool other characters on the stage. Our emotions are continually divided between seeing things from the point of view of the person fooled, and seeing things from the point of view of our knowledge of the disguise.

In fact, the idea of disguise and pretence is not necessarily comic at all. In Handel's *opere serie* it is usual for at least one character to be in disguise, and the revelation of true identity does not necessarily have a comic effect. Furthermore, acting itself is a matter of disguise, and disguise-situations on the stage can create complexities beyond the action. In both Mozart's *Le Nozze di Figaro* and Richard Strauss' *Der Rosenkavalier* a female singer plays the part of a boy, who during the opera takes on the disguise of a girl. Interestingly enough, in good performances of these operas, we accept the initial girl-playing-boy disguise, and only really notice the girl/boy-disguised-as-girl pretence. At the same time, it is our very willingness to suspend disbelief, to accept the essential pretence of drama, that enables disguise as comic device to work. A man dressed up as a woman is acceptable on the stage in a way he/she might not be in the street. To see the latter may send a shiver of horror through us, for we are not prepared to question reality when we are living in it: the basic pretence of the stage provides an opportunity for the imagination to operate more freely on the implications of transvestism.

Disguise essentially makes the point that things are not always what they seem to be. It raises that same possibility of an alternative reality which lies at the basis of tragedy. Comedy is absurd, an irrational bringing together of things which do not belong together. But to see the essential absurdity of human life is the starting point of Existentialism, as described by Camus in *L'Étranger* and Sartre in *La Nausée*. In works such as these the tightrope between comedy and horror is stretched taut: the characters inhabit a world which combines the frozen moment of comic bisociation and the frozen moment of tragic catharsis. The mind is on the brink of reality, unsure, trembling, trying to understand. A passage such as the following from *L'Étranger* hovers between comedy, tragedy and enlightenment. The speaker, Meursault, is in the funeral parlour of an old people's home: his mother has died. He sits in vigil, and dozes off.

177

I was awakened by an odd rustling in my ears. After having had my eyes closed, I had a feeling that the light had grown even stronger than before. There wasn't a trace of shadow anywhere, and every object, each curve or angle, scored its outline on one's eyes. The old people, Mother's friends, were coming in. I counted ten in all, gliding almost soundlessly through the bleak white glare. None of the chairs creaked when they sat down. Never in my life had I seen anyone so clearly as I saw these people; not a detail of their clothes or features escaped me. And yet I couldn't hear them, and it was hard to believe they really existed.

Nearly all the women wore aprons, and the strings drawn tight round their waists made their big stomachs bulge still more. I'd never yet noticed what big paunches old women usually have. Most of the men, however, were thin as rakes, and they all carried sticks. What struck me most about their faces was that one couldn't see their eyes, only a dull glow in a sort of nest of wrinkles.

On sitting down, they looked at me, and wagged their heads awkwardly, sucking their lips in between their toothless gums. I couldn't decide if they were greeting me and trying to say something, or if it was due to some infirmity of age. I inclined to think that they were greeting me, after their fashion, but it had a queer effect, seeing all those old fellows grouped round the porter, solemnly eyeing me and dandling their heads from side to side. For a moment I had an absurd impression that they had come to sit in judgement on me.[4]

The scene, and Meursault's comments, are not just comic or tragic, but rather both. His experience is similar to the one we have in the theatre, a state of heightened perception in which even the most trivial things seem to be important. It is a state beyond comedy or tragedy, an eternal moment of hovering on the edge of laughter or tears.

Meursault's problem is that neither tears nor laughter ever come. In tragedy and comedy they do: emotional tension is released as we succeed in uniting the two forces that draw us up and drag us down. It is this notion of unity that brings us to our final distinction between and similarity between tragedy and comedy.

Tragedy draws us up from the reality of everyday to a higher reality, but at the climax reminds us of what we wish to escape. Comedy reminds us of the reality we know and at the climax (of the scene, or the joke) suddenly makes us look at that reality from a new point of view. This is essentially what music-drama has always been about: solving the problem of here-and-now (life) by wondering about nowhere and no-when (death). The ritual music-drama of primitive man arose out of moments when the two worlds of life and death interacted; he sought to explain the connection by reproducing that interaction. In their different ways, comedy and tragedy attempt to do the same thing. Both aim at reconciling the factual and the possible, tragedy by fusion in the cathartic moment, in which the possible dominates the factual, and comedy through fission in the comic climax, in which the factual and possible clash like cymbals.

Michael Tippett suggests[5] that comedy is always concerned with 'the barriers to marriage'. This is generally true on the level of what comic plots are superficially about, but it is also true on a deeper level. Marriage is an image of unity and integration, and the comic plot which deals with attempts to bring together a man and a woman despite circumstantial difficulties is an image of man's attempt to bring together the factual and the possible. Often, in a comic plot, the successful overcoming of difficulties in the final scene seems to be less than convincing, and one is inclined to think that the marriage between hero and heroine might not be as perfect as one would hope. Thus the marriage between Count Almaviva and Rosina in Beaumarchais' *Le Barbier de Séville* turns out to have been a misalliance in *Le Mariage de Figaro*; and, despite their reunion at the end of that story, one suspects that the future may hold further problems for them. It is in this sense that comedy is concerned with the barriers rather than the marriage: the plot pivots upon the desire to achieve marriage, but the desire is seldom shown to be properly achieved. The cymbals clash, but rebound apart.

Both tragedy and comedy are rooted in human experience. We continually aspire to the heights, but we also know we cannot easily achieve them. In the end, the terms tragedy and comedy lose their meaning, for both are concerned with the same thing: aspiration and downfall. That is one reason why great drama and great music-drama can make us want to weep and laugh at the same time.

Though tragedy and comedy may have the same goal, they approach it by different paths. Comedy essentially concentrates on everyday reality: in consequence comic characters tend to be more realistic (though not necessarily more *real*) than tragic characters. The action of comic plots too tends to concentrate upon contemporary and everyday events, often those occurring in ordinary houses rather than in palaces. A comic text tends to be written in everyday speech rather than in elevated poetic language. Imagery is often earthly rather than heavenly; sexual and scatological humour have the effect of reminding us of our earthbound nature.

These tendencies, when they appear in comic music-drama, have an important and inevitable effect on the role of music. Music is by its very nature the language of an alternative reality: it therefore has an awkward relationship to the sort of drama which makes its effects in terms of everyday reality. Musical images have the function of universalizing the specific: comedy makes its effects by means of a bisociation of specifics. Comic characters exist in a world where everyday reality has become a dramatic image, and comedy depends for its effect on the presentation of that dramatic image, which music can all too easily replace with something else. Music, moreover, has a sustaining function. Musical sounds create their own time continuum, which is different from the time continuum of everyday reality, and usually slower. A comic text whose dialogue proceeds at a

179

naturalistic pace can completely lose its effect if it is sung.

This is not to say that music has no role to play in comedy. Certain types of music, whose simplicity makes them easily and swiftly absorbed, interact with the speed and realism of comedy in a thoroughly effective way. But the use of more complicated textures and musical sounds — such as are generally used in tragic music-drama — may be more difficult to relate to the world of comedy. Here music's role is inevitably restricted to moments where an alternative reality asserts itself, and has time to assert itself. In *Le Nozze di Figaro*, for instance, Mozart keeps a tight rein on the humour in the final scene. Here the Count discovers a whole bevy of hidden witnesses to his foolish amorous exploits. Music could only present this succession of farcical revelations in a superficial way (orchestral gasps of surprise, absurd juxtapositions of chord or textures, vocal 'laughter' and the like) and Mozart wishes instead to build to a climax that music can penetrate and reveal: the final confrontation between the Count and the Countess when he asks her forgiveness and she grants it. Although this is the climax of the entire comic opera, there is nothing 'funny' about it at all, for the music is not witty here, but as deadly serious as the Count and Countess.

Comic music-drama certainly existed in the time of the Greeks, if not before. In the seventeenth century we can find examples in Lully's works, and in occasional scenes in tragic opera. But 'comic opera' really came into its own in the eighteenth century, perhaps because recitative and aria offered an extremely appropriate variety of forms to meet the different demands of comedy and music. In recitative, naturalistic dialogue could be sung without disturbing its pace; the aria was a means to explore a sustained moment of emotional tension. In fact, in *opera buffa* a third musico-dramatic ingredient was developed, the ensemble, by means of which the two could be brought together in the form of an exploration of the developing situations of various characters simultaneously. Until the eighteenth century, however, music's role in comedy was considerably less important than it was in tragedy.

Aristophanes and Menander

The earliest extant Western European comedies are those of Aristophanes. He lived from about 445 B.C. to after 388 B.C., and of his forty-four plays eleven have survived. His working life coincided with the last twenty years of Euripides, whom he frequently attacked for turning tragedy from morality to cleverness, and with the Peloponnesian War, which forms the subject-matter for many of his plays. As with tragedy in the case of Aeschylus, comedy appears to emerge suddenly with the plays of Aristophanes: we know little of his predecessors.

Comedy was established as a *genre* for dramatic competitions at the Great Dionysia in 486, approximately fifty years after the establishment of tragedy. Why there was a delay is difficult to determine: perhaps it was thought inappropriate at first to include works with such an obviously secular approach to life in what was essentially a religious festival, although, bearing in mind Greek attitudes to religion, this argument is not altogether convincing. Perhaps the introduction of comic drama was a product of the relaxation that must have followed the successful defeat of the Persian army at Marathon in 490; perhaps, indeed, it was captured Persians who introduced comic drama to Athens.[6] The particular origins of Athenian comedy are not important: what is important is that comic drama as such must have had its origins in the distant past.

Comedy, like tragedy, has its ultimate source in the special experiences of man and men, and we might seek for its beginnings in those occasions when circumstances occurred that might have prompted primitive man to laugh. Imagine, for instance, the hunter who disappears beneath a herd of stampeding buffalo. His fellows see the herd rush over him; the rumble of hooves fades into the distnace. Then, out of the swirling dust, emerges the man, stumbling slightly, but unscathed. The bisociation between what his fellows had expected and what they see would surely lead to laughter. The explanation of how and why such an 'accident' happened would have given the tribe, later, pause for thought: was that particular hunter especially favoured by the buffalo gods? Did he have some special magical power? Was the incident planned by the gods to reveal some truth about the man or about buffalo? Of course, there was a 'rational' explanation: the man had fallen into a hollow in the ground which protected him, but that only raises the questions of why the hollow was there and whether circumstances and events were not still guided by the gods.

Perhaps, in an attempt to understand the incident, or to describe it to the other members of the tribe not present when it happened, the hunters re-enacted the story of The Man who Wasn't Trampled by the Buffalo. Perhaps they were able to do it so imaginatively that, although the audience knew the man would survive (they had seen him return from the hunt) they were able to share in the astonishment of his fellows. Perhaps they, too, laughed.

Let us take another example. The tribe prepares for a buffalo-dance. The 'actors' don their buffalo robes and appear on the dancing-ground. The drums strike up and the ritual begins. And then something goes wrong: anyone who has taken part in drama of any kind knows that things can go wrong. Perhaps someone stumbles, and accidentally trips up one of his fellows. Perhaps a buffalo mask slips to the side of a performer's head, or falls off. Perhaps one of the performers finds it difficult to keep in time. Perhaps a deadly or dangerous insect gets trapped inside a costume and the performer becomes more interested in getting rid of it than in performing the ritual. Any of these incidents could produce laughter from those observ-

181

ing: a visual bisociation has occurred.

What of the man to whom these incidents occur? Suppose he discovers he becomes popular when other people laugh at him. Suppose he is 'accident-prone', one of those people who cannot walk down a path without stumbling over his own feet. Might he not be tempted to exploit his ability (or inability)? And suppose someone else in the tribe imitates him in order to shift popularity to himself. The wish to be admired is age-old in man: there is no reason why a primitive man should not discover that his ability to imitate actions which provoke laughter arouses the admiration of his fellows.

It was probably early in his history that man discovered the potential humour and potentially serious implications of 'accident'. Indeed, the spiritual and creative leader of the tribe, the shaman, might well have deliberately used laughter-provoking 'accident' for serious purposes. There is evidence that shamans were practical jokers,[7] and their practical jokes presumably had some ultimately serious intent. A practical joke is often played on someone in order to make the victim perceive a truth through the eventual realization of comic bisociation. It also often relies on other people being 'in the know'; they too share a bisociative awareness: the practical joke is the source of dramatic irony. The essential atmosphere of both is the superiority felt by those in the know over him who does not know: the latter is an outsider-victim, the former are insiders. Here again we see the emotional shift: the victim of tragedy is a victim for whom we feel sympathy; the victim of comedy does not arouse our sympathy.

Thus comedy is often directed at the person who is not a member of the in-group; the man who suffers from physical deformity, for instance. Often, as Rigoletto suggests, the only way for the physically (or mentally) deformed to become accepted as members of the community is for them to encourage others to see them as butts of humour. The village idiot, the hump-backed man, even the town drunk, are all images of comedy; they are also, often, images of incomprehensible wisdom; legend and literature are full of examples of the wise simpleton, or the clever dwarf.

Wisdom can often be presented in a comic disguise. Alexander the Great is reported to have made a special trip to visit the famous philosopher Diogenes, whom he admired, and who lived in a barrel. Alexander respectfully asked the worthy sage if there was any service the mighty Emperor might do for him. 'Just one thing,' replied Diogenes. 'Would you move out of my sunshine?' It is hardly the request we or Alexander would expect, but the unexpectedness of it only adds to its wisdom. And just as the sage's perception of the world and its values has comic overtones, so a comic writer's or actor's jokes often have undertones of wisdom.

All these ingredients — meaningful accident, comic imitation, laughter at a victim, and at deformity, the prod of simple wisdom — are present in the comedies of Aristophanes, but had their origins in the natural humour and delight in pretence of man. Aristophanes' plays also contain two other ingredients of importance: political satire and sexual humour.

Aristophanes was sharply critical of particular Athenian politicians, and of the conduct of the Peloponnesian War. The personal criticisms he makes in his plays would, nowadays, immediately provoke libel and slander actions, but through them all he holds a consistent attitude, opposing corruption, the misuse of power, and, on many occasions, the self-destructiveness of the war itself. Three of the eleven surviving plays (*The Acharnians, Peace* and *Lysistrata*) are concerned with ways of making peace with Sparta. Five plays are concerned with important political issues: *The Knights* deals with the political activities of Cleon, leader of the pro-war faction in Athens, who also appears in *The Wasps*, which deals with the issue of payment for public service. *The Clouds* attacks Socrates' educational methods, and *Lysistrata, Thesmophoriazusae* and *Ecclesiazusae* discuss feminism. Both this last play and *The Birds* propose alternative societies. It is worth noting, in relation to the broader issue of censorship, that although Aristophanes' plays are in general severely critical of the government, they were performed under the auspices of the state Dionysia. Contemporary figures were included as characters in many of the plays, presented in a most unflattering light: Cleon himself in *The Knights* and *The Wasps*, Socrates in *The Clouds*, and Euripides (one of Aristophanes' favourite targets) in *The Acharnians, Thesmophoriazusae* and *The Frogs*. Dramatic satire is, in some respects, a safe way to criticize a government: there is always the ultimate defence that it is only a play. Political satire is also a method guaranteed to win an audience's sympathy for one's play: no one governs without arousing some complaint. But on the whole Aristophanes' satire is written not just for its own sake: he is urging his audience to consider political and philosophical issues in a new light.

In *The Birds* Aristophanes proposes an alternative society. Pisthetaerus and Euelpides, weary of life in Athens, climb up to the kingdom of the birds, and persuade the birds to recognize that they are in a position to hold the balance of power between the gods and men. Their arguments fall on receptive ears. The birds block off the sacrificial smoke from rising to the gods, who are thus starved into submission, and give up their authority for a spoonful of stew. A poet, a priest, a civil servant, lawyer and a soothsayer ascend from earth, hoping to exploit the inhabitants of the new kingdom, but are swiftly disposed of. Finally, Pisthetaerus consolidates his position in a marriage ceremony with Iris, daughter of Zeus.

The play is essentially a utopian fantasy, full of humour, topical reference and spectacle. But it also has its serious side. Much of the action is contained in fast, witty dialogue (presumably spoken) but the choral passages for the birds (undoubtedly sung) are lyrical and sustained, and not aimed at evoking laughter. Here the text is written (appropriately enough) in a more elevated

183

style and presents the serious theme of the play. In the central choral passage, the chorus begins by addressing its female *aulòs*-playing accompanist, who has just entered to the admiring and suggestive comments of Pisthetaerus and Euelpides.

CHORUS

Golden one, beloved!
O fairest of birds to me,
Playmate, mistress of melody,
Late, so late, thou appearest.
Come, my own, my dearest,
Sound thy silvery flute to sing
Songs in tune with the voice of spring,
Music poured from thy heart to bring
Charm to verse anapaestic.

Dim creatures of earth, who attain unto birth like leaves, in blind fecundation,
Ye men of a day, frail figures of clay, mere phantoms in wild agitation,
Ungifted with wings, poor suffering things whose life is a vision diurnal,
I beg you, attend unto us, the unending, the truly and only eternal,
Who airily fly, and the years defy, whose thoughts are the thoughts of the ages.[8]

The birds explain their ancestry, the way men depend on them to show the passage of seasons, and point out their importance to sacrifices. They continue:

If, then, you will only believe us divine,
We shall serve you as prophets and musical Nine.
The winds and the weather, in spring, in fall,
In winter and summer, will be at your call.
Nor ever, like Zeus, will we sit on a cloud,
Indulging in lofty disdain of the crowd;
But, near you, we'll see that the life of each one —
Both you and your wife and your son and *his* son —
Is a round of good fun.
With health, with wealth, with peace and with play,
Youth, laughter, and dances, and banquetings — yea,
Bird's milk for your breakfast — I venture to say
That, embarrassed with riches, fatigued, blasé,
You will pray
For a stay
Of good fortune!

Muse of the woodland
(*Tio tio tio tiotinx*),
Changeful ever is thy singing,
Through the valleys and hilltops ringing

(*Tio tio tio tiotinx*),
Where, amid greenery tresses beside thee I raise
(*Tio tio tio tiotinx*)
From my fawn-yellow throat, in melodious praise,
Hymns unto Pan of the forests and fountains,
Dances to Rhea, the Queen of the mountains
(*Tototo tototo totototinx*),
Whence, like honey-bee from flower,
Phrynichus drank, in my lyrical bower,
Nectar so sweet that its savor
All his song doth flavor
(*Tio tio tio tiotinx*).[9]

They invite men to join them in their new kingdom, to lead a life free from
the strains of life in Athens, and conclude:

Such was the music
(*Tio tio tio tiotinx*)
Made by swans for Phoebus' greeting,
Quire of voices and pinions beating
(*Tio tio tio tiotinx*).
Wafted afar from the moors above Maritza's bed
(*Tio tio tio tiotinx*),
To the clouds of high heaven the melody sped.
Beasts of the wilds were crouching in wonder;
Breathless, the billows were quenching their thunder
(*Tototo tototo totototinx*).
Gods were awed. Olympus' portal
Rang, when the Muses and Graces immortal
Sang, to the birds replying,
Hail! Hosanna! crying
(*Tio tio tio tiotinx*).

Naught is better, naught more pleasant, than to grow a pair of wings.
At the theater, for instance, they'd be quite convenient things.
Bored with tragedies, and hungry . . . never mind, you needn't stay;
You could wing it home, eat luncheon in a comfortable way,
Then, replete, fly back among us for a comic matinée.
If a Patrocleides present got the gripes, would he in pain
Sit here sweating? Not a moment! Up he'd soar with might and main,
Blow off steam with sighs of rapture, and cavort back here again.
Or an ardent lover, haply, is on tenterhooks because
Down in front he spies her husband, seated with the Senators.
Well, he'd ruffle up his feathers and away from you he'd go;
Then, when he had loved his lady, back he'd fly to see the show.
Are not wings a priceless blessing? 'Tis as plain as plain can be.[10]

The birds advocate liberation. Briefly, the tragic vision is evoked: the idea of man aspiring beyond his earthbound existence. Man is seen from the viewpoint of an alternative reality. He is described as blind, frail, transient and doomed to suffer. He is encouraged to don wings, to share in the eternal life of the birds, which will bring him a life of pleasure instead of suffering. Birdsong itself is praise of the great mother-goddess and of Pan, the primitive nature-deity.

In short, this chorus provides a serious counterpart to the comic plot. Pisthetaerus and Euelpides are seeking an alternative reality and a renewing of their lives in practical terms; the chorus of birds here proposes the same in spiritual terms: a Dionysiac rebirth. But the chorus is set in the comic context: the final lines bring us back to practical matters, offering the possibility of the wings of imagination and wish actually becoming available to the Athenian in the theatre audience. They cannot be: and the tragic vision is abruptly bisociated into comedy.

The transition back from the tragic world is achieved by means of three jokes. One is at the expense of tragedy, one is scatological, and one makes reference to sex. The anti-tragic joke here is, in context, self-mockery, a deflation of the pretensions of the chorus. The imagery of all three jokes is ascent and travel followed by descent and return, an instant image of the aspiration of tragedy and the comic return to reality. The scatological and sexual references have the same effect, for they remind us of our basic biological functions, which the aspiring tragic character in all of us would like to forget. 'Dirty' jokes and 'blue' jokes are frequent in comedy, for this reason: they oppose the spiritual by reference to the physical.

The actor in Aristophanes' comedies wore a padded costume with a large artificial phallus. Sexual references therefore were not coy but, rather, open to graphic illustration. In *Lysistrata,* for instance, much is made of the frustration of the men who are denied sexual satisfaction by their wives; the actors' costumes were able to make this explicit. For 'official' drama to include such sexual explicitness may seem odd to us; it shows that the Greeks had a more open attitude to sex than ourselves, and lends support to the theory that Dionysos-worship was an important source of Greek music-drama.

The defeat of Athens at the end of the Peloponnesian War brought about changes in the city. The old boisterousness and arrogant confidence wavered, to be replaced with a tamer sobriety. Athenians became less concerned with political and philosophical issues and more interested in trade, the pursuit of wealth, and family life. A bourgeois culture evolved. By Alexander's time, the Old Comedy of Aristophanes had given way to the New Comedy, of which Menander (343–292) was the leading exponent. Here comedy is cleaned up and sentimentalized and sticks firmly to the everyday world. Aristophanes' fantasy, vulgarity and boisterousness are purged: the comedy of manners is born. The chorus no longer plays an important role. Plots are tightly knit rather than expansive and have the general theme of romantic love battling against the barriers to marriage. Characters tend to be types: the pseudo-heroic lover and his beloved, whose naiveté and purity are almost unbelievable, the suspicious, touchy and misanthropic old man, the intriguing servant, and the cowardly braggart. Much is made of disguises and misunderstandings and practical jokes. The actors no longer wear the extravagant costumes of Old Comedy, but contemporary everyday dress.

Menander wrote over a hundred plays: eight won the prize for comedy. Only one has been preserved complete — *Dyskolos,* discovered in Egypt in 1957; the remainder are available only in fragments and in Roman adaptations. Music played very little part in Menander's plays: they can hardly be termed music-dramas. Nevertheless they were very influential upon Roman writers, particularly Terence, and this influence was passed on to the reborn literary comedy of the seventeenth and eighteenth centuries.

The bawdiness and satire of Aristophanes and the character-types of Menander passed through Rome into the groups of travelling comedians of the European Middle Ages, and thus to the *Commedia dell'Arte*, which provided the foundations of both 'modern' pantomime and 'modern' farce. The same sources led to *opera buffa,* where music made its reappearance, to make reborn comic music-drama.

The Commedia dell'Arte

The *Commedia dell'Arte* (Comedy of the Masks) came into prominence in Italy during the second half of the sixteenth century. It was, essentially, comic drama, improvised to specified plots by stock, masked characters. Its origins seem to lie in the Atellan farces of the Roman theatre, but connections are difficult to prove. We know there were groups of 'mummers' — mimers — throughout the Middle ages, but the exact nature of their drama is not clear. In any event, during the early sixteenth cetury in Italy the popular Roman comedies of Plautus — themselves strongly influenced by Aristophanes — were resurrected in translation, and these, performed by comic actors with a talent for improvisation, seem to have been the spark that set alight the *Commedia dell'Arte* tradition. It was to last until the late eighteenth century, when more organized forms of comedy took its place.

There were six stock male characters in the *Commedia dell'Arte*. Three were 'zanni': Arlecchino, Pulcinella, and Brighella, and three were 'old men': Pantalone, the Doctor, and the Captain. Each had his own qualities: Pulcinella his cruelty and cynicism (Punch of 'Punch and Judy'), Arlecchino his acrobatics, Brighella his self-interested intriguing, Pantalone his miserliness, touchiness and gullibility, the Doctor his excessive dignity and pedantry, and the Captain his extravagant boasting. Descendants of these

187

characters can be found in many eighteenth-century comedies and comic music-dramas.

Other characters were involved in the *Commedia* plots too: the female servant Colombina, lady *inamorate* like Isabella, gossipy old women, dashing, fatuous male lovers, often ridiculously naïve, and occasional extras like Tartaglia the stuttering lawyer.

Commedia plots were drawn from a variety of sources, often reflecting or parodying more serious dramatic forms of the day. They might be based on Classical comedies, or Renaissance versions of them; they might be based on pastoral drama, even on tragic themes. The scenarios, which are all that was written down, preserve some of the hilarious details of these plots. Conventionally, the list of characters was followed by a list of properties: the following is the list of characters and properties required for one *Commedia pastorale* entitled *La Maga,* or *The Enchantress:*[11]

('Serious' characters)
Jove
Enchantress
Spirit
Uranio, Sireno (shepherds)
Clori, Filli (nymphs)

('Comic' characters)
Pantalone
Gratiano
Coradellino
Zanni

Chorus of nymphs and shepherds

Properties
A ray of lightning; sausage; cudgel; cords; two bladders; a ladder; plate of macaroni; grotto; rock to open; tree to drop fruit; artificial fire; fountain.

The main ingredients in the *Commedia* plays were the typical ingredients of farce: practical jokes, intrigue, satire, disguise and mistaken identity, and vulgarity. Added to these were love and acrobatics, pathos and juggling, raised hopes, dropped trousers, awkwardness, grace, gluttony, seduction, magic, compromise, discovery, topical reference, mock funerals, animals, recipes, men dressed as women, women dressed as men, both dressed as birds or animals, blows, kicks, thunderstorms, and occasional moments of compelling drama.

The role which music played in the *Commedia* seems to have varied from troupe to troupe. With the Italian troupe in Paris it was evidently of considerable importance, and the French *Commedia* was a great influence in the development of *opéra comique.* In other countries and groups it may have been less important, but it is evident that the typical *Commedia* performance included at least several songs. The *Recueil Fossard*, only recently discovered, contains engravings of French *Commedia* scenes from the reign of Henry III in the mid-sixteenth century. Some of these engravings show music being performed, the texts being printed beneath.

In one engraving, for instance[12] three figures are shown: Harlequin and 'Il Segnor Pantalon' with books of music, and 'Zany Corneto' playing the viol. All three are standing in formal poses.

HARLEQUIN:	Let us sing, Pantalone, this song well;
	If you would gain your lovely mistress,
	The certain way to get her in the end
	Is to be a *museau de chien* (a dog's nose), that's a
	mu-si-cian
CORNETO:	Let us three be in harmony, that we may
	Send her to sleep to the sweet sound of my lyre;
	And though, like you, I never learned to read,
	That won't stop me playing eagerly.
PANTALON:	Be brave, my friends, I'm singing the bass
	Of this delightful trio, composed for my lady,
	The sweetness of my voice will pierce her soul,
	For my part is neither crooked nor hump-backed.

The interesting feature of this (besides its vulgarity) is that the song is, apparently, both a part of the plot (a serenade to Pantalone's *inamorata*) and a comment on the situation. The delightful comic situation of three vulgar comedians assembling formally as if to delivery a concert is further bisociated by the inappropriateness of their words to this formality.

One of the occasional characters in the *Commedia* cast was La Cantarina, the female singer, who apparently combined the roles of comic servant and music-hall artiste. She would at times step out of the action to dance, sing and play musical instruments, for the delectation of the audience. Beyond these few facts, our information about music in the *Commedia* is a blank.

The rise of the *Commedia dell'Arte* did not go unnoticed by composers of serious music-drama; many seventeenth-century operas contain comic scenes, though seldom as bawdy as pure *Commedia*. At the turn of the eighteenth century in Naples, some comic operas were being written in Neapolitan dialect, and were strongly influenced by popular comedy, but Scarlatti's *Il Trionfo d'Onore* of 1718 seems to have the distinction of being the first *opera buffa* in Italian. The plot is typical *Commedia* of the senti-mental variety, an entanglement of emotional relationships, involving stock characters. Riccardo (a young lover) has seduced Leonora (an *inamorata*). Leonora's brother Erminio (a second young lover) loves Doralice (a second *inamorata*) who falls in love with Riccardo. Riccardo's

189

uncle, Castravacca (a Pantalone-type) is engaged to Cornelia Buffacci (an old woman), who is Doralice's aunt. Riccardo also has a servant, Captain Rodimarte Bombarda; Cornelia has a maid Rosina . . . and the stage is set for a comedy of love on several levels, of intrigue, deceit and tomfoolery. Scarlatti sets the plot in recitative and nineteen musical numbers, most of them in *da capo* form. Ten musical numbers for the 'serious' characters include one duet and one quartet; eight numbers for the comedians include three duets and a quartet.

Commedia influence is also evident in the comic intermezzi written for performance between the acts of *opere serie*. Pergolesi's *La Serva Padrona* (1733) is the most famous intermezzo of this type, and was performed in the intervals of an *opera seria*, his own *Il Prigionier Superbo*. Here a Colombina-type comic servant inveigles her master (a Pantalone) into marrying her, by frightening him with the appearance of Capitan Tempesta (really a fellow-servant in disguise). The musical structure consists of eight *da capo* musical numbers, including three duets, and linked with recitative.

By the middle of the century, *opera buffa* as such was becoming well-established in Italy and gradually expanding into the countries to the north. This evolution was due in no small part to the development of comic drama, which led to the writing of complete comic texts, many of which were extremely suitable to musical setting. The man chiefly responsible for this was Carlo Goldoni (1707–93). Goldoni came from the *Commedia* tradition, and his plays reflect this influence. He wrote over two hundred and fifty plays and libretti, and there is little difference, apart from the aria verses, between his plays for music and his purely spoken plays. His libretti, and libretti arranged by others from his plays, provided a staple diet for *opera buffa* composers for fifty years. They mostly concern plots of intrigue amongst the bourgeoisie and their servants — with, thus, some similarity to Menander's plays — and include many of the *Commedia* comic devices, but without the *Commedia's* vulgarity or its improvisatory element. The names and characteristics of the *Commedia* character-types are often retained. Goldoni's 'reform' of the *Commedia* was bitterly opposed by Carlo Gozzi (1720–1806) who tried to retain the improvised *Commedia* play in Italy, without much success.

In France the *Commedia* tradition lies behind the plays of Molière (1622–73), who, like Goldoni, blended it with comedy of manners. Marivaux (1688–1763) continued this blend, writing works with obvious references to the *Commedia* and infused with sentimental love. The plays of Beaumarchais (1732–99) are more polished and witty than these of Marivaux, and contain an element of political commentary, but there are still obvious traces of the *Commedia dell'Arte*. In *Le Barbier de Séville* and its sequel *Le Mariage de Figaro* (both of which became celebrated operas in the eighteenth century — the former in Paisiello's setting), characters retain traces of their *Commedia* origins: Figaro is Brighella, Bartholo is a Doctor figure, and Suzanne is a Colombina.[13] In *Le Barbier* Count Almaviva is the naïve young lover, and adopts the *Commedia* pseudonym of Lindoro.

The *opera buffa* that flourished in Italy and Vienna in the last thirty years of the eighteenth century was therefore strongly influenced by the *Commedia*. Many of the traditional plot features were retained: disguise and mistaken identities, practical jokes and hoaxes, unfortunate arrivals, secrets and revelations. But the influence of the comedy of manners and the comedy of sentiment removed much of the extravagance, and characters had become individuals rather than types. This last development reflected the mood of the time: a new idea was gaining a hold, the idea of progress.

Progress and music
The traditional view of the classicist of the Renaissance and Baroque periods was that the Classical Age of Ancient Greece was superior to the present age, and that man should attempt to emulate it. This idea lay behind the attempts of the 'Second Florentine Academy', whose aim was to imitate the 'superior' art-form of Greek tragedy. But during the eighteenth century man came to view his history in a different manner. Abbé St Pierre's writings (for instance the *Discours sur le Polysynodie* 1718) took the advanced view that man can plan his own future, with the assistance of the social sciences. Man today, he argued, is not necessarily inferior to the 'ancients': on the contrary, man's rational investigations build upon the past, and an unreasoning admiration of the distant past can be an obstacle rather than a help. Turgot, in his *Discours sur les progrès de l'esprit humain* (1750) regarded history as 'heritage augmented', arguing that each age progresses beyond the previous one.

This switch in attitude, from looking back, or looking round, to looking forwards, gave new impetus to the eighteenth century's classical delight in Reason. Diderot and his fellow-*Encyclopédistes* saw the establishment of knowledge and truth not just as an academic exercise, but as a task equipping man to plan a better future.

The idea of progress was also developing in terms of the progress of the individual. Indeed, the whole idea of the individuality of human beings was growing in importance. Voltaire had passionately advocated liberty of conscience: 'I disagree profoundly with your views, but I will fight to the death for your right to express them.' Rousseau went further: men are equal, not as feudal slaves, but as free-thinking individuals with their individual natural emotions, and have an influence over their own destinies. Political and social structures should aim to reflect this equality of men, and education should seek to develop individual abilities. These ideas were to lead to the more positive aspects of the French revolution in the last fifteen years of the century.

191

People were discovering, too, that there were opportunities to progress, both socially and materially. The Industrial Revolution was drawing men from the countryside into the cities where, they believed, they could better themselves materially. America, too, was offering opportunities to the emigrant.

The acceptance of the idea of progress signalled a fundamental change in attitudes to life. It offered the possibility that things could change, that the history of man and of individual men was not fixed within a dogmatic structure, that life next year might be different from life this year. The idea was not new: it had been recognized by those who had come into contact with Greek attitudes, but now it was no longer just a scholastic theory but the spirit of an age.

The new spirit was reflected in a new approach to musical forms, and is illustrated in the primary difference between Baroque and Classical musical structures. Baroque musical structures were essentially explorations in depth within fixed limits. Thus the *da capo* aria explored one emotional moment; although there might be some internal progress, it rarely moved outside the primary experience. Similarly, Baroque instrumental forms, such as those of the concerto grosso, were discussions of single issues; even fugue, while it appears to 'develop', has a single theme to which all else relates, either directly or in partnership. The Lutheran cantata too, though a succession of numbers, was usually bound together by the chorale which motivated it.

Classical forms tend in another direction. A movement in Sonata form (which may be taken as the typical form of the later eighteenth century) uses two deliberately contrasting musical ideas: they interact, and, by the end, one of them at least has changed in part. The situation at the end of a Sonata-form movement is not the same as it was at the beginning. This new structure was made possible by the simplification of small-scale melodic shaping, which meant that melodic ideas were clear-cut and easily recognizable. Ornamentation, which of itself is static rather than dynamic, became less important, a matter of emphasis rather than of exploration, and there grew the idea of musical development, of progress through the interaction of contradictions.

Sonata form, with its inherent possibilities of progress, contradiction, and development, was obviously extremely suitable as a means of reflecting narrative dramatic action. It is no coincidence that the *opera buffa* narrative ensemble and symphonic Sonata-form movements should have developed simultaneously. Which influenced which is a matter for argument: essentially they reflected a common attitude towards life and art. Some symphonic movements in Haydn's and Mozart's works sound like comic opera ensembles without the words: Mozart's comic opera ensembles use some of the devices of Sonata form to create developing music-drama.

192

Mozart's Le Nozze di Figaro

Wolfgang Amadeus Mozart spent the last ten years of his life in Vienna, from 1781 to 1791. He moved there from Salzburg, not only because his patron, Archbishop Colloredo, refused him artistic freedom, but also because Vienna was a centre of musical and operatic life in Europe.

Vienna was a natural staging-post in the migrations of musicians across Europe, particularly from Italy, the homeland of *opera buffa*, to St Petersburg, whither Catherine the Great was inviting the leading *opera buffa* composers of the age. As the capital of a large Empire, ruled by an educated aristocracy, Vienna had quite naturally developed strong cultural traditions, more so in opera than in anything else, owing to the wider acceptance of Italian rather than French or German influences: Austria herself ruled most of northern Italy. As a cosmopolitan capital in the confident days before the French Revolution, Vienna attracted the great operatic talents of the age.

Here Metastasio lived, succeeding Apostolo Zeno as Court Poet from 1730 to 1782; he developed *opera seria* libretto-writing to a fine art. Here too lived Johann Hasse (1699–1783), the most prolific of *opera seria* composers. Calzabigi and Gluck had written their first 'reform' operas in Vienna in the 1760s. At the time of Mozart's arrival, the Court Kapellmeister and Theatre Music Director was Antonio Salieri, a composer of considerable talent, only six years older than Mozart. Early in 1782 there also arrived in Vienna Lorenzo da Ponte, ex-diplomat and spy, and, some would say, the greatest *opera buffa* librettist. Other important figures in the vicinity were Joseph Haydn, based at Esterhaz but visiting Vienna fairly often, his brother Michael Haydn, Karl Ditters von Dittersdorf, the leading composer of operas in German (*Singspiele*, with spoken dialogue and usually comic), Ignaz Umlauf, musical director of *Singspiele* to the Court, Leopold Kozeluch, Court ballet composer, and some of the best singers in Europe, hired by the Emperor Joseph II.

When Mozart arrived in March 1781, the Court theatre (the *Burgtheater*) was in the midst of a five-year attempt to establish 'national' comic-opera — *Singspiel*. Mozart made his contribution in 1782 (July) with *Die Entführung aus dem Serail*, whose plot and a good part of whose text had been stolen by the otherwise reputable librettist and opera producer Stephanie the Younger from an opera text by one Bretzner, who was not pleased. The so-called *National-Singspiel* attempt at the *Burgtheater* was called off early in 1783, not because it had failed — it had not — but because it was felt it was time to return to Italian *opera buffa*. Two other theatres were operating in Vienna, and were primarily devoted to comic opera: one at the *Kärntnertor*, under he aegis of the court opera direction, and the *Theater in der Leopoldstadt* (a suburb). Another theatre, the *Theater auf der Wieden*, was about to open too, playing a repertoire of popular comedy.

193

Despite the importance of its 'highbrow' culture, Vienna was also the home of a late survivor of the *Commedia dell'Arte*. This was the *Hanswurst* comedy, which blended vulgarity, farce, popular song, and acrobatics into 'plays' which were mostly extemporized. It was extremely popular with all classes. Mozart undoubtedly attended performances, probably those given by Johann Joseph Laroche at the Leopoldstadt theatre. Nor can there be much doubt that Mozart enjoyed it, vulgarity and all: young Wolfgang was no elegant courtier. Besides being the best billiards-player in Vienna, he had a fine appreciation of the dirty joke, and himself wrote words and music for some of the most scatologically disreputable songs ever written (see, for example, K.560[14]).

The sheer range of operatic performances in Vienna during Mozart's years there is amazing. *Opera buffa, opera seria, Singspiel, opéra comique* all made regular appearances on one or other of the growing number of opera-stages in the city and its suburbs.[15] Mozart was able to hear works by the leading composers of Europe, operas originally composed in Naples, St Petersburg, northern Germany and Paris. In 1783 Paisiello's *Il Barbiere di Siviglia* was performed at the Burgtheater; Mozart must have missed it, since he was in Salzburg on a visit at the time, but he doubtless saw other performances in the next few years.

Beaumarchais' play, on which Paisiello's opera was closely based, had been originally written as a comic opera libretto in 1772: the *Opéra-Comique* in Paris had refused it and Beaumarchais had rewritten it as a comic play, first performed in February 1775. An immediate success, it was soon translated into nearly every European language for performance in the major cities of the Continent. Paisiello's opera had been first performed in St Petersburg in 1780.

Somewhat to everyone's astonishment, Beaumarchais produced a sequel in 1784: *La Folle Journée, ou le mariage de Figaro*. It had been accepted by the *Comédie Française* in 1781, but censorship difficulties — it was less than polite to the doctrine of absolutism — had led to considerable delays. Unlike most sequels, *Figaro* was even more of a triumphant success than *Le Barbier*: it spread equally quickly throughout Europe. At this time Mozart was casting about for a new operatic subject, and he seized avidly on Beaumarchais's new play. What Paisiello had done with *Le Barbier* he knew he could do — and better — with *Le Mariage de Figaro*, especially with Lorenzo da Ponte as librettist. We do not know much about the actual composition of the work. Our two sources, da Ponte's *Memoirs* and the *Reminiscences* of Michael Kelly, Irish tenor and the first Curzio, are delightfully entertaining but unreliable. In any event, the first performance took place in the *Burgtheater* on 1st May 1786. Its success was enormous, but short-lived, for the work appeared during what was perhaps the golden year of opera in Vienna, and soon had rivals. Martin y Soler had enjoyed one triumph in January with *Il Burbero di Buon Core*; he was to have another in November with *Una Cosa Rara*. In the *Kärntnerthor* theatre Dittersdorf's *Doktor und Apotheker*, a *Singspiel*, appeared in July, and was hailed as a masterpiece. In May the Leopoldstadt theatre was re-playing *La Contessina*, an immensely popular *opera buffa* by Gassmann. Even *Le Nozze di Figaro* could not vanquish all these competitors.

Da Ponte's libretto from Beaumarchais' play stands firmly in the *Commedia* tradition. The characters have recognizable antecedents in the *Commedia* character-types: Figaro and Susanna, the servants, as Brighella and Colombina; Bartolo (the Countess's ex-guardian and a physician) as the Doctor; Marcellina (housekeeper in the chateau of the Count and Countess Almaviva) as the old-woman figure, with a streak of *inamorata*; Cherubino (the Countess's page) as a naïve and very young lover; Don Curzio (the lawyer) as a stuttering Tartaglia, at least in Kelly's first performance; Don Basilio (the singing-teacher) as a hybrid *zanni*, the fop plus the scandal-monger; Antonio (the gardener) as the stupid *zanni* plus the drunken *zanni*.

Two characters stand apart: the Count and Countess Almaviva. We can loosely trace *Commedia* sources: the Count is perhaps the young lover on the way to becoming a Pantalone; the Countess is perhaps an *inamorata*. But both are distinct individuals, more characters than character-types. The same is perhaps true of Susanna — in the last act at any rate. The others however, including Figaro, remain, in the libretto, more types than characters. It is Mozart's music that brings them to life; exactly how we shall see in a moment.

The far from simple plot of *Le Nozze di Figaro* is essentially concerned with two marital problems: (1) the wish of Susanna and Figaro to marry, which is challenged by (a) Count Almaviva's pursuit of Susanna, and (b) Marcellina's pursuit of Figaro; and (2) the collapsing marriage of the Count and Countess, with strains being caused by (a) the Count's interest in Susanna and (b) Cherubino's pursuit of the Countess. Although these two basic strands are interwoven in a very complex way, Da Ponte avoided utter confusion by driving the action on in a series of quickly developing situations. He also structured the work with extreme care, and, presumably with Mozart's help, organized the musical numbers to reflect that structure.

The *Grundgestalt* of dramatic action[16] in *Le Nozze di Figaro* is as follows: proposition — consequence or reaction — interruption by new event — solution. This microcosmic 'drama' includes the basic Aristotelian ingredients of reversal, discovery and calamity, at the point of interruption (though on an apparently rather less high-flown level). It also includes within it the comic structure of the joke: expectation — clash — explosion of tension. The four acts of the opera can be seen to be arranged according to this formula: Act I presents four propositions: (a) Susanna wants to marry

Figaro (b) the Count wishes to seduce Susanna (c) Cherubino wishes to seduce the Countess (d) Marcellina and Bartolo wish to 'get' Figaro (in their different ways). Act II presents the consequences and reactions to these four propositions: the Countess's misery at the Count's infidelities, the Count's accusations of the Countess's infidelity with Cherubino, the resort of Marcellina and Bartolo to the law, and the Count's determination to prevent Figaro and Susanna from marrying. In Act III the *peripeteia* occurs, with the discovery that Marcellina and Bartolo are Figaro's parents: this puts a new complexion on everything, and the plot switches into a united intrigue by all against the Count.[17] In Act IV he is brought low: in consequence, a solution is found for the two marital problems.

This four-part *Grundgestalt* is evident on the small-scale too, and here it is obvious that Mozart is attempting to reflect the *Grundgestalt* in the tonal relationships between musical numbers. The musical numbers in *Le Nozze di Figaro* are organized in pairs. Each pair uses keys related closely to each other. Each pair is related to the next pair much less closely. The archetype of this pattern is four successive musical numbers in the following keys: E flat major, B flat major; G major, C major. This sequence of keys occurs three times in the opera: Nos. 6, 7, 8, 9; Nos. 10, 11, 12, 13; and Nos. 15a, 15b, 15c, 15d (see Fig. 16). It is hinted at in Nos. 20, 21, 22, and Nos. 28c, 28d, 28e, 28f. This pattern of four keys reflects the shape of the basic unit of dramatic action: the first two closely related keys reflect 'proposition' and 'consequence'; the move to a more distant third key reflects the *peripeteia* of the new event, which leads to solution in a closely related key. The fourth key, moreover, often has a close relationship to the first.

Fig. 16   Musical numbers in *Le Nozze di Figaro*, Acts I and II

Act I

	Overture: 'The Marriage of Figaro'	D major	PROPOSITION
1	Susanna and Figaro measure their future bedroom and inspect Susanna's wedding-hat.	G major	CONSEQUENCE
2	Susanna suggests the bedroom is too near the Count's for her safety.	B flat major	INTERRUPTION
3	Figaro is determined the Count will not get the better of him.	F major	SOLUTION
4	Bartolo plans vengeance on Figaro (for the events in *Le Barbier*).	D major	
5	Susanna and Marcellina confront each other with insulting politeness.	A major	

6	Cherubino sings of the passion of his love (for the Countess).	E flat major	PROPOSITION
7	The Count accuses Susanna of hiding Cherubino and discovers it to be true. Basilio enjoys the situation.	B flat major	CONSEQUENCE
8	The chorus ask the Count to bless Figaro's and Susanna's marriage.	G major	INTERRUPTION
9	Figaro teases Cherubino, who has been banished to a regiment.	C major	SOLUTION

Act II

10	The Countess laments her lonely state.	E flat major	PROPOSITION
11	Cherubino sings of his love for the Countess.	B flat major	CONSEQUENCE
12	Susanna dresses up Cherubino as a woman.	G major	NEW EVENT
13	The Count knows the Countess is hiding someone: Cherubino or Susanna?	C major	SOLUTION / NEW EVENT
14	Susanna and Cherubino swap places.	G major	SOLUTION
15a	The Count accuses the Countess of hiding Cherubino.	E flat major	PROPOSITION
15b	Susanna emerges: the Count is warned not to jump to conclusions.	B flat major	CONSEQUENCE
15c	Figaro arrives to finalize the wedding arrangements.	G major	NEW EVENT / PROPOSITION
15d	The Count asks Figaro to explain various odd happenings.	C major	CONSEQUENCE
15e	Antonio the gardener reports seeing a man in the garden (Cherubino); Figaro says it was him.	F major / B flat major	NEW EVENT / PROPOSITION / CONSEQUENCE
15f	Bartolo, Marcellina and Basilio arrive, demanding satisfaction.	E flat major	NEW EVENT

Figure 16 shows the musical numbers in the first two acts of *Le Nozze di Figaro*, with indications as to the use of key to reflect the structure of developing action. It will be seen that several sequences of four musical numbers follow the *Grundgestalt* and are arranged in pairs of keys. Two sequences occur in Act I: the first concerns the Figaro-Susanna relationship, the second the Cherubino-Susanna relationship. In Act II Nos. 10 and 11 are concerned with the Countess-Cherubino relationship; the intervention of Susanna, and then the Count, leads to an extension of the *Grundgestalt*. The lengthy Finale, No. 15, progresses by a series of interruptions which become new events; the act ends with no solution.

In Act III the structure becomes more complex. Here da Ponte conflated two acts of Beaumarchais's play, and the result is a succession of short scenes necessary to the pursuit of the various intrigues. The musical numbers are as follows:

16	The Count amorously makes an assignation with Susanna.	A minor A major
17	The Count determines he will defeat Figaro.	D major
18	Sextet: the discovery of Figaro's parents.	F major
19	The Countess is heart-broken but hopes to regain the Count's affections.	C major
20	Susanna and the Countess concoct a letter inviting the Count to meet a lady.	B flat major
21	The chorus (including Cherubino dressed as a girl) bring flowers to the Countess.	G major
22	The engagement celebrations for Susanna and Figaro, and Marcellina and Bartolo. The Count receives the letter from Susanna.	C major

This is the order in the printed score. Robert Moberley and Christopher Raeburn[18] however maintain that the act makes better sense if No. 19 (the Countess' aria) follows No. 17 and precedes No. 18. The case they make out includes the transferring of a short recitative scene too, and is convincing in that in their version some of the intrigue seems to be more credibly conducted. In their view, the transposed order was Mozart's original, and our printed version arose at the first performance because of the need to allow Francesco Bussani, who played both Bartolo and Antonio, sufficient time to change his costume.

They also argue that the key sequence in their version is 'better', presumably because a sequence of falling fifths occurs in the keys of No. 19's C major to No. 18's F major to No. 20's B flat major. This would be reasonable if the dramatic action moved consequentially from one number to another (as it does in Act II's No. 15). Indeed, if this is our criterion, we might more credibly see No. 17 (the Count's aria) and No. 19 (the Countess' aria) as a pair; but their respective keys of D major and C major are not closely related.

Any dramatic analysis of the act shows that two main plots are being pursued: (1) the Count is determined to seduce Susanna; (2) the Countess is determined to regain the Count. As it happens, both plots come together in No. 22: at the Countess's instigation, and in pursuit of her plot, Susanna agrees to meet the Count in the garden later in the evening. Thus No. 22 provides the 'solution' to the 'propositions' of both Count and Countess. The third important element in the act is the unexpected discovery of the identity of Figaro's parents. This affects the Count's plot but not the Countess's.

The musical numbers of the act may therefore be analysed as follows:

Count's plot

No. 16	A minor/major	PROPOSITION
No. 17	D major	CONSEQUENCE
No. 18	F major	INTERRUPTION
No. 22	C major	SOLUTION

Here the key relationships show a typical PCIS shape.

Countess's plot

No. 19	C major	PROPOSITION
No. 20	B flat major	CONSEQUENCE
No. 21	G major	INTERRUPTION
No. 22	C major	SOLUTION

Here the key relationships are less typical.

In this analysis, it matters little whether we accept the printed score's order of numbers, or the order suggested by Moberley and Raeburn.

Printed score

COUNT			COUNTESS		
16	A	P			
17	D	C			
18	F	I			
			19	C	P
			20	B flat	C
			21	G	I
22	C	S	22	C	S

Moberley and Raeburn

16	A	P			
17	D	C			
			19	C	P
18	F	I			
			20	B flat	C
			21	G	I
22	C	S	22	C	S

In either case an 'elegant' structure emerges. Indeed, if Mozart and da Ponte did rearrange the numbers of the act, then one can see that this had little

199

effect on the integrity of the dramatic *Grundgestalt*.

In Act IV (see Fig. 17) the *Grundgestalt* is evident in the Finale (No. 28) which proceeds like Act II's Finale by extension, but here sections are clearly paired into sequences in which first Susanna and then the Countess are mistaken for each other. The issue here is the Count-Countess relationship, and its parallel in the servants' world, the Figaro-Susanna relationship; in short, we have returned to the two central marital problems of the opera.

Fig. 17   Musical numbers in *Le Nozze di Figaro*, Act IV

23	Barbạrina has lost the pin she was supposed to give Susanna from the Count.	F minor	
24	Marcellina: contrary to nature, woman is man's slave.	G major	VARIATIONS
25	Basilio: to be a fool is a good way to survive.	B flat major	ON
26	Figaro: men are made fools of by women.	E flat major	A
27	Susanna awaits the arrival of her lover. (The Count? Figaro?)	F major	THEME
28a	Cherubino attempts to seduce 'Susanna' (really the Countess).	D major	PROPOSITION
28	The Count does the same thing.	G major	CONSEQUENCE
28c	Figaro pretends to attempt to seduce 'The Countess' knowing it is really Susanna.	E flat major	NEW EVENT PROPOSITION
28d	They repeat it for the Count's benefit.	B flat major	CONSEQUENCE
28e	The Count interrupts them; the masquerade is revealed; the broken Count is forgiven by the Countess.	G major	NEW EVENT
28f	General celebrations by all.	D major	SOLUTION

In the opera there are two groups of musical numbers which cannot be easily arranged into the *Grundgestalt*. In Act I Nos. 4 and 5 (a pair) could be regarded as the second half of a *Grundgestalt* of Nos. 2, 3, 4 and 5; more properly, they go with Nos. 18 and 18a to make a *Grundestalt* on the Bartolo/Marcellina — Figaro/Susanna relationships. In Act IV Nos. 24 to 27 are four arias, all concerned with the same theme, the relationship of man to woman (i.e. 'marriage'). It was a stroke of genius for da Ponte and Mozart to insert these here, for they raise in an absolutely clear way the central issue of the work, and thereby prime us with the possibilities of solution to that problem. Can the plot of Susanna and the Countess succeed against the Count? That is the question implied in No. 24. Is it better to be passive and let other people sort things out (No. 25)? No. 26 takes the opposite point of view to No. 24. No. 27 raises, in perhaps the most appealing moment in the opera, the experience of aspiration behind the comic intrigue, and also brings us back to the plot.

In reflecting the dramatic *Grundgestalt* through his choice of keys — or, more precisely, in the 'modulations' between the keys of numbers — Mozart gives evidence of his wish to communicate narrative drama in music. The same wish is evident on the small-scale too, within individual numbers. Of the thirty-nine musical numbers in *Le Nozze di Figaro* (including each section of the finales as a separate number) eighteen are 'narrative', dynamic numbers, in which the action of the plot moves forwards. Of these eighteen, the most celebrated is No. 18, the Sextet in Act III, in which the discovery of Figaro's parents is celebrated by the family, viewed with horror by the Count and Curzio, and explained to Susanna. The Sextet too follows the dramatic *Grundgestalt*. The 'proposition' — Marcellina's confession that she is Figaro's mother, and her statement that Bartolo is the father — occurs at the end of the preceding recitative. The first part of the Sextet proper shows the consequent reactions to this revelation; then Susanna enters and witnesses Figaro and Marcellina in an embrace (interruption). Eventually the situation is explained to her and she joins in the family celebration (solution).

Example 14 shows the recitative which precedes the Sextet. On the Count's instructions, Curzio the lawyer has been asked to give a legal decision on Marcellina's suit against Figaro for debt. He, Marcellina, Bartolo and Figaro appear before the Count, and Curzio reports his verdict. Mozart structures the recitative using a recurrent melodic *motiv*, which

Ex. 14   Mozart: *Le Nozze di Figaro*

occurs in bars 1–3, 6–8, 10–12, 15–18, 20–2, and 27–37 (my translation is literal). Significantly, these passages of text are precisely those which drive the action forward: they are the most important phrases in the dynamic narrative.

This melodic *motiv* is carried over into the Sextet itself, just as the basic dramatic issue of Marcellina and Figaro's relationship is carried over: see the first five bars of Ex. 15[19] (again, the translation is literal). Mozart clearly lays stress upon the first three notes, through the orchestral figure. This falling triad permeates the whole Sextet, and may be found in passages as diverse as bars 14 and 15 (in the orchestra and in the Count's part), bars 47 to 58 (in the orchestra), bars 86 and 87, and bar 103 (in Bartolo's part). In a form with a rising sixth replacing one or other of the falling thirds it can be seen in bars 44 to 45 (in Susanna's part), in bars 48 to 57 (in the orchestra) and in bars 116 and 120 (in the Count's and Don Curzio's parts). The second three notes of the *motiv* undergo greater transformation: they appear in retrograde inversion at the top of the orchestra in bars 13 to 15, determining the material of these bars, which present the astonished reactions of Don Curzio and the Count. Don Curzio's vocal line here augments the intervals while

204

preserving the shape. This same passage reappears in bars 29 to 31, suggesting the unspoken reaction of the Count and Don Curzio to Susanna's entry. In a revised form, the passage returns to show Susanna's astonished reaction to the news that Figaro has found his parents, in bars 80 to 85 and 89 to 94. Out of the six-note melodic *motiv*, then, Mozart derives melodic material to represent the central dramatic situation and the reactions of amazement it causes. Such a technique, whether conscious or unconscious, reveals Mozart's skills and instincts as a music-dramatist.

Analysing Mozart's music in this way, by using twentieth-century techniques, and interpreting the music in terms of the dramatic ideas, is not often done. Some readers may find it incredible that such apparently effortless and inspired musical flow should contain rigorous structural organization. Others may argue that the particular *motiv* involved in this scene is so ordinary a musical shape that its appearance here is in no way unusual. The first point can only be countered by saying that rigorous structural organization and apparent effortlessness are not strange bedfellows: a great artist in any field has a mastery of technique (including structural techniques) which is vital to the creation of satisfying images; it is the art concealed in art. The second point can only be answered by repeating the evidence of the drama. The scene presented in the recitative is a conversation in which certain lines of dialogue are more important than others. They lead forward, one to another, from the start of the scene to the end; they are the lines crucial to the development of the dramatic situation. Is it, then, coincidence that Mozart should have used the *motiv* for each of these lines and for none of the others? Certainly the *motiv* is not melodically unusual; but it is not its rarity or originality that matters, but the use made of it to make a musico-dramatic structure. Nor should we be surprised if a music-*dramatist* as masterly as Mozart has carried the *motiv* over into the Sextet. The ensemble is a natural continuation from the recitative (as the integrated cadence shows); the dramatic situation has not fundamentally changed, so there would seem no reason why the musical material should change.

Mozart was fortunate in that da Ponte's libretto for the Sextet is well-structured: the actions and reactions of the characters are clear-cut in the text. Essentially we have an opposition between Figaro, Marcellina and Bartolo on the one hand, and Don Curzio and the Count on the other. Into this confrontation steps Susanna: at first she sides with the Count, but later joins the family. The musical structure shows this clearly, and in so doing also shows Mozart's skills in reconciling the demands of musical recapitulation and dynamic narrative.

The musico-dramatic sections of the Sextet are partitioned in Ex. 15. In terms of musical structure, the 'exposition' can be said to last from bar 1 to bar 40. Bars 1 to 13 present the 'first subject-group', in F major, using triadic material, and representing the reunion of the family. Bars 13 to 17 present a

205

Ex. 15 Mozart: *Le Nozze di Figaro*

contrasting 'second subject', moving from the tonic to the dominant, and representing the Count's and Don Curzio's astonished reactions. Bars 17 to 24 repeat the dramatic and musical materials of bars 1 to 13, but accept the final harmonic shift to the dominant of bars 13 to 16: in other words, elements from both sides are presented. Bars 24 to 40 repeat this tripartite ABA structure, but with some thematic and tonal differences. Susanna's entry shifts the key to C major. Bars 24 to 29 use triadic material; bars 29 to 33 the 'astonished reaction' material, and bars 33 to 40 the material from bars 17 to 24. We may summarise thus:

1 — 13	A	(F major)	⎫
13 — 17	B	(F → dominant)	⎬ F major
17 — 24	A/B	(F → dominant)	⎭
24 — 29	A varied	(C major)	⎫
29 — 33	B	(C → dominant)	⎬ C major
33 — 40	A/B varied	(C → dominant)	⎭

The pattern is repetitive enough to ensure a recognizable musical structure, but adaptable enough to show a developing dramatic situation.

The 'development' section can be said to occur from bar 40 to bars 72 or 74. The significant dramatic development begins in bar 40 too, with Susanna's outburst. Thematically her rising scale in C minor can be related to the 'second subject' and to the rising scale she used on entry (bars 26 and 28). At bar 44 outburst turns to accusation; Figaro's attempts to appease anticipate the orchestral support he receives from bar 48. Here Mozart uses a two-bar sequence whose repetitions have a calming effect. Susanna's final outburst and slap act as a dramatic effect *against* the musical sound. Mozart again shows his musico-dramatic ability. In order to write 'dramatic' music a

209

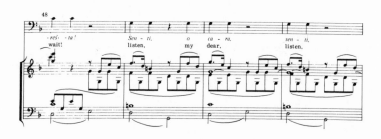

composer does not need to illustrate every single action: in this case Mozart sticks to the prevailing mood, and is thus able to make the effective point made in the text, that the slap has no effect upon Figaro or Marcellina (or Bartolo). It is for this reason — that the slap has been ignored — that Susanna imitates the Count in bar 56.

These bars, from 54 to 72, mark the point of greatest division between Figaro and Susanna: Mozart expands the moment to give it emphasis, and to prepare us for the reconciliation.

Appropriately, it is Marcellina who makes the first approach to Susanna, thus giving Mozart the dramatic opportunity to 'recapitulate' the opening material of the Sextet. Although Marcellina's vocal line is new, the orchestra repeats its own and her material in bars 74 to 78. Susanna's 'astonished reaction' repeats the B section of the 'exposition' with the same move to the dominant. Figaro again takes up triadic material as he introduces his father (in F major). Again Susanna's 'astonished reaction' uses B material and moves to the dominant. Figaro reintroduces both his parents: Susanna is convinced.

213

The 'recapitulation' can thus be summarised:

74 — 80	A	(F major)	
80 — 85	B	(F → dominant)	
85 — 90	A clarified	(F major)	F major
91 — 94	B	(F → dominant)	
95 — 102	A extended	(F major)	

Opera in Perspective

The 'coda', bars 102 to 140, shows Marcellina and Bartolo sharing the triadic theme (bar 103) while Susanna's lyrical melody expresses her happiness (and relief) in discovering the truth. The Count and Don Curzio are united in opposition: their *d* flats and *g* flats show their lack of sympathy with the prevailing F major, but the family is able to ignore such chromatic disturbances without difficulty. Finally the Count storms out; bars 136 and 137 recapitulate in F major the short *motiv* used for his attempted departure in C major at bar 24, while simultaneously the reiterated *c* from bars 2 and 4 and the harmonic progression of bars 103 to 104 are sounded — musico-dramatic characterization on a microcosmic level.

The scene is however not yet over. Example 16 shows the recitative which follows (translated literally). Here it can clearly be seen that Mozart continues to use the basic melodic *motiv* for as long, and for only as long, as the issue of the Figaro-Marcellina relationship is discussed. The melodic material alters as the text turns to the giving of money to Figaro, and finally, as Susanna rejoices in her happiness and they all realize the opportunity afforded by the new events, the musical material is based on a new *motiv* of a

Ex. 16   Mozart: *Le Nozze di Figaro*

rising fourth. Again Mozart's skill is shown: the culmination of the dramatic events here, which closes the dramatic structure, is presented in the form of new musical material, which again drives the music-drama forward.

Our musico-dramatic analysis of this scene has shown how Mozart is able to reconcile the conflicting demands of closed structure and dynamic narrative in a thoroughly convincing way. Music and drama are linked fairly obviously in the structure of the Sextet, but beneath this and through the whole scene musical ideas are used to represent the central musico-dramatic issue. The musical material thus used has, simultaneously, an expressive and a structural function, and succeeds both in satisfying our desire for comprehensible forms and in moving the action forward.

The 'comedy' in this scene lies in the unexpected revelation of who Figaro's parents are; we perceive the Figaro-Marcellina relationship, in particular, in a new light. But Mozart clearly shows that he is less concerned with an abrupt bisociation in the comic manner, and is more concerned with exploring the implicit experience. The musical idea announced in the recitative is expanded into the Sextet: as a result, we are drawn into the experience that lies behind the moment of 'comic' revelation. In the end, the Sextet is not 'comic'; rather it is pure music-drama, an expansion and exploration of that moment of complete psychological transformation experienced by Figaro and Marcellina in particular, but also by Bartolo, and later by Susanna.[20]

The universality of the experience is reinforced by the way in which Mozart emphasises the human life of the characters. They may be born from *Commedia dell'Arte* types, but each is endowed with individual life. A glance at Susanna's vocal lines in the Sextet shows how clearly they express her changing attitudes to the situation. But their expressiveness not only brings Susanna to life; it also operates upon us and draws us into a direct apprehension of her experiences. The reactions of all the characters in the Sextet are our own potential reactions: by potentially experiencing them all, sometimes simultaneously, we move beyond the limits of everyday reality and beyond the limits of our own conscious selves.

Le Nozze di Figaro is not just 'comic entertainment'. Comic and entertaining it is, but it goes beyond that. Its surface characteristics, in the way it presents a story involving 'historical figures', are governed by the manners of the later eighteenth century, just as the music proceeds according to the conventions of the later eighteenth century style. But the musical and dramatic outer clothing conceals experiences which are essentially human and no different from those we can experience in the twentieth century. Thus it is that we are moved: not by the explicit, but by the implicit. Mozart's images are powerful ones, images structured not only by convention, but by his creative imagination as a music-dramatist, and it is this that gives them their power.

7   Romantic Opera

The sources of Romantic Opera

The latter half of the eighteenth century saw not only the triumph of international European *opera buffa*, but also the development of French and German comic opera styles. In Germany the *Singspiel* evolved as a spoken text interspersed with songs: the South German/Austrian variety was heavily influenced by *opera buffa* and became, in Dittersdorf's hands, virtually German *opera buffa* with spoken dialogue rather than recitative. In France *opéra comique* emerged, again with spoken dialogue and songs.

In general, the plots of *Singspiele* were similar to those of *opere buffe*, but with a tendency towards greater sentimentality on the one hand and naïve moralizing on the other. Young love was the emotion driving the plot forward, and any opportunity to sing a simple song which expressed the moral in a situation, or simply a general moral truth, was eagerly seized. Dittersdorf's *Doktor und Apotheker* presents the simple, Menander-like plot of a young lover and his intriguing servant trying to outwit a Pantalone and his awesome wife, in order to win their daughter and her serving-maid. The events that occur hinge on intercepted letters, disguises and an attempted elopement, although they are far less complicated than those of *Le Nozze di Figaro*. Other character-types from the *Commedia dell'Arte* are present, notably a bragging, cowardly soldier, who, in one delicious scene, falls asleep while on vigil: Dittersdorf depicts his yawns in the music, and finally his snores.

The two ingredients of sentimental love and moralizing were evidence of a changing outlook on life. The intellectual combat of intrigue, present in *opera buffa,* was beginning to seem an irrelevance. Plots based upon codes of behaviour, proper manners and the like also seemed to be irrelevant. What was becoming important was to gain one's freedom from traditional restraints: young love should not have to bow to the strictures of an older generation; on the political front, in France, the banner of freedom was being raised against tyrannical government.

More and more man was coming to think of himself as a free individual. No longer was it easy to accept the traditional view that he had a fixed political and economic position in a feudal system, that his behaviour should conform to fixed codes, that his feelings of love should be confined within a social system of engagement and marriage. Nor did it seem any longer necessary to confine musical expression within a fixed code of traditional musical structures: on the contrary, suitable structures must be found to meet the demands of individual expression. In France the Revolution occurred in part because of bad harvests and incompetent government, but it was the new spirit of the age which provided the justification for men taking matters into their own hands and acting as free individuals. In the rest of Continental Europe, the new ideas of freedom from restraint received expression primarily in artistic media, at least until Napoleon's armies spread the Revolution. The forces of reaction were to set in after Waterloo, but however Metternich might try to put the political clock back to 1780, men could not be persuaded to resume the outlook of their grandfathers. The convulsion had produced 'Romanticism', perhaps the most difficult to define of all aesthetic terms.

The period of maximum political turmoil in France, from 1789 until 1804 when Napoleon was crowned Emperor, was also the time when eighteenth-century music-drama began to mould itself into something new. During his reign, from 1804 to 1815, experiments were made in the new style, and by 1821, when he died, 'early Romantic opera' was established, its aesthetic features providing the basis of music-drama for a further seventy years or so.

In Vienna between 1789 and 1804 important operatic developments were occurring not so much in the *Burgtheater* as in a small theatre in a suburban slum, the *Theater auf der Wieden*. It had been taken over in 1789 by Emanuel Johann Schikaneder, a popular comedian with his own company, who had decided to give up touring around provincial cities and to settle in the capital. In November of that year he staged *Oberon*, a 'magical' *Singspiel* by Paul Wranitzky, one of Haydn's violinists at Esterhaz. Magic had often played a part in the *Commedia* scenarios; here it was elevated, with considerable success, to be an important ingredient in music-drama with a fully written spoken text and music. In 1791 Schikaneder won a permanent place in history for himself and his theatre with the first performance of *Die Zauberflöte;* it was his own text, and starred himself, and had music by Wolfgang Amadeus Mozart.

Die Zauberflöte (The Magic Flute) is a pot-pourri of almost every 'new' idea floating in the cauldron of European music-drama at the time. It contains fairy-tale magic, sentimental romantic love, the rescue of a heroine, Masonic symbolism, villains and villainesses, simple popular tunes, complex virtuoso arias, *opera buffa* ensembles, spoken dialogue, supernatural beings, animals, *Commedia* comic devices, and a glockenspiel. Its world is no longer the world of courtly, bourgeois, or lower-class intrigue; rather it is a world in which anything can happen and nothing is accidental. In short, it is an attempt to imitate the world of myth, while at the same time retaining elements of *Singspiel* and popular comedy. The result is astonishing. A princely hero acquires a comic servant who is a magical creature, half-bird and half-man; he sets out to free a beautiful maiden from a man we expect to be a villainous Pantalone-figure but who turns out to be the High Priest of an Egyptian temple. Instead of a complicated pattern of comic intrigues we find a series of ritualistic and magical initiations into the mysteries of the temple, and instead of hero and heroine simply finding happiness together, they find virtue and honour as well. Through it all floats Mozart's music, shifting styles as appropriate, but somehow filling the characters with life, and encouraging us to open our minds to the mysteries that lie behind the work. Apart from the hurriedly-composed and rather ordinary *La Clemenza di Tito*, this was Mozart's last opera; one wonders what he might have written next.

In 1792 Ludwig van Beethoven arrived in Vienna: a new spirit was awakening in music. By 1804 he had written his Third Symphony, the 'Eroica', in which traditional musical structure is forced to submit to expression. The late eighteenth-century composer had usually accepted a structure and expressed himself within it; Beethoven's new attitude opened the door to Romanticism in music. It was a reflection of the ideas of the age in its assertion of individuality against traditional systems, and therefore was to be expected, but it required a man of Beethoven's talent and self-confidence (not to say egoism, at this date anyway) to put idea into practice. Beethoven's uncompromising assertion of what *he* felt and thought, and his consequent struggles to find *a way of saying* what he felt and thought, inspired and stimulated generations of composers to do the same. But Beethoven provided them with a musical means, in his attitude to structure and in his use of musical resources, to create a type of music-drama that reflected the new spirit of the age.

France, between 1789 and 1804, was preoccupied with political issues. But this is not to say that there was no music-drama; on the contrary. The leading figure in Paris was an Italian, Cherubini (1760–1842), who, besides being a learned teacher of counterpoint, also helped to develop music-drama in keeping with current thought. French Romantic opera was built out of the traditional materials of Gluck's 'reform' opera and *opéra comique*. Cherubini's operas were chiefly 'number' operas with spoken dialogue, in the *opéra comique* tradition; but they had serious themes and contained moments of Gluckian grandeur. Cherubini was influenced in his musical language by Beethoven, though he was not capable of Beethovenian indi-viduality. Perhaps his most important work, historically, was *Les Deux Journées* (1800, usually entitled in English *The Water-Carrier*): it is a 'rescue

225

opera'.

'Rescue opera' was a type of drama whose plot revolved around last-minute rescues, hair-breadth escapes, suspense and relief, punctuated by high-flown moral statements of a political kind. It was a true child of the French Revolution — though Grétry's *Richard Coeur de Lion* of 1784 is usually regarded as an antecedent: there, however, the emotions are more sentimental than political. The most famous rescue opera of all is Beethoven's *Fidelio* (1805, in its first version), which may be described as a magnificent hymn to human aspiration. The work includes some scenes which are musically and dramatically stunning, and others in which dramatic content and musical craftsmanship fall short of Beethoven's lofty aims. His lack of musico-dramatic experience made it difficult for Beethoven to judge the value of some scenes and of parts of the text despite constant re-workings of the score; in consequence *Fidelio* must be seen as a flawed masterpiece.

Germany's contribution to music-drama at this time was mainly in the fields of theory and aesthetics. The literature of the latter part of the eighteenth century espouses classical and rational aesthetics, with some notable exceptions: Johann Georg Hamann had suggested in his *Sokratische Denkwürdigkeiten* of 1759 that reason could not be trusted, and his pupil Johann Gottfried Herder emphasized the importance of enthusiasm and inspiration in poetic composition. 'The true knowledge is love, is human feelings'[1] he proclaimed in 1779. Herder's ideas gave rise to the *Sturm und Drang* school of poets who opposed rationalism, enlightenment and the classical emphasis upon form, and sought inspiration in their own liberated emotions. (The term *Sturm und Drang* is frequently applied to Haydn's symphonies written in the early 1770s, but this appears quite absurd if his music is compared with the far more intense personal expression and iconoclastic disregard of convention of the *Sturm und Drang* poets.)

In the field of drama, Germany produced Goethe and Schiller. Goethe's *Faust* Part I was completed in 1801. Its theme — that man exists only for as long as he continually strives after something new — its erratic, anti-formalistic shifts of scene, its emphasis upon emotion and the supernatural, and its theme of salvation through love, created an enduring definition of Romantic attitudes. Schiller's plays were masterpieces of emotional tension within more rigorous structural bounds.

Italy kept itself aloof from such Germanic developments. Between 1789 and 1821 opera continued very much on eighteenth-century lines: *opera buffa* was still being written, and even old-fashioned *opera seria*. But Simon Mayr, a Bavarian, settled in northern Italy at the turn of the century and began slowly to persuade his audiences to accept new ideas. Choruses and ensembles grew more important; structures were expanding into more large-scale patterns. The aria itself was coming under new musical influences: harmony was growing simpler to allow the voice to soar in melodies with poignant chromatic inflections or to leap in dazzling displays of '*bel canto*' ornamentation. Rhythms, especially in the orchestral accompaniment, were becoming simpler, providing a context for the individualist expression of the human voice: as ever, the Italians were maintaining the supremacy of vocal melody, their chief contribution to European music-drama.

Back in France, Cherubini's ideas had been picked up and developed by another Italian, Gasparo Spontini. (Perhaps the lack of interesting Italian opera at this time is the result of all the good Italian musicians going to Paris.) The imperial coronation of Napoleon had shifted French attitudes from iconoclasm to self-aggrandisement: France now believed herself to be the leader of Europe, and a suitably spectacular form of music-drama was required. Spontini provided exactly that with *La Vestale* in 1807, a work which had the dubious distinction of being Napoleon's favourite opera. The Emperor may have had little choice: Spontini's chief supporter and patron was the Empress Josephine. The story is set in Ancient Rome (regarded by the French as a true prototype for their own republic). Julia, a Vestal Virgin, falls in love with the victorious young general Licinius: in paying attention to him, she lets the sacred temple flame go out. Her 'crimes' are discovered, but she refuses to divulge the name of her lover. As she is about to be buried alive for perjuring her vows and profaning the temple, a flash of lightning re-ignites the sacred flame; she is saved and marries Licinius. This story, in which love triumphs over all, is arranged in a Gluckian manner with spectacular scenes structured on a large scale. But the librettist, Étienne de Jouy, added the excitement and tension of 'rescue opera', Spontini responded appropriately, and the result was a triumph. Its importance in the development of French, Italian and German Romantic opera was immense: to an audience hearing it today (though performances are unfortunately rare) it is full of musical techniques that one normally associates with the operas of twenty years later.

In Vienna, France, Germany and Italy, the ingredients of 'Romantic' opera were gradually being assembled. The form of comic opera (spoken dialogue and sung numbers) was generally employed, but Gluck's through-composed 'reformed' opera was there as a model, and was used by Spontini in *La Vestale*. A more chromatic musical language was developing as a result of the growing emphasis on expression at the expense of shape. Attention was being drawn in operatic plots to the plight of individuals in the midst of great events, and to the passions driving individuals rather than their reasoned motives. Great human issues were being raised, and simple solutions put forward: the eternal validity of human love, dominating all else; the idea that nature is a dynamic force that cannot be tamed and formalized as in the gardens of Versailles; the idea that human aspiration and striving — the Prometheus image — is what constitutes man's essential worth. Man's

227

emotions and instincts were being liberated from moral and intellectual constraints, and he saw his own dynamic nature reflected in nature around him.

Essentially, Apollo was being overthrown by Dionysos. The content of images was beginning to dominate the shapes of images. A composer like Mozart had almost always accepted conventional musical shapes, expressing what he wanted to say within those formal limitations. The Romantic composer found that what he wanted to say could not (and, to the iconoclast, should not) be confined within Apollo's traditional structures: he was therefore obliged to experiment with new ways of expressing his musical ideas. It is for this reason that the harmonic language of music developed at such high speed during the first half of the century, for harmony is the small-scale structuring of basic musical ideas. Expression was now self-expression, and what a particular composer wanted to express was a product of his individuality: it could not be expressed with the same methods that another composer had employed.

There came a time, however, when composers discovered that the Dionysiac basis to their music was having a Dionysiac effect upon their audiences: swiftly they realized that this Dionysiac effect could be roused by the use of quite simple devices. And so Romantic music developed in two directions simultaneously: towards passionate sincerity and towards fraudulent charlatanism. Audiences, then as now, often had difficulty in distinguishing between the two. They went to the opera to have their passions roused, but they were often incapable of judging whether or not their passions were roused in the service of truly worth-while experiences or merely for trivial thrill. For this the musicians must take much of the blame.

Music and symbol
The Romantics regarded music in a different way from their immediate predecessors. Firstly, music was the Romantic art *par excellence*. 'No colour can be as romantic as a musical note', said the German writer Wackenroder.[2] Music 'is the most romantic of all the arts', wrote E. T. A. Hoffmann.[3] The quality of music which most attracted the Romantics — writers as well as composers — was its very lack of definition, its inability to be explicit, and its supreme ability to communicate the implicit. Words and pictures could not communicate feelings as precisely as music could, simply because they pin emotions down, and emotions are vague and complicated things.

This quality of music was acknowledged by Schopenhauer, in whose philosophical system music plays an important part. 'Music . . . is in the highest degree a universal language that is related to the universality of concepts. . . Yet its universality is by no means that empty universality of abstractions, but is of a quite different kind; it is united with thorough and unmistakable distinctness.'[4] Bettina von Arnim suggested that music was above even philosophy: 'Music is a revelation of a higher order than any morality or philosophy.'[5]

The idea of the universality of musical images is one we have met already. In Chapter 1 we investigated the nature of musical images, and came to the conclusion that its attraction for primitive man lay in music's ability to communicate 'what lies behind' reality, whether that be the reality of the everyday world or the reality of dramatic text and action. For primitive man, music was a magical, mysterious force through which, when it was linked to the more specific images of drama, he could explore the otherwise inexplicable. At the same time, musical images have a structure, in which sound is enclosed and organised. To these two sides of music, the direct, irrational impact of experience through music, and the more objective, rational structures of music, we gave the Nietzschean names Dionysos and Apollo.

From our investigations of Western European opera since 1600 it has been clear that composers have used music on two symbolic levels: as a Dionysiac, instant communication of the experiences lying behind the text and action; and, by employing Apollonian structural devices, as a means of symbolizing patterns of thought and emotion behind the text and action. Peri's recitative had the aim of symbolizing in music the emotions of the characters; but his organization of the recitative also symbolized the patterns of emotion of the characters. A similar phenomenon occurs in Monteverdi's *L'Orfeo*: since Orfeo himself is an Apollonian figure, his inclination towards structure influences the structure of the work via Monteverdi. In Handel's use of *opera seria* conventions, the *da capo* aria directly communicates the emotions of the characters, but Handel's manipulation of tonal structures also reflects the underlying moral-emotional motivation of the characters. In Gluck's *Orfeo ed Euridice* too, key is used as an underlying expression of the issues of the opera. In *Le Nozze di Figaro* Mozart presents through the sounds and structures of the music the experiences behind the comic situations.

In all these examples music is operating symbolically through its Dionysiac and through its Apollonian aspects. As in the myths of primitive man, and in Greek tragedy, it is not only the events which are symbolic of human experiences; the way they are presented is also equally symbolic. This was the idea that gave rise to rhetoric, the theory and practice of how to say things persuasively; it is also the reason why artistic creativity requires craftsmanship as well as inspiration or talent. In the end — as in the music-dramas we have discussed — inspiration and craft combine into art, and expression and structure are seen as indistinguishable because structure expresses something too.

But not all composers of music or music-drama have seen things in quite this way. Music can be pseudo-expressive: it can seem to communicate the superficial symptoms of an experience rather than its deeper meaning. The Second Florentine Academy groped towards a rebirth of music-drama precisely because they felt the conventional madrigal was pseudo-expressive: when the text said 'descend', descending scales were used; when the word 'ascend' appeared, the music 'ascended'. Mention of a nightingale produced 'nightingale' music. Peri and Rinuccini set out to find a means of presenting *real* expression symbolically in music: they were less interested in the fact that someone mentioned a nightingale than in the experience that led to the mention of the word.

Algarotti and Gluck, too, found themselves with the same problem all over again. The *opera seria* of the 1740s and 1750s seemed full of pseudo-expression, with cliché piled upon cliché, and emotion trampled on by the pseudo-emotion of rhetoric. Like Peri, Gluck sought to re-establish the deeper experiences behind a text.

The issue comes up a third time in the Romantic period, at the beginning of the nineteenth century. Romantic aesthetics placed emphasis upon an individual's emotions without necessarily paying much attention to the context of those emotions. Music, moreover, was often seen as symbolic in its Dionysiac sound-effects rather than in its Apollonian structural aspects. It was therefore only too easy for the Romantic composer to communicate single emotions with devastating effect, but without placing them in a psychological context: in short, it was easy for his music to be pseudo-expressive, to be pictorial.

Pictorial music had received a boost in the early years of the century, through the use of music to portray nature. Beethoven's *Pastoral* Symphony had done just this, but had raised a problem. The Romantics believed that the forces of external nature and those of man's inner nature were similar, if not reflections of each other. So, was the *Pastoral* Symphony about the countryside, or about human nature, or both? Berlioz' *Symphonie Fantastique* raised the same question: Berlioz remained equivocal about whether his music was intended to depict the scenery and outward events in this series of 'episodes from the life of an artist', or was in some way meant to portray the feelings of the artist himself. The dividing-line between pictorialism and expression was thin: once it was accepted that music could express nature pictorially, the door was open to a pictorial representation of human emotions. An audience could be thrilled through a 'picture' of the externals of anger in the same way as it could respond to a musical 'picture' of a thunderstorm; indeed, both might use the same musical material.

In addition to the 'nature and pictorialism' issue, a further aspect of Romanticism made musical symbolism a problem, particularly in music-drama. Characters were seen to be motivated more and more by their emotional attitudes, less and less by reasoned judgment. In *Le Nozze di Figaro* hardly anyone acts impulsively except Cherubino. In Romantic opera, if it is not impulse which motivates the characters it is at least their daemonic natures, the compulsion of their emotions. And emotion is what music most obviously communicates. How easy, therefore, to fabricate the dramatic tension which explodes into action by using clichés of musical tension. At the same time, and alternatively, the opportunities were there to portray complexities of emotion, and to create musical symbolism on a deeper level.

What differentiated the superficial, the pseudo-expressive, from the deeply and truly expressive, was the extent to which symbolism extended to the musical structure. It is important to emphasize the significant role of structure in nineteenth-century music for two reasons: firstly, many musical historians, especially those writing before the 1920s, tended to think that Romantic music was 'formless' or nearly so; and secondly, Romantic music is so overtly emotional and Dionysiac that we tend to forget that Apollo might have a hand in matters.

As we turn to Romantic opera, then, we must bear in mind a number of things. Firstly, the idea that music can symbolize non-musical ideas or even objects is not new, at least in the history of music-drama. Secondly, musical symbolism can be superficial and pseudo-expressive, or deeply expressive of human experiences. Thirdly, musical symbolism can extend beyond Dionysiac sound-effect to Apollonian sound-structures. Now let us separate the wheat from the chaff.

French Grand Opera

After *La Vestale* Spontini remained in Paris until 1820; none of his later operas achieved the same success. But a model had been suggested which combined the structures of Gluck with Romantic ideas and emotionalism.

During the later 1820s, Parisian audiences saw the first plays of Victor Hugo; the preface to *Cromwell* (1827) was a manifesto of Romantic drama: anti-classical, pro-Shakespearean, and advocating a drama which heightens reality, blending comedy and tragedy, and in which action results from high-powered emotion. *Ernani* (1830) caused a furore nightly for months as pro-Hugo and anti-Hugo claques fought it out with cheers and boos in the auditorium. The play itself was typical of its *genre*. 'Blood-and-thunder here holds the stage. . . Amid confusion, the story passes from thrilling episode to thrilling episode.'[6] The pro-Hugo faction won the battle, for they more accurately reflected the mood and taste of the Parisian audiences of the time. Thrills, sensations, extravagance, spectacle, intense emotion — these were the commercially acceptable elements of drama.

Music-dramatists responded. In 1829 Auber's *La Muette de Portici* appeared, to be followed the following year by Rossini's *Guillaume Tell*, and French Grand Opera was inaugurated. It can be said, with some justification, that the two best French Grand Operas of the period were *Guillaume*

Tell, written by an Italian, and *Rienzi*, written by Wagner, a German. In fact, the most typical French Grand Operas were written by Giacomo Meyerbeer (originally Jakob Beer), who was essentially an eclectic cosmopolitan in his music, as he was in his name and career. His two most successful contributions were *Robert le Diable* in 1831 and *Les Huguenots* in 1836.

The *genre* was unashamedly commercial: the director of the Paris *Opéra*, Louis Veron, was determined to run the theatre at a profit, and certainly Meyerbeer's operas made a great deal of money. Meyerbeer's librettist was Eugène Scribe, who was also a playwright of considerable reputation. To Scribe has been awarded the honour, by some historians, of being the 'inventor of the well-made play'.[7] What mattered to him was the plot, and theatrical effectiveness; most authorities doubt his sincerity as a playwright. Scribe certainly had an eye on commercial success: 'he was able to set up what amounted to a play-factory, in which stories were found, invented, or paid for and turned, like sausages, into comestibles for which the public was eager to expend its money.'[8] Scribe wrote, regularly, ten plays a month for ten months of the year, and then had a two-month holiday, undoubtedly deserved.

Although Meyerbeer was conscious of the commercial possibilities of Scribe's libretti, he was not a slick composer. He took the greatest pains over his compositions, reworking passages endlessly, even up to the night of the first performance, and often revising thereafter. His last opera, *L'Africaine*, was twenty years in composition. The trouble that Meyerbeer took cannot be disputed, although ever since Wagner the results of his pains have been held in low esteem. Meyerbeer's brand of craftsmanship served the view of music-drama prevalent at the time; it worshipped the gods of sensationalism and theatrical effect. Consequently Meyerbeer's operas are impeccably written, magnificent examples of a kind of opera that is ultimately worthless.

Les Huguenots has a typical Scribe plot. The setting is historical, and the story takes place at the time of the wars between the Catholics and Protestant Huguenots in France: its climax is the Catholic massacre of the Huguenots on 24th August 1572, St Bartholomew's Day. Against this conflict is set the love of Raoul, a Huguenot, for Valentine, a Catholic. Scribe produces a libretto that is full of stirring, exciting and sensational events; the chorus groups of Catholics and Huguenots play a large part. Act I takes place during a Catholic party, with maximum opportunity for drinking- and love-songs. Act II, set at the Queen's court, includes the then notorious bathing chorus, and the first of many choral confrontations between the religious factions. Act III includes a wedding procession, a duel which turns into a general brawl between the factions, and the unexpected (and unmotivated) appearance of a group of gypsy dancers. In addition to a thrilling love duet, Act IV contains the scene of conspiratorial plotting and the blessing of the conspirators' swords. Act V includes the St Bartholomew's Day massacre itself, as well as a court ball. Amidst these spectacular scenes occur scenes of personal confrontation, for the love affair of Raoul and Valentine is a stormy one; as a Catholic, she is engaged and then married to the Comte de Nevers, a Catholic nobleman, while Raoul himself is amorously tempted by the Queen. No opportunity is missed by Scribe to exploit the developing situations for maximum theatrical effect; that is, for the greatest tension and excitement.

Indeed, there are enough thrills and spills and spectacular moments in *Les Huguenots* to satisfy the requirements of a modest Hollywood epic. Since Scribe is more concerned with these aspects of the drama, he tends to neglect motivation and the portrayal of character. Raoul and Valentine remain cardboard characters, merely going through the motions of heroism. Meyerbeer's music does little to provide what is missing: it superbly reflects the outward gestures of emotional tension, but goes no further than that. In the end *Les Huguenots* is escapist entertainment. It recreates the superficial aspects of music-drama but never penetrates beneath to explore the universality of human experience. Why is this so?

In the first place, Meyerbeer, although in his way a clever craftsman, and a leading Grand Opera composer, was not a great music-dramatist. His music admirably reflects the superficialities of the text, and the superficialities of emotion, but he was not able to get beneath the skins of his characters and to look out at the world through their eyes. He was unable to get beyond what the words say to what they mean. His music is, therefore, like that of the late sixteenth-century madrigalists, and like that of the general run of *opera seria* composers: it is merely pictorial and illustrative, though admirably effective in that purpose. It portrays emotion but does not express it.

The love-duet in Act IV is generally reckoned to be the best moment in the opera. Raoul, hidden in Valentine's bedroom, has overheard the Catholics plotting to massacre the Huguenots. He emerges, and declares to Valentine that he must go and warn his fellows and fight beside them. Valentine begs him not to go: it might lead to his killing her father and husband, and to his own death. Raoul is resolute, until Valentine declares her love for him. At once Raoul forgets his honour, sinking into ecstasy, begging her to repeat her declaration. Valentine is stunned by the effect of her words. Raoul suggest they run away together, but Valentine demurs. The sound of a bell in the distance brings Raoul back to reality: now he is full of remorse for his suggestion, and again determines to go. Valentine again pleads with him not to go – she will die if he leaves her – but Raoul resists her and finally departs.

The reactions of the character here are increasingly contrived. The first step follows naturally from the preceding scene: Raoul's determination to go, coupled with Valentine's fears of the consequence. But Raoul's *volte-*

face is absurd, its absurdity only magnified by Valentine's. One suspects it was placed here by Scribe only in order to provide an opportunity for the expression of the emotions of love. When Raoul returns to his former attitude, it is Valentine's return to her first attitude which is absurd: does she or does she not want him to stay? Essentially, Scribe is attempting to portray dilemmas, but he fails abysmally, particularly in Valentine's case, and leaves us with the conclusion that both characters are weak.

Meyerbeer's response to the text suggests that he was quite unaware of all this. The music follows the emotional states of the characters without justifying them: as a result it makes us believe them without believing in them. It is perfectly calculated to squeeze every ounce of emotional effect out of situations which are in the end fraudulent.

The characters in *Les Huguenots* purport to act in accordance with religious and moral principles, but really they are following the dictates of their feelings, in typically Romantic fashion. Meyerbeer's music reflects these feelings, and therefore appears to show character motivation. But it lacks the kind of Apollonian musical structures that have represented a moral and dramatic continuum in the previous operas we have discussed. Meyerbeer's craftsmanship is devoted to the moment, and he has no long view of the springs of musico-dramatic action.

The final scene of the opera illustrates the essential triviality of the work (see Ex. 17). Catholic soldiers swarm into the street, led by St Bris, Valentine's father. Raoul, his companion Marcello, and finally Valentine are shot. Queen Marguérite appears. Here action is presented in the crudest way: Valentine's final words offer an opportunity, however brief, for some exploration of what is after all the crucial situation of the opera, but Meyerbeer produces only eight bars of rather ordinary music. One has only to compare this with the final scene from Verdi's *Aida* (a parallel situation) or the final scene of Verdi's *Rigoletto* (a parallel text — see Ex. 23) to see that in *Les Huguenots* Meyerbeer is chiefly interested not in human situations, communicated with relevance to our own, but in large-scale

Ex. 17   Meyerbeer: *Les Huguenots*

'effects without causes', in Wagner's words. French Grand Opera such as this misuses the language and tradition of music-drama.

Italian Romantic Opera

Mayr's 'Romanticised' Italian operas appeared during the first fifteen years of the century. By 1813, however, another Italian composer was beginning to make a name for himself: Gioacchino Rossini. In that year appeared his serious opera *Tancredi,* and *L'Italiana in Algieri,* an *opera buffa* composed in three weeks. Rossini's reputation as a comic opera composer was established with his *Il Barbiere de Siviglia* in 1816; it has in the end proved a more lasting reputation than his fame as a composer of serious opera, which was confirmed in the same year by his *Otello.* Rossini's last opera, *Guillaume Tell* (1829) was written for Paris; he wrote no opera in the last forty years of his life.

Il Barbiere di Siviglia is certainly the most popular and famous of Rossini's operas, and is still one of the two or three most popular comic operas ever written. It therefore deserves some attention. The work had a notable precedent, Paisiello's setting of the Beaumarchais play, composed in 1782 and still considered in 1816 to be a masterpiece: Rossini was faced with considerable opposition — not from Paisiello himself, who was seventy-six years old — but from Paisiello's supporters and those who believed Rossini to be a worthless upstart. Rossini himself publicly stated his respect for Paisiello, but was obviously determined not to be overshadowed: his opera was not a work of homage to his elder, but a work designed absolutely for the taste of the day. According to a notice in the published libretto, sold before the first performance, Rossini 'expressly asked. . . that some new situations for musical pieces be added, and he further asked that these be to the modern theatrical taste. . .'[9] He went further, conscious of 'the need to insert choruses into the subject itself, either because they are required by modern usage or because they are essential for producing a musical effect in a theatre of notable capacity.'[10]

This last reason — the size of the theatre — is a poor one. Rossini's *Il Barbiere di Siviglia* was written for the Teatro Argentina in Rome, whose stage was smaller than that of the Hermitage Theatre in St Petersburg, where Paisiello's opera — without choruses — was performed.

The main reason for Rossini's alterations was his wish to conform to 'modern theatrical taste'. Like Meyerbeer, he was aware of his public, perhaps more aware of that than of anything else. But where Meyerbeer took the greatest pains over composition, Rossini composed the whole of *Il Barbiere di Siviglia* in two and a half weeks. He was a naturally fluent composer, but to have written the first act in eight days and the second act in five days (the remaining week being spent on writing out the full score) is an astonishing feat. It also suggests that Rossini was either an instinctive musico-dramatist genius, or was merely concerned with superficialities, with portraying emotion rather than expressing it.

The general tide of opinion is that Rossini was an instinctive musico-dramatic genius. Unfortunately the evidence suggests that the other possibility is more likely. Of the eighteen numbers in the opera, seven contain borrowings from his own earlier works or from other composers (including the use of material from the second act finale of Spontini's *La Vestale* for the first act finale of *Il Barbiere*). The overture had already been used for at least two of Rossini's operas.[11] The idea of 'borrowing' material for an opera was not new: it was for instance a habit for *opera seria* composers. John Gay's *The Beggars Opera* of 1728 deliberately used tunes already well-known to the audience: much of the effect was in the bisociation (comic or tragic) between the expectation of familiar, often vulgar words, and the hearing of Gay's new texts to these melodies. For *opera seria* composers, the 'borrowing' of their own and other people's tunes was not usually done with the intention to parody: it was often the result of a need for haste. In the case of *Il Barbiere di Siviglia* we can detect the same reason. Such 'borrowings' (it would be discourteous to use any other term) suggest that the composer does not see his characters as individual human beings, nor their situations as deeply-felt personal experiences.[12]

This is not to say that there is no evidence of Rossini's music reflecting dramatic situations, either superficially or on a deeper level. He does appear to be using key-associations, for example. G major is used in Act I to represent Count Almaviva's wooing of Rosina (the Countess in *Le Nozze de Figaro*), his plans with Figaro to achieve success, and Rosina's and Figaro's similar plans; at the end of Act II it is the key in which all sing of the triumph of faithful love. It also appears, ironically perhaps, as the key in which Bartolo sings of his love for Rosina. B flat major seems to be used to represent Figaro and the Count deceiving and triumphing over Bartolo, while E flat major is twice used for Bartolo's pride and anger (though its other appearances seem not to fit this association). The sharp keys of E major and A major are used when firstly Rosina, and later Bertha (one of Bartolo's servants) sing of love.

These hints of a long-term use of tonality by Rossini suggest he was, perhaps, anxious to communicate the narrative developments of the plot in his music. But the music makes its impact above all through its surface sparkle and polish, its rhythmic vitality and its melodic invention. It is this which rouses the admiration of an audience, this and the vocal ornamentation. But, in fact, the sparkle and polish are a form of superficial Romantic rhetoric, all too easily substituting for musico-dramatic truth. There are some moments in *Il Barbiere di Siviglia* when one wonders whether the ornamentation in particular is dramatically necessary or real.

In a comparison with *Le Nozze di Figaro*, *Il Barbiere di Siviglia* comes off considerably the worse. Rossini's characters are less finely drawn; the comedy in situations is emphasized over and above the potential psychological transformations underlying them. Such expansions as occur in the musical fabric are devoted solely to the outpouring of emotion, and their structures contribute nothing to the expression. At times, indeed, the music seems unrelated to what underlies the text. Example 18 is a passage for the Count, newly arrived in disguise at Bartolo's house in the hope of seeing his beloved Rosina. The text may be translated as 'Ah would that she were here, the dear source of my happiness! O come to your beloved, who now awaits you filled with love.' The ornamentation is brilliant, and the harmony naïve: one wonders whether either has anything at all to do with the Count's

Ex. 18   Rossini: *Il Barbiere di Siviglia*

238

obvious longing. He may be 'bubbling over' with excitement, or even swept away in an ecstasy of anticipation, but Rossini's music is a combination of such clichéd naîveté and such gross exaggeration that it trivializes the Count and his situation to the level of *Commedia dell'Arte* buffoonery. All it produces in the audience is the kind of excitement and fun aroused by watching the bubbles in a glass of champagne.

It is moments such as this in Rossini's works and in others of the nineteenth century that have encouraged audiences to see opera as 'beautiful' or 'thrilling' (and sometimes 'witty') music but not as dramatic experience. Intensity of expression within simple structure is, however, no substitute for dramatic truth. It holds our attention on the surface, but in the end prevents us from penetrating beyond. It is also a rather easy way to compose opera,

239

and perhaps explains why Rossini was able to compose his operas so quickly.

Although Paisiello gave Rossini his blessing in 1816, he had earlier called his successor 'a 'licentious' composer who paid little attention to the rules of his art, a debaser of good taste, a man whose great facility in composition was in part the result of a very tenacious memory.'[13] Paisiello was himself a competent but not a great music-dramatist, and his remarks about Rossini might be merely resentment of a younger man's success. But the charges are accurate: Rossini did not have the late eighteenth-century composer's awareness of the proper relationship between a whole and its parts, which is a symptom of good taste, and which is reflected in music-drama through the integrating of content and structure.

Rossini's contemporaries and successors in Italy were Vincenzo Bellini, remembered most for his two operas of 1831, *La Sonnambula* and *Norma*, Saverio Mercadante, now inexplicably forgotten outside Italy, and Gaetano Donizetti. Donizetti, born in 1785, five years younger than Rossini, wrote both comic and serious operas; his major achievement is the tragedy *Lucia di Lammermoor* of 1835, which is chiefly remembered for its 'Mad Scene'.

The serious operas of Donizetti, Mercadante and especially Bellini communicated emotion above all through vocal melody. This was very much in the Italian tradition: Peri had wished to communicate the expression behind a text by means of expressive melody; the early seventeenth-century opera composers had added a more rigorous structure to create the aria, and Italian *opera seria* had seen the aria as the only means of communicating emotion. Italian *opera buffa* had developed the ensemble as a kind of *mélange* of arias, or an aria for several people. But Bellini and his contemporaries developed the vocal line in arias according to the new Romantic musical language, while preserving the traditions of ornament. The result was an original, and very influential musical cantilena.[14]

To emphasize the vocal line in music-drama is to focus attention on the emotions experienced by the characters singing: by involving us through highly expressive vocal melody, with a simple accompaniment, the composer enables us to identify with the experiences of the character — unless, of course, the vocal line degenerates into cliché, which unfortunately has been known to happen in Bellini's operas. As a result, Bellini's arias, like those of *opera seria* composers, are often used as vehicles for the star singer, merely opportunities for vocal display. That this should happen to Bellini's music, in particular, is a pity, for despite his melodic clichés he was a composer who painstakingly sought to write 'dramatic' music in the best sense of the term; his reputation now has largely become that of a 'dramatic' composer in the worst sense — a composer who makes everything submit to sensationalism.

Donizetti, with his experience in comic opera, tended to keep his feet rather more firmly on the ground than did Bellini. Above all, he was conscious of the importance of structure in music-drama. This is evident from an investigation of *Lucia di Lammermoor*. The plot (taken from the novel by Sir Walter Scott[15] is one of almost Gluckian simplicity, in contrast to the plots of Scribe and Meyerbeer, for instance. Lucia (to use the Italian names) is in love with Edgardo of Ravenswood, the enemy of her brother Enrico, who would prefer her to marry a friend of his, Arturo Bucklaw. Enrico succeeds in achieving his aim by devious means; but Lucia murders her Arturo on their wedding night, goes mad, dies, and Edgardo in despair commits suicide. This story of love and violence develops fairly slowly, though intensely, through a series of arias and duets and larger choral scenes. Each number is organized, broadly, in '*cavatina-cabaletta*' structure: an initial, more meditative section is followed by an interruption leading to a faster and more active section. Both the main sections rely for their effect primarily upon vocal melody.

The *cavatina-cabaletta* structure shows its derivation from the patterns of comic action in *opera buffa*, here developed within the framework of the aria.[16] Donizetti however is clearly concerned with the total structure of the scene surrounding the high points of *cavatina* and *cabaletta*: the notes of the vocal melodies are not chosen merely for their temporary impact. This can be illustrated in the duet in Act I between Lucia and Edgardo. Lucia awaits his arrival; he appears to the material shown as Ex. 19 (a), containing two motives, *x* and *y*. These motives provide the remaining vocal material in the scene. Edgardo suggests, in recitative, that he and Lucia flee together to France. He swears eternal war on Lucia's family, swearing 'by the tomb which holds my ancestors' traditions' (Ex 19 (b)). Lucia placates him (c): 'calm yourself, restrain yourself', turning his G minor to G major. The interruption after this cavatina comes with Edgardo switching from angry thoughts about Lucia's family to a demand that she bind her fate to his (d); Lucia agrees, and together they sing that 'only death can end our love' (e). Edgardo announces he must go, and they sing a cabaletta exchanging vows of love (f). Example 19 shows how the motives *x* and *y* are developed, opposed and finally integrated through the scene.

Donizetti extends this kind of structural organization onto the larger scale. *Lucia di Lammermoor* is particularly suitable for this, for in Lucia's

Ex. 19   Donizetti: *Lucia di Lammermoor*

(b) Larghetto

Sul-la tom-ba   che rin - ser - ra,   il tra - di - to ge - ni - to - re ...

(c)

Deh!   ti __ pla - ca, deh! ti pla - ca,   deh! ti fre - na...

(d) Allegro

Qui, di   spo - sa e-ter - na __ fe-de, qui mi giu - ra al cie - lo in - nan-te

(e)

Ah! sol - tan - to il no - stro __ fo - co spe-gne-ra di mor - te il gel ...

(f) Moderato assai

Ver - ran - no a te sull' au - re i miei sos-pi - ri ar - den - ti

'Mad Scene' after having murdered her husband, she imagines she is getting married to Edgardo. She remembers her meeting with him (the duet discussed above): Donizetti quotes directly the cabaletta theme (Ex. 19 (f)). She pictures a wedding ceremony, and Donizetti sheds light on Lucia's tortured mind by using material sung by Arturo before their marriage contract was signed. The vocal line during the whole of the first part of the scene is dominated by a falling four-note pattern. This pattern has appeared only three times before in the opera: once in the Lucia-Edgardo duet (Ex. 19 (c)), once to represent Enrico's basic motivation (in Act I, scene 1), and once as the theme for Edgar's curse, when he discovered that Lucia had married Arturo (Finale, Act I). The final section of the Mad Scene is a cabaletta for Lucia using a triadic motive (see Ex. 20) 'shed bitter tears for me. . .'. Vocal material initiated by this shape has occurred three times in the opera: twice sung by Lucia herself, and all three times in situations when Lucia's love for Edgardo is at issue.

242

Ex. 20 Donizetti: *Lucia di Lammermoor*

Spar - gi d'a - ma - ro pian - to il mio ter - res - tre

ve - - lo

Previous appearances of  shape

(1) Lucia's vision (Act One)

Larghetto

Reg- na-va nel＿ si - len - zi - o ... ... e l'onda pri-a si lim - pi - da ...

(2) Lucia to Enrico (Act Two)

Larghetto

Sof - fri - - va nel pian - to lan - gui - a nel do -lo - re...

(3) Edgardo and Enrico quarrel over Lucia (Act Three)

Marziale

O so - le, più rat - to a sor - ger t'ap - pre - sta...

Further appearance
(4) Edgardo's suicide

Larghetto

Fra po - co a me ri - co - ve-ro da - ra ne -glet-to a-vel - lo...

In *Lucia di Lammermoor* Donizetti shows that, unlike Meyerbeer and Rossini, he was concerned with the psychological structure of music-drama. This is certainly a feature of the composer who towers over every other Italian music-dramatist in the later years of the century: Giuseppe Verdi.

243

Opera in Perspective

Verdi's Rigoletto

Verdi's two great works in the purely Italian operatic tradition of Bellini and Donizetti were *Rigoletto* (1851), and *La Traviata* (1853). Of his other masterworks, *Il Trovatore* (1853) and *Aida* (1871) were strongly influenced by French Grand Opera, *Otello* (1887) uses the Italian tradition but extends beyond it, and *Falstaff* (1893) was Verdi's version of *opera buffa*.

Rigoletto is taken from Victor Hugo's play *Le Roi s'amuse*, first performed in 1832. The plot concerns the physically-handicapped court jester, Rigoletto (Triboulet in the play), whose daughter falls in love with, and is seduced by, Rigoletto's master the Duke of Mantua (Francois I, King of France, in the play).[17] Rigoletto plans, in revenge, to have the Duke murdered; his plot goes awry, and it is his daughter who is murdered instead.

The final act of the opera, in which the tragedy occurs, is superbly constructed by Verdi. The action takes place on a divided stage set, inside and outside an inn: Rigoletto has employed a villainous Burgundian called Sparafucile to murder the Duke, who is due at the inn for an assignation with Sparafucile's sister, Maddalena. (Sparafucile, incidentally, literally means 'shoot-gun') Rigoletto has also brought Gilda with him to observe the Duke's behaviour, to prove that her 'beloved' is a relentless womaniser.

The Duke arrives, and asks for wine and Maddalena. While he waits he sings the famous song '*La donna è mobile*' — woman is fickle. Maddalena appears, and a quartet follows in which the Duke and Maddalena flirt inside the inn while Rigoletto and Gilda comment as they watch from outside the inn (Ex. 21). The quartet is probably the best example of the Italian Romantic version of a Mozartian ensemble: it is a static rather than a dynamic musico-dramatic situation, but it shows Verdi's powers of musical characterization. The progress of each character can be explored through musico-dramatic analysis.

The Duke begins passionately but without using all his powers of persuasion: his melodic line is not the sole melody of interest, for it intertwines with the theme in the orchestra. It is only after he has gone so far as to

Ex. 21   Verdi: *Rigoletto*

sen - ti del mio co - re il fre-quen - te, pal - pi - tar ————— Con un
feel my heart swiftly beating, With a

det - to, un det - to sol tu puo — — i le mie pe - ne, le mie pe - ne con - so -
word alone you could soothe my anguish.

GILDA

Ah ——— co - si par - lar — d'a -
Ah, thus he spoke of

MADDALENA

Ah! ah! ri - do ben di co - re, che tai ba - je cos - tan po - co:
Aha! I laugh; such words are cheap.

IL DUCA

- lar.

- li - ce / betrayed — cor — tra -

po - co; / cheap; — quanto valga il vostro gio - co mel crede - te, so apprez - / the value of your jests I know very

son de' vez - zi tuo - - i; / slave to your charms, — con un / with a

- ti - - va, / liar, — ch'ei / that — men - / he's a

- di - to, / heart. — ah! / ah,

- zar. / well. — So no av - vez za, bel si - gno - re, ad un si - mi - le scher - / I am used, dear sir, to such

det - to un det - to sol tu puo - - i le mie / word alone you could soothe

- ti - - - va, sei si - / liar you may be

253

259

(almost in an aside) propose to Maddalena, and has been refused, that he must bring all his persuasive charm to bear, in the D flat major section. Here he adopts a vocal line very similar to the song he sang on hearing that his followers had successfully kidnapped Gilda. There the text read 'when love's power calls me, I must yield to it'. Here he addresses Maddalena as 'lovely child of love'. The connection is obvious. Through the rest of the quartet the Duke sticks to this theme, musically and dramatically.

Maddalena begins by matching the Duke in her vocal line; in the game of flirtation she is as practised as he. When the Duke launches into his D flat tune, on the other hand, she finds she has considerably more to cope with. Her words suggest she is dismissing him, but her semiquavers mark the beats definitively, suggesting that she is anxious that matters (like time) should proceed in a controlled way: such deliberate clinging on to regular tempo would not be necessary were she not frightened of losing control, and succumbing to the Duke's *rubato*. By bar 81 her control is in so much danger of slipping (the Duke has turned his tune on her twice by this time) that her 'ah! ah!' occurs on the off-beat. By the end she is still fighting, clinging to the reiterated semiquavers, now only on one note for even greater safety. (Maddalena also knows that her brother has agreed to kill the Duke, therefore any liaison she might enjoy with him must perforce be brief. This fact may help her to resist, or it may offer a deliciously wicked temptation to succumb.)

Gilda's reaction to seeing her 'faithful lover' busy seducing someone else is characterized by Verdi through falling phrases of lament and gasps of horror. At bar 75 she is clearly more under control, briefly at least, for she sings in two-bar phrases, a triadic parody of the Duke's theme; after reaching a top B flat in bar 79 she plunges a tenth in bar 80, and then resumes her gasps. A musical identification with the Duke's love-making has brought the horror of the situation home to her again.

Rigoletto says nothing until bar 42: the situation is plain enough for Gilda to see. 'Have you seen enough?' he asks, to a grimly functional rising and falling semitone. The Duke's D flat major theme makes no impression at all on Rigoletto: in bar 68 he picks up the same notes he used in bar 42, as he curtly tells Gilda that weeping will do no good. But he is sympathetic: when Gilda grows more lyrical in bar 75 so does he. From bar 81 he is once again firm, his semiquavers moving on to the emphatic first beat of the bar; in bars 85 and 86, while the others chatter, gasp or lyrically persuade he marches from beat to beat, expressing his cool and relentless determination for vengeance. Only in bar 88 does his emotion burst through — or 'explode' as the word *fulminar* says. In bars 97 to 100, while Gilda gasps on the off-beat he maintains the beat.

Verdi's expression of the emotional situations and reactions of the characters in this quartet is so clear that even in the hands of the dramatically un-trained professional opera-singer the scene can be guaranteed to work on the stage. The lengthy scene which follows is rather more difficult. The Duke curiously but conveniently goes to sleep in his room, yawning his way through a reprise of '*La donna è mobile*', Rigoletto sends Gilda away, and gives Sparafucile a down-payment on the fee for murder. Gilda returns, unknown to Rigoletto, and overhears Sparafucile and Maddalena discussing the murder. Maddalena, attracted by the Duke, persuades Sparafucile that they should cheat Rigoletto; instead of murdering the Duke they could murder someone else — for instance, the first person to arrive at the inn. Gilda, who has overheard this, resolves to sacrifice herself, knocks on the door, and is admitted. A storm which has been threatening suddenly bursts out in all its fury. When it has subsided, Sparafucile emerges from the inn, carrying a body in a sack, and delivers it as promised to Rigoletto. Rigoletto is triumphant. Suddenly, he hears from the inn the voice of the Duke singing '*La donna è mobile*'. He tears open the sack and discovers it contains his dying daughter.

The action in this scene was not conducive to conventional Italian operatic techniques. To dwell lengthily on individuals' emotional reactions would hold up the pace of the action; at the same time, to treat the entire scene as recitative would be contrary to Romantic aesthetics. Verdi therefore conceived of an orchestrally-accompanied free structure, containing two musical ideas which could bind the scene together and at the same time express something of the atmosphere (see Ex. 22). The first is a bell-like motive, with a sound quite different from those of conventional Italian opera; the absence of a third in the chord (except in one bar) creates an empty and rather sinister mood. The second is storm music: lightning, thunder and wind. Elemental forces are at work, not only climatically, but in

Ex. 22   Verdi: *Rigoletto*

terms of human nature too; the link is provided by the chorus humming the 'wind' effect. Thus Gilda's murder occurs when the storm is at its height. To the Romantic, this is no coincidence.

Only three times in the scene does Verdi insert more 'traditional' music into this framework, firstly when the Duke falls asleep singing '*La donna è mobile*' and secondly and thirdly (the music is the same) when Sparafucile and Maddalena agree on the new murder plan and Gilda overhears and seizes her opportunity. The theme used here (see Ex. 22 (c)) has precedents in two places in the opera. A similar theme was used when Monterone, whose wife had been seduced by the Duke, cursed Rigoletto for mocking him. The chorus, aghast at the curse, sang 'Oh you who dared to disturb our feast, guided by an infernal power. . .' The theme is also anticipated (in the same key of D minor) in Rigoletto's denunciation of the Duke and the court, when he speaks of 'the young woman you stole from my house last night. . .' Both these anticipations can be seen to be relevant to the present situation, and show Verdi's long-term structural methods.

Following the second, and musico-dramatically superb, reprise of '*La donna è mobile*' by the supposedly dead Duke, the opera comes to a climax with the duet between an anguished, broken Rigoletto, and the dying Gilda. Gilda is unrepentant, and sings of heaven with a beautiful theme in D flat major (the key of the Quartet). Verdi's expertise in handling music-drama is shown in his treatment of her death (see Ex. 23). She dies just before she can arrive at the final note of her cadence in D flat major: we are held in suspense, and Rigoletto's words maintain that suspense. When *he* reaches the required *d* flat on the word 'morta', the orchestra sounds a diminished seventh, which leads to a cadence, as Rigoletto remembers Monterone's curse, in D flat minor.

This moment is a perfect example of tragedy in music-drama. Gilda's D flat major aria has been one of aspiration beyond this world, as was her act of self-sacrifice. We are with her, involved in the aspiration. But we are returned to reality with Rigoletto's reminding us of the curse of reality; D flat major must become D flat minor. Our involvement switches to Rigoletto, the victim; we are reminded that we are all victims of the everyday world. Aspiration lingers while reality returns: we therefore finally experience the tragic bisociation between higher and lower realities.

Ex. 23   Verdi: *Rigoletto*

263

German Romantic Opera

The growth of German Romantic Opera during the first half of the nineteenth century owed something to influences from Italy and France, more to the influence of Beethoven's 'new' symphonic techniques, but most to the development of specifically German aesthetic and philosophical attitudes. The *Sturm und Drang* school, with its emphasis upon intuition and feeling in opposition to classical, rational, structural considerations, had evolved a series of ideas whose influence can be traced through to the German Romantics proper, but other considerations were important too.

Chief amongst these was an interest in the 'supernatural'. It arose, firstly, from a growing nationalism, evident particularly in collections of German folk-tales, in which supernatural forces play a large part. Germany was not conquered by the Romans, and from the German forests had arisen the first tide of barbarian invasions that overran Western Europe as the Roman Empire collapsed. Greco-Roman Classicism was not part, therefore, of the cultural heritage of Germany; the German Romantic attitude to the supernatural is closer to 'primitive' ideas of the relationship between man and nature. German aesthetic attitudes to classical Greece in the post-Winckelmann later eighteenth and early nineteenth centuries emphasized, therefore, its more pagan, Dionysiac aspects in contrast to the prevalent European attitude which had traditionally stressed the Christian, Apollonian aspects.[18]

A Dionysiac, pagan attitude was entirely in keeping with Romantic ideas in general, in which the emotional life was stressed, and in which man's inner nature was seen to reflect and be reflected in the natural world about him. But it led to a more positive emphasis upon symbolism: connections were made between natural, psychological and moral forces, and these forces could be symbolized as human figures, in keeping with the ideas of primitive man. Thus, in Goethe's *Faust* one of the two main characters is Mephistopheles, not a human figure at all (though he has very human characteristics) but the personification of an idea — 'der Geist der stets verneint' (the spirit of negation) — and a modern version of that primitive nature deity who became in Christian theology the Devil. *Faust* also contains magical and mysterious inexplicabilities that belong to the world of myth rather than to the historical world of Hugo, Meyerbeer and Rossini.

The close relationship between the world we live in and this other, primitive world is exemplified in the Märchen (folk-tales) of E. T. A. Hoffmann, published between 1810 and 1820, the prototypes of the nineteenth-century ghost story, and similar to the English Gothic novel. Hoffmann was a novelist, dramatist, poet, critic and musician, and in 1816 his opera *Undine* was performed in Berlin. It was quite natural that he should see music as a way of connecting the two worlds, for, in his words, 'music discloses to man an unknown realm, a world that has nothing in common with the external, sensual world that surrounds him, a world in which he leaves behind him all definite feelings to surrender himself to an inexpressible longing.'[19] Hoffmann argues in the same essay that music cannot deal with specific things, but 'guides us out of life into the realm of the infinite', a realm which was also represented through the supernatural.

Undine is not an opera that deserves detailed analysis: its importance lies not in its quality but in the fact that it exists, as the first attempt to write German Romantic Opera. In the same year, Ludwig Spohr's *Faust* was produced in Prague; it betrays similar tendencies — though the plot bears little resemblance to Goethe — and further illustrates the way that the traditional *Singspiel* was being developed in response to new aesthetics.

The new aesthetics stressed the role of music as a Dionysiac force, but no German could entirely neglect the demands of ordered structure. What German composers were to contribute to music in the nineteenth century was, above all, a new method of structuring music, born out of Beethoven's symphonic forms, based upon ideas that had appeared with some frequency in music-drama, and essentially concerned with providing a structure that allowed for dynamic narrative.

Although symphonic music-drama, as the new structure is customarily called, was essentially a musical invention, it reflects an idea that was gaining force throughout the first half of the nineteenth century, the idea of evolution. In 1790 Goethe published a book on the metamorphosis of

265

plants, in which he put forward the fundamental concept of continuous, ordered development.

> Whatever forms we examine, especially organic ones, we never find anything standing still, resting or finished, but rather that everything is in a state of continuous motion. We customarily use the word 'structure' to describe what has occurred rather than what is occurring; if we wish to introduce the concept of morphology [the study of change], we should think of 'form' as something held fast in our experience for only a moment. . . Nothing that lives is a single unit, it is a combination of many things; even though it appears to us to be individual, it remains a collection of living, independent entities, similar in idea and predisposition, but in appearance able to be alike or unalike. These entities are sometimes united from the start, sometimes join together eventually. They separate, find each other again, and bring about endless development in every way and in every direction.[20]

Goethe's description fits the development section of a Beethoven Sonata-form movement, or a late Beethoven quartet. It characterizes the tendency of Romantic music to use small musical entities, which react with each other to create overall structures, and reflects the Romantic dislike for closed forms.

This idea was to reach its climax in Wagner, but is already anticipated in his German predecessors, especially Spohr and Weber. In its stress upon 'organic' music, that is to say upon music as continually changing sounds, it is essentially a Romantic idea, built upon the notion of life as progress and the concept of music reflecting the changing emotional life of the individual. It has a more distant musico-dramatic ancestory in Greek tragedy and the *dramma per musica* of the early sixteenth century, and had been present, beneath the surface, in much of eighteenth-century opera as well, as we have seen. But through the German Romantic opera composers it was to emerge into full view, and provide a means for music-drama to throw off the shackles placed upon it by the Italian delight in aria and the French delight in spectacle.

Weber's Der Freischütz

The first really significant German Romantic Opera was Weber's *Der Freischütz*, composed between 1817 and 1820 and performed in Berlin in 1821. Its success was immediate and lasting. The story is taken from German folklore and contains a strong supernatural element. Max, a forest ranger, is anxious to marry Agathe, the daughter of the head ranger, Cuno; she has been promised to him on the condition that he wins the annual marksmanship contest. Max has had little success, but a guaranteed method of winning is suggested to him by Caspar, a fellow ranger. Caspar has struck a bargain with Samiel, the sinister and devilish god of huntsmen, selling his soul to him in exchange for seven magic bullets which never fail to hit their mark. He is now due to forfeit his life and soul, but can defer this if he finds another victim for Samiel. He therefore persuades Max to join him in the gloomy and frightening Wolf's Glen, where together they manufacture the magic bullets for Max. The following day, Max is invited to display his marksman's skills: he shoots at a dove, which turns out to be Agathe — however. Agathe's love and purity are sufficient to deflect the bullet, which instead wounds Caspar. Samiel appears and claims Caspar; a saintly hermit intercedes on Max's behalf, and he is awarded Agathe's hand after a year's probation.

The story has a simple moral theme: Agathe, the symbol of innocent goodness and love, and Caspar and Samiel, symbols of evil and exploitation, battle for Max, and the good wins. The battle takes place where the worlds of everyday and the supernatural meet, a forest, inhabited by the innocent, Romantic-Arcadian rangers and villagers and by the ghostly supernatural forces of Samiel. It is also the world of myth, in which events proceed not according to the laws of logic, but with hidden meaning. Agathe is sitting in her room one day when a portrait of one of her ancestors falls off the wall: accident it might appear, but the text makes it clear that this is no coincidence, but an omen. At appropriate moments Samiel appears, and without any adequate dramatic preparation, the hermit appears at the end to personify the victory of the forces of good. Clearly, the plot is not mere history, nor just a good story: beneath the surface powerful and mysterious forces are at work.

The primitive ancestory of the story is evident. Max's shooting at a target is a symbolic allegory of his wish to win Agathe; in order to attain this end he uses sympathetic magic. In invoking supernatural forces to aid his marksmanship he is really asking for aid in gaining Agathe. This is made clear in the identification between the dove (Max's target) and Agathe herself. The magical force invoked by Max is Samiel, the god of huntsmen; the fact that Samiel is an ancestor-god is shown in the ominous fall of the ancestor-portrait, which injured Agathe slightly, just as the Samiel/ancestor-inspired shot at the dove is to seem to hit Agathe.

The return to myth in *Der Freischütz* was not intended to resurrect primitive music-drama; rather it was the natural outcome of certain themes in Romantic thought. For Weber to use music to reflect, represent and express the mysterious and magical forces beneath the action was quite in keeping with contemporary attitudes to music. In so doing, he not only creates 'pictorial' sounds to represent the supernatural world and the world of forest huntsmen, but also uses music to 'express' the underlying patterns of interrelated forces which are battling beneath the surface conflict. The music is, like the story and characters, symbolic; all three are more meaningful than they at first appear. This was a departure from the French

267

and Italian traditions, where the characters are rarely more than historical figures, the story always explicable within the historical framework of the plot, and the music expresses the individual emotions of the characters but seldom anything more.

In composing music which takes us beneath the surface of the drama, Weber uses two structural devices: recurring melodic themes and key-associations. Although the opera uses the conventional *Singspiel* structure of musical numbers separated by spoken dialogue, the music is concerned less with isolated situations and experiences than with the underlying meaning of the legend as a whole.

The essential conflict in *Der Freischütz* is between Agathe, symbol of innocence and purity, and Caspar/Samiel, symbolizing corruption and evil: the two forces are battling for the soul of Max. Weber symbolizes each of the forces with a theme, shown in Ex. 24. (a) is announced whenever Samiel appears: it is a chord of the diminished seventh.

The diminished seventh chord is a peculiar one, in that it is tonally ambiguous. In theory, it stands for a dominant seventh, whose root is raised by a semitone.[21] Thus the chord of Ex. 4 (a) is analytically a chord of *d natural − f sharp − a* natural *− c* natural, a dominant seventh leading to a chord of G major, but with the *d natural* actually raised to an *e flat*. The resulting diminished seventh chord *e* flat *− f* sharp *− a − c* is a string of minor thirds; it can be shifted up on position to give the chord *f* sharp *− a − c − e* flat and still sounds the same. If we do this, we can then regard the *f* sharp as the 'lifted' root, and can call the chord an altered dominant seventh of *f* natural *− a − c − e* flat, the dominant seventh leading to B flat major. The process can be continued: as a result, the basic diminished seventh chord is four possible dominant sevenths leading to four different keys.

In using a diminished seventh to represent Samiel, the supernatural force, Weber stresses its undefinable or ambiguous quality: the supernatural does not belong to a world of logic and order. Once Max surrenders to it, it can take him in a number of directions over which he has no control. Psychologically, this resembles a condition in which the ego surrenders to the forces of the unconscious, and we can make the same connections between the world of the supernatural and the world of the unconscious which we have made in discussing earlier music-dramas.

Agathe, on the other hand, is characterized by theme (b) in Example 24, a lyrical, triadic, clearly tonal melody in E flat major. Her innocence and purity are a force for order. This theme occurs four times in the opera: twice in the overture, in E flat major and in C major, once in her aria in Act II in E major, and once at the very end of the opera, in C major again.

The system of key-associations used by Weber in the opera builds upon what is implied by these two themes. Samiel's diminished seventh, with its minor third intervals, leads to minor keys, in general associated with the

Ex. 24   Weber: *Der Freischütz*

(a)   (Slow tempo)

(b)   (Allegro)

forces of supernatural evil, particularly C minor. Against C minor is pitted C major (the tonic major), E major (which turns the major third note of C major into an emphatic tonic), and E flat major, the relative major. Figure 18 shows the key associations in more detail.

The outer circle shows the major keys used in the opera, and indicates the positive, benevolent forces they represent. The inner circle shows the minor keys used, arranged, so that each is opposite its relative major, the minor third relativity being suggested bySamiel's diminished seventh. The diminished seventh chord *a — c — e* flat — *f* sharp is shown in the Maltese cross figure. It will be noted that the 'evil' minor keys from B flat minor to C sharp minor are not used by Weber (they are thus shown in brackets): they are in the segments of the circle whose major keys offer the most serious challenge to evil. The 'battle' takes place chiefly in the oppositions between C minor and E flat major, A minor (the key of Max's forebodings) and C major, F sharp minor (the framing key of the Wolf's Glen scene when the magic bullets are cast) and A major (the key in which Agathe and her companion Ännchen sing of happy marriage at the beginning of Act Two.

Der Freischütz contains many musical numbers of quality, but the two most useful to consider here are the Wolf's Glen scene and the Overture.

The Wolf's Glen scene occurs at the end of the second act (the opera is in three acts), the position where, in conventional *opera buffa* and *Singspiel*, occurred the most lengthy ensemble of intrigue and confusion. Nothing could illustrate better the difference between eighteenth- and Romantic nineteenth-century attitudes to music-drama than Weber's replacing comic intrigue at this point with a scene of supernatural horror, set in a rocky glen, and centred around magic spells and incantations, with ghostly apparitions and spectacular stage effects. A key-analysis of this scene is shown in Fig. 19; although it seems on first hearing and sight to be merely a scene of spectacle

269

Fig. 18   Key-associations in Weber's *Der Freischütz*

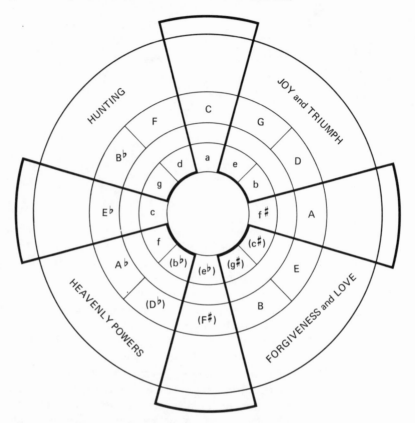

and thrill, with music which pictorializes each supernatural event in turn, there is nevertheless a strictly ordered key-structure beneath. Narrative and dynamic aspects appear to determine the progress of the music, but even here, in the domains of Dionysos, Apollo has a part to play. Within an overall framework of F sharp minor, the main events of the action occur in C minor: the summoning of Samiel, the preparations, Max's descent, and the casting of the final three bullets. The central point occurs when Agathe appears, providing an opposition to the events of the scene, and presented by Weber in C major. Overall, the scene is structured in an arch-like way; narrative structural techniques and ceremonial structural techniques proceed hand in hand. The material used also makes reference, directly or indirectly, to material already presented in earlier numbers, thus reflecting Weber's approach to the opera as an overall structured music-drama.

The Overture is worthy of consideration because it presents the music-

Fig. 19 Wolf's Glen scene from Der Freischütz

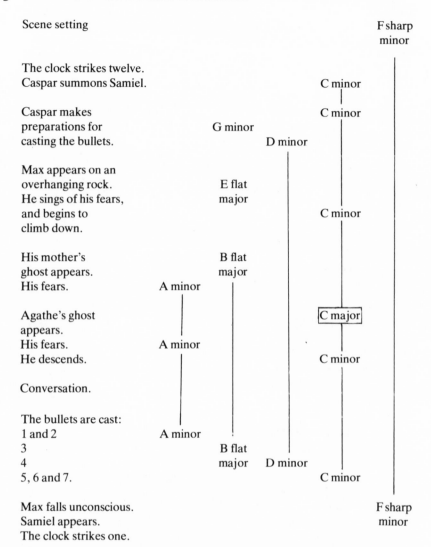

Scene setting					F sharp minor
The clock strikes twelve. Caspar summons Samiel.				C minor	
Caspar makes preparations for casting the bullets.		G minor	D minor	C minor	
Max appears on an overhanging rock. He sings of his fears, and begins to climb down.		E flat major		C minor	
His mother's ghost appears. His fears.	A minor	B flat major			
Agathe's ghost appears. His fears. He descends.	A minor			C major C minor	
Conversation.					
The bullets are cast: 1 and 2 3 4 5, 6 and 7.	A minor	B flat major	D minor	C minor	
Max falls unconscious. Samiel appears. The clock strikes one.					F sharp minor

drama in microcosm while at the same time following a Sonata-form structure. In this it is a descendant of the Mozartian ensemble and the Beethoven symphony, and creates a textless music-drama of its own. Fig. 20 shows the Sonata-form structure together with the texts later sung to the musical material. The first subject material is associated with Max's confrontation with evil, while the second subject material is associated with love, innocence and purity, the forces which oppose evil and which will finally

271

Fig. 20 Overture to Der Freischütz

Thematic references	Musical structure	Key
Forest and huntsmen	Slow introduction	C major
Samiel theme		C minor
	Sonata Allegro:	
	EXPOSITION	
Max (Act I): 'Dark powers surround me. . .' *and* music for the seventh bullet	First subject	C minor
Max's entry into the Wolf's Glen: 'Fearfully gapes the dark abyss. . .'	Bridge passage	E flat major
Agathe (Act I): 'I feel a sweet attraction for him. . .' *and* Act II Finale: 'Whoever is pure and innocent in life. . .'	Second subject	E flat major
	DEVELOPMENT	
'Seventh bullet'		E flat major
		C major
Caspar (Act I): 'Surround him, dark spirits. . .'		C minor
		B flat minor
		D minor
		C minor
Agathe (Act I): 'I' feel a sweet attraction. . .'		G major
	RECAPITULATION	
Max's 'Dark powers surround me. . .' *and* 'Seventh bullet' *and* Samiel theme	First subject	C minor
Agathe (Act I):: 'My pulses beat, my heart seethes; I feel a sweet attraction. . .' *and* 'Whoever is pure and innocent. . .'	Second subject	C major

redeem him.

Der Freischütz is a remarkable work. It blends together operatic elements from *Singspiel*, and from Italian opera (in some of the arias); it is thoroughly Romantic in its emotionalism and its relating of inner emotion to the forces of nature; it resurrects myth and thus reactivates music-drama as an exploration of the inexplicable; it has great dynamic narrative pace, but is structured on the long term; it contains in the Wolf's Glen scene a German Romantic version of a Dionysiac rite, and in the overture an example of symphonic music-drama. Above all, it looks back to primitive music-drama, the ultimate source of all the rebirths of European music-drana, and thereby provides an immediate source for the music-dramas of Wagner.

Romantic Opera as music-drama

Romantic opera is, to many people, the model for all opera. Its particular characteristics have come to be regarded as typical of opera as a whole: emotionally exciting music, historical plots in spectacular settings, a large orchestra and chorus, and virtuoso singing. But our investigation of music-drama has defined the *genre* in rather different terms, and we must therefore ask in what way Romantic opera is related to the basic features and developing traditions of Western European music-drama.

From its beginnings, music-drama has been concerned with the exploration of the mysteries of human existence, in particular with the psychological transformation we have called death-rebirth. This exploration is effected through the use of images, and different sorts of images have been employed at different times by Western Europeans in reflection of the cultural and aesthetic values and attitudes of a particular period. In Romantic opera, the images have tended to be those of a historical setting and even a historically-based (if fictional) plot, in contrast to some other forms of opera which chose myth or the 'everyday reality' of the comic vision. Only *opera seria* shared Romantic opera's predilection for political history. It can be argued that history is less immediately helpful than myth as a veil through which to explore the inexplicable: historical settings present the 'everyday world' of the past, and actions in a historical context may be highly explicable in historical terms. Both *opera seria* and Romantic opera therefore placed a considerable emphasis upon individual emotional expression, as a means of pointing to the universality of the human experiences occurring in a historical context. Thus both *opera seria* and Romantic opera have laid stress upon the individual singer and the impact of vocal melody, showing the depth of emotion (at least theoretically) through ornamentation. By these means the Dionysiac experience speaks through Apollonian history, the eternal through the transient. The agent for this expression in *opera seria* was the *da capo* aria: its equivalent in Italian Romantic opera was the *cavatina-cabaletta*. The two forms reflect a change in attitude: while the

273

da capo aria balances closed structure and narrative development, the cavatina-cabaletta lays much greater stress upon overt progress and development.

Not all Romantic composers succeeded in using current approaches to get to the heart of the matter. History was often seen less as a veil for universals than as an end in itself; the emotionalism of the aria often became less a medium for the transmission of deep human experiences than a vehicle for emotional display. Similarly, the chorus in Romantic opera often acts as merely another individual or a collection of individuals in the plot, rather than being a medium whose function it is to link the characters and the audience in the Greek fashion favoured by Monteverdi and Gluck. The most significant error of the Romantics, however, was in confusing 'important' with 'large'. An important issue, one suspects they felt, will be shown to be important if it is stated in a large enough way. This confusion between the depth of an experience and its size led to music-drama that was impressive without actually saying anything, an exaltation of matters that are essentially trivial, and finally a weakened ability in audiences to distinguish between the worthless and the worthwhile. We are still experiencing the consequences of this Romantic error.

· The inability to distinguish between what matters and what does not matter is paralleled by and reflected in many Romantic composers' inability to balance the parts and the whole. The overall text and subject of an opera was treated in terms of the opportunities it gave for thrilling moments, whereas composers like Monteverdi and Gluck saw the individual moments as parts of a more important whole.[22] Thus we find in Romantic operas little evidence of long-term musical structures.

The 'great' music-dramatists have always perceived that the structure of an image is finally as much part of its meaning as its content. Thus we have noted composers' perpetual struggle with the problem of finding an overall shape to dramatic narrative, for success here determines the success of the overall image. The Romantic composers' emphasis upon narrative as such, born of an aesthetic attitude which lauded progress, frequently led them to neglect overall structural aspects; again, this flaw is often disguised by the impact of the moment. While the Romantic music-dramatists were moving more and more away from the idea of closed numbers and towards the idea of continuity (at least in France and Italy) they rarely succeeded in re-creating the structural virtues of the set-number on the large scale.

There are of course notable exceptions. Verdi and Donizetti both produced great music-dramas within the perhaps unlikely framework of Romantic opera. Here a historical setting is a means and not an end: neither *Lucia di Lammermoor* nor *Rigoletto* needs authentic historical sets and costumes in performance.

Two other operas we have mentioned in this chapter are not ultimately historic at all: *Die Zauberflöte and Der Freischütz.* Both are mythic, with magic and the supernatural playing an important part. The heroes undergo ordeals in order to win the heroines, and these ordeals are the 'deaths' necessary to be 'reborn'. In *Der Freischütz,* Max undergoes his ordeal in the service of Agathe, the Maiden-Goddess of the Hunt, Artemis in another disguise. His descent into the Wolf's Glen parallels, too, Orpheus' descent into the underworld; it is an archetypal image from the collective unconscious.

Such mythic images are far removed from the world of everyday. They are not *realistic* in the sense that the St Bartholomew's Day Massacre is *realistic.* But they are profoundly *real* in that they arouse a response from our subconscious minds. That response cannot be verbalised in the same way that we might verbalise a moral from witnessing a reconstruction of the St Bartholomew's Day Massacre. But if we cannot verbalise our response, that response is no less valid.

It is perhaps ironic that the Romantic period should by and large have tended more towards realistic, historical music-drama than towards inexplicable, mythic music-drama, for one of the cornerstones of Romantic aesthetics was the belief in the inexplicability of artistic images. In fact the apparent dichotomy between explicability and inexplicability in Romantic music-drama can be explained in terms of the development of Western European thought.

The great expansion in scientific discovery and investigation during the seventeenth and eighteenth centuries was based on two principles: firstly that the universe is governed by absolute laws, and secondly that cause and effect, 'causality', lies at the heart of the structure of the universe. The idea of absolute scientific law was summed up in Newton's *Principia* (1687), which was based above all upon the notion that time is absolute. The doctrine of causality can be summarized in the dogma that 'there is in nature and history a causal law so binding that every event is a necessary result of what has gone before and a necessary cause of what will come.'[23] Not all philosophers subscribed wholeheartedly to these doctrines (notably David Hume) but they remained the fundamental props of scientific and philosophical thought. We have met both ideas before, in a different context: the doctrine of absolutism as political theory, and the doctrine of causality in terms of the idea of developing, structured progress. Goethe's morphological theories attempted to show the absolutes behind the processes of change.

The theories of causality and absolute natural laws enable explanations to be offered for the phenomena we perceive in the everyday world; what happens is the result of what has happened, in accordance with scientific law. Thus an apple on the ground is the result of the apple falling from a tree in accordance with the law of gravity. This is the rational, scientific approach to the world. From it there follows the belief that the meaning of what we perceive is explicable.

Primitive man had a different view. Seeing an apple lying on the ground, he could imagine a number of reasons for it being there; the 'meaning' of what he perceived lay, for him, in areas beyond pure scientific explanation. As we have noted, myth does not proceed according to scientific, causal laws, and the events which occur in myth may be impossible to interpret according to 'scientific truth'. The scientific, rational method starts from the assumption that the universe is explicable in absolute terms, and seeks explanations which can be expressed verbally. But man from his earliest times has accepted that many things in the world are inexplicable in verbal terminology, and can only be explored irrationally; it was from this idea that music-drama sprang.

Romantic aesthetics opposed what was thought of as the excessive rationalism of eighteenth-century aesthetics. Early nineteenth-century poets, writers and musicians believed that art was an expression of things beyond or above causality. In a pre-Freudian era, personal emotion and behaviour were seen to be inexplicable, *acausal*, not open to scientific investigation. In short, the Romantics were emphasising the acausal in a causal world.

Thus it is that we can see why magic and the supernatural, as acausal 'explorations' of events, should be stressed. We can also see why Romantic music-drama stressed the acausal phenomenon of intense emotional expression, even though in a work like *Les Huguenots* the causality of history is employed as an explanation of events. Even more significantly, we can see why Romantic music-dramatists — and composers and poets — had problems with structure. Artistic images are combinations of the inexplicable, in the content of the image, and the explicable and analysable, in the structure of an image. In stressing the acausal content of images, they came up against the problem of how this could be preserved within the causal structure of images. And the more the musical language developed in the service of acausal expression, the more the causal structure of the language was disturbed.

It was a dilemma to which there was no easy solution. But one man came up with an answer, a way of bringing together causal and acausal elements, of providing a renewed integration between the irrationality of acausal experience in dramatic images and the rationality of causal musical structures. The man was Richard Wagner; but his solution, like all solutions to this problem in the history of opera, was so rooted in the temporary cultural attitudes of Romanticism that it could not be a final answer, however much he might wish.

8 Wagner and after

Wagner and Romanticism

With Wagner we reach the culmination of Romantic thought. Almost every characteristic of Wagner's art can be seen to have its antecedents in one or other of his predecessors' works; but what makes Wagner exceptional is that he was able to bring the various trends and ideas together into a coherent system. Like his contemporaries Darwin and Marx, Wagner created out of the various strands of his time a single entity of ideas which was immensely persuasive, and influenced patterns of thought for several generations.[1]

By 1859 Wagner was thoroughly schooled in current operatic methods. While a student at Leipzig, he had come under the spell of Beethoven, Shakespeare, Schiller and Weber. As a vocal coach and chorus trainer in Würzburg, he had immersed himself in the current operatic repertoire. Between 1837 and 1839, as musical director of the theatre at Riga, he had spent much of his time conducting Italian Romantic operas and French *opéras comiques*. From 1839 to 1841 he was in Paris, attempting without success to break into the world of French Grand Opera. From 1843 to 1849 he was musical director at the Dresden opera, and here were performed the works in which he first showed his musico-dramatic abilities: *Rienzi, Der fliegende Holländer* and *Tannhäuser;* here too *Lohengrin* was composed. In 1849 he became involved in an abortive revolution in Dresden, whence he fled rather abruptly to Switzerland. Here, from 1849 to 1852, he occupied himself with writing about opera, re-thinking its problems, and producing solutions drawn from his personal experiences in the operatic and political worlds. Chief amongst his writings was *Oper und Drama*, which, as the title suggests, distinguishes between the sort of 'opera' currently being written and the 'music-drama' which he believed should supplant it. During these years he also worked on the libretto and music of what was to be *Der Ring der Nibelungen*, his epic series of four music-dramas drawn from Northern European myth.

Wagner was an extraordinary man: egotistical and arrogant, impossibly

277

extravagant, often at odds with conventional morality, utterly dedicated to the truth as he saw it but at the same time willing to comprise his theoretical principles if that would help get his works performed. There were in him the typically Romantic ingredients of charlatanism, utter sincerity, self-pity, self-aggrandisement, a delight in the decadent and grandiose, deviousness, brutality, fanaticism, eccentricity and devotion. He aroused in those around him sycophancy and hatred, adoration and disgust. For those composers who admired him, he became an idol, a terrible peril, and an almost insurmountable problem.

In addition to composing music-drama, Wagner was a theoretician. Although his practice did not altogether coincide with his theories, it is remarkable how closely they are related, in most important respects. Wagner's essential standpoint was that opera should not be mere entertainment, but (and he drew on Greek tragedy to support this) a fundamentally educative and ennobling experience. In his view, Romantic opera (like much of eighteenth-century opera) had debased the form, allowing 'drama' to serve music: everything was subordinate to music's power to thrill. Like Algarotti, he advocated the opposite extreme, that music's proper place was to serve the 'drama'. In fact, as his own works show, by 'drama' he did not mean the non-musical ingredients of opera such as text, scenery, lighting and so forth; 'drama' was for him the totality of opera, the whole series of experiences arising from, reflecting and commenting on the human condition that formed, he believed, the only proper subject and object of opera.

In reforming opera, therefore, Wagner felt it necessary to reform every part of it. The story should be taken from myth and presented in a series of simple actions, supported by a text written in short phrases and providing through its alliterations a series of pathways to the roots of human experience. Romantic music was the means through which what lies behind the action could be communicated: in speaking to our feelings, the music would give us a deeper knowledge than mere text and action can do. But the 'drama', the inner action beneath the surface, unfolds continuously, not in a series of sudden emergencies; therefore the musical texture must be continuous. A vocal melody, he believed, is too closely related to the text to be able to communicate properly what lies behind it: that function must be performed by the orchestra, the modern equivalent to the Greek chorus in its ability to universalize specific emotions and to comment on the action. Furthermore, Wagner believed, if opera is to make its full impact as total drama, all the ingredients must be integrated to serve a common purpose, as a *Gesamtkunstwerk* (a collective work of art). The libretto should be written by the composer. Acting must be related to music — therefore Wagner produced his own operas and let others conduct them. Above all, the music-drama must be performed in the right environment, in which an audience is totally concerned with the images presented to it; accordingly, he built the opera-house at Bayreuth, with the seats arranged in the fashion of the Greek amphitheatre, and with the orchestra hidden below the stage, so that the mechanics by which the inner action was evoked should be invisible.

In his practical aspirations, Wagner sounds like an idealist with 'impossible' aims, which he was; but his energy, his good fortune, and the worth of his music-drama enabled him in the end to attain the fulfilment of many of his ideals. Wagner's moral and artistic idealism was, moreover, firmly grounded in the everyday world: he believed that music-drama was so relevant to the human condition that through it mankind might be brought to a better life — which he defined according to his own political philosophy. Such a naïve Romantic view might bring a smile to the thin lips of the twentieth-century cynic. Like the arts in general, music-drama is usually less a vehicle for the reform of man than a reflection of the views he already holds. Auber's *La Muette de Portici* might, as the story goes, have caused the Belgian Revolution of 1830; but it could hardly have done so unless its revolutionary sentiments (which are by no means the central theme of the opera) had corresponded with sentiments already felt and voiced. Wagner's 'reformed' music-drama is best seen, not as 'The Art-Work of the Future' (as he called it) or even as part of a revolutionary programme, but rather as a symptom of Romantic thought.

On the purely musical level, Wagner's theoretical ideal of continuously developing orchestral music without set numbers was scarcely easy to put into practice. In emphasizing musical narrative, he was faced, like Peri, with the problem of structure. But, unlike Peri, Wagner had a number of precedents to go on: Beethoven's symphonic structures, the Mozart ensemble, Gluck's setting of whole scenes as units, and the possibilities inherent in German composers' use of classical tonality as a unifying element.

Accordingly, he evolved a system of musical structure based upon melody and modulation. Both these methods of shaping continuous music had been experimented with by Wagner's immediate predecessors. Out of the melodic style of the late eighteenth century, early nineteenth-century composers had evolved the melodic germ, a small, easily memorable idea which could be developed, expanded, altered and placed in different harmonic and rhythmic contexts without losing its essential identity. In Wagner's hands, this became the *leitmotiv*.

The *leitmotiv* does not have a purely musical function: it is a musico-dramatic device. It is no coincidence that it should be called a 'motive', for the *leitmotiv's* function is to express the motives of the drama, the ideas and feelings which motivate the characters to action. Many of the *leitmotiven* in Wagner's operas have been given names for convenience (for instance the 'Sword-motive' in *The Ring*); Wagner disapproved of this idea, for it

279

suggests the sort of pictorial approach to music-drama which he considered corrupt. (Although in the following discussion we, too, conveniently give names to *leitmotiven*, it must be remembered that music is not an explicitly descriptive medium.)

Wagner's use of modulation as a structural ingredient also owes much to his predecessors. The requirements of intense Romantic expression had led composers to experiment with ever more daring modulations from key to key; ambiguous chords such as the diminished seventh were increasingly used to express the indefinite quality of Romantic feelings. For Wagner to use modulation as a structural ingredient was therefore not a restrictive practice: on the contrary, in establishing principles of modulation he was able to keep control over an expanding tonal idiom.

Wagner's theory of modulation is essentially a system of key-associations: to the best of my belief he was the first composer to point out in cold print the advantage of this sytem in the composition of music-drama, although, as we have seen, the system had been extensively and naturally used throughout the history of Western European opera. Wagner's outline of a theory of modulation in *Oper und Drama* has received less attention than it deserves, with the result that many have believed Wagner's music to be lacking in tonal organization. It is therefore worth quoting it in full, even in Wagner's rather turgid prose.

> To the sensitive ear, as we have observed, alliteration (*Stabreim*) can unite the speech-roots of words of opposing emotional expression, as in *Lust und Leid* (joy and pain), *Wohl und Weh* (well-being and grief), and thus present them to the emotions in a family relationship. On a higher level of expression, musical modulation can make such a relationship obvious to the feelings. If we take, for example, an alliterative line of single emotional meaning, such as *Liebe gibt Lust zum Leben* (love gives joy to life), then, just as the alliteration stresses the single emotion, so the musician has no reason to quit his chosen key. If we now take a line of mixed emotional meaning, such as *die Liebe bringt Lust und Leid* (love brings joy and pain), then, just as the alliteration combines two contrary emotions, so the musician is compelled to modulate from the first key, representing the first emotion, to another key, representing the second emotion, the second key being determined according to the relationship between the two emotions. The word *Lust* in this example is the climax of the first emotion and presses on towards the second, and must be treated with an emphasis quite different from that in the former example *die Liebe gibt Lust zum Leben*. The note to which it is sung will automatically turn into a note leading into the second key representing *Leid*.
>
> This combination of *Lust und Leid* presents a special emotion, whose individuality lies in the point where two emotions interact, relate and influence each other. Such a phenomenon is only possible in music, because of music's talent for harmonic modulation. Out of this it can create emotional tension as no other art can.

280

Let us now see how musical modulation hand in hand with poetic content can lead back to the original emotional stance. If we follow the first line *die Liebe bringt Lust und Leid* with *doch in ihr Weh auch webt sie Wonnen* (yet even in her grief she weaves blisses), then *webt* (weaves) becomes the note leading back to the first key, for here the second emotion returns, enriched, to the first. . .

We can best understand the immensity of music's power [to show the structure of emotion] if we imagine that, between the move away from the first emotion and the return to it in the second line, a longer sequence of lines occurs, expressing the various crescendos and blends of intervening emotions — now strengthening, now conciliatory — until the final return of the main emotion. Here, to realize the poetic intention, we must pass through and back from the most various keys; all the keys touched on must however appear in exact family relationship to the original key. . .[2]

Example 25 is a home-made musical illustration of modulation-theory, showing its application in four ways. (a) is a simple setting of the text at a fast tempo: F major is employed for 'Liebe', and D minor for 'Leid'. At 'webt' the chord acts as a pivot, returning us to F major. Only one *motiv* is used, the ascending arpeggio figure, and it appears in both keys. In (b) a more moderate tempo is used, and a more complex approach. The same keys are used: this time the word 'Leid' as a D minor chord in first inversion, the root position being reached on 'Weh', where however the seventh is added. The

Ex. 25   Wagner's Modulation Theory

(d) Sehr mässig

Die Lie - be bringt Lust und Leid; Doch ____

____ in ihr Weh _____ auch Webt sie Won - nen.

(copyright: John D. Drummond)

return to F major is achieved through a typical Wagnerism: in bar 9 we have the dominant of the dominant of F major, which moves in bar 11 to a second inversion chord of F major. Two motivic ideas are used, the rising chromatic scale, which generates the need for a theme, and the descending diatonic scale (bars 3, 11 and 13) which is more of a *motiv*. In (c) a further step is taken: the *motiv* in bar 1 itself suggests a modulation from F major to D minor, and thus sums up the harmonic-expressive idea of what is said. At 'Wonnen' a new *motiv* is introduced — the 'bliss-*motiv*', to carry the musico-dramatic action forward. Finally, in (d), we see the effects of using a more advanced chromatic idiom, that of *Tristan und Isolde;* indeed, this version is based on a *Leitmotiv* from that work although Wagner would scarcely have used it as naîvely as here. In this version the second key is A flat minor; it will be seen that the chromatic harmony is such as to make the prevailing tonalities less distinct.

As outlined in *Oper und Drama*, Wagner's modulation theory clearly provides a method for structuring tonality on the small-scale. It is also applicable to large-scale organization, for keys can be used with long-term associations, and the return of dramatic ideas at a much later date in an opera can result in the return of particular tonal areas. Indeed, it is the large-scale tonal structures which are most evident in Wagner's music-dramas (see the analyses of Lorenz, George and others); on the small-scale,

283

analysis is made more difficult by the chromatic inflections of Wagner's musical language.

Wagner owed much to his immediate predecessors, not only in his ideas, but also in his musical style. His ease with melody can be traced to his thorough experience with the Italian opera that he later so despised. His ability to match theatrical effect with appropriate music he learned from the French Grand Opera he later scorned. His harmonic language is developed from that of Spohr, Marschner, Schumann, and later, Liszt. His predilection for German subject-matter derives from Weber and his successors. Many of his theoretical ideas can be found in earlier writings in music-drama. But he owed much more to his own abilities. Wagner was gifted not only with musical talents, but with a vision of music-drama as a powerful and distinctive art-form. How and where he acquired it we do not know: as a boy he was passionately interested in drama; perhaps something might be built on the fact that in 1847, just before his own ideas were hardening into theory, he spent some considerable time editing — and drastically altering — Gluck's *Iphigenia in Aulis.*

Dramatic themes in Tristan and Isolde

The story of Wagner's *Tristan und Isolde* (composed 1857–9) can be summarized briefly, but depends on knowledge of preceding events. Tristan, the champion of King Marke of Cornwall, defeated and killed in battle Lord Morold, the betrothed of Princess Isolde of Ireland, but was himself dangerously wounded in the combat. Isolde, finding him, at first determined to kill him, but was unable to, because of the look in his eyes. As a mistress of the arts of magic, she healed Tristan's wounds, and he abruptly left her to return to Cornwall, where he had told King Marke of Isolde. The king then resolved to take Isolde as his queen, sending Tristan to Ireland to fetch her.

When the opera opens we are on board ship: Tristan is bringing Isolde to Cornwall. Isolde, furious at Tristan's treatment of her, invites him to drink with her. She has prepared a poison, and is willing to sacrifice herself to bring about Tristan's death. But her maid Brangäne has substituted a love-potion for the poison. Isolde and Tristan drink (Tristan perceives Isolde's plan and is willing to die): but instead of dying, they fall in love. At this moment the ship docks, and the populace is heard hailing the approach of King Marke.

In Act II we learn that Tristan and Isolde have kept their love a secret. It is evening, and King Marke is out hunting with Lord Melot and his other attendants. Isolde has arranged to meet Tristan, and awaits him in a glade. He arrives; they confess their love for each other, and realize that their love can be consummated only in death. As they embrace, King Marke arrives, warned of the meeting by Melot. Tristan refuses to recant and provokes a fight with Melot, allowing himself to be stabbed.

In Act III we are at Tristan's castle in Brittany, whither his faithful servant Kurwenal has taken the wounded hero. Isolde is due to arrive by ship to join him. Tristan, delirious, imagines her arriving, but when she does so it is only in time to see him die. Her ship is closely followed by one bearing King Marke and Melot; as they force entry into the castle Kurwenal succeeds in killing Melot, at the cost of his own life. King Marke offers forgiveness to Isolde, but she prefers to join her beloved Tristan in death: singing of their love, she falls unconscious on his body.

This story contains some obvious Romantic ingredients: the glorification of (sexual) love, the challenge of love to convention and honourable behaviour, the sacrifice of a heroine to her beloved. But Wagner's view of love here extends beyond the conventions of Romantic opera. For him, love is closely related to death: Tristan and Isolde find love in place of death in the first act, agree that love can only be comsummated in death in the second, and achieve the unity of love in death in the third act. Love-death, in German *Liebestod*, is the central theme of the opera.

It is also an apt description of the Dionysiac experience, and as such relates to what has been called the pagan element in German Romantic literature. Love and death are both moments involving the loss of identity; combined, they become a symbol of psychological transformation. The German pagan Hellenist writers such as Schlegel and Heinse promoted the idea of love and death, symbolized in the single image of *Nacht* (night) as against the classical Hellenist Enlightenment idea of Apollonian *Tag* (day) as a symbol of reason and clarity. The supreme example of this Dionysiac view in the works of the German Romantic poets is the *Hymnen an die Nacht* of Novalis. This series of poems purports to be inspired by a vision Novalis had at the grave of his fiancée.

> The unity of death and love, the 'synthesis of eternity and temporality' is the central theme of *Hymns to the Night* (1799). The great symbol of this integration is night. It is the emblem of the unconscious, out of which, by means of wilful forgetting, divine elements arise in the soul, and in which the soul strives through Eros towards the divine. . .[3]

That Wagner drew the idea of *Liebestod* from this Romantic tradition is clear, and can be shown by placing side by side two passages of text, one from a hymn of Novalis, and one from Wagner's *Tristan und Isolde*. 'I cross the frontier of death, each stab of anguish a spur to rapture; soon I shall be free and lie intoxicated in the embrace of love.'[4] 'Then shall we die together, eternally, endlessly together, with no awakening, no fearing, anonymous in love's embrace, lost in each other, our lives but love.'[5]

Wagner went further and adopted the symbolism of *Tag* and *Nacht* in the opera. The lovers abhor the world of honour, proper behaviour and moral codes symbolized by King Marke and by *Tag*, and together seek the world of

285

Nacht. And since this is music-drama, not poetry, Wagner is able to create the symbols visually on the stage. Thus Isolde plots to kill Tristan on board the ship with the curtains which surround her 'apartment' closed; they remain closed while the potion is drunk, but are thrown open to admit bright daylight as the ship docks and the ceremonies of arrival are forced on Tristan and Isolde. Act II takes place in the evening; night falls as the lovers declare their love for each other, and day dawns as they are discovered by Marke and Melot. On a textual level, too, *Tag* and *Nacht* symbolism is used, often in a rather dense and impenetrable manner. The second act contains a lengthy philosophical discussion between Tristan and Isolde, in which the issue discussed is essentially that of *Tag* versus *Nacht.* Thus Isolde, speaking of her desire in Act I to poison Tristan, interprets it in the following way: 'I wanted to escape from the light of *Tag*, to take you with me into *Nacht*, where my heart promised there would be an end of deceit, where the foreboding delusion of deceit would dissolve, and there to drink to you eternal love, and, united with you, to dedicate us both to death.'[6]

The association between night, love and death is an extremely ancient one. The reader is reminded of the rites of the Marind-Anim tribe, and of the typical fertility-rite involving sex and symbols of death and marriage. Indeed, the imagery of *Tristan und Isolde* is obviously associated with Dionysos and rituals of death and rebirth. We may regard the drinking of the potion in Act I as the primary death-rebirth symbol in the opera: the lovers believe they are dead and reborn. Following this symbol of adolescent initiation, Act II brings the death-rebirth image into association with a symbolic marriage: the death and rebirth is musical, for it occurs between and within Tristan and Isolde in their long love duet. The third act reaches its climax with the symbolic and actual moment of physical death for the two lovers; their rebirth is forecast in Isolde's closing lines, which leave us in the audience aspiring towards rebirth ourselves.

In between these moments of death-rebirth *Tag* continually reasserts itself; aspiration is, up until the last moment, continually followed by the sudden appearance of everyday reality. Technically speaking, this is more usual as a comic device, but within the work as a whole it operates each time in much the same way as at the end of Verdi's *Rigoletto*, by reinforcing our sympathy with those who aspire and who now become victims.

The descent of Tristan and Isolde into the world of *Nacht*, which brings the promise of their being truly united, has some similarity with the moment in the Orpheus legend when Orpheus descends into Hades in the hope of regaining unity with Euridice. But the Tristan story is not the whole of the Orpheus legend: we can find a long-term version of it spread over the whole of Wagner's output of operas from 1850 until his death.[7] Figure 21 gives a brief resumé of this. It should be noted that rough sketches of the story-lines of all these works were made before 1856. Of all the moments in the

Orpheus legend, the descent into Hades, the world of the supernatural, is the moment most likely to appeal to a Romantic composer like Wagner, and in *Tristan und Isolde* Act II he explored with compelling power the Dionysiac experience which he believed lay at the heart of music-drama.

Fig. 21   Wagner's operas and the Orpheus legend

RHEINGOLD and DIE WALKÜRE
Acts I and II
(composed 1853–5)
Wotan (Old Orpheus), to preserve   Orpheus seeks and
his power, consults the Earth-   finds the nature-nymph,
Mother and begets by her   Eurydice.
Brünnhilde.

DIE WALKÜRE Act III
(composed 1855–6)
Wotan 'loses' Brünnhilde.   Eurydice dies.

SIEGFRIED Acts I and II
(composed 1856–7)
Siegfried (Young Orpheus)   Orpheus defeats
defeats the dragon and   Charon and
enters its cave.   enters Hades.

TRISTAN und ISOLDE
(composed 1857–9)
Tristan (Young Orpheus)   Orpheus seeks
seeks unity with Isolde   unity with Eurydice
in love-death.   in Hades.

DIE MEISTERSINGER
(composed 1861–7)
Hans Sachs (Old Orpheus)   Orpheus is told
teaches Walther (Young Orpheus)   that he must
the need for control over emotion   control his desire to look
in art.   and speak to Eurydice.

SIEGFRIED Acts II and III
(composed 1865–9)
Siegfried finds and wins   Orpheus finds and regains
Brünnhilde.   Eurydice.

GÖTTERDÄMMERUNG
(composed 1869–72)
Siegfried loses his memory. . .   Orpheus 'forgets' the condition. . .
loses Brünnhilde. . .   loses Eurydice. . .
remembers her too late. . .   remembers too late. . .
and he and Wotan are   and returns alone,
'destroyed'.   in despair.

PARSIFAL
(composed 1877–9)

Parsifal (Young Orpheus) rejects women. Gurnemanz' (Old Orpheus) Kingdom and the Grail are saved by the sign of the Cross.	Orpheus rejects women. Apollo intervenes and rescues Orpheus.

DIE SIEGER (The Victors)
(plot sketched 1856)

Lovers are united only if the condition of chastity is observed.	Orpheus and Eurydice renounce Dionysos and are united in Apollo's heaven.

Musico-dramatic structure in Tristan und Isolde

Wagner's two methods of structuring symphonic, continuous music, the *Leitmotiv* and his modulation-theory, are more than merely structural devices for music: they are musico-dramatic, for each is strictly related to text and inner action. It follows therefore, that the recapitulation of melodic materials and keys depended to a large extent upon the organization of text and plot: it is small wonder that Wagner felt he should write his own libretti, for in doing so he would be making pre-compositional decisions about the music. It is this that explains his curious comment that he had the music in his head when writing his texts.

Figure 22 shows the system of key-associations used by Wagner in *Tristan und Isolde*. It will be seen that C major (*Tag*) extends its influence to F major and G major, which represent the virtues of the *Tag*-world. The sharpest and flattest keys are those associated with love and *Nacht*. Any analysis of keys used in the opera is fraught with danger, and fig. 22 has been arrived at only after very detailed study of the opera, particularly of Act II, the centre of the work in more ways than one. The basic assumption of the tonal analysis leading to this conclusion is that Wagner's harmony is based upon the use of substitute-chords,[8] and further that he uses ambiguous chords according to their pure sound-effect. This can be illustrated in an analysis of the opening bars of the opera, a series of chords which have challenged analysts for a century. Example 26 analyses the opening bars, the so-called Potion-*motiv*, by means of deducing a series of steps by which Wagner might have subconsciously arrived at their individual sound. (a) represents a straightforward tonal progression A minor, F major as a Neapolitan chord to E major, B major as the dominant of E major, and E major itself; in short, a four-bar progression in A minor from tonic to dominant, with natural tonal balance: the second bar moves in a flat direction, the third in a much sharper direction, and the fourth to a flatter position just sharp of the tonic, giving the shape ⌐_⌐¯⌐_

Fig. 22   Key-associations in Wagner's *Tristan und Isolde*

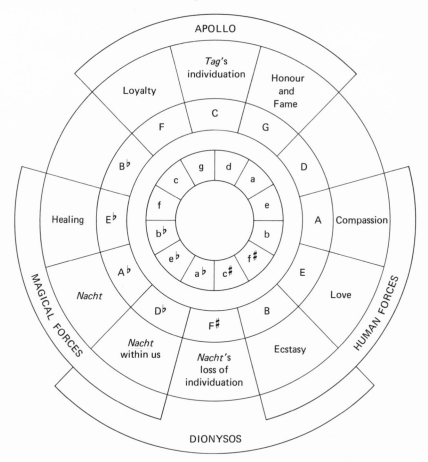

In (b) a chromatic alteration is made: the third bar holds over the *a* and *f* from the second bar to make an augmented sixth chord (a 'French' sixth) in E major.

Ex. 26   Wagner: *Tristan und Isolde*

289

In (c) the harmony to the 'tune' of bars one and two is elided: the crucial *f* natural in the bass in bar three is now 'prepared' by the single held *f* natural in the tune of bar two. In (d) the opening *a* is shortened in order to throw greater emphasis onto the held *f*; but in so doing the implied A minor chord in bar one is reduced in value: to compensate, a seventh is added to the final chord, turning E major into a dominant seventh in A minor. The chords in bars three and four have their parts rearranged, in order that the *d* natural in bar four should follow clearly from the preceding *d* sharp; in consequence, there arises a four-note *motiv f – e – d sharp – d natural* of descending semitones in the alto part. In (e) this *motiv* is applied to the uppermost part

290

in inversion. In (f) a time signature of 6/8 is added, and we arrive at what Wagner actually wrote. It becomes obvious that we have a chromatic progression in A minor, using two ambiguous chords: in the second bar an implied Neapolitan chord, and in the third bar an augmented sixth chord.[9]

Wagner's harmony in *Tristan und Isolde* can nearly always be deciphered in this way, by 'removing' its chromatic alterations and seeking its implications. At the same time, it is important to note that the actual surface of sound is more important than the scaffolding which supports it: these opening bars have a Dionysiac sound-effect of unfulfilled yearning which characterizes Tristan's and Isolde's yearning for the world of *Nacht*. The impact of this emotion is, however, strengthened and finally justified by the Apollonian structure which underlies it.

The long duet in Act II between the lovers is in two sections. In the first, they discuss their relationship and its history, in terms of *Tag* and *Nacht*. The whole section is closely structured by Wagner, using *leitmotiven* and key associations. Example 27 is a short extract (bars 682 to 713) in which this is revealed.[10] The text literally translated, reads 'To *Day* [*Tag*], to *Day*, to malicious/*Day*, to our fiercest enemy all hate and indictment!/As you [extinguished] the torch, o might I the light, to avenge love's sufferings in [the face of] insolent *Day*, extinguish!/Is there any distress, any anguish that it does not awaken with its shining? Even in *Night's* [*Nacht*] twilight splendour/my beloved shelters it at home and threatens me with it!' The diagonal lines

Ex. 27   Wagner: *Tristan und Isolde*

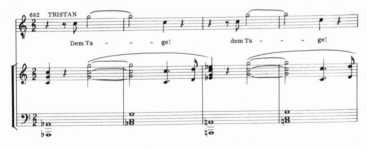

hegt ihn Lieb - chen am Haus.   streckt mir dro - hend ihn aus!

above, and in the musical example, indicate the divisions of the passage as analysed below:

682–7   Quasi-A flat major, ending with E flat 7;

688–93 E major,[11] including the Potion *motiv* (Ex. 26) in 690–1, and the two augmented sixth (German) progression E to E flat 7 in 691–2; the passage ends on E flat 7;

694–701 E major, including 'sounds' of A flat (bars 695 and 697), and an augmented sixth (French) progression E to E flat 7 in 700–701; the passage ends on E flat 7;

702–9   E major, with parodies of the Potion *motiv* in 702, 703 and 704; augmented sixth (German) progressions, from F7 to E7 in 707–8 and from E7 to E flat 7 in 708–9; the passage ends on E flat 7;

710–12 A flat major, including the Potion *motiv* progression in 712.

713   Orchestra begins next section; Isolde sings in the following bar.

Despite the fact that this section *sounds* unstructured (there is only one perfect cadence, in 709–10), it is evident that beneath the surface a rigorous structure is being used. Tonally, the passage is based on an E major/A flat major polarity, summarized in the augmented sixth progression E7 to E flat 7, which has its source in the Potion *motiv*. Thematically, the *Tag motiv* is almost constantly present: its falling and rising shape is shown in the orchestra in bars 681–4 (as well as in the home-made Ex. 25 (e)).

The musical structure is also a musico-dramatic structure: *Tag* is what Tristan is discussing, and he views it from the point of view of *Nacht* (A flat major) and E major (love).

In the second part of the duet discussion gives way to an embrace of tender love. Tristan draws Isolde down onto a bank of flowers (says Wagner's stage direction), kneels before her and she cradles his head. Together they sing the following text:

O sink upon me, night (*Nacht*) of love,
Make me forget that I may live;
Receive me into your womb;
Set me free from the world!
Now the last lights are extinguished;
All we thought about, all we imagined,

293

All our memories, all our recollections;
Holy twilight's sublime foreboding
Obliterates the horror of delusion,
Liberating us from the world.
Hidden the sun, in our hearts,
Stars of bliss shine and smile.
Caught in the web of your magic,
Sweetly dissolved in your gaze;
Hearts united, lips united,
United in a single breath,
My glance is broken, blinded by love;
The world and its brilliance have faded,
All that *Tag* deceitfully showed us;
[I stand] opposed to deceit and illusion,
I myself am the world,
Sublime, blissful intermingling,
Life sanctified to love,
[I am] that desire
From which there is no re-awakening,
That is free from delusion,
That knows only beauty.[12]

This passage describes the Dionysiac experience, and Wagner's music for this Hymn to *Nacht* (see Ex. 28, bars 1102 to 1213 of Act II[13] deliberately creates a mood of dreamy yearning. At the same time, it too is rigorously structured.

Bars 1102 to 1121 accompany the sinking of the lovers onto the bank of flowers. The passage begins in A major (the first chord being in the subordinant, D major); at bar 1107 we arrive on that very augmented sixth

Ex. 28   Wagner: *Tristan und Isolde*

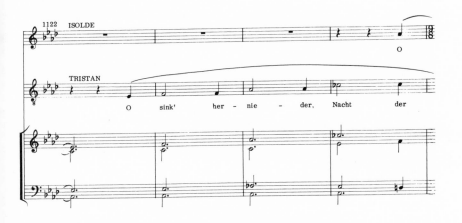

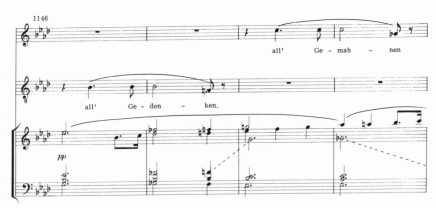

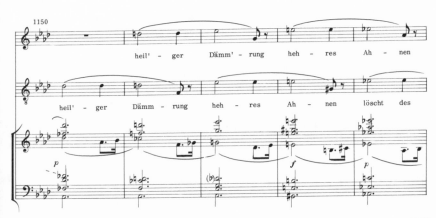

chord which was 'altered' to give the first chord of the Potion *motiv*. This resolves, as in the Potion *motiv*, into E7 in bar 1110, and we move on into E flat 7 as in the passage analysed in Ex. 27. *Mässig langsam* (moderately slowly) marks the beginning of the Hymn to Night, in A flat major; but note that A major still makes its presence felt in the final preparation (aurally, if not notationally; these bars are here shown enharmonically): in bars 1115 and 1116, over an *e* flat dominant pedal in A flat major, the chords of F sharp minor and E major are sounded, respectively the relative minor and dominant major of A major.

Indeed, the whole of the Hymn to Night through to bar 1211 uses the A flat major/A major (notated by Wagner as B double flat) juxtaposition in much the same way as had the earlier discussion of the lovers: see bars 1137–8, 1152–5, 1162–7, and 1202–5. Also present is the Potion *motiv*, stated in its archetypal form at the climax, bars 1192–4. The altered augmented sixth chord which gives that *motiv* its particular identity is sounded in bars 1144, 1156, 1198 and 1199; its constituent notes form Tristan's opening melodic line in bars 1122–6. Unaltered augmented sixths used as pivots occur in bars 1139, 1143, 1147, 1174 and 1176.

An opposition between A major and A flat major is extreme. The one key which is closest to and equidistant from both of them is B major (sub-dominant major of the relative minor of A, and relative major of the tonic minor of A flat). It is not surprising, therefore, that the climax to the love-duet occurs in this key: the text begins 'how can we grasp it, how let it go, this bliss, far from the sun and the harsh parting caused by *Tag*?' B major is the key in which *Nacht* and the love of Tristan and Isolde can be brought together and united: it is the symbol for *Liebestod*, the consummation of love in death. After Tristan's death in Act III Isolde resumes this B major passage from the love duet and the opera ends with a cadence in B major as Isolde falls lifeless on Tristan's body.

Wagner's solution to the problem of writing music-drama was a simple one. He concentrated the action, and expanded and explored the human feelings and experiences behind the action: in this sense he was more purely Romantic than some of his Romantic predecessors, and also more Gluckian. He took the view that the only way in which music could express the 'drama' was through structured musical narrative, and he achieved this aim through the use of *leitmotiven* and key-associations. In fact there was nothing new in this method: it had been used by every major Western European music-dramatist (if not by every opera composer) since Peri.

Yet *Tristan und Isolde* was considered by many to be a 'formless' work. Even the usually level-headed critic Eduard Hanslick, who was not in fact the ogre Wagner portrayed as Beckmesser in *Die Meistersinger*, had this to say of *Tristan und Isolde:* 'Musical form, already considerably relaxed in *Tannhäuser* and *Lohengrin,* is totally destroyed, making way for a type of dramatic representation reminiscent of a boundless flood, and governed not by the musical idea but by the word.'[14] What Hanslick and others failed to recognize was that the Dionysiac message of the opera could only be communicated with overwhelming power *because* the opera is tightly structured.

The Apollonian structure behind the Dionysiac sounds is not evident to the hearer: in listening to (or preferably seeing and listening to) *Tristan und Isolde* we are swept into the Dionysiac experience.[15] Wagner achieves this effect through the way he disguises the structure. The music, for Tristan and Isolde at least, 'sounds' like continual transformation — as Hanslick perceived. Wagner deliberately avoids, as far as he can, establishing fixed points of reference: he evades perfect cadences, 'closed' melodic and harmonic ideas, easily perceived closed structures. The music leads the listener ever onward to the next sound, reaching points of relative rest only in the Act II love-duet (Ex. 28) and in Isolde's final *Liebestod* passage, where the concept of transformation is most clearly stated in the text!

There is an obvious connection between the musical effect of 'transformation' and the underlying dramatic theme of the work — psychological transformation through love-death, an archetypal image of death and rebirth. The music not only supports and communicates the dramatic theme, it is itself an expression of it. The symbol of transformation extends over the work as a whole: the music *is* the drama.

This kind of connection between music and drama is essentially acausal. It is not a cause-and-effect connection because both drama and music happen simultaneously. One does not determine the other; both are determined by common symbolism. A single idea or experience is expressed in both. There is nothing new about this: it lies, as we have seen, behind the earliest music-drama, and behind the best of Western European opera. Indeed, man's wish to open his mind to a world of acausal connections may be the primary reason for music-drama.

The point that *Tristan und Isolde* emphasizes, which is that acausally-connected events can have meaning, needs to be stressed as we turn now towards a discussion of music-drama in the twentieth century. The physical sciences in the first seven decades of the nineteenth century took as their fundamental hypothesis that meaning lies in causal relationships; for them causality was an absolute. This view, born in the Rationalist eighteenth century, was scornful of the possibility of acausality.

> In Joshua's World anything could happen. Magic played a most important part in everyday life. Happenings were determined by the caprice of ruling powers whose whims and intentions varied from day to day. Ours is a world of law. Effect follows cause with unvarying relations. Order and regularity reign where formerly magic and caprice held sway. The law of gravity operates relentlessly, the same yesterday, to-day and to-morrow, regardless of bribe or entreaty.[16]

303

What *Tristan und Isolde* does is to assert the sway of magic and caprice, and thereby appeals to that part of us which refuses to accept the absolutism of causality which otherwise tends to rule our attitudes to life.

The twentieth-century confusion

The extent to which causality governs the way we look at life can be shown by examining the curious story of M. Deschamps and the plum-pudding.

> A certain M. Deschamps, when a boy in Orléans, was once given a piece of plum-pudding by a M. de Fortgibu. Ten years later he discovered another plum-pudding in a Paris restaurant, and asked if he could have a piece. It turned out, however, that the plum-pudding was already ordered — by M. de. Fortgibu. Many years afterwards M. Deschamps was invited to partake of a plum-pudding as a special rarity. While he was eating it he remarked that the only thing lacking was M. de Fortgibu. At that moment the door opened and an old, old man in the last stages of disorientation walked in: M. de Fortgibu, who had got hold of the wrong address and burst in on the party by mistake.[17]

How do we react to this story? The first question to ask is whether it is fact or fiction. The reader will probably tend to regard it as fiction, because it involves a chain of three coincidences so outrageous that we can scarcely believe them to be true. The whole story, we might say, is so unlikely that it must be fiction.

Why should we react with such suspicion? Because the three events cannot be explained causally, and we are conditioned to think causally. In point of fact, the story is a true one, insofar as I can ascertain: certainly the astronomer Camille Flammarion and the psychologist Carl Jung believed it to be true, and I have no reason to suppose that they were misled, gullible or lying.

What troubles us about the story is *a* there seems to be a connection between the three events, and *b* the connection is, by our normal rational processes, inexplicable. It is especially troubling because it is about the everyday world: it raises the possibility, in Jung's words, that in addition to causality there is 'another factor in nature which expresses itself in the arrangement of events and appears to us as meaning.'[18] Were this story, however, the synopsis of a three-act play or music-drama, we would find ourselves less troubled. It is easier to accept the possibility of acausal but meaningful connections in the images of drama.

We must acknowledge the possibility that what we can accept as 'meaning' in dramatic images is acceptable precisely because there is, and we know deep down that there is, another connecting factor in nature besides causality. If this is the case, it lends support to the idea that myth is a way of explaining things, and its acausal explanations have some ultimate validity. The rational sceptic will always scorn an idea of this kind, for it suggests a return to Joshua's World. But Joshua's World is the world of music-drama; the rational sceptic may well also scorn Monteverdi's *L'Orfeo,* Gluck's *Orfeo ed Euridice,* Weber's *Der Freischütz* and Wagner's *Tristan und Isolde.* The person familiar with Oriental patterns of thought may, on the other hand, find the idea of acausal, meaningful connections not at all difficult to accept.

In fact, although the Rationalist viewpoint, with its doctrines of absolute natural law and the 'unvarying relations' of cause and effect, purports to be the scientific viewpoint, developments in theoretical physics over the past century have suggested that both doctrines are in fact invalid. Firstly there developed the idea that absolute equals statistically probable: Heisenberg put forward the Principle of Uncertainty, arguing that no event can be described with absolute certainty. Einstein developed the Theory of Relativity, which argues (amongst other things) that the meaning we find in what we see depends on the point of view we have. Anxious to determine how absolute are the dimensions of space and time, which interact to give 'meaning' to the idea of motion, he almost regretfully concluded 'it is impossible to determine absolute motion by any experiment whatsoever'.

Despite these new ideas, causality remains a basic assumption in our thought processes. We pride ourselves on our ability to think logically — if *a* then *b*. Our everyday experience, of course, confirms that causality is, generally, a valid interpretation of the world we live in. Apples do fall from trees because of the law of gravity. But causality may not be the exclusive truth: it may have limits, and there may be alternative explanations. The acceptance of limits to absolutism, of alternatives, of uncertainty, is both a new experience and the oldest experience: to explain this we must take a wider view.

For primitive man, life was full of uncertainty and alternatives. He perceived his world as ruled by the interaction of various forces, none of which was absolute, all of which could be comprehended only through what we would call anthropomorphic techniques. His world was dominated by invisible gods who could yet be perceived. The events of his life held a meaning he could only dimly grasp at, by means of ritual and myth. The establishment of Sumer, however, changed all that. Man now came to believe in a supreme order to the Universe, a single authority. While primitive man interacted with the forces around him, Sumerian man (and his successors) began to dominate his environment, taking authority from 'above'. In ancient imagery, the World of the Goddess becomes the World-Mountain of the Goddess, with the city of Man, the Lord of Earth, on its summit.[19]

The belief in some ultimate and absolute authority beyond himself has been the basis of Western European man's civilization ever since. This belief has had two effects: firstly it has provided a basic certainty about his position

305

in the Universe, and secondly it has provided him with a frame of authority for his own actions and activities. One of those activities has been the exercise of his intellectual powers, and we have followed the dialogue between reason and faith through the history of Western European man from the Greeks to the nineteenth century. At first, reason was regarded as a servant of faith — it sought to discover the nature of the absolute order. From time to time, authority was challenged by reason: but, at least until the nineteenth century, some reconciliation was always possible. This inter-action and challenge created the particular character of Western European music-drama, in which reason in the form of musico-dramatic structures sought to reconcile itself with the 'absolutism' of musico-dramatic experi-ence; and all the while the primitive irrational, acausal, view of the world asserted itself beneath the surface.[20]

During the eighteenth century, reason began to exert a real authority of its own: the doctrine of causality became an absolute in its own right. The developments in the natural sciences of the nineteenth century confirmed the new faith in reason. Through Darwin's theory of evolution, rational man broke free, finally, from divine authority as communicated through the 'absolutes' of Scripture. The new technological breakthroughs of the Indus-trial Revolution were regarded as part of man's mastery over his environ-ment, a mastery no longer exercised in the service of divine order, but in the interests of man's own planned progress towards a Golden Age. Meanwhile, perhaps as part of the liberation from divine absolutism, man began to assert his non-rational side with new freedom, in the emphasis on emotional expression in the arts during the Romantic period. Faust, the striving individual damned in the Medieval versions of his legend, now achieved salvation.

But faith in the absolutes created by reason has turned out to be shaky. Applied science, the pride of man liberated from God, turns out to be leading us through technology to a Golden Age that does not answer to our conditions as human beings. Theoretical science, through Uncertainty and Relativity, challenges our rational absolutes. 'There is nowhere any certainty more, any solid rock of authority, whereon those afraid to face alone the absolutely unknown may settle down, secure in the knowledge that they and their neighbours are in possession, once and for all, of the Found Truth.'[21]

Out of the maelstrom one new idea has emerged: the application of reasoned investigation to the inner processes of the human mind. Psycho-logy may not be everyone's favourite subject, but what makes it important is that it shows man approaching his position vis-à-vis the universe in a new way. In psychology the emphasis is thrown upon the apparently non-rational aspects of man, even though it may seek causal explanations for them. In Jungian psychology, the emphasis upon dreams and symbols, and the notion of 'the collective unconscious', re-asserts ideas of 'basic human experiences' and of 'acausal connections' which have received scant attention for centuries. This change of direction, towards the inner world of Man, seeking to find 'meaning' and 'truth' therein, is 'not so much a question of superstition as of a truth which remained hidden for so long only because it had less to do with the physical side of events than with their psychic aspects.'[22]

The new interest in the inner world is reflected also in the renewed interest of Western European man in Oriental philosophy. Here the 'inexplicable' and the acausal are not matters to cause concern. Here also it is accepted that symbols and images are more significant than facts and proofs. Mystery is not something to be investigated, analysed, and rationalized, but something to be accepted as it is. 'The faith in Scripture of the Middle Ages, faith in reason of the Enlightenment, faith in science of modern Philistia belong equally to those alone who have yet no idea of how mysterious, really, is the mystery even of themselves.'[23]

We may seem to have strayed rather far from our subject of music-drama. In fact, the topics discussed here are the threads that make up the tangled skein of Western European man's twentieth-century world-view, and therefore lie behind the tremendous variety of approaches and styles used by twentieth-century music-dramatists. Many of those styles and approaches were not, of course, evolved out of a direct consideration by music-dramatists of the issues we have raised here. Many composers were more pre-occupied with technical musical problems; others had a firm image of opera fixed in their minds, and simply conformed to it without question. But as we now turn to a survey of Western European music-drama since Wagner, we shall see how it reflects man's attempts to cope with an increasingly confused world.

The nineteenth century continues

In the previous chapter, Romantic opera was described as conforming to many people's image of 'opera'. Several music-dramatists of the twentieth century have accepted the image, and written 'modern' 'Romantic' operas. The works they have produced have consequently been popular with the opera-going public: they have a comforting air of familiarity, since they make their points in terms we understand.

Giacomo Puccini was a music-dramatist of this kind. *La Bohème, Tosca* and *Madame Butterfly* are amongst the most widely performed operas today. Their subjects are taken from history, or from the everyday world, or occur in some spectacular exotic setting, and although the characters may be cardboard cut-outs, the situations are milked for maximum emotional tension and excitement. Puccini can be regarded as the climax of Italian Romantic opera, more of a Bellini than a Verdi. His own psychological peculiarities influenced his choice of plots and his treatment of the charac-

307

ters, and some critics have had a fascinating time psycho-analysing his operas in Freudian terms.[24] Despite this 'contemporary' feature, and a musical language which shows some influence of Wagner and piquantly exotic colours, Puccini's operas remain firmly entrenched in the aesthetic tradition of the early nineteenth century. High emotion, musical excitement and sentimental lyricism rule the stage, at the expense of musico-dramatic truth.

A more convincing music-dramatist in the nineteenth-century tradition was Benjamin Britten. Britten burst on the operatic scene in 1945 with *Peter Grimes*. The plot centres round an outsider-figure, Peter Grimes, who lives in a fishing village on the Suffolk coast. He is regarded with deep suspicion by the rest of the community, for two reasons: his view of life is different from that of his fellows, and he mistreats his boy apprentices. It is this second reason which eventually leads the villagers to hunt him to his death, or more precisely, to his suicide.

Grimes' 'peculiar' vision of life is expressed in an aria in Act I, scene 2.

> Now the Great Bear and Pleiades, where earth moves,
> Are drawing up the clouds of human grief,
> Breathing solemnity in the deep night.
>
> Who can decipher, in storm or starlight,
> The written character of a friendly fate,
> As the sky turns, the world for us to change?
>
> But if the horoscope's bewildering,
> Like a flashing turmoil of a shoal of herring,
> Who, who can turn skies back,
> And begin again?[25]

The key-word in this passage is 'horoscope'. Grimes sees an acausal, astrological meaning behind 'the changing world', a meaning which cannot be logically deciphered, and can only be accepted. His fellows in the village (called 'The Borough'), are causalists to a man. Grimes' first boy apprentice was lost overboard mysteriously in a storm; Grimes is questioned at the inquest, but cannot give a rational, logical explanation; for him events do not have 'causes' — they simply occur.

The second element in Grimes' outsiderness, his mistreatment of his boy apprentices, arouses the moral distaste of The Borough not on the grounds that apprenticeship at a young age is wicked (Balstrode, the most sympathetic of characters, remarks 'Something of the sort befits/Brats conceived outside the sheets'); nor is it simply that they dislike his use of physical violence; it is essentially because Grimes is a homosexual (though this never surfaces as an open accusation). Homosexuality, like a belief in astrology, is a form of behaviour that stimulates the moral outrage of those who cling to the tenets of religious absolutism: it is because Grimes is a homosexual that he is driven out of the community. Grimes' behaviour and his attitudes to others in the opera conform closely with Havelock Ellis' classic descriptions of typical homosexual behaviour.[26] At first, together with the local schoolteacher, Ellen Orford, Grimes tries to ignore this fact about himself; he struggles to be accepted as a normal member of the community. But the attempt is hopeless, as Ellen eventually points out (in Act II, scene 1), and Peter realizes he must accept the way he is. 'So be it,' he cries, 'and God have mercy upon me!'

Britten sets these words to a melodic *motiv* which recurs throughout the rest of the opera: see Ex. 29. Grimes's homosexuality, symbolized in this theme, is accepted by him (a), and arouses the moral outrage of the village, (b) and (c), — note that, earlier, one of Grimes's chief persecutors remarks 'his exercise is not with men but killing boys'. It underlies the gathering momentum of the plot (d), and brings him sympathy from Balstrode and (in inverted form) from Ellen (e). The *motiv* occurs in the interlude devoted to Grimes' disturbed mind as the pursuers close in on him (f). It is used to represent his inevitable challenge to The Borough (g). At the end of the opera, when normal village life is restored, someone hears that there is a boat sinking out at sea; in fact it is Grimes' boat, and he is committing suicide, returning to the great symbol of the mother-goddess. The villagers ignore the report: Auntie (the local madame) says it is 'one of these rumours', but her vocal line

Ex. 29   Britten: *Peter Grimes*

309

(b)

Act II, 19 bars after [18]

Act II, 3 bars before [28]

(d)

Act II, [44]

(e)

(f)

(g)

(h)

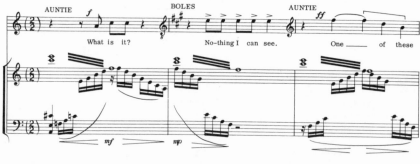

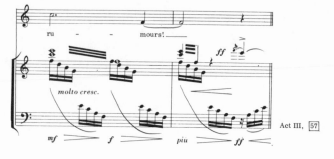

(Reproduced by permission of the Copyright Owners, Boosey & Hawkes Music Publishers Ltd.)

uses the *motiv* of Grimes' homosexuality (h): this is what he will be remembered for.

Peter Grimes is essentially a message-opera, a plea for tolerance. Britten portrays his outsider-hero sympathetically, partly by pointing out the hypocrisy of the intolerant villagers, but mostly by giving Grimes the most effective music. The opera is structured according to nineteenth-century practice: set-numbers joined together in a more or less continuous fabric,

312

with the use of thematic reminiscence. The emphasis is thrown on vocal melody, especially in Grimes's music, and on extensive and powerful choral passages. The orchestra contributes six interludes: four are directly pictorial of aspects of the sea, while two are expressive of the pressures on Grimes, from outside and inside. This connection between pictorialism and 'dramatic music' is thoroughly Romantic. The opera is, in short, designed to appeal to an audience which accepts the nineteenth-century Franco-Italian view of opera, and in those terms it is eminently successful. Because of this, it probably does not succeed as a work with a message, for that type of opera is one which places a greater emphasis upon the effectiveness of the moment than on establishing a moral continuum.

The message of the opera is, moreover, too specific, even though it may be important. It does not demand a response from the deepest levels of our being because the issue is essentially relevant only to the everyday world. *Les Huguenots* too carries a message pleading for tolerance and under-standing, but neither Grimes and Ellen nor Raoul and Valentine finally become symbols of us all. They undergo no psychological transformation and neither do we.

Peter Grimes was Britten's first mature opera; in some respects his later works are less marked by a nineteenth-century approach. The chamber operas, such as *The Turn of the Screw* and *The Rape of Lucretia*, use more experimental dramatic and musical techniques; so do the Church Parables such as *Curlew River*, which attempt to marry the Japanese Nō play and the medieval miracle-play. In *Owen Wingrave* Britten attempted television opera. In *Death in Venice* the dramatic techniques of the chamber operas, with the addition of dance, are transformed to the larger stage of the opera-house. These changes of approach, large or small, reflect the dilemma of an essentially nineteenth-century composer faced with the need to respond to changing conditions and ideas. What is most remarkable about Britten is that he managed to retain a personal style, however derivative or however irrelevant it may be, in a world where 'the new' is constantly required and in which, having discovered the invalidity of traditional absolutes, we tend to reject all absolutes out of hand.

While Puccini and Britten continued the Italian tradition of nineteenth-century opera, other composers, particularly between 1880 and 1914, con-tinued the German tradition of Wagner. Wagner had pronounced his music-drama to be the Art-work of the Future, but while lesser composers accepted the doctrine and turned out pale imitations of Wagner's works, others developed their own music-drama in their own Wagner-influenced way.

Richard I (Wagner) was succeeded by Richard II (Strauss). Strauss accepted the Wagnerian doctrine of continuous music structured by *Leitmotiv* and key-association. But he also accepted the view of many of his contemporaries, that *Tristan und Isolde* is a glorification of extremist behaviour, represented in extreme emotion communicated through extreme chromaticism. In *Salome* (1905) and *Elektra* (1909) Strauss went further, to create two music-dramas in which pathological insanity provides the motivation of plots of a blood-curdling kind. Salome's sexual advances to John the Baptist are rejected, so she relieves her frustration by having him decapitated and kissing his dead lips, and by attempting to seduce her father. Elektra hates her ageing, sadistic nymphomaniac of a mother (Klytemnestra) for taking a lover (Aegisthus) and killing her husband Agamemnon: she has buried an axe, and persuades her brother Orestes to wreak vengeance, almost collapsing with mortification when she discovers that he is only stabbing Klytemnestra and Aegisthus to death with a sword instead of hacking them to death with the axe.

These two charming ladies are, as it were, the children of Isolde, but badly brought up. Like Isolde they must follow the dictates of what they feel, but in seeking to imitate their mother they lack her awareness of broader issues. While Isolde says 'What I feel is right because it is what makes the world go round' (in the deepest sense), they say 'what I feel is right because I feel it'. Here the Romantic absolutism of feeling is revived, in a more extreme form. Salome is motivated by lust, and Elektra by revenge; neither is concerned with the deep forces of life which motivate Isolde. Thus Salome's death (she is crushed to death with shields) and Elektra's death (having only her revenge to live for, she collapses in ecstasy when it is achieved) are not doors opening to a new world of life transformed. Although the subject matter of both operas is taken from 'myth' (Biblical or Greek) it is not treated mythically but historically and causally.

But the plots are presented with immense persuasion. In both operas the moments of horror are communicated through music which sends a shiver of horror through us, and the moments of tenderness, even though they are expressed by monstrous people, have all the musical sensuality and warmth necessary to engage and involve us. Like Wagner's harmony, Strauss's harmony is analysable in terms of traditional tonality, which he returns to for his more tender pages, and to which he adds chromatic alterations and decorations for his horrific moments. He makes his characters fascinating — and the more insane they are the more fascinating they become — but they do not in the end stand for everyman. Their appeal is to only part of us, not to the whole.

The preoccupation with minds on the verge of insanity is also shown in Schoenberg's *Erwartung* (1909), a musico-dramatic monologue (mono-drama) for female voice and orchestra. A woman searches for her lover in the woods, and finds his dead body: that is basically all that 'happens' in the sense of stage events. But the real drama occurs beneath the surface, in the extraordinary way that the woman's spoken thoughts capture the intensity

314

of her emotions, her shifting impressions, and the complexity of her psychological state. The text of the first short scene, for instance, is as follows.

> (*Hesitantly*) Along here? . . . The path is invisible. . . How the trees shimmer, silver. . . like birches. . . (*staring at the ground*) oh, our garden. . . the flowers for him are surely faded. . . The night is so warm. (*Suddenly anxious*) I am afraid. . . (*listens to the wood, tensely*) how heavily the air breathes. . . As if a storm. . . (*wrings her hands, looks back*) so horribly silent and empty. . . But here at least it is bright. . . (*looks up*) the moon was so bright earlier. . . (*cowers down, listens, looks ahead*) Oh, always these fancies. . . with their song of love. . . Don't speak. . . it is so sweet with you. . . the moon is setting. . . (*getting up*) you are cowardly. . . don't you want to look for him?. . . Then die here. . . (*turns towards the wood*). How menacing the silence is. . . (*looks nervously around*) the moon is full of horror. . . Does it see in? . . (*anxiously*) I alone. . . in the damp shadows. (*Taking heart, goes quickly into the wood.*)

In the fourth and final scene (by far the longest) we finally learn something specific about the situation: her lover was, apparently, unfaithful to her, and the possibility is raised that she murdered him. Whether she did or did not is beside the point: what is important is that the music-drama up to the moment when she discovers the body has been built entirely upon hint and suggestion. We are drawn into circumstances with no obvious causal explanation: what are communicated to us are the disorganized fancies of the woman, linked by no logical connection, apparently random thoughts and feelings arising from deep in her unconscious. Indeed, some commentators have pointed to the similarity between the *Erwartung* text (by Marie Pappenheim) and the speech of patients on the psychiatrist's couch or under hypnosis.

Schoenberg wrote the music for *Erwartung* in seventeen days. Like the text, it is structured as a continuous stream of musical thoughts and ideas. Various musical cells return in more or less recognizable form — usually less — and correspond with the central images in the woman's mind which give rise to her words. The musical fabric is extremely fluid: Schoenberg alters tempo and dynamics to follow the detailed stage directions, and his material tends to avoid rhythmic regularity. The avoidance of strict rhythm, strict tempo, and tonal structure leads to musical sounds which reflect the acausal text.[27] Here, musically and musico-dramatically, the Romantic impulse towards emotionalism reaches its most extreme point; the drama consists of little more than a fluid series of changing emotional states connected by the unconscious rather than the conscious.

The thread of Romanticism in music-drama comes to an end in our survey with *Erwartung*.[28] We can see in it a stress on the irrational, in response to

315

the Rationalism of the eighteenth century. Romantic Irrationalism in music-drama took the form of an emphasis on personal emotion, sometimes within a causal, historical context, but at other times as a means towards communicating the deepest human experiences, which we perceive as acausally meaningful through their impact upon our unconscious minds. The former type of Romantic music-drama is represented by the French and Italian schools, by Strauss, and by *Peter Grimes*; the latter type is represented by *Der Freischütz, Tristan und Isolde* and *Erwartung*.

In both types Dionysos is worshipped. In early Romantic opera he and Apollo are opposed: personal emotion as universal experience exerts itself against the specifics of historical causality, and melodic expression tends to be Apollonianized into vocal virtuosity. In *Tristan und Isolde* Apollo and Dionysos are united — although there is a clear Dionysiac message — because the structural method is at the service of the idea lying behind the work. In Strauss's *Salome* and *Elektra* Dionysos is triumphant in the field of expression, but the Dionysiac experiences lack a meaningful foundation.

The resurgence of Dionysos in Romantic opera is a renewal of *enthusiastic music-drama*, but we have noted that the enthusiasm has often been an end in itself rather than a means to bring us a deeper appreciation of our own potential for psychological transformation. *Enthusiasm,* in short, is not always tempered by *ceremonial* in Romantic music-drama, for *ceremonial music-drama* provides the structure which relates content to the archetypal images of the unconscious. In few Romantic operas do we sense the presence of a ritual, of a central controlling idea which casts its influence over all. Wagner's operas after 1850 are exceptional in this respect. Since Romantic opera accepts the idea of progress, and was born in an age of Rationalism, it is obviously *narrative music-drama,* exploring issues through developing plot. But, again, the *narrative* aspects often become ends in themselves; an issue is explored for its own sake (as in *Peter Grimes*) rather than as an image of deeper problems; plot can become an end in itself (as in *Les Huguenots*) and a justification for events rather than merely one particular sort of connection between them.

The central technical problem of Western European opera, the problem of structuring narrative, was solved in different ways during the nineteenth century. By the end of the century, the demands of emotional expression had placed intolerable stress upon the conventional techniques of identifiable theme and recognizable tonality. By about 1910 it was clear that some new solutions must be found: each of these solutions brought with it, or was influenced by, particular aesthetic opinions about the nature of music-drama in twentieth-century culture. It has been in the area of musical technique that the confusions of the twentieth-century world view have been most clearly displayed.

316

New formal principles

1925 saw the first production of *Wozzeck,* an opera in three acts by Alban Berg. Berg's solution to the problem of structuring narrative was, in the first instance, to play down narrative as the means of connecting the events of the plot. His source for the work was *Woyzeck,* a play left in fragmentary form by Georg Büchner at his death in 1837. The story tells of the simple soldier Wozzeck, something of an outsider-figure, who suspects his mistress Marie of infidelity: he stabs her and commits suicide. The characters inhabit a distorted everyday world: its distortions are Wozzeck's distortions, for, like the Woman in *Erwartung,* he is on the edge of insanity. He finds it difficult to make causal connections; events to him seem to occur without much point; he does not seem to think the same way as other people; he responds to environments in an odd way. He is perhaps a simpleton, or a shaman, or a lunatic. In a humanitarian modern society he would be 'taken into care'.

In the first act we learn the nature of Wozzeck's outsiderness, in relation to three characters. In scene 1 he is shaving the Captain. They discuss morality, which Wozzeck argues is a matter of one's class position. In scene 2 he is in the woods with his friend Andres; while Andres's response to the environment is to sing hunting songs, Wozzeck sees visions, magic and horror in the world about him. In the fourth scene Wozzeck visits the Doctor, a Super-Rationalist with a touch of the *Commedia* doctor about him: he is employing Wozzeck for medical experiments (of a fairly harmless kind). Here we are given real insight into Wozzeck's mind. The Doctor maintains that we can control all our physical actions: to say we are forced by nature to do certain things is 'superstition'. Wozzeck replies:

> But see, Doctor, sometimes a man has that sort of character and disposition, but with Nature it's different. Do you see, with Nature. . . it's. . . how shall I put it. . . for example: if nature is out of things, if the world is so gloomy that you have to grope around in it with your hands, and you think it'll melt like a spider's web, ah, if things are, and yet aren't. . . ah, Marie! If everything is dark and there's only a red glow in the west like a forge, what is there to cling to? Doctor, when the sun stands at noon and it's as if the world were going up in flames, a terrifying voice speaks to me. . . The mushrooms! Have you seen those rings of mushrooms on the ground? Straight-line circles, figures — if only someone could read them![29]

Wozzeck sees more in the world around him than scientific cause and effect. What he sees he cannot explain — it is inexplicable.

In telling the story of Wozzeck, Berg takes Wozzeck's point of view. The events are related in fifteen scenes, with some connections and more or less in chronological sequence, but in general one scene does not lead causally to the next. The five scenes in Act I have considerable independence, which Berg reflects in his musical structures of Suite (Prelude, Pavane, Gigue, Gavotte, Prelude), Rhapsody with songs, March and Lullaby, Passacaglia,

317

and Rondo. The five scenes in Act II develop more from one to another, as Wozzeck comes to learn that Marie is unfaithful; here the musical structure is a five-movement symphony. In Act III we have the dénouement, the murder of Marie and suicide of Wozzeck; Berg uses here more experimental, less traditional ways of creating musical structure, in which certain basic elements of music (a note, a chord, a rhythm, a *moto perpetuo*) are explored. The progress of these structures, from the eighteenth century through the nineteenth century to the twentieth century, illustrates well Berg's constant search for suitable ways of organizing music-drama: this is an extremely 'twentieth-century' approach, for Berg is accepting different structural absolutes for different sorts of scene.

In December 1914 Schoenberg underwent a psychological, philosophical and aesthetic crisis. During the first fortnight of January 1915 he wrote a text called *Totentanz der Prinzipien,* planned as the third movement of a symphony. The *Totentanz* (The Death-dance of Principles) was conceived as a monologue recited at a graveside, and perhaps has its source in Novalis *Hymnen an die Nacht,* but it is entirely twentieth-century in that it reveals Schoenberg's disaffection with absolutes, a sudden realization that there is nothing to cling on to, not even the absolute of time. 'All is lost!' cries the narrator, and thirteen chimes are heard.

Schoenberg had been brought up in the Jewish faith, and in order to find a way out of the crisis, he turned to the mystical writings of Judaism, in particular to the Qabalah. The first exposition of a solution is given in Schoenberg's text to *Die Jakobsleiter* (Jacob's Ladder), written a little later in January 1915.[30] The image of Jacob's Ladder — Jacob fell asleep and dreamed of a ladder stretching between earth and heaven, with angels ascending and descending on it — gave rise in Schoenberg's mind to the idea of man progressing through life in eternal striving to reach God. The Faustian idea of the absolute of striving was inevitably accepted by Schoenberg the Romantic, but to it he added the Qabalah idea of the reincarnation of souls.[31]

According to this idea, man has a soul which is absolute, but which is reincarnated in a series of temporary bodies. The soul is an element in a World of Truth, at the head of which stands God, while the body is an element in the everyday world. The belief that a soul is continually reincarnated in a series of bodies could be expressed in terms of an idea that is incarnated in a series of images, and it was this connection between the religious and the aesthetic which brought about Schoenberg's revolution in musical structural methods. A more primary source is the Qabalah itself.

> The basic *Qabalah*. . . is a. pattern of co-ordinated symbols and concepts subsumed under a single comprehensive idea. The idea is the idea of the One God. . . It takes itself up, and simultaneously reveals itself in ten spheres or Sephiroth, which classify the co-ordinated symbols and concepts. . . they are

related to one another as equal members of the basic ground plan (a) of the life of the cosmos, (b) of the collective and individual mental life, and (c) of the integrated, individuated consciousness of the fully-evolved God-man.[32]

In relating idea and images, absolute and particular, the Qabalah shows its ancestry, for these ideas are not unlike those of Sumerian and Meso-potamian thought. How curious, indeed, that the source of Schoenberg's twelve-note method may lie in the world-view of five thousand years ago.

Twelve-note music is structured around a Row: the twelve notes of the chromatic scale are arranged in a particular order, with all included and none repeated. The Row in twelve-note music takes over the functions of key and thematic material in conventional tonal music. Every Row can have forty-seven variants: it can be played backwards (retrograde), upside-down (inversion) and backwards-and-upside-down (retrograde inversion), and can be transposed to begin on any of the twelve notes. Figure 23 shows this diagrammatically; the particular Row chosen is that used by Schoenberg in his music-drama *Moses und Aron*. The diagram consists in fact of forty-eight variations of themselves (each horizontal Row can be read in either direction), a group of self-reflecting images. They are forty-eight incarnations of an idea, or soul, which lies behind them. In composing according to Schoenberg's twelve-note method, one moves from variant to variant according to the dictates of the composition and one's own personal 'style'.

A twelve-note Row is important not so much for its notes as for the intervals between the notes; it is these that determine its character. In other words, it is the connections between events which give them their meaning; and since these connections are a function of the Row itself — unlike the note-relationships in tonality, which are conventional and apply to all tonal music — they create an absolute for one piece of music only. In this way, Schoenberg establishes an absolute causality which is relative to a particular piece of music. This is 'the truth' for this piece, he says, and it does not exist outside this piece. In the Row tabulated in Figure 23, note the extreme economy in the intervals, reflecting Schoenberg's desire for maximum control.

Schoenberg's major opera written according to the twelve-note method is *Moses und Aron*, written between June 1931 and March 1932. The libretto is complete in three acts, but Schoenberg set only the first two acts to music and, despite an occasionally reiterated wish to complete the work, left it unfinished at his death in 1951. In the opera, Schoenberg is evidently still concerned with the same aesthetic problems that led to the invention of the twelve-note method, that is, the relationship between absolute and par-ticular, and between idea and image. The issue is this: how can the Jewish people, newly liberated from Egypt, be brought to a full understanding of

319

Fig. 23   Row-table for *Moses und Aron*

	BASIC ROW →								← RETROGRADE		
Number of note	1	2	3	4	5	6	7	8	9	10	11	12
	A	B♭	E	D	E♭	C♯	G	F	F♯	G♯	B	C
	B♭	B	F	E♭	E	D	G♯	F♯	G	A	C	C♯
	B	C	F♯	E	F	E♭	A	G	G♯	B♭	C♯	D
	C	C♯	G	F	F♯	E	B♭	G♯	A	B	D	E♭
	C♯	D	G♯	F♯	G	F	B	A	B♭	C	E♭	E
	D	E♭	A	G	G♯	F♯	C	B♭	B	C♯	E	F
	E♭	E	B♭	G♯	A	G	C♯	B	C	D	F	F♯
	E	F	B	A	B♭	G♯	D	C	C♯	E♭	F♯	G
	F	F♯	C	B♭	B	A	E♭	C♯	D	E	G	G♯
	F♯	G	C♯	B	C	B♭	E	D	E♭	F	G♯	A
	G	G♯	D	C	C♯	B	F	E♭	E	F♯	A	B♭
	G♯	A	E♭	C♯	D	C	F♯	E	F	G	B♭	B

Transpositions

Number of semitones in interval between neighbouring notes: 1 6 2 1 2 6 2 1 2 3 2 3

G♯	G	C♯	E♭	D	E	B♭	C	B	A	F♯	F
G	F♯	C	D	C♯	E♭	A	B	B♭	G♯	F	E
F♯	F	B	C♯	C	D	G♯	B♭	A	G	E	E♭
F	E	B♭	C	B	C♯	G	A	G♯	F♯	E♭	D
E	E♭	A	B	B♭	C	F♯	G♯	G	F	D	C♯
E♭	D	G♯	B♭	A	B	F	G	F♯	E	C♯	C
D	C♯	G	A	G♯	B♭	E	F♯	F	E♭	C	B
C♯	C	F♯	G♯	G	A	E♭	F	E	D	B	B♭
C	B	F	G	F♯	G♯	D	E	E♭	C♯	B♭	A
B	B♭	E	F♯	F	G	C♯	E♭	D	C	A	G♯
B♭	A	E♭	F	E	F♯	C	D	C♯	B	G♯	G
A	G♯	D	E	E♭	F	B	C♯	C	B♭	G	F♯

Transpositions

Number of note	1	2	3	4	5	6	7	8	9	10	11	12

INVERSION → ← RETROGRADE INVERSTION

the One God? Moses understands, but is unable to find the right way to communicate; Aron is an expert communicator, a manipulator of images, but does not understand. In Moses' view, the One God cannot be communicated through images; as the commandment says, 'thou shalt not make unto thee any graven image'. Aron takes a different view: people can only understand something if it is presented in images they can comprehend. One can see the force of both arguments.

In Act II the confrontation between the brothers reaches a climax. Aron and the people have been worshipping the image of the Golden Calf in a Dionysiac orgy; Moses storms down from Mount Sinai with the Ten Commandments carved in stone, and shatters the Golden Calf, rebuking Aron for letting the Truth be distorted in images. Aron responds by saying that images are the only thing people can grasp and points to the stone tablets in Moses' hands. 'They too are only an image,' he says, 'a part of the Idea.' In despair Moses shatters them, and collapses.

Aron is of course right, and Schoenberg knew it. Ever since primitive times, man has used images and symbols to explore and express the deep mysteries of life. But Moses is right too, for an image must accurately — or as accurately as possible — reflect the Idea that lies behind it. Empty images say nothing; the empty vocal imagery of much early Romantic opera becomes the Golden Calf of virtuosity before which audiences bow down in worship. It was in order to establish a rigorous control over images that Schoenberg evolved the twelve-note method; not only are the constituent notes controlled by the absolute of the intervals between them, but the forty-eight rows are similarly controlled by their self-reflecting relationship.

In Act III, Aron is a prisoner of Moses (the Idea controls images). He pleads for his life — 'I was to speak in images while you spoke in concepts; I was to speak to the heart while you spoke to the head. . .'[33] — but Moses is resolute. 'You have betrayed God to idols, Idea to images. . . You were chosen to have a gift so you could fight for the divine Idea; when you use your gift for false and negative purposes. . . when you give up the renunciation of the wilderness and let your gifts raise you to the summit [of egoistical self-expression], then, as a result of your misuse, you will always be hurled down to the wilderness.'[34] Aron is released, but falls dead. 'But in the wilderness', says Moses, 'you shall be invincible, and shall reach the goal of unity with God'.

The moral is confirmed: images for their own sake are worthless. And thus Schoenberg throws off the shackles of Romanticism[35]; the Aron part of him, the musical expressionist, dies and leaves the Moses part of him, the musical structuralist.

Or that is the way it is in theory: in fact Schoenberg did not set this Act III scene to music. What sort of music could he, after all, have provided? Perhaps he realized that there is always an Aronic side to music; Aron is the

321

Dionysos-figure and Moses the Apollo-figure, and purely Apollonian music is perhaps as empty as purely Dionysiac music. Certainly Schoenberg's own music, despite its twelve-note structure, creates images that are highly expressive, and in many of his later works he used the twelve-note method less strictly.

As in *Tristan und Isolde*, the musical fabric of *Moses und Aron* communicates the ideas lying behind the work. Firstly, and obviously, the twelve-note structure is a manifestation in forty-eight images of Schoenberg's Idea. Secondly, since the row substitutes for key and theme, various versions of it are used as if they were key-associations or thematic ideas, returning at appropriate moments in the drama. The basic association of this kind is provided in Aron's opening words. He makes four statements, each of which expresses one of the vital relationships in the opera.

(a) 'O son of my fathers, did the great God send you to me?' [The God-Moses relationship]

(b) 'My brother, did the Almighty give me to you as His vessel. . .' [The Moses-Aron relationship]

(c) '. . . to shed on our brothers His eternal grace?' [The Moses/Aron-People relationship]

(d) 'Happy people, belonging to a single God, whom no other has the power to assail.' [The People-God relationship]

As Ex. 30 shows, Schoenberg sets (a) to the basic row, (b) to the inverted row, (c) to the retrograde, and (d) to the retrograde inversion. Thirdly, Schoenberg uses the sound-effects of music for expressive purposes. Moses' role is a *Sprechstimme* one; instead of singing he speaks in defined rhythms and with the pitches approximately notated. Only in one passage may he optionally sing, when he tells Aron 'Purify your thinking, free it from worthless things, dedicate it to truth.' It is the nearest he comes in the opera to being able to communicate his Idea. Aron, the expert communicator, is a lyrical tenor, and his vocal line is often very expressive in a nineteenth-century way. Indeed, those parts of the music-drama where images triumph over Idea (as in the Golden Calf scene) have music of an immediate emotional appeal, appropriately enough, while scenes where the Idea dominates (as in the opening scene where Moses receives his instructions from God) have a more conceptual, patterned, Apollonian effect.

The return to the past

While Schoenberg explored his own new way of structuring music, and established his own 'relative absolutes' for music, other composers sought to recapture the absolutes of the past. Under the influence of his librettist Hugo von Hofmannsthal, Richard Strauss turned back from the extreme

Ex. 30   Schoenberg: *Moses und Aron*

(Reproduced by permission of Schott & Co. Ltd.)

emotionalism of *Elektra* and in 1911 produced a Romanticized eighteenth-century 'comedy' called *Der Rosenkavalier*. It is his most popular opera. In it Strauss captures the spirit of eighteenth-century Vienna, although the scene is viewed through the rose-tinted glasses of a sentimental Romantic. Hofmannsthal and Strauss apparently thought of the work as a modern *Le Nozze di Figaro,* in which Octavian (Cherubino) abandons a love-affair with the Marschallin (the Countess), in favour of Sophie, the pretty, ingenuous daughter of a rich merchant. But the action centres less round Octavian and Sophie than on the Marschallin and on the deliciously *buffo* Baron Ochs von Lerchenau, who like something out of Viennese popular comedy, clumsily woos everything in a skirt (including the disguised Octavian) and becomes the butt of a gigantic and cruel practical joke.

Strauss's music is partly in the post-Tristan idiom of lush chromatic harmony, especially for the love-scenes between Octavian and the Marschallin; partly in a kind of Rossinian *opera buffa* style; partly in the style of the nineteenth-century Viennese waltz; and partly in a pseudo-eighteenth-century style, which attempts to recapture the sophistication, balance and taste of Mozart. It was this last element which particularly

323

attracted Strauss and Hofmannsthal as a way of reintroducing a sense of formality and ceremonial into music-drama. The stage action continually reinforces ceremonial, in the Marschallin's levée in Act I, in the presentation of the rose (an engagement ceremony) in Act II, and in the *opera buffa* formality of the seduction scene in Act III. In the end, however, it was Strauss who envisaged the most effective moment of the opera, the trio for Sophie, Octavian and the Marschallin, where a visually and musically busy final act comes at last to a moment of statuesque stillness, in which the feelings of the three characters are movingly explored.

Der Rosenkavalier was an attempt to solve the problems of post-Romantic music-drama by recapturing the spirit of the past, though in a rather sentimental and nostalgic way. A more serious effort to reinstate pre-Romantic ceremonial was undertaken by Igor Stravinsky.

Stravinsky's 'opera-oratorio' *Oedipus Rex,* first performed in 1927, shows him returning to the roots of European music-drama and presenting a version of Sophocles' play in a highly ritualistic fashion. The original Greek text was translated into French by Jean Cocteau, and then from French into Latin by Jean Daniélou. Stravinsky wanted a Latin text because Russian, his native language, was too unfamiliar to European audiences, and other Euro pean languages were 'temperamentally alien' to himself,[36] while Latin, a 'dead language', had the advantages of being ritualistic and remote. Curiously, however, Stravinsky modelled his vocal rhythms on the original Greek text. Before each scene, a narrator steps forward and explains the forthcoming events in the language of the audience. He opens the work by addressing the audience as follows:

> You are about to hear a Latin version of King Oedipus. To spare you the trouble of listening and remembering, and because our stage presentation is rather static, I shall remind you of Sophocles' drama from time to time as we proceed.

> Without knowing it, Oedipus is at odds with the forces that watch over us from the far side of death. When he was born, they set a trap for him, and here you shall see the trap spring shut. . .[37]

Three things in this speech are worth noting. Firstly, Stravinsky does not want us to pay much attention to the words. If we were to do so, we would be drawn into an identification with the characters speaking them, and, as he himself remarked (in *Dialogues and a Diary*), 'my audience is not indifferent to the fate of the person, but I think it far more concerned with the person of the fate, and the delineation of it which can be uniquely achieved in music.'[38] It is the abstract quality of the music which can communicate the idea behind the action. Secondly, the staging of the work was planned as monumental and static. The characters do not move on the stage, but simply appear at and disappear from fixed points in a constant tableau. This is the 'oratorio' aspect of the music-drama. Thirdly, we are made immediately aware of forces of magic and mystery when the narrator speaks of 'the forces that watch over us from the far side of death' (the words are Cocteau's).

In short, Stravinsky is opposing all the elements in music-drama which would lead us to become emotionally involved in the characters portrayed and particular events narrated on the stage, and is directing our attention directly to what lies behind them. Since the visual side is extremely Apollonian, we might expect the music to communicate the issues in a Dionysiac fashion: far from it. Stravinsky's music is tightly structured, in accordance with attitudes he later explained in *Poetics of Music*, viz.,

> Art in a true sense is a way of fashioning works according to certain methods acquired either by apprenticeship or by inventiveness.[39]

> For myself, I have always considered that in general it is more satisfactory to proceed by similarity than by contrast. Music thus gains strength in the measure that it does not succumb to the seductions of variety.[40]

> The unity of the work (of art) has a resonance all its own. Its echo, caught by our soul, sounds nearer and nearer. Thus the consummated work spreads abroad to be communicated and finally flows back towards its source. The cycle, then, is closed. And that is how music comes to reveal itself as a form of communion with our fellow man — and with the Supreme Being.[41]

The Supreme Being is, of course, Apollo. He is the god of craftsmanship in the arts, of similarity rather than contrast. For Stravinsky, the deepest, most mysterious experiences of man are not perceived through loss of self in an involvement with the content of images, but through the resonance of their structural and expressive unity. For him *ceremonial* outweighs both *narrative* and *enthusiasm*.

The view is an interesting one; we have not met it in music-drama since we discussed the Mass. Traditionally, an emphasis on *ceremonial* would indicate a view that artistic structures reflect absolute, universal order; here, however, Stravinsky seems to maintain that artistic structures can reflect an acausal structure of the world, not the structure explicable in holy writ or scientific textbook, but something whose echo is caught by our souls. And thus we can see that Stravinsky and Schoenberg have much in common: both are concerned with finding a pattern behind the world, in an age when causal connections seem an insufficient or unimportant explanation. Each believes that musical structures can express the absolute order he believes must exist in the Universe. Each writes music that is intellectually appealing in its rigorous control over the content of images, but each believes that music finally communicates to that part of us that is beyond both intellect and emotion.

325

9 Alternative realities

Music-drama as dream

In the previous chapter we raised, in twentieth-century terms, the issue of causality versus acausality. The issue is not a new one; only the terminology is new. From the start we have argued that music-drama is founded on man's wish to explore the 'inexplicable': in twentieth-century terminology we can define this as a wish to explore 'what is inexplicable according to causal patterns of thought'. The 'inexplicable' may be quite explicable in acausal terms.

In short, we have continually implied the existence of two alternative realities: the reality of the everyday world, which Western European man since the development of the natural sciences has interpreted according to causal theory and scientific absolutes, and the reality of a 'hinterworld', a hidden world beneath the surface of things with which primitive man sought to communicate through myth and magic, and with which Western European man has sought to communicate through the arts — and in particular, for our purpose, through music-drama. The relationship between the two realities has also been the concern of religion and philosophy, especially the latter, since Western European man has come to place greater reliance upon his reasoning powers than on organized religion.

The two realities occur together in *Tristan und Isolde* in the symbols *Tag* and *Nacht*. We have noted a poetic influence upon this symbolism, but must now turn to note a philosophical influence too, through Wagner's immersion (in 1854) in the writings of Arthur Schopenhauer (1788–1860).

In *Die Welt als Wille und Vorstellung* (1819) (*The World as Will and Representation*), Schopenhauer maintains that we experience two levels of reality, or two worlds as he calls them. The first world is the 'world of representation', the world of phenomena and events: it includes the things we see and the thoughts we have. But, Schopenhauer argues, these are reflections or images of a second world, 'the world as Will' which creates them. The Will

326

is the innermost essence, the kernel, of every particular thing and also of the whole. It appears in every blindly acting force of nature, and also in the deliberate conduct of man, and the great difference between the two concerns only the degree of manifestation, not the inner nature of what is manifested.[1]

In considering the various activities of the human mind, and the arts, Schopenhauer concluded that most are concerned with the 'world as representation', but one art is, in his view, much more closely related to the Will, and that art is music. Music 'never expresses the phenomenon, but only the inner nature, the in-itself of every phenomenon, the will itself.'[2]

It is for this reason that music is finally inexplicable, for 'the composer reveals the innermost nature of the world, and expresses the profoundest wisdom in a language that his reasoning faculty does not understand, just as a [woman hypnotised] gives information about things of which she has no conception when she is awake.'[3]

According to Schopenhauer, music provides one path to a direct experience of the Will. There are three other paths, however: meditation, love, and dreams. Love, in its total loss of individual identity in union with another person, is a move out of the pluralistic world of representation into the universal world as Will (see *Über die Grundlage der Moral, On the Foundation of Morality*, 1840). This idea was clearly influential upon *Tristan und Isolde*. Dreams offer us a direct perception of and participation in the world as Will.

> Life has long been recognised [as] and often declared to resemble dream. And indeed, this comparison with dream permits us to perceive, even if only as at a misty distance, how the hidden power that directs and moves us towards its intended goals [the Will] . . . might yet have its roots within the very depths of our own unfathomable being.[4]

> In dreams. . . the circumstances that motivate our acts seem to befall us from without, as independent, often repulsive, completely accidental occurrences, and yet there is a concealed purposeful continuity throughout: for there is a hidden power, to which all those accidents of the dream conform, which is actually directing and coordinating its incidents. . .[5]

Schopenhauer argues that our dream experiences are not false, but prove to us that events can be connected in a way different from the way events are connected according to the laws of the world of representation.

> Every event in every individual life must then be implicated in two fundamentally different orders of relationship: first, in the objective, causal order of the course of nature, and second, in a subjective order relevant only to the experiencing individual himself and as subjective, consequently, as his dreams — *where the sequence and content of the occurrences are as predetermined as the scenes of a drama*. . . (My italics)[6]

Schopenhauer here imples that there is a relationship between dream and drama. The scenes of a drama unfold before us with something of the authority of the world as representation, but they are, literally, the product of a creative Will, that of the dramatist. If we add Schopenhauer's idea that music is also a direct expression of the Will, we may conclude that, in a Schopenhauerian interpretation of the two realities, music-drama gives us direct access to the hinterworld.

Schopenhauer's *The World as Will and Representation* was published in 1819, and belongs properly to the Romantic period in music. We have noted its influence upon Wagner, and it can be seen that it is 'Romantic' in the emphasis it places upon music and upon dream. The Romantic artist (in whatever field) accepted without question the existence of alternative realities of one sort or another: if he had one single attribute it was a continual search for 'something else', a something which could only be understood through the feelings.

A more practical connection between drama, music, dream and the hinterworld was made by the *symbolistes,* a group of writers — primarily poets — active in France in the last thirty years of the nineteenth century. The *symbolistes* in fact acknowledged more of a debt to Wagner than they did to Schopenhauer, whose influence was therefore second-hand. For Baudelaire, Wagner's music was like a drug stimulating the imagination, leading the mind into a dream-like state. Wagner's symbolism he saw as not merely allegory, to be understood intellectually, but as a means of arousing unconscious thoughts. Wagner's use of legend he regarded as marvellously anti-historical, for it illustrates Wagner's interest in the eternal rather than the temporal.[7]

The *symbolistes* were concerned with trying to create (usually in poetry) the world behind the world we live in. C. M. Bowra suggests they 'attempted to convey a supernatural experience in the language of visible things, and therefore almost every word is a symbol and is used not for its common purpose but for the association it evokes of a reality beyond the senses.'[8]

The *symbolistes* sensed that the world we live in is essentially a reflection of the hinterworld. In this Schopenhaurian view, any object or event functions not only within the framework of this world, but connects with the hinterworld: it is a symbol. The objects of this world are both finite and infinite. Words, for instance, were used by *symboliste* poets in such a way as to avoid the specific meanings they might have. Mallarmé believed that music was the most 'infinite' art-form in this sense, and that poetry should attempt to be 'musical', should attempt to grasp 'that character of music which releases us from the need for logical comprehension and leads us towards the universal Idea.'[9]

It was in the form of drama that the *symboliste* view of alternative realities could best be experienced, for here a visual element was added, engaging the audience more deeply in the dream-world. Here too could be shown that even what we see in life has a symbolic side: scenery and costumes in *symboliste* drama are not merely decorative, but should somehow reflect the influence of the unseen, unknowable forces that lie behind the play. *Symboliste* drama also rejects 'dramatic action' in the accepted sense, for the aim is not to show human beings undergoing crises and conflicts, and arming themselves against a sea of troubles. In a play like Maeterlinck's *Pelléas et Mélisande,* the characters are passive rather than active, submissive to the forces of the hinterworld that control their 'destiny', just as in dreams we are at the mercy of whatever forces control the sequence of events.

Debussy's Pelléas et Mélisande

The *symbolistic* dream-world, and the *symboliste* emphasis on music, quite naturally led composers to set *symboliste* texts. In 1894 Debussy wrote an orchestral piece on Mallarmé's poem *L'Aprés-midi d'un Faune.* The story is told of Debussy informing Mallarmé he had turned the poem into music, to which Mallarmé replied: 'Oh? I thought I had done that myself already.' Debussy was also intrigued by Villiers de l'Isle-Adam's play *Axël.* He 'felt himself drawn to this poet, who lacked [the prevalent] banality [of dramatists of the time], who had a taste for mystery, for moods of foreboding, for obsessive, haunting feelings, for everything in the human soul that remains obscure and impenetrable. . .'[10] Ever since 1889 Debussy had had in mind ideas about music-drama that could be called *symbolist.*

> Music begins where words end, and translates the inexpressible; it should emerge from the shadows and be discreet. The poet [in music-drama] should be he who only half-says things. Two associated dreams, that is the ideal. No place, no time. No 'making scenes'. No pressure on the musician: he makes [the dream] complete. . . [There should be] no musical development, for a prolonged development does not, cannot, stick closely to the words. . . in dramatic music, tints and colours should be predominant; as for the libretto, [there should be] short verses, shifting scenes, varying in place and character. . . as to the characters, no speechifiers, no debaters, but poor creatures, submitting to life and fate. . .[11]

To these requirements Maeterlinck's play *Pelléas et Mélisande* fitted admirably.

Very little happens in *Pelléas et Mélisande.* The story is the familiar one of the eternal triangle: Mélisande is married to Golaud, but she and Golaud's brother Pelléas fall in love. What makes the work original is not the story but the way it is told. In the dream-world of the play nothing is 'accidental', as can be seen in the following synopsis. Environment, event, and text collaborate to suggest some secret meaning. *Act I, scene 1:* Golaud, hunting in the forest, finds Mélisande weeping by a well. She will not say who she is, merely

329

that she has run away from somewhere. She is lost, and so is he, but they leave together. *Scene 2*: a room in the castle. Geneviève, Golaud's and Pelléas' mother, reads to Arkel, their grandfather and king, a letter from Golaud telling them he has married Mélisande. Arkel does not object: 'we only ever see the other side (*l'envers*) of destiny, even of our own . . . he may do as he wishes: I have never set myself against someone's destiny; he knows his future better than I. Perhaps there are no such things as unnecessary events.' Pelléas appears: he has had a letter from his friend Marcellus: 'he is going to die, and is calling for me . . . he says he knows exactly the day when death must come to him. . .' *Scene 3*: a terrace outside the castle and overlooking the sea. Geneviève, Mélisande and Pelléas watch a ship set sail. It is the ship that brought Mélisande. A storm is brewing out at sea.

Act II, scene 1: Pelléas and Mélisande are walking in the park. They stop by a fountain. Mélisande takes off her wedding ring, plays with it, and loses it in the fountain. It is noon. *Scene 2:* Golaud's and Mélisande's room in the castle. Golaud is in bed, recovering from an accident: while he was riding in the woods at noon, his horse suddenly threw him. Mélisande is unhappy; when Golaud asks her what is wrong, she replies 'it is something stronger than I. . .' Golaud notices her ring is missing: she tells him she lost it by the sea. *Scene 3:* Pelléas and Mélisande visit a cave by the sea. They are pretending to look for the ring. In the darkness they see three old people in rags, asleep.

Act III, scene 1: outside a castle tower. Mélisande stands at a window combing her hair. Pelléas arrives. Mélisande's long hair cascades down; Pelléas caresses and fondles it passionately. Doves fly out of the tower. Golaud arrives and tells them not to be foolish children. *Scene 2:* Golaud leads Pelléas down into the castle vaults. 'Do you see the chasm, Pelléas?' *Scene 3*: having emerged from the vaults, Pelleas tells Golaud: 'I thought I would fall.' It is nearly noon. *Scene 4:* Golaud questions Yniold, his son by a former marriage. Has the boy seen Pelléas and Mélisande together? He holds him up to a window: can he see Pelléas and Mélisande together now? Yniold tells him they are sitting silently looking at the lamplight.

Act IV: scene 1: a room in the castle. Pelléas asks Mélisande to meet him in the castle gardens that evening. He is going away. 'I shall be so far away that you won't be able to see me.' They hear voices. *Scene 2*: Arkel visits Mélisande. He hopes she will bring happiness to the castle. 'I have gained some sort of belief in events, and I have always seen that a young and beautiful being creates around her young, beautiful and happy events.' Golaud arrives: he is deeply suspicious of Mélisande. 'I am nearer to understanding the great secrets of the other world than the small secret of her eyes.' Her innocence is no normal innocence. He forces her to kneel in prayer. *Scene 3:* Yniold is trying to find a toy ball near the fountain in the park. He hears sheep bleating, and watches a shepherd driving them. The shepherd tells him the sheep are crying because they are going not to the sheep-fold but to the slaughter. *Scene 4:* Pelléas and Mélisande meet by the fountain in the park. They declare their love for each other. Pelléas says 'I have played like a child around something I could not imagine. . . I have played, in a dream, around the snares of destiny. . .' Golaud surprises them and stabs Pelléas with his sword.

Act V: a room in the castle. Mélisande has just given birth to a child, and is dying. Golaud asks her about Pelléas: she confesses she loved him, but says their love was innocent. 'I no longer understand the things I say. . . I do not know what I say. . . I do not know what I know. . . I no longer say what I want. . .' Serving-women gather unbidden, and fall to their knees as Mélisande dies. Arkel says of her: 'she was a little creature so quiet, so timid, so silent. . . she was a poor little creature as mysterious as everyone is. . .'

This synopsis can do no more than hint at the overall mood of mystery and dream in the work. Maeterlinck encourages us to open our minds to the possible associations of events, to their symbolic cross-connections. He deliberately avoids being specific: Golaud's suspicions, for instance, are based on hints rather than facts. He senses what is going on although he can find no proof: but his 'senses' are right. The characters all remain enigmatic: their lives are somehow unreal, as if they only exist as figments of our imaginations. They speak in hints and suggestions, as if they are only the mouthpieces for words that spring from beyond their thoughts. 'Since there is no definite answer to the great questions and mystery of life, the ambiguity of symbol and discourse. . . effectively replaces the conversational chatter of ordinary theater. . .'[12]

Debussy read *Pelléas et Mélisande* in 1892, and immediately jotted down musical ideas for a setting. When he attended the first performance, in May 1893, he was resolved to write it as a music-drama. Maeterlinck granted his permission, Debussy began work. The task was, however, not an easy one, for two reasons. Firstly, Debussy had been an ardent Wagnerian for some years, and although he intellectually rejected Wagner, the power of Wagner's music still had a strong hold on him. Secondly, the theory of writing deliberately non-developing music was bound to cause certain problems in practice. Debussy himself was aware of these difficulties. In a letter to Ernest Chausson he apologizes for not writing earlier.

> It is Mélisande's fault! Forgive us both! I have spent days pursuing the nothing of which she is made, and I'm not brave enough to tell you all about that; it's the sort of struggle you know about, but I don't know if you have ever gone to bed with a kind of desire to cry, rather as if you've not been able to see someone you love very much during the day. Now it's Arkel who torments me: he is *from beyond the grave,* and he has this uninvolved, prophetic tenderness for those who are about to vanish – and he has to say all that with *doh, ray, me, fah, soh, lah, te, doh*!!! What a life![13]

In September 1893 he writes again to Chausson that he has completed the love-duet in Act IV (scene 4), but is critical of it.

> It's rather like some duet by A Certain Gentleman, never mind who — and the ghost of old Klingsor, *alias* R. Wagner would always appear round every bar; so I tore everything up and started by finding an organic collection of more personal musical phrases and forced myself to become both Pelléas and Mélisande: I've been trying to find the music behind all the accumulated veils. . . I've used, more spontaneously than ever before, a means that seems to me rather unusual, that is to say silence — don't laugh — as a means of expression, and perhaps the only way to put across the emotion of a phrase. . .[14]

In fact Debussy did not fully avoid the Wagnerian influence in the Act IV love duet: the situation is so similar to Act II of *Tristan und Isolde* that musical parallels inevitably occurred.

The Wagnerian moments are few in *Pelléas et Mélisande:* certainly the prevailing mood is Debussyan and *symboliste*. The work was completed in 1895, but only received its first performance in 1902. Debussy spoke of the production in the following terms:

> The stage production of a work of art, however beautiful it may be, always contradicts one's inner dream. . . That lovely delusion in which the characters lived for so long, as you did yourself, and in which it often seemed they might arise from the mute page, able to be touched — doesn't that explain the terror one feels when one sees them brought to life before ones eyes through the agency of some artiste or other? . . From this moment on, nothing seems to remain of your old dream. An alien will places itself in between it and you: the scene shifters make the décor explicit, and the forest birds nest in the 'wood' of the orchestra; the chandeliers are lit, the curtain rises and falls, halting or prolonging our emotions; applause, or angry noises, sound like a distant carnival. . . This year, 1902, when the *Opéra-Comique* staged *Pelléas et Mélisande* with their well-known care, I experienced feelings like these. . . The character of Mélisande I had always thought difficult to portray. I tried hard to capture in music her fragility and distant charm, but there was still her physical appearance, and those long silences which a false gesture could ruin or even make meaningless. . .[15]

From these remarks it is clear that Debussy had serious doubts about staging the work: he was frightened that his dream-world of *Pelléas et Mélisande* might be shattered when it came to production in a theatre. In fact the first performance was a success only amongst those who were already sympathetic: most of the audience found the work un-dramatic, un-musical, and at times hilarious. The spirit of Hugo was still very much alive.

The lack of enthusiasm for *Pelléas et Mélisande* is perhaps understandable, for Debussy made no concessions to popular musico-dramatic taste. On the contrary, he wished to do nothing else than reinforce the indefiniteness, mystery and deeply meaningful inconsequentiality of Maeterlinck's dream-world. The musical sounds are fleeting, imprecise, mysterious; the large orchestra is used to give a wide range of delicate instrumental colour, and not as a Meyerbeerian or Wagnerian emotional battering-ram; silence is widely used as a musical ingredient; the vocal lines are close to naturalistic speech, far from Italian *bel canto*, often almost whispered. Rhythm is fluid, harmony dwells on chords of potential rather than chords of resolution, melody is fragmentary. Debussy does use *Leitmotiven,* although they do not create the musical fabric in a Wagnerian way: they occur to prick our memories, to lead us to an awareness of associations and connections between things that reflect the structure of the hinterworld.

Example 31 consists of three extracts from the love duet in Act IV, scene 4. Here can be seen Debussy's deliberate avoidance of large theatrical gesture, and his concentration upon 'the other side of destiny', upon the mystery and wonder of events.

(a) is the beginning of the scene: Pelléas enters, and waits for Mélisande's arrival.

> 'It is the last evening, the last evening . . .' he says. 'Everything must come to an end. I have played like a child around something I could not imagine . . . I have played, in a dream, around the snares of destiny. . . Who suddenly woke me? I shall flee, crying with joy and grief, like a blind man fleeing his burning house. I shall tell her that I shall flee. . .'

Ex. 31   Debussy: *Pelléas et Mélisande*

(a)

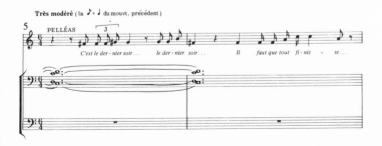

The vocal line proceeds according to the dictates of naturalistic declamation: it is the orchestral accompaniment that provides the hinterworld. As Debussy maintained, 'musical development' as such does not occur: short phrases of a bar or two are juxtaposed, but no 'development' does not mean there is no structure.

The relationships between notes are primarily determined by whole-tone scales — the flurry on the last beat of bar 11 is an example. In a whole-tone scale there is no 'tonic' and therefore no hierarchy amongst the notes: all are equal, in the same way that all events in the world of dream are 'equal'. There is a similarity here with the 'equality' of the twelve notes of the chromatic scale in Schoenberg's method, but while Schoenberg creates a 'law' in his arrangement of the notes into a row, Debussy uses the whole-note scale more fluidly. Nor does he confine himself to the notes of one whole-note scale: he uses the intervening semitones as appoggiaturas and passing-notes to create fragments of melodic material. Wagner had done much the same in the context of tonal harmony. The musical motive associated with Pelléas, for example, occurs in bars 12 and 13.

Example 31 (b) includes the moment of Mélisande's arrival to meet Pelléas. In Wagner's opera the parallel is the arrival of Tristan in Act II, a moment of climax after long preparation. Here the orchestral statements in bars 1 and 3 support the growing intensity of Pelléas' vocal line, but Mélisande's first notes do not confirm the crescendo: the climax becomes, typically, anti-climax. Bars 8 to 13 show two statements of similar three-bar-long material. Again, a non-developing, mosiac pattern is being used, providing a context of acausal meaning in which the remarks of the characters gain symbolic force, as in Mélisande's 'Let me stay in the light'. A translation follows.

PELLÉAS   I must gaze one last time into the depths of her heart! I must tell her all that I have not told her.

335

MÉLISANDE	Pelléas!
PELLÉAS	Mélisande! Is it you, Mélisande?
MÉLISANDE	Yes.
PELLÉAS	Come here. Don't stay at the edge of the moonlight, come here, we have so many things to say to each other . . . come here into the shade of the lime-tree.
MÉLISANDE	Let me stay in the light. . .
PELLÉAS	They could see us from the tower windows. Come here; here we have nothing to fear.

(b)

(c) is the climax of the duet.

339

(Reproduced by permission of Durand and Cie. Paris/ United Music Publishers Ltd.)

PELLÉAS	Don't you know what I am going to tell you?
MÉLISANDE	No, no; I don't know anything.
PELLÉAS	Don't you know why I must go away . . . don't you know it is because . . . I love you?
MELISANDE	I love you too.
PELLÉAS	Oh, what did you say, Mélisande? I almost didn't hear it. . . The ice is shattered with burning swords! . . You said that in a voice coming from the end of the world! . . I almost didn't hear you. . . You love me? You love me too? Since when have you loved me?
MÉLISANDE	Since always. Since I first saw you. . .

Again the important statements are made quietly, and unaccompanied. Again the material is 'organized' rigorously, but non-developmentally. The four-note theme in bar 1 (it occurred too in extract (b) in bars 1 and 3) is a determinant of much of the material, explicitly or implicitly.

Debussy's musical structures in *Pelléas et Mélisande* create a fabric of meaning beneath the surface. But, unlike Schoenberg, Debussy has no absolute principle to govern his structures: he does not establish a hinter-world order and produce his music accordingly. The music attempts no more than to open our minds to the hinterworld. It transmits the *symbolisme* of the text not more explicitly, but more forcefully: it forces us to find our own meanings, which was precisely the aim of the *symbolistes* themselves. Neither they nor Debussy seek to explain the inexplicable: they wish us merely to be aware of a meaning in events which lies deeper than the causal connections of our everyday lives.

The clash of worlds

Symbolisme was perhaps the most important influence on *surréalisme*, another movement based in France, which flourished between 1924 and the Second World War. Like the *symbolistes*, the *surréalistes* sought to portray the greater reality behind the reality of everyday, but they took a more extreme position, and deliberately opposed the scientific thinking, materialism and morality that belong to the everyday world. Consequently, by the 1930s many *surréalistes* declared themselves to be working for political ends.

André Breton's *Manifesto du surréalisme* of 1924 was the first focus of *surréaliste* ideas. The manifesto begins by attacking realism in literature, particularly as it is displayed in the novel. Breton regarded the novel as scarcely superior to a game of bridge, an entertainment in which events occur according to the rules of causality, and in which the characters are banal puppets. The novel is, he argued, based on a world of logic: the emotions portrayed in novels are mechanical and contrived. (He had not, presumably, read James Joyce's *Ulysses,* recently published in Paris.)

Language, says Breton, is a way to give shape to the imagination, which is our only means to penetrate the deep mysteries. Imagination indicates to us a realm of *what can be,* and thus stands opposed to realism, which is the realm of *what is.* Imagination can lead us to the state of 'innocent madness', and ultimately to a perception of what is 'marvellous' and 'beautiful'. Imagination already offers us the world of dreams, in which events occur in a way they never could in the world of realism. But language also belongs to the everyday world. It is this ambiguity of language which gives it its artistic potential: through it the contradiction between reality and dream can be resolved.

> I believe in the future resolution of these two states, in appearance so contra-dictory, which are dream and reality, in a kind of absolute reality, *surreality,* one might call it. It is toward this conquest that I proceed, certain of not attaining it but too unconcerned with my own death not to count somewhat on the joys of such a possession. . .[16]

In order to achieve this goal, the writer must fight against 'talent', which is, to the *surréaliste,* the ability to adjust, re-work, and invent material, and tends to place barriers across our access to the imagination. Anyone can open himself to the imagination: it requires no specialist training. Revelation can be produced by the simplest method.

> Secrets of surrealist magic art. Written surrealist composition, or first and last attempt: Have someone bring you writing materials after getting settled in a place as favourable as possible to your mind's concentration upon itself. Put yourself in the most passive, or receptive, state you can. Forget about your genius, your talents, and those of everyone else. Tell yourself that literature is the saddest path that leads to everything. Write quickly, without a preconceived subject, fast enough not to remember and not to be tempted to read over what you have written. The first sentence will come by itself. . . It is rather difficult to make a decision about the next. . . But it shouldn't matter to you anyway. Continue as long as you like. Trust in the inexhaustible character of the murmur. . .[17]

Such a method of writing is entirely dependent upon what may be the nature of the hinterworld. The writer merely becomes the channel through which the content and structure of the hinterworld will flow. It therefore depends upon an acceptance of the hinterworld itself, and upon the hinterworld having a content and structure which can communicate itself. The technique of 'automatic writing', as it is called, is consequently not regarded with much approval by those who reject anything beyond the reality of this world, those who are unwilling to open themselves to the hinterworld, or those who believe that the hinterworld is revealed to us through our powers of reason. It is a step beyond *symbolisme* along the path towards the direct perception of the hinterworld.

'Automatic writing' also has the quality of improvisation, and as such is an important source of some contemporary musical techniques. *Surréalisme* itself was hardly influential at all upon the musicians of the twenties and thirties, and only became a musical technique in this respect after the Second World War.

But *surréalisme* did have an impact upon drama. One of its important antecedents was Guillaume Apollinaire (1880–1918), whose *drame surréaliste, Les Mamelles des Tirésias*, (The Breasts of Tiresias) was written as early as 1903 and published in 1917. In 1947 the composer Francis Poulenc set the play as an opera. The story concerns Thérèse, and her attempt to liberate herself from her social position as wife and mother. But the method she chooses is not a socio-political one. In the first scene, she performs a symbolic act: she opens her blouse, and her breasts (two balloons) float up above her head, attached to her with string. Determined to free herself from these symbols of her feminine role, she bursts the balloons. Here we have moved away from *symbolisme* into a *surréaliste* device: there is a visual opposition and contradiction between reality (breasts are breasts, balloons are balloons) and imagination (breasts are balloons, balloons are breasts), a contradiction which alters our view of reality.

The scene is unavoidably comic, and deliberately so. Our minds are bisociated in the effort to understand. The *surréalistes* often used comic devices as means to bring us to an understanding of the hinterworld. 'Laughter,' wrote Alfred Jarry, one of the great precursors of *surréalisme*, 'is born out of the discovery of the contradictory.'[18] Through the *surréalistes* the comic vision returns to drama, not the polite comedy of manners or even the bedroom farces of realism, but as the moment of absurdity in which we suddenly realize the contradiction between realities. Comedy is itself at root surreal, for in it we perceive the *surréaliste* clash of realities.

Thérèse's bursting of the balloons has the immediate consequence that she grows a beard and moustache. To her husband's astonishment, she adopts the name Tirésias. The following scene is brief.

VOICE OF TIRÉSIAS, INSIDE THE HOUSE   I'm moving house.
A chamber pot is thrown out of the window.
HUSBAND The piano. *Then a urinal.* The violin. The situation's getting serious. *He goes into the house with heavy shoulders.*

The absurdity of this scene is followed by that of the next, in which two characters argue whether they are in Paris or Zanzibar, and shoot each other. Thérèse returns in man's clothes, her husband in a dress. A policeman appears, and idiocy is piled upon idiocy: the husband decides to produce on his own the children necessary to 'Zanzibar'.

In a world such as this the causal structure of the everyday world is abandoned; and yet we in the audience see the characters and actions as at least partly realistic. Poulenc's music in the opera reinforces this realism: he uses conventional means, a musical language that is easy to understand, and tunes and rhythms that are easy to grasp. The effect of the work therefore lies in its totality, as an experience full of contradiction and bisociation. What we make of it is our own affair. We cannot accept it either in terms of everyday reality or in the terms of conventional music-drama; we are knocked off balance by the clash of worlds, of associations, of symbols. We may take refuge in laughter; we may hurriedly regain our former balance and consider the experience — and the work — either immoral, or insane, or a waste of time. Or we may open our minds to the experience and seek what we can within it. If this latter course seems the most difficult of all, it is because somewhere along the line between childhood and adulthood our minds have been conditioned by a particular view of the world: but that view is only two centuries old and may be of limited validity.

The avant-garde

'Avant-garde' or 'contemporary' music is often regarded as virtually incomprehensible. The names Stockhausen and Cage are liable to provoke reactions of terror or disgust amongst even the more 'cultured' of music-lovers, although they are often more enthusiastically received by the young. The reason for this musical apartheid is not difficult to find: avant-garde music is based upon aesthetic premises different from those of 'conventional' Western European music since the Renaissance (although, significantly, medieval music has had considerable influence upon some contemporary composers).

To summarize the ideas of the avant-garde is no easy matter, but one thread running through much of what contemporary composers have to say is a rejection of traditional musical methods, an opposition to traditional ideas about music. Many contemporary composers believe that the music written in the eighteenth and nineteenth centuries is not 'relevant' to man in the twentieth century. In taking this line, the avant-garde composer believes that the traditional surface characteristics of music (conventional instruments, conventional forms, the conventional way of organizing pitch and time), which grew up as part of the European dedication to rationalism, are too closely associated with the rationalist view to be of much service in an age where rationalism is coming to seem more of a barrier than a path to truth. Even the conventions of 'composing a piece of music', and of 'performing a piece of music' in the concert-hall, are challenged as being too closely associated with a view of the relationship of the arts to life which is false and finally of no benefit.

In order to break away from these traditions and conventions, avant-garde composers have adopted some radically new techniques. Some are designed to allow the composer to use sound without the traditional restrictions, as for instance in the use of electronic musical instruments and machines. Others are intended to avoid the absolute, fixed quality of a musical 'composition', allowing performers the freedom to create sounds as a function of their time and place, or as a function of the moment of performance before an audience.

Ideas such as these spring from the ideas of the *surréalistes:* they too rejected tradition, and were anxious to allow their own ideas to determine the form of their works. Moreover, they too were concerned to communicate ideas that are 'relevant' without being cast in the mould of causal, developmental artistic structures. But while the *surréalistes* grasped at portraying that hinterworld which they sensed intuitively to be important, avant-garde musicians are much more aware of the developments in scientific thought that have so radically altered the old absolutist view. Thus Karl H. Wörner remarks that

> modern compositional practice is founded on the relativity of the concept of time. Stockhausen has always stressed the concept of multitemporality — plurality of time. Musically this is founded on the phenomenon according to which each sound has its own time. Proceeding from this fact, one has to think in terms of strata of time.[19]

Along with multitemporality modern compositional practice has also adopted multispatiality, the idea that sound sources may be arranged so as to impinge upon the ear from different directions.

Multispatiality is of course not a new idea in music. The most notable ancestor is the music written in the sixteenth century for two choirs facing each other in different lofts of St. Mark's Cathedral in Venice, itself a development of plainsong antiphony. A performance of multi-spatial music does however create a new situation for an audience, particularly if it wishes to watch the sound being made, for it has more than one location to look at. The relationship between the sound-sources thus sets up a visual environment; and if the sound-sources move, the audience is in fact witnessing music-drama. (The Sextet from *Le Nozze di Figaro* is, after all, six sound-sources — seven if one includes the orchestra — who have a shifting multispatial relationship.) In much contemporary 'music' therefore, the line between 'music' and 'music-drama' is a very narrow one.

An extreme example of this is Stockhausen's *Musik für ein Haus* (1968), which, although it is not called a music-drama, is in fact one.

> The acoustical happenings were located in four rooms situated on two floors. Directions for improvisation were given to the individual instrumentalists; their various improvisations were now picked up by microphones in each room, fed to a mixing desk, partly distorted by electronic means, then played back again on the loudspeakers of the other rooms, so that amongst the musicians themselves there was constantly an experience of reciprocal stimulation. The public had the opportunity to move around freely in all the rooms. Listening was intuitive, freed from the pursuit of interrelations. A fifth chamber provided the opportunity of listening simultaneously to the musical processes in all four rooms.[20]

Urban man's house here substitutes for primitive man's tribal dancing-ground. The public's move from room to room substitutes for the opera house's scene-changes. Conventional musical interrelations are avoided, and the sounds made by conventional instruments are distorted, in order that we may be forced to open our minds to a new musical reality. And the aim of the exercise is to bring about in us a clash of worlds: the four rooms, into which we walk as we do in the everyday world, and in which sounds are being made apparently independently, are in fact interrelated on a deeper level. The world of everyday reality clashes with an implied hinterworld. The house itself becomes (in Schopenhauer's terminology) more than the world as representation: it becomes the world as Will.

Many of John Cage's works show his belief in the importance of a visual, spatial element in music. The published score of the notorious *4'33''* (1952) consists of three movements, each marked *tacet* (do not play), and each given a duration in minutes and seconds that together add up to four minutes and thirty-three seconds. No sound is made, although the performer is of course required to enter and sit at the instrument. The work arouses our expectations, and, deliberately, does not fulfil them. Instead of being guided as usual by a composer into the hinterworld, we are left to find the hinterworld ourselves, in the visual and aural events that may occur during those four minutes and thirty-three seconds. It is, of course, a *surréaliste* trick, but it also deliberately stimulates our imaginations. If we find it an experience impossible to accept, that may be partly because we are embarrassed, but more because what is absent from the work is the element of human Apollonian image-making: the experience lacks the imagic shapes which control and focus the magic experience.

In Cage's *Water Music* (1952) theatrical elements are more in evidence, and this time sound is used. The score is mounted on a large poster visible to the audience, and consists of instructions to a pianist to make sounds using water in a variety of ways. *Sounds of Venice* and *Water Walk* of 1959 both use stage properties. But it is Cage's *Theatre Piece* of 1960 which can lay most

345

claim to be an avant-garde music-drama. Up to eight performers are involved, each working in some aural or visual medium — music, dance, acting, mime and so on. Each performer provides and organizes his own material in accordance with a series of general instructions, his resulting score to have a duration of thirty minutes. In performance, each performer gets on with his own programme, which may or may not include interaction with other performers. The result is somewhat astonishing: often the most intriguing cross-relations occur between the separate events on the stage. Cage regarded *Theatre Piece* as an image of 'reality'.

> If you go down the street in the city you can see that people are moving about with intention but you don't know what those intentions are. Many things happen which can be viewed in purposeless ways. . . If there are only a few ideas the piece produces a kind of concentration which is characteristic of human beings. If there are many things it produces a kind of chaos characteristic of nature.[21]

The material provided by the performers reflects an interaction between world and hinterworld, and this time Cage's own structural determinants attempt to reflect the hinterworld's order behind 'the chaos of nature'.

In fact Cage perceives little distinction between the everyday world, the hinterworld, and the world of drama.

> 'Theatre is all the
> various things going on at the
> same time.'
> 'Theatre takes place
> all the time wherever one is and art simply
> facilitates persuading one this is the case.'[22]

It is for this reason that he has tended to use what most authorities call 'chance determination processes' in making decisions about the organization of material. In *Theatre Piece,* for instance, the performer writes his material upon a series of twenty cards, which are then shuffled. Whatever principles govern the arrangement of cards in shuffling therefore determine the order in which the material is used.

When a deck of cards is shuffled, it might seem that the order that results is entirely random. However, modern scientific research indicates that various factors may intervene. Well-documented evidence suggests that 'chance' can be influenced, consciously or unconsciously, by a person who conducts exercises of this kind (throwing dice, and the like).[23] There is no clear explanation for this phenomenon, but that it can occur is not in doubt. This is not to say that the performers in *Theatre Piece* will inevitably influence the ordering of their materials despite the apparent randomness of the shuffling exercise. But it does offer the possibility that some mysterious hinterworld forces may operate in creative experiences of this kind, and it may provide the beginnings of an explanation as to why *Theatre Piece* often turns out in performance to be less chaotic and more meaningful than one might rationally expect.

The most forceful argument in favour of there being hidden meaning in the so-called 'chance determination processes' of avant-garde music is provided by Cage's use of the *I Ching* in making organizational decisions — for *Music of Changes* (1951) and *Mureau* (1971). *Music of Changes* is a piece for piano, and Cage composed it by taking a large amount of piano material and assembling it according to the answers he obtained from consulting the Chinese *Book of Changes* or *I Ching*.

The *I Ching* is some three thousand years old, and consists of a series of oracular statements, which act as the answers to questions. Annotations to these statements have been assembled over many centuries. In order to discover the answers to a particular question, patterns are created by the dividing of yarrow stalks or the tossing of coins: it is in this way that 'chance determination processes' are involved, although the basis of the *I Ching* is that there is nothing chancy about the operation at all. The *I Ching* is essentially a method of divination, of discovering truth by using means beyond the logical and rational. Its appeal to twentieth-century man, suspicious of his rational tradition, is obvious.

What Cage, and many other avant-garde musicians (or music-dramatists) are attempting to do is to bring the hinterworld to our immediate awareness. This is what the *symbolistes* also attempted, in their own terms. But to the contemporary creative artist, the attempt involves a more radical rejection of tradition, and an effort to break out of accustomed ways of thought. Before we dismiss his efforts, it is as well to consider whether or not what he is trying to do might not have considerable value, and whether or not it might be less of a 'new view' than the oldest view of man.

Paths to the hinterworld

In discussing various examples of Western European man's music-drama, we have focussed upon two aspects: content — what the opera is about, and structure — how the materials are shaped and organized. Opera has been examined as music-drama, and in the context of the particular cultural environment of each period. From these investigations a number of conclusions can be drawn.

1 *The surface aspects of a music-drama are created in accordance with prevailing cultural conditions.*
   Amongst the surface aspects we can include
   a the surface content of the drama — the sort of plot chosen, the sociological behaviour of the characters;
   b the surface structure of the drama — the organization of time, place, and events;

347

    c the surface content and structure of the music — the relationship between voice and instruments, the type of musical material used, the sorts of musical forms that are apparently employed.

2 *The inner aspects of a music-drama are created in accordance with man's constant need to explore the otherwise inexplicable.*
Amongst the inner aspects we can include:

    a the inner content of the drama — the meaning behind the plot and behaviour of the characters, which may have mythological or psychological power;

    b the inner content and structure of the music – the underlying power of the musical sounds, which may open us to the processes of psychological transformation;

    c the inner content and structure of the music-drama — the underlying relationship of musical sound to dramatic meaning, which may open us to the hinterworld.

As the history of opera has progressed, this last-named aspect has often been more heavily or less heavily veiled: it is more obvious, for instance, in works like Monteverdi's *L'Orfeo* and Gluck's *Orfeo ed Euridice,* Wagner's *Tristan und Isolde* and Debussy's *Pelléas et Mélisande,* than it is in works like Handel's *Rodelinda,* Mozart's *Le Nozze di Figaro,* or Berg's *Wozzeck.* But even in these latter works its presence can be traced. Its consistent presence argues that man's need for some path to the hinterworld is a permanent one.

That man is able to establish some kind of relationship with a world behind the world is not seriously in doubt, although for the past two hundred years this idea has been largely dismissed. The belief in magic and the supernatural held by what we are pleased to call 'primitive' tribes and cultures, and shared by some of the finest minds of the Middle ages, has been written off by rational, scientific, Western European man as superstition. We prefer to think of the world as explicable according to conventional scientific thought. And yet, even during the last two centuries, the creative artistic minds of Western Europe have accepted non-rational connections between man and nature. It is consequently by no means inappropriate that some scientists have recently conducted extensive investigations to discover whether there is any truth in 'superstitions' such as psychokinesis (the ability to move objects with the mind), telepathy, clairvoyance, and similar phenomena. Somewhat to the surprise of many investigators, the ability of man to go beyond rationality in these curious ways has turned out to be not mere superstition, but fact. It seems that we do possess curious and irrational abilities to relate to and even influence the world about us. Rather less controversial research has also shown that nature can influence us, in ways hitherto unsuspected by scientists.[24]

Oriental thought has always taken such matters for granted. While Western European man's scientific, rational approach has been concerned with explaining nature in terms of its particular ingredients, the Chinese mind, as illustrated through the *I Ching,* is concerned with grasping the totality of nature. Jung makes this clear.

> Unlike the Greek-trained Western mind, the Chinese mind does not aim at grasping details for their own sake, but at a view which sees the detail as part of the whole. For obvious reasons, a cognitive operation of this kind is impossible to the unaided intellect. Judgment must therefore rely much more on the irrational functions of consciousness, that is on sensation . . . and intuition . . . This grasping of the whole is obviously the aim of science as well, but it is a goal that necessarily lies very far off because science, whenever possible, proceeds experimentally and in all cases statistically. The experiment, however, consists in asking definite question which excludes as far as possible anything disturbing and irrelevant. It makes conditions, imposes them on Nature, and in this way forces her to give an answer to a question devised by man. She is prevented from answering out of the fullness of her possibilities. . . The workings of Nature in her unrestricted wholeness are completely excluded.[25]

The Western epitome of man's knowledge of the world about him is the Encyclopedia, in which nature is divided into alphabetical sections. The Oriental epitome is the Indian seer Aruni's formula 'thou art that' — what is within you and what you perceive outside you are one.[26]

And yet there is no essential difference at all between Oriental and Occidental human beings. The Chinese are just as able to conduct scientific research — and make an atom bomb — as Europeans. And Europeans are just as capable of experiencing the wholeness of nature as are the Chinese. Indeed, it becomes clear that the path to the hinterworld has been constantly trodden by the creative artists of western Europe: not only through poetry and painting and music but also, and perhaps even primarily, through the medium of music-drama.

The paths to the hinterworld are taken by those who seek to explain the inexplicable. For the primitive man who evolved music-drama, the close relationship between world and hinterworld was obvious. The buffalo-dance of the I-khun-uh-kah-tsi and its accompanying myth makes this clear, as do the Mysteries of Eleusis. These music-dramas included *narrative,* by means of which events are related in terms of this world, and a context is set up in which we may be prepared to detect the workings of the hinterworld, *ceremonial,* in which the conditions are established through which we may perceive a structural connection between world and hinterworld, and *enthusiasm,* in which we desert the world and enter the hinterworld.

In chapter 2 we introduced these three terms in the context of a distinction between Occidental and Oriental ways of thought. There we noted Campbell's distinction between the two: that Oriental thought is based upon the search for identity with the hinterworld, while Occidental thought takes as its starting point that man and hinterworld are separate and have some

349

kind of relationship. Man's search for a new music-drama in the century since Wagner illustrates the distinction neatly. Schoenberg and Stravinsky, in their different ways, confirm the Occidental way, by establishing a relationship between absolute and particular; Debussy, the *surréalistes* and the avant-garde adopt the Oriental way by seeking to bring us to a direct identification with the hinterworld.

Campbell maintains that the 'Oriental' way is man's earliest response to the world he lives in: it lies behind the mythology of the primitive hunter and planter. It was the establishment of the Sumerian civilization, he argues, that introduced the idea of a separateness and relationship between man and the hinterworld. Perhaps, indeed, the avant-garde, despite its obvious reliance on technological tools, is leading us back to a view of the world which we have had since our earliest beginnings, but which centuries of 'civilization' have now submerged.

In chapter 1 we introduced the symbols of Apollo and Dionysos, to describe the two sides of musico-dramatic images. Apollo we have described as the symbol of shapes and structures, and Dionysos as the symbol of our liberation from shapes and our identification with what lies behind them. We have noted Nietzsche's idea that the work of art is a product of the mating of the two. The Dionysiac aspects we can now see as part of that ancient allegiance of man to the Earth-Mother, to the belief in the possibility of loss of self in the womb of nature — perhaps even of the denial of the will-to-live, exemplified by the experience of love. The Apollonian aspects can be seen as part of the Sumerian tradition, in which the lines of demarcation between man and Nature are clearly set out. Greek culture, the cradle of Western European civilization, placed the two gods in meaningful opposition, and that opposition inevitably persists to this day. But we must beware of seeing Apollo as a means of preventing the Dionysiac experience: on the contrary, he provides a means by which we can gain that experience. Nietzsche describes Apollo as the god of the world of dream, and we have noted that the dream-world — whether it be the world of human dreams or the musico-dramatic dream-world — is a recognized and sure path to the hinterworld. Apollo, in short, provides — in space-age terminology — the capsule in which we explore the cosmos: and without his Apollo capsule the astronaut cannot survive.

In investigating the effect music-drama has upon us, we have used the term psychological transformation. Music-drama arose out of man's wish to understand moments of transformation within himself: birth, adolescence, marriage and death. It is precisely at these moments that the hinterworld most closely impinges upon us, and what primitive man sensed, science is at last beginning to confirm. There is, it seems, a marked increase in the number of births during magnetic storms, which are themselves caused by the positions of sun, moon and planets.[27] It even seems to have been proved

350

that the 'superstitious' belief that we select marriage partners in accordance with astrological compatibility is not without basis,[28] The evidence mounts, to challenge our scepticism, that our lives are somehow mysteriously connected to universal forces we only dimly comprehend.

One belief has remained constant throughout man's history: that music is somehow a direct counterpart of the hinterworld. For primitive man music was magic; for the Greeks it was universal harmonia; for medieval man it was the music of the spheres of the universe; for Bach it was the worship of God; for Schopenhauer it was the resonance of the Will. This belief is both mysterious and important, for it does suggest why music-drama can have such a powerful effect upon us. In defining music as the most abstract of the arts, as we have, we must not think that abstract signifies an absence of meaning. On the contrary, a musical exploration of a dramatic experience may discover the real meaning in it; we may discover the real universals behind the explicit images, and if we cannot explain that meaning rationally in words, it may nevertheless have permanent validity.

What next?
To forecast the future of music-drama is a fool's errand. We have the music-drama we deserve: its particular forms derive from prevailing views of the world. Plato put it accurately enough when he said that music changes when the laws of man change. In a time such as the present, ruled by one philosophy and grasping towards another, any prediction is unwise. At the same time, certain trends can be indicated.

Faced with serious problems in this world, and conditioned to find solutions in this world, twentieth-century man has a predilection for seeking political and ideological answers. This tendency has had its adherents in the arts, in the belief that the arts can be, or should be, political and ideological. Wagner can perhaps be blamed for this to a certain extent, as can the *surréalistes*. In music-drama the best examples are the collaborations of Bertolt Brecht and Kurt Weill, notably *Der Aufstieg und Fall der Stadt Mahagonny* (1930). Here urban man is viewed from a socio-political viewpoint; Brecht chose to attribute man's faults to economic and environmental factors. This message was transmitted by Weill through the agency of music based on popular styles, setting up a contradiction between the biting, satirical text and the lazy, easy-going music. The effect is a *surréaliste* one, but is used for ideological purposes: the audience is not encouraged to seek the hinterworld but to accept a message about this world which is of this world. This is not to say that *Mahagonny* does not take us into the hinterworld in spite of its aims: it can do, for music-drama is bigger than any single ideology, although that is not a view that any totalitarian government finds it easy to accept.

The arts, including music-drama, can also be used as an escape from the

351

problems of this world into a fantasy Arcadian world. Such escapist music-drama is evident in the Viennese operetta and the saccharine European and American musicals of the twentieth century, although some of the latter, at least, have used the stage world as a means to comment upon the everyday world (notably *West Side Story*). Others have used the power of contemporary pop-music in an attempt to renew our myths (for instance *Jesus Christ Superstar*).

Contemporary pop-music arouses in many the same sort of reactions as contemporary avant-garde classical music does. But our reaction to pop-music is often compounded by fear. We sense, in the musical experiences of the pop-festival or discothèque, the same sort of mind-blurring, hypnotic, total loss of self that Pentheus sensed in the rites of the worshippers of Dionysos. And yet the appeal of that experience to the young is unquestionable, just as it was to the women of Thebes; indeed, it is an experience common in many forms of 'primitive' ritualistic music-drama, for what it does offer is an immediate and total escape from this world into the hinter-world. In the resulting trance 'impossible' things can happen — men can walk on fire without being burnt; the body can be contorted into abnormal positions; and, sometimes, the truth can be spoken. Whether or not those who flock to pop-festivals and discothèques and submit to the deliberately banal and ear-shattering sounds of contemporary pop-music are in fact gaining any deeper appreciation of the mysteries of life, or whether the experience is being used to close minds rather than to open them is a moot point. The profit of pop-music may be merely financial and not psychological. But even if this is the case, even if most of the music written in contemporary pop idioms contributes nothing to human experience, and is a cosmetic rather than a cure for our ills, we should not suppose that it is *per se* incapable of more.

One thing is certain. Opera as we know it is becoming increasingly more difficult to mount, for economic reasons. No Western European opera-house or opera company can survive without financial assistance beyond its box-office takings. Most rely on assistance from the state — that is, from every tax-paying member of the community. In a democratic society, such assistance depends upon the tax-payers being convinced of the value of opera, and, however much we might argue that music-drama is a way of fulfilling man's basic needs, this is not quite the same as saying we all should pay taxes for opera. For one thing, televison offers us powerful cosmetic music-drama, in its fantasy pseudo-world. For another, opera is not the same as music-drama, but merely one kind of music-drama, one that has associations with particular views of reality that may no longer be relevant.

It is this argument which lends support to the idea that the opera-house is a museum (stated with most impact by Pierre Boulez). This is not, of course, an argument against supporting opera-houses; after all, we support other kinds of museum. Museums, moreover, can be very stimulating places to visit. Even if we attended a performance of *Le Nozze di Figaro* merely to satisfy our curiosity about the way the later eighteenth century looked at life, such an experience would hardly harm us, and might benefit us.

But the idea that opera is a product of outdated cultural attitudes ignores the other aspect of opera — its relationship to music-drama as a branch to a tree. From all we have discussed so far, it is clear that opera as music-drama can and often does communicate meanings beyond the surface. There is an eternal, universal quality about the best opera that takes no account of its date of composition, the linguistic peculiarities of its text, the costumes its characters wear, or the instruments used in the orchestra. Even if we find the amorous intrigues of *Le Nozze di Figaro* trivial, and the philosophical assumptions of the characters irrelevant, we have not fully described the opera if we only take into account those attributes. There is more to it, and if opera is to die, it should not be allowed to do so merely on the grounds of its superficial characteristics.

The avant-garde offers a radical alternative. In place of the conventional view that opera is a branch of music, contemporary composers are inclined to say that 'music' and 'drama' are inevitably closely related. The performance of musical sounds cannot be divorced from a visual, spatial dimension. This is an argument with considerable historical validity, if we take the widest historical perspective, and may offer the most hope for the future. But the avant-garde's radical opposition to tradition carries with it the danger that no concession will be made to the audience on whose behalf the path to the hinterworld is being trodden. The result could be — and often is — the formation of a musical priesthood without a congregation.

Technology has had a marked effect upon our attitudes to music and music-drama. We now have the opportunity to hear a symphony orchestra or opera-singers perform in our own living-rooms. Gramophone records have brought to music and to opera a larger audience than ever before: in theory, the bringing of these 'paths to the hinterworld' directly into the everyday world of our own living-rooms ought to be a reason for celebration. In practice, however, there arises the danger that we treat music and music-drama only as part of the everyday world, like the wallpaper and furnishings of our living-rooms. It can further be argued, with considerable justification, that listening to the gramophone records of an opera is far from an ideal way to experience the work: it leads to the belief that opera is music, not music-drama, and ignores the vital ingredient of a good opera production — the relationship between sound and visual images.

Some scientists and philosophers, and many of the articulate young, believe that our view of the world is in the process of radical change, and that it is because of this that we cling so desperately to the ideas of the past. Certainly in music and music-drama we expend much more time and energy

353

on the works of the past than we do on those of the present: it is as if we are so frightened of being deprived of our familiar patterns of thought that we will not yield them up at any price. One consequence of this is that we deprive ourselves of the wider view.

The wider view of music-drama is what we have explored in this book. Opera in its various forms can be seen to be a branch, and only a branch, of music-drama. If man moves into a different world-view, then 'opera' may no longer serve him: other forms of music-drama may emerge. We, rooted in the present time, may lament, but in the wider view it is not opera that matters but music-drama. 'Opera', as we said at the beginning, is a *genre* only some three hundred and eighty years old, and is essentially a regional manifestation. Music-drama, in its various forms, is far, far older and more widespread. The passing of 'opera', if it occurs, should be an occasion for mourning, because it has proved to be a type of music-drama full of vitality and meaning, but its death might bring about a rebirth of music-drama in some new form.

In the end, of course, what happens next in music-drama will not be determined by books like this, by Ministries of Culture, or by committees. It will be born out of the inevitable conviction of him, her, or those who create music-drama. Books can assist, as can intellectual argument — they helped Peri, Gluck and Wagner — but in the final analysis it is up to the shaman, who sees his visions of the hinterworld, and finds a capsule into which he can entice us, so that we too can share his voyage of exploration.

Notes on the text

CHAPTER 1 THE ORIGINS OF MUSIC-DRAMA

1 And to catalogue dance as a branch of physical education.
2 Some anthropologists, notably Lévi-Strauss (in *Structural Anthropology*), question the validity of using surviving primitive cultures to determine what were the cultures of prehistory. Many problems are involved, including the possibility that a surviving primitive culture has regressed from a more advanced stage, and may therefore contain features alien to its apparent prehistoric equivalent. While the method of cultural cross-reference cannot guarantee sure answers, it may however suggest valid *possibilities*.
3 Notably Lewis R. Binford and Sally R. Binford.
4 Marshack, *The Roots of Civilisation*, p. 78.
5 *The History of Man*, pp. 55–6.
6 See Radcliffe-Brown, *The Andaman Islanders*.
7 Ibid., p. 129.
8 Campbell, *Primitive Mythology*, p. 370.
9 Arranged from Grinnell, *Blackfoot Lodge Tales*. I make no apology for quoting this at length; it is the primitive equivalent of an opera scenario.
10 Quoted in Campbell, *Primitive Mythology*, p. 22.
11 Quoted in Huizinga, *Homo Ludens*, p. 23.
12 Stanislavsky, *Building a Character*, chapter 2.
13 Campbell, *Primitive Mythology*, p. 170.
14 J.R. Firth, *The Tongues of Men;* and *Speech*, p. 25.
15 Nietzsche, *The Birth of Tragedy*, p. 128.
16 An account by a Siberian peasant, noted in Campbell, *Primitive Mythology*, pp. 265–6.
17 See Campbell, ibid., pp. 254–63.
18 Nor can a committee write an opera: the result is likely to be a pantomime. The experiment of composition by committee has been recently attempted in Communist China, without great success, at least so far as the quality of the composition is concerned.
19 Birds are the traditional familiars of shamans, for they have a freedom of movement which aptly parallels the shaman's ability to leave earthbound life behind him and soar in flights of the imagination.

20 Frazer, *The Golden Bough*, pp. 518–19. A poetic translation of Homer's original may be found in Hine: *The Homeric Hymns*, pp. 4–16.

21 Ibid., pp. 429–30.

22 A bull-roarer is a slip of wood fastened to a thong.

23 See Cambell, *Primitive Mythology*, pp. 170–1.

CHAPTER 2   THE MUSIC-DRAMA OF ANCIENT GREECE

1 Campbell, *Primitive Mythology*, p. 147.

2 A plucked stringed instrument.

3 Translated from Joseph Gregor, *Kulturgeschichte der Oper*, pp. 21–2. Gregor gives no source for his information. His history of opera is, however, the only one I have seen which treats the pre-Greek history of opera in any detail at all. Allardyce Nicoll, in his history of *World Drama*, p. 25, refers to this Egyptian music-drama which 'celebrated the death of Osiris, and apparently told how his limbs were torn apart, to be brought together again by Isis, his sister and wife'. Nicoll, unfortunately, misses the point in commenting that 'we remain unsure whether this presentation was truly dramatic — whether it may not have been, after all, merely a piece of expanded ritual'.

4 See Kirk, *The Songs of Homer*. See also West, 'Greek Poetry 2000–700 B.C.', *Classical Quarterly* 1973, p. 182.

5 Campbell, *Occidental Mythology*, p. 7.

6 See Campbell, ibid., pp. 162–77 for a detailed analysis of Odysseus' journey in these terms.

7 Apuleius, *The Golden Ass*, pp. 228–9.

8 Aeschylus, the first dramatist whose plays are preserved, was a native of Eleusis, and, according to Aristotle, was tried and acquitted of the charge of revealing secrets of the Eleusinian Mysteries in one of his plays.

9 Ridgeway, *The Origin of Tragedy* and *The Dramas and Dramatic Dances of Non-European Races*.

10 Reese notes that the Greeks had twenty-one pitches within the octave (*Music in the Middle Ages*, pp. 23–4). Sachs observes that they had at least three major thirds, five minor thirds, seven seconds, thirteen semitones and nine quarter tones (*The Rise of Music in the Ancient World*, p. 213).

11 Aristotle, *On the Art of Poetry*, in *Classical Literary Criticism*, p. 48.

12 Aeschylus, *Prometheus Bound. . .*, p. 127.

13 Ibid., p. 145.

14 *The Greek Tragic Theatre*, p. 75.

15 Sophocles, *The Theban Plays*, p. 62.

16 *Primitive Mythology*, p. 328.

17 *The Golden Bough*, p. 185.

18 Sophocles, *The Theban Plays*, p. 26.

19 Ibid., p. 31.

20 Ibid., p. 46.

21 Campbell, *Primitive Mythology*, pp. 165–6. A description of the self-mutilation of the god-king of the south Indian province of Quilacare in Malabar.

22 Sophocles, *The Theban Plays*, p. 55.

23 Such chronology is within the legendary version of Greek history and not in any

way accurate historical dating.

24 Euripides, *The Bacchae and other plays*, pp. 183–4.
25 *New Oxford History of Music*, ed. Wellesz, Volume 1, p. 396.
26 Ibid., p. 396.
27 See ibid., p. 397.
28 *Occidental Mythology*, pp. 3–4. What follows is a paraphrase of Campbell's ideas, so far as mythological and religious distinctions are concerned.
29 *The Republic*, Book VII, 514–21.

CHAPTER 3 ROME AND THE MIDDLE AGES

1 I Corinthians 15: 22. (New English Bible).
2 See Campbell, *Occidental Mythology*, pp. 371–3.
3 Fifty-two years before, Wagner had reformed music-drama with the slogan 'music must serve the drama, not drama serve music'.
4 In 1054 there occurred the schism between the Eastern Orthodox Church and the Roman Catholic Church. Our investigations are concerned with the latter.
5 See 'The Mass as Sacred Drama', Essay II in *Christian Rite and Christian Drama in the Middle Ages*, by O.B. Hardison, Jr., pp. 35–79.
6 See Axton, *European Drama of the Early Middle Ages*, chapters 1 to 3.
7 Lea, in *Italian Popular Comedy*, traces a continuing tradition from Roman mimes to the Italian *Commedia dell'Arte* of the sixteenth century.
8 Axton, op. cit., pp. 33–4.
9 Quoted in ibid., p. 31.
10 The *Visitatio Sepulchri* play was popular but not necessarily the first. Axton, op. cit., p. 61 discusses an eighth-century 'oratorio' on the subject of The Harrowing of Hell.
11 From the Limoges Manuscript, 923–4 A.D.
12 Discussed by Axton, op. cit., p. 78 *et seq.*
13 From Woolf, *The English Mystery Plays*, p. 85.
14 The Feast of Corpus Christi was introduced as a special day upon which Christian music-drama might be performed. It occurs on the first free Thursday after the octave of Pentecost, that is, in late spring or early summer, and therefore at the same time of year as the Great Dionysia Festival in Athens.
15 See Brown, 'Musicians in the Mystères and Miracles' in Taylor and Nelson, *Medieval English Drama*.
16 Purvis, *The York Cycle of Mystery Plays*, p. 100.
17 Ibid., pp. 101–2.
18 See Carpenter, 'Music in the Secunda Pastorum' in Taylor and Nelson, op. cit., pp. 212–17.

CHAPTER 4 REBIRTH

1 See Harry Elmer Barnes, *An Intellectual and Cultural History of the Western World*, Vol., 2., p. 552.
2 No respectable church was without its relics. Even in 1929 it was estimated that Catholic churches in Europe contained fifty-six fingers of St. Peter the Dominican, thirty bodies of St. George, twelve heads of St. John the Baptist, and

seventy veils of the Virgin Mary. Erasmus (1466–1536) suggested there were enough Relics of the True Cross in European churches to build a ship. See Barnes, op. cit., p. 583.

3 Quoted in Barnes, op. cit., p. 559.

4 See Sachs, *The Rise of Music in the Ancient World*, pp. 222–3 for an explanation of Greek note-names.

5 *Pagan Mysteries in the Renaissance*, Penguin edition, p. 265.

6 Ibid., pp. 265–6.

7 According to Reese, *Music in the Middle Ages*, p. 152.

8 Giulio Caccini, *Le Nuove Musiche*, edited by H. Wiley Hitchcock, p. 103.

9 Edited from Jacopo Peri, *Le Musiche sopra L'Euridice*, p. 17. *Notes:* bars 1–26: two bars here equal one bar in source; bar 21: *g* sharp in bass in source. Source gives vocal line, bass line, and figures only. Organ realization by J.D.D.

10 Edited from ibid., pp. 12–13. *Notes:* bars 2–4 written in source as one bar; bars 5–25: two bars in edition equal one bar in source. Organ realization by J.D.D.

11 Note that Dafne's heart is frozen because of the Aristotelian experience of 'terror and pity'.

12 Edited from ibid., p. 30. *Notes:* two bars in edition equal one bar in source. Organ realization by J.D.D.

13 *L'Orfeo*, edited by G.F. Malipiero, footnote to p. 2.

14 Taken from Claudio Monteverdi: *L'Orfeo, favola in musica*, edited by Denis Stevens, pp. 2–3, bars 18–26.

15 The vocal line, barring and bass taken from ibid., p. 9, bars 1–24. Stevens's editorial vocal ornamentation has been omitted. The continuo realization and translation are my own.

16 It is important to distinguish between a key and a chord. A *chord* consisting of a 'tonic triad' in D minor (the notes *d*, *f* and *a*) could be regarded as a chord of the supertonic in C major; it does not indicate the *key* of D minor unless the crucial notes of D minor (a *g* natural and a *c* sharp) have been previously announced. Here we are concerned exclusively with key-relationships, not with chord-relationships. (That there can be misunderstandings is the result of the inherent ambiguities in tonal musical sounds; such ambiguities are the very stuff of musical expression.)

17 Op. cit., p. 21, bars 165–80.

18 Ibid., pp. 52–3, bars 225–40.

19 Ibid., p. 57, bars 312–20. The problems involved in realizing a continuo of this period are particularly trying here. Did Monteverdi intend that the continuo player should try to accommodate the dissonances of the vocal line (e.g. the *g* sharp in bar 6)? Should an editor 'fill in gaps' such as the first two bars with movement in the continuo part? Scholars and editors have differing views on questions of this kind. In my opinion, the crucial thing to remember is that the continuo player's task is to create sounds at rehearsal and in performance which contribute to the dramatic interpretation by the singer, while following such instructions as the composer has given, and observing the particular dramatic style of the production. Continuo playing is essentially a form of creative improvization. No editorial, printed realization should be regarded as gospel. In all my realizations in these musical examples I have attempted to provide a

minimal harmonic skeleton in order to show the chords Monteverdi either definitely specifies or seems to imply. Very occasionally I have used a chord which is not indicated by the figures (or absence of figures) — as for instance the D major chord in bar 5 here; in all such cases I must stress that it is my chord, and I might well change it if I were engaged in playing continuo in a production of *L'Orfeo*.

20 Ibid., p. 119, bars 225–31.
21 Ibid., p. 119, bars 235–8.
22 *A Short History of Opera*, p. 7.
23 Quoted in Strunk, *Source Readings in Music History*, p. 374.

CHAPTER 5   OPERA SERIA

1 In *The Baroque,* Part 1, chapter 4.
2 See illustration in Nagler, *A Source Book in Theatrical History*, p. 82, and photograph in Nicoll, *World Drama*, facing p. 193.
3 In *Venetian Opera in the Seventeenth Century*, chapter 3, Worsthorne shows that the early opera-houses in Venice (and elsewhere in Italy) were of the 'tiered-boxes' type.
4 Such criticism arises from our twentieth-century theatrical experiences, born of nineteenth-century melodrama and fostered by the commercial cinema. If we are willing to accept the rules of the game in French Classical Tragedy and in *opera seria,* we discover that the apparently unexciting dilemmas of the characters can speak to our own condition in a very powerful way, even more powerful perhaps than the spectacle of John Wayne rescuing a stage-coach from marauding Indians.
5 One suspects the musical director might well have had some say too, especially if he was respected, and/or the composer of the work and/or the singer's vocal teacher.
6 As presented in the Chrysander edition, ignoring all arias in Appendices, but including the optional (?) aria for Rodelinda on pp. 89–90.
7 Quoted in Strunk, *Source Readings in Music History,* p. 661.
8 It is doubtful whether Algarotti actually knew any of the early Baroque operas, but his text makes it clear that he knew of them by name and had a good idea of what their composers were trying to achieve.
9 Quoted in Strunk, op. cit., p. 664.
10 Ibid., p. 664.
11 Ibid., p. 670.
12 There are thus two versions of each opera, a Vienna one and a Paris one. Most published vocal scores are hotch-potches of both: the Complete Edition of Gluck's works publishes the versions separately.

CHAPTER 6   COMIC MUSIC-DRAMA

1 Oscar Wilde, *The Importance of Being Earnest*, Act I.
2 See Arthur Koestler. *The Act of Creation*, chapter 2.
3 *The Use of Lateral Thinking.*
4 Albert Camus, *The Outsider*, translated by Stuart Gilbert. Penguin ed. pp. 19–20. Reprinted by permission of Hamish Hamilton Ltd., and Alfred A. Knopf, Inc.
5 In *Moving into Aquarius.*

6 So far as I know, this intriguing possibility has never before been suggested.
7 See 'On the Psychology of the Trickster-Figure', in *Four Archetypes* by C.G. Jung.
8 *The Birds*, translated by R.H. Webb. *The Complete Plays of Aristophanes*, pp. 254–5. Reprinted by permission of University Press of Virginia.
9 Ibid., pp. 256–7.
10 Ibid., pp. 258–9.
11 K.M. Lea, *Italian Popular Comedy*, Vol. II, p. 618.
12 Reproduced in Duchartre, *The Italian Comedy*, p. 325.
13 For the first performance of Mozart's *Le Nozze di Figaro* Michael Kelly, who played the part of the lawyer Don Curzio (Brid'oison in Beaumarchais' play), turned the character into an authentic Tartaglia by using a stutter.
14 In the 'New' Mozart Complete Edition; the 'Old' Complete Edition censors the texts.
15 I have so far discovered 117 different operas performed in Vienna in the decade 1781–91, on average one 'new' (to Viennese audiences) opera a month.
16 *Grundgestalt* means basic shape, and is used in music analysis to signify a sequence of notes lying behind a composition and from which the material is derived.
17 The facts of Figaro's parenthood has been given in Beaumarchais' introductory letter to *Le Barbier*.
18 In *Music and Letters*, Vol. LXVI, 1965, pp. 134–6.
19 From the *Neue Mozart Ausgabe*, II/5/16, *Le Nozze di Figaro, Teilband 2*, pp. 375–401. The piano realization is my own.
20 Mozart's original (manuscript) tempo marking for the Sextet was *Andante*, not *Allegro moderato*. His later decision to increase the tempo suggests that he may have felt that he had over-sentimentalized the family relationships, or that the outbursts of Susanna, and the Count and Curzio, required a tempo with more pace. Whether or not the sextet is 'funnier' at the faster tempo is a moot point.

CHAPTER 7   ROMANTIC OPERA

1 'Das wahre Erkennen ist Lieben, ist menschlich Fühlen' (*Vom Erkennen und Empfinden der menschlichen Seele*, 1779, I, 3). Quoted in *The Romantic Tradition in Germany, An Anthology* by Ronald Taylor, p. 1.
2 Quoted in Thorlby, *The Romantic Movement*, p. 152. See also Strunk, *Source Readings*.
3 Quoted in Strunk, *Source Readings*, p. 775.
4 *The World as Will and Representation*, III, 52, p. 262.
5 *Goethe's Briefwechsel mit einem Kinde*, II. Quoted in Thorlby, op. cit., p. 152.
6 Nicoll, *World Drama*, p. 471.
7 See, for example, Freedley and Reeves, *A History of the Theatre*, p. 341.
8 Nicoll, *World Drama*, p. 488.
9 Quoted in Weinstock, *Rossini*, p. 58.
10 Ibid., p. 58.
11 See Weinstock, op. cit., pp. 56–7 for details of the borrowings.
12 It is of course possible that a musical number previously composed will 'fit' a new dramatic situation like a glove; it remains however extremely unlikely that the

musical material will coincide with any thematic continuum there may be in the new opera. In Rossini's case it becomes impossible to justify his borrowings in musico-dramatic terms, simply because there are so many of them.

Reference should also be made here to Gluck, who like many eighteenth-century composers, occasionally borrowed from himself, even at crucial moments in his 'reform operas'. Gluck remains a puzzling case: as we have noted, his dedication to reform seems not always to have been absolute.

13 Weinstock, op. cit., p. 47.
14 Influential on Chopin, for example.
15 English (and Scottish) novels and events were very much in vogue as opera subjects after the Battle of Waterloo!
16 Some arias in early *opera buffa* (for instance in Pergolesi's *La Serva Padrona*) are organized in alternating slow and fast sections. Mozart's operas contain arias structured as a slower section followed by a faster one (for instance the Countess's aria in Act III of *Le Nozze di Figaro*).
17 The action takes place in the sixteenth century, which leads one idly to wonder whether the opera intends the 'Duke' to refer to Federigo, first duke (1500–40), patron of the painter Romano and the poet and dramatist Aretino, who together created a series of notoriously lascivious engravings and sonnets. To judge by the Duke's behaviour in the opera, such artistic fancies would be to his taste. The plays of Aretino are of some historical interest, since they show the blending of *Commedia* vulgarity with Menander-like intrigue.
18 See Henry Hatfield, *Aesthetic Paganism in German Literature*.
19 Quoted in Strunk, *Source Readings*, pp. 775–6.
20 Translated from *Morphologie, Bildung und Umbildung organischer Naturen*. Collected Works, Vol. 9, p. 332.
21 It may also be regarded as a dominant minor ninth chord without its root.
22 Wagner's argument that in the opera of this period drama had become the means and music the end is a rather different conclusion from the same evidence. His view supposes a division between drama and music which is not, finally, valid, although it is possible to view his terminology as deliberately chosen for convenient effect.
23 Barnes, *An Intellectual and Cultural History of the western World*, Vol. 2, p. 736.

CHAPTER 8   WAGNER AND AFTER

1 See Barzun, *Darwin, Marx, Wagner*.
2 My translation from *Oper und Drama*, Part III, chapter 3, pp. 256–8.
3 My translation from Rosteutscher, *Die Wiederkunft des Dionysos*, p. 85.
4 My translation from Novalis' Fourth *Hymn to the Night*.
5 My translation from *Tristan und Isolde*, Act II, scene 2.
6 My translation from ibid., loc. cit.
7 I am indebted to Martin Hindmarsh for his collaboration in the formulation of this idea.
8 As suggested by Kurth and by Lorenz, and shown in (d) of Ex. 25.
9 It is unusual to apply the inductive method to musical analysis. The reader who prefers to use the deductive method is advised to read Ex. 25 upwards, from the bottom to the top. One reader of the manuscript of this book maintains (as would

others) that the source of the chords in bars 3 and 4 is the Phrygian cadence of modal music (*f—a—d* to *e—b—e*). The Phrygian cadence acquired, in the late sixteenth century, by chance or design, a sharpened *d* in the first chord and a *g* sharp in the second, thus preparing the way for the augmented sixth chords of the seventeenth and later centuries. It could be argued from these indubitable facts that the *f* to *e* of bar 2 is a forecast of the crucial bass notes of bars 3 and 4, and that to suggest a Neapolitan implication to bar 2 is going too far. This may well be the case, and it is certainly true that Wagner wished us to be kept in suspense through bars 1 to 3, only resolving our expectations into an itself unresolved chord in bar 4. My purpose in implying chords in bars 1 and 2 is not to turn Wagner's exciting Dionysiac sounds into dull, explicable Apollonian formulae, but merely to point out that one can find an Apollonian structure in the Dionysiac image: in all Wagner's music it is this hidden structure which makes the images so compelling. In this case, I would argue, the very first note, *a*, determines structurally, and predisposes us aurally for, the chord in bar 4 of a dominant seventh in A minor. Many analysts misinterpret the opening chord progression in *Tristan und Isolde* because they do not take into account the musical events of the first two bars.

10 The accompaniment has been simplified to show the tonal progressions more clearly.

11 The E major here, at 694 and at 702, is written by Wagner as F flat major. This raises the thorny question of enharmonics: is the key of F flat major really the same as the key of E major? For all practical purposes it is: only an extraordinarily subtle aural perception would notice the difference. Whether it matters to a composer is a moot point: presumably he chooses to write an *f* flat for some good reason. That reason might be that it is more convenient to write flats rather than sharps in the context of a prevailing tonality or key signature — in which case the difference between *f* flat and *e* is not a matter of musico-dramatic expression. If, however, *f* flat is used *inconveniently,* we can deduce that there is an expressive purpose. In this case, the tonality is predominantly flat, and it would have been less convenient for Wagner to use E major. If he had done so, then key-interpretation would be easy; that he has not done so merely leaves the question open.

In general, in his works Wagner does not notate keys inconveniently. In *Tristan und Isolde,* for instance, E major tends to be used in a natural or sharp tonal context, and F flat major in a flat context. Richard Strauss does often write chords inconveniently and this is *prima facie* evidence (which can be supported by analysis) that he uses such keys as G flat major and F sharp major with quite different associations (a practice which may work only on paper and not in a listener's head).

Here, and in the later analysis of an extract from *Tristan und Isolde,* I have taken the line that enharmonic keys are equivalent in their associations. I would add, however, in reference to the key-associations displayed in fig. 22, that to represent E major as F flat major might suggest a 'magical' view of 'human love', which would not be inappropriate to this scene or to the whole work.

12 Wagner's poetry is extremely difficult to translate: this translation has of necessity sacrificed metre and rhyme to concentrate upon specific and implicit meanings.

13 Again, the accompaniment texture has been simplified for clarity.

14 From a criticism of the first performance of the work in Vienna, October 1883. *Music Criticisms 1846–99*, p. 222.

15 Hence those who object to being 'swept away' find *Tristan und Isolde* obnoxious and immoral.

16 Professor K.F. Mather, in *World Unity*, October 1927, quoted in Barnes, *An Intellectual and Cultural History*, Vol. 3, p. 981.

17 Quoted in Jung, *Synchronicity*, footnote to p. 21.

18 Ibid., p. 95.

19 See Campbell, *Creative Mythology*, p. 574.

20 The experiences which provide the content of music-drama are absolute in that they are part of everyone's human experience, and irrational in that they are neither rationally explicable nor communicated intellectually.

21 Campbell, *Creative Mythology*, pp. 620–1.

22 Jung, *Synchronicity*, p. 119.

23 Campbell, *Creative Mythology*, p. 609.

24 See Mosco Carner, *Puccini, a Critical Biography*, Duckworth, London, 1958.

25 The text is by Montagu Slater. I have added commas in order to draw the sense out of the passage, and divided the passage into three 'verses' as Britten does.

26 See *Psychology of Sex*, pp. 188–219.

27 Schoenberg's music of this period is usually described as 'atonal': it might therefore seem suitable to make an equation between 'atonal' and 'acausal' and between 'tonality' and 'causality'. The sounds created in tonal music are explicable according to an absolute system of note-relationships, and in that sense tonality can be called causal. On the other hand, the reason why tonal music can be so expressive is that the system is full of ambiguities: the causal explanation for a chord of G major in a particular piece, for instance, depends upon the context in which the chord appears (it might be a tonic chord, a dominant chord, a subdominant chord, a relative major chord, or function in a number of other possible ways). In other words, tonality is a system in which a sound may have many causes and many effects. On another level, however, to an audience accustomed to seeing causally structured drama presented in tonal music, 'atonal' music seems vividly to express drama which is 'acausal'.

28 Debussy's *Pelléas et Mélisande* is of considerable relevance to a discussion of late-Romantic operas which have the fluidity of *Erwartung* or the apparent inconsequentialities of *Wozzeck*. I have however reserved discussion of this work to the following chapter, for reasons which will be clear.

29 My translation.

30 See Willi Reich, *Schoenberg, a Critical Biography*, pp. 97–105.

31 See Barford, 'Urphänomen, Ursatz and Grundgestalt', and Drummond, 'The Background, Shape and Meaning of Twelve-Note Music.'

32 Barford, op. cit., pp. 227–8.

33 My translation.

34 My translation.

35 There is a trace here of the Principle of 'Renunciation', an idea that plagued Wagner after he read Schopenhauer and that considerably confused his attempts to find a satisfactory ending to *The Ring*.

36 See *Dialogues and a Diary*, pp. 21–31.

37 My translation.

38 See *Dialogues and a Diary*, pp. 21–31.

39 *Poetics of Music*, pp. 24–5.

40 Ibid., p. 33.
41 Ibid., p. 146, the closing words of the book.

CHAPTER 9   ALTERNATIVE REALITIES

1 *The World as Will and Representation*, II, 21, p. 110.
2 Ibid., III, 52, p. 261.
3 Ibid., III, 52, p. 260.
4 From *On Apparent Design in the Fate of the Individual*, an essay in *Parerga and Paralipomena*. Quoted in Campbell, *Creative Mythology*, pp. 340–1.
5 Quoted in ibid., p. 341.
6 Quoted in ibid., p. 344.
7 See Balakian, *The Symbolist Movement*, chapter 3.
8 *The Heritage of Symbolism*, p. 5.
9 Balakian, op. cit., p. 85.
10 My translation from Vallas, *Claude Debussy et son temps*, p. 140.
11 My translation from ibid., p. 141.
12 Balakian, op. cit., pp. 124–5.
13 My translation from Vallas, op. cit., p. 157.
14 My translation from ibid., pp. 157–8.
15 My translation from ibid., pp. 224–5.
16 Quoted in Nadeau, *The History of Surrealism*, footnote to p. 89.
17 Quoted in Nadeau, ibid., p. 90.
18 Quoted in Roger Shattuck's introduction to Nadeau, ibid., p. 25.
19 Karl H. Wörner, *Stockhausen*, p. 159.
20 Wörner, ibid., pp. 170–1.
21 Quoted in Nyman, *Experimental Music*, p.61.
22 From *45' for a Speaker*, in *Silence*, pp. 146–93.
23 See Jung, *Synchronicity*, pp. 22–9 and Watson, *Supernature*, pp. 252–3.
24 Lyall Watson's *Supernature* is a sober investigation of recent scientific research in these fields. One of the more intriguing features of such research it that it seems to confirm what the Romantics believed: that man's inner nature and the outer world of nature are closely related.
25 Jung, *Synchronicity*, pp. 49–50. We may note that Jung considers the combination of sensation and intuition to be one of the chief psychological characteristics of the creative artist. (See *Psychological Types*.)
26 Aruni, about six or eight centuries B.C. Quoted in Campbell, *Creative Mythology*, p. 346.
27 See Watson, *Supernature*, pp. 58–61.
28 See Jung, *Synchronicity*, chapter 2.

Bibliography

The following list gives the titles of works consulted in the preparation of this book. A more regular bibliography of operatic history may be found in Grout's *Short History of Opera*.

AESCHYLUS, *Prometheus Bound, The Suppliants, Seven against Thebes, The Persians.* Trans. Philip Vellacott. Penguin Books, London, 1961.

APULEIUS, *The Golden Ass,* Trans. Robert Graves, Penguin Books, London, 1950.

ARISTOPHANES, *The Birds.* Trans. R.H. Webb, in *The Complete Plays of Aristophanes,* Ed. Moses Hadas. Bantam Books, New York, 1962.

ARISTOTLE, *The Rhetoric.* Trans. Sir R.C. Jebb. Cambridge University Press, 1909.

ARISTOTLE, HORACE, LONGINUS, *Classical Literary Criticism.* Trans. T. S. Borsch. Penguin Books, London, 1965.

AXTON, Richard, *European Drama of the Early Middle Ages,* Hutchinson, London, 1974.

BALAKIAN, Anna, *The Symbolist Movement, a Critical Appraisal.* Random House, New York, 1967.

BALDRY, H.C., *The Greek Tragic Theatre.* Chatto and Windus, London, 1971.

BARFORD, Philip, 'Urphänomen, Ursatz and Grundgestalt,' in *Music Review* 28, 1967, pp. 218–31.

BARNES, Harry Elmer, *An Intellectual and Cultural History of the Western World.* Vol. II: *From the Renaissance through the Eighteenth Century.* Vol. III: *From the Nineteenth Century to the Present Day.* 3rd revised ed. Dover, New York, 1965.

BARROW, R.H., *The Romans.* Penguin Books, London, 1949.

BARZUN, Jacques, *Darwin, Marx, Wagner; Critique of a Heritage.* 2nd ed. Doubleday, New York, 1958.

BAZIN, Germain, *The Baroque.* Trans. P. Wardroper. Thames and Hudson, London, 1968.

BOWRA, C.M., *The Heritage of Symbolism.* Macmillan, London, 1943.

BRONOWSKI, J., *The Ascent of Man.* BBC and Book Club Associates, London, 1973.

BROWN, Howard Mayer, 'Music — How Opera Began; an introduction to Jacopo Peri's *Euridice* (1600)', in Eric Cochrane (ed.), *The Late Italian Renaissance 1525–1630.* Macmillan, London, 1970.

BROWN, Howard Mayer, 'Musicians in the Mystères and Miracles', in Taylor and

Nelson (eds.), *Medieval English Drama, Essays Critical and Contextual.* University of Chicago Press, 1972.

BURCKHARDT, Jacob, *History of Greek Culture.* Trans. Palmer Hitty. Constable, London, 1963.

BUTLER, James H., *The Theatre and Drama of Greece and Rome.* Chandler, San Francisco, 1972.

CACCINI, Giulio, *Le Nuove Musiche.* Ed. H. Wiley Hitchcock. A–R Editions Inc., Madison Wisconsin, 1970.

CAGE, John, *Silence.* Wesleyan University Press, Connecticut, 1961.

CAMPBELL, Joseph, *The Masks of God.* Vol. I: *Primitive Mythology* (1969 edition). Vol. II: *Oriental Mythology* (1962). Souvenir Press, London, 1973. Vol. III: *Occidental Mythology* (1964). Vol. IV: *Creative Mythology* (1968). Souvenir Press, London, 1974.

CAMUS, Albert, *L'Étranger.* Editions Gallimard, Paris, 1942. Trans. (*The Outsider*) Stuart Gilbert. Hamish Hamilton, and Penguin Books, London; Alfred A. Knopf, Inc., New York.

CARCOPINO, Jérôme, *Daily Life in Ancient Rome.* Trans. E.O. Lorimer. Penguin Books, London, 1941.

CARPENTER, Nan Cooke, 'Music in the *Secunda Pastorum*' in Taylor and Nelson (eds.), *Medieval English Drama, Essays Critical and Contextual.* University of Chicago Press, 1972.

COON, Carleton S., *The History of Man, From the first Human to Primitive Culture and Beyond.* Jonathan Cape, London, 1955.

CORRIGAN, Robert W. (ed.), *Comedy: Meaning and Form.* Chandler, San Francisco, 1965.

DA PONTE, Lorenzo, *Memoirs.* Trans. Arthur Livingston. Orion, New York, 1959.

DEAN, Winton, *Handel and the Opera Seria.* O.U.P., London, 1970.

DE BONO, Edward, *The Use of Lateral Thinking.* Jonathan Cape, London, 1967.

DRUMMOND, John, 'The Background, Shape and Meaning of Twelve-Note Music: an Examination via *Moses und Aron.*' *Soundings* 3 (University College, Cardiff), 1973.

DUCHARTRE, Pierre Louis, *The Italian Comedy.* Trans. Randolph T. Weaver. Dover, New York, 1966.

DURANT, Will, *The Life of Greece.* Simon and Schuster, New York, 1939.

ELLIS, Havelock, *Psychology of Sex.* Heinemann, London, 1933.

ERLANGER, Philippe, *The Age of Courts and Kings; Manners and Morals 1558–1715.* Weidenfeld and Nicolson, London, 1967.

EURIPIDES, *The Bacchae and other plays.* Trans. Philip Vellacott. Penguin Books, London, 1954.

FARNELL, Lewis Richard, *The Cults of the Greek States*, Volume V. Clarendon Press, Oxford, 1909.

FIRTH, J. R., *The Tongues of Men* and *Speech.* O.U.P., London, 1964.

FRANCE, Peter, *Rhetoric and Truth in France, Descartes to Diderot.* Clarendon Press, Oxford, 1972.

FRAZER, J.G., *The Golden Bough,* Abridged edition. Macmillan, London, 1960.

FREEDLEY, George, and REEVES, John, A., *A History of the Theatre.* Crown, New York, 1941.

GAFORI, Franchino, *Practica Musicae* (Milan, 1496). Republished by Gregg Press, Farnborough, 1967.

GEORGE, Graham, *Tonality and Musical Structure*. Faber and Faber, London, 1970.

GOETHE, Johann Wolfgang von, *Sämmtliche Werke*. 10 volumes. Verlag der J.G. Sotta'schen Buchhandlung, Stuttgart, 1875.

GREGOR, Joseph, *Kulturgeschichte der Oper: thre Verbindung mit dem Leben, den Werken des Geistes, und der Politik*. Gallus Verlag, Vienna, 1941.

GRINNELL, George, B., *Blackfoot Lodge Tales: The Story of a Prairie People*. University of Nebraska Press, 1962.

GROUT, Donald Jay, *A Short History of Opera*. 2nd ed. Columbia University Press, New York, 1965.

GUTHRIE, W.K.C., *The Greeks and their Gods*. Methuen, London, 1950.

HANSLICK, Eduard, *Music Criticisms 1846–99*. Trans. and ed. Henry Pleasants, 1950. Penguin Books Ltd., London, 1963.

HARDISON, O.B. Jr., *Christian Rite and Christian Drama in the Middle Ages*. The John Hopkins Press, Baltimore, 1965.

HATFIELD, Henry, *Aesthetic Paganism in German Literature from Winckelmann to the death of Goethe*. Harvard University Press, Cambridge, Mass., 1964.

HENDERSON, W.J., *Some Forerunners of Italian Opera*. John Murray, London, 1911.

HINE, Daryl, *The Homeric Hymns*. Atheneum, New York, 1972.

HOMER, The Iliad. Trans. E. V. Rieu. Penguin Books, London, 1950.

HUIZINGA, J., *Homo Ludens*. Trans. R.F.C. Hull. Routledge and Kegan Paul, London, 1949.

HUXLEY, G.L., *The Early Ionians*, Faber and Faber, London, 1966.

JUNG, C.G., *Four Archetypes*. Trans. R.F.C. Hull. (Extracted from Jung's Collected Works, Vol. IX). Routledge and Kegan Paul, London, 1972.

JUNG, C.G., *Psychological Types, or The Psychology of Individuation*. (1920). Trans. H. Godwin Baynes. Kegan Paul, Trench, Trubner, London. n.d.

JUNG, C.G., *Synchronicity, An Acausal Connecting Principle*, (1952). Trans. R.F.C. Hull. Routledge and Kegan Paul, 1972.

JUNG, C.G. and KERÉNYI, C., *Introductions to a Science of Mythology. The Myth of the Divine Child and the Mysteries of Eleusis*. Trans. R.F.C. Hull. Routledge and Kegan Paul, London, 1951.

KELLY, Michael, *Reminiscences*. Roger Fiske (ed.). O.U.P., London, 1975.

KERMAN, Joseph, *Opera as Drama*. Random House, New York, 1956.

KERR, Walter, *Tragedy and Comedy*. The Bodley Head, London, 1967.

KIRK, G.S., *The Songs of Homer*. Cambridge University Press, 1960.

KITTO, H.D.F., *Greek Tragedy, a literary study*. 3rd ed. Methuen, London, 1961.

KOESTLER, Arthur, *The Act of Creation*. Danube edition, 1969. Pan Books, London, 1970.

KURTH, Ernst, *Romantische Harmonik und ihre Krise in Wagners Tristan*. Max Hesses Verlag, Berlin, 1923.

LANG, Paul Henry, *Music in Western Civilization*. Dent, London, 1942.

LANG, Paul Henry (ed.), *Stravinsky, A New Appraisal of His Work*. Norton, New York, 1963.

LEA K.M., *Italian Popular Comedy, a Study in the Commedia dell'Arte, 1568–1620 (with special reference to the English Stage)*. Russell and Russell, New York, 1962.

LÉVI-STRAUSS, Claude, *Structural Anthropology*, Trans. Claire Jacobsen and Brock Grundfest Schoepf. Beacon Press, Boston, 1963.

LIPPMANN, Edward, A., *Musical Thought in Ancient Greece*. Columbia University

Press, New York, 1964.

LORENZ, Alfred Ottakar, *Das Geheimnis der Form bei Richard Wagner*. Vol. 1: *Der Ring der Nibelungen*, 1924. Vol. 2: *Tristan und Isolde*, 1926. Vol. 3: *Die Meistersinger*. 1930. Vol. 4: *Parsifal*, 1933. Max Hesses Verlag, Berlin.

MAHR, August C., *The Origins of the Greek Tragic Form, a study of the early theater in Attica*. Prentice-Hall, New York, 1938.

MARSCHACK Alexander, *The Roots of Civilisation*. Weidenfeld and Nicholson, London, 1972.

MERRIAM, Alan P., *The Anthropology of Music*. North Western University Press, 1964.

MOBERLY, Robert and RAEBURN, Christopher: 'Mozart's 'Figaro': the plan of Act III', in *Music and Letters,* Vol. XLVI, 1965, pp. 134–6.

MONTEVERDI, Claudio, *L'Orfeo, favola in musica*. Ed. Denis Stevens. Novello, London, 1968. *L'Orfeo, favola in musica*. Ed. G.F. Malipiero. Chester, London, 1923.

NADAL, Octave, *Le Sentiment de l'amour dans l'oeuvre de Pierre Corneille*. Gallimard, Paris, 1948.

NADEAU, Maurice, *The History of Surrealism* (1964). Trans. Richard Howard. Jonathan Cape, London, 1968.

NAGLER, A.M., *A Source Book in Theatrical History (=Sources of Theatrical History, 1952)*. Dover, New York, 1959.

NELSON, Robert J., *Corneille: His Heroes and their Worlds*. University of Pennsylvania Press, Philadelphia, 1965.

NICOLL, Allardyce, *World Drama from Aeschylus to Anouih*. Harrap, London, 1949.

NIETZSCHE, Friedrich, *The Birth of Tragedy from the Spirit of Music*. Trans. Francis Golffing. Doubleday, New York, 1956.

NYMAN, Michael, *Experimental Music, Cage and beyond*. Studio Vista, Cassell and Collier Macmillan, London, 1974.

OREGLIA, Giacomo, *The Commedia dell'Arte* (1964). Trans. Lovett F. Edwards. Methuen, London, 1968.

PALISCA, Claude V., *Baroque Music*. Prentice-Hall, New Jersey, 1968.

PALISCA, Claude V., 'Girolamo Mei: Mentor to the Florentine Camerata,' in *The Musical Quarterly,* Vol. XL, No. 1, January 1954, pp. 1–28.

PERI, Jacopo, *Le Musiche sopra L'Euridice*. Facsimile edition. Forni Editore, Bologna, 1969.

PIRROTTA, Nino, 'Temperaments and Tendencies in the Florentine Camerata' (trans. Nigel Fortune), in *The Musical Quarterly,* Vol. XL, No. 2, April 1954, pp. 168–89.

PURVIS, J.S., *The York Cycle of Mystery Plays, a complete version*. S.P.C.K., London, 1957.

RADCLIFFE-BROWN, A.R., *The Andaman Islanders*. Second edition. Cambridge University Press, 1933.

REESE, Gustave, *Music in the Middle Ages*. Dent, London, 1941.

REICH, Willi, *Schoenberg, a Critical Biography*. Trans. Leo Black, Longman, London, 1971.

RIDGEWAY, William, *The Dramas and Dramatic Dances of Non-European Races in special reference to the origin of Greek tragedy*. Cambridge University Press, 1915.

The Origin of Tragedy, with special reference to the Greek tragedians. Cambridge University Press, 1910.

ROSTEUTSCHER, J.H.W., *Die Wiederkunft des Dionysos, der Naturmystische Irrationalismus in Deutschland.* A. Francke Verlag, Bern, 1947.

SACHS, Curt, *The Rise of Music in the Ancient World, East and West.* Norton, New York, 1943.

SCHOPENHAUER, Arthur, *The World as Will and Representation.* 2 vols. Trans. E. F. J. Payne. Dover, New York, 1966.

SOPHOCLES, *The Theban Plays.* Trans. E.F. Watling. Penguin Books, London, 1947.

STANISLAVSKI, Constantin, *Building a Character.* Trans. Elizabeth Reynolds Hapgood. Methuen, London, 1968.

STERNFELD, F.W. (ed.), *A History of Western Music.* Vol. I: *Music from the Middle Ages to the Renaissance.* Weidenfeld and Nicholson, London, 1973.

STRAVINSKY. Igor, *Poetics of Music in the form of six lessons.* (1942) Trans. Arthur Knodel and Ingolf Dahl. Random House, New York, 1947.

STRAVINSKY, Igor and CRAFT, Robert, *Dialogues and a Diary,* Faber. London, 1968.

STRUNK, Oliver (ed.), *Source Readings in Music History.* Norton, New York, 1950.

TAYLOR, Ronald, *The Romantic Tradition in Germany, an Anthology with critical essays and commentaries.* Methuen, London, 1970.

THORLBY, A.K., *The Romantic Movement (Problems and Perspectives in History).* Longmans, London, 1966.

TIPPETT, Michael, *Moving into Aquarius.* Routledge and Kegan Paul, London, 1959.

TOYNBEE, Arnold, *Mankind and Mother Earth.* O.U.P., 1976.

TRAVLOS, J., *Pictorial Dictionary of Ancient Athens.* Thames and Hudson, London, 1971.

VALLAS, Léon, *Claude Debussy et son temps.* Albin Michel, Paris, 1958.

WATSON, Lyall, *Supernature, A Natural History of the Supernatural.* Hodder and Stoughton, London, 1973.

WEINSTOCK, Herbert, *Rossini,* a biography. O.U.P., London, 1968.

WAGNER, Richard, *Oper und Drama,*Deutsche Bibliothek in Berlin, n.d.

WELLESZ, Egon (ed.), *New Oxford History of Music,* Vol. 1: Ancient and Oriental Music. O.U.P., 1957.

WEST, M.L., 'Greek Poetry 2000–700 B.C.' *The Classical Quarterly,* New Series Vol. XXIII, 1973, pp. 179–92.

WIND, Edgar, *Pagan Mysteries of the Renaissance,* Faber and Faber, 1958, and Penguin Books, 1967.

WOOLF, Rosemary, *The English Mystery Plays.* Routledge and Kegan Paul, London, 1972.

WÖRNER, Karl H., *Stockhausen, Life and Work.* Trans. and ed. by Bill Hopkins. Faber, London, 1973.

WORSTHORNE, Simon Towneley, *Venetian Opera in the Seventeenth Century,* Clarendon Press, oxford, 1954.

Index